THE MIDWEST BOOK REVIEW

JAMES A. COX
Editor-In-Chief
mwbookrevw@aol.com
http://www.execpc.com/~mbr/bookwatch/

278 Orchard Drive
Oregon, WI 53575
(608) 835-7937
mbr@execpc.com

Flying High In Iowa
Howard W. Greiner
Indian Hills Publishing
100 Highway 34 East, Albia, IA 52531
0-9672141-0-6 $24.95   1-800-728-4286

Flying High In Iowa is the autobiography of Howard Greiner in which he chronicles his life from h
an Iowa farm in 1923 through his years growing up in the Great Depression, his becoming a pilot in
Air Corps, being shot down over Germany in World War II and imprisoned in a POW camp, to his r
Iowa at the end of the war to become a farmer and business entrepreneur with the attendant struggles
and successes. Grein talks about meeting the love of his life while stationed with his flight crew in C
Wyoming and their 38-year marriage and their six children, including the story of their one special c
his wife's battle with breast cancer. It is also the story of an Iowa farm boy with no formal education
on to become a trustee and chairman of the board of one of Iowa's foremost community colleges. Th
memoir is enhanced with 180 illustrations and spans 76 years of a remarkable life, including nine bri
death. Howard Greiner is articulate and engaging as he relates his accomplished life and turbulent tir
High In Iowa will be of intense interest to students of the history of Iowa, World War II, farm life, r
entrepreneurship, and the art of biography.

1

DO NOT BUY THIS BOOK

IF YOU DO NOT WANT TO KNOW HOW AN
   IOWA FARM BOY WAS RAISED DURING THE
   DEPRESSION, OF THE 1923-40 PERIOD.
IF YOU DO NOT WANT KNOW HOW THIS YOUNG
   MAN GOT THROUGH ARMY AIR CORPS TRAINING
   TO BECOME A BOMBER PILOT AND A PRISONER OF
   WAR WITH NO FORMAL EDUCATION.
IF YOU DO NOT WANT TO KNOW ABOUT BEING A
   SUCCESSFUL FARMER, AN ENTREPRENEUR
   STARTING MANY BUSINESSES. THEN LOSING
   EVERY THING AND STARTING ALL OVER AGAIN.
IF YOU DO NOT WANT TO KNOW HOW HE HANDLED
   LOSING THE LOVE OF HIS LIFE AND BEGINNING
   A NEW LIFE AGAIN.
IF YOU DO NOT WANT TO READ HOW HE ESCAPED
   THE CLUTCHES OF DEATH NINE TIMES. HOW LUCKY
   CAN YOU BE."THANK YOU GOD"
IF YOU ARE LOOKING FOR A PERFECT WRITTEN
   BOOK. IT IS NOT A PERFECTLY WRITTEN BOOK.
IF YOU WANT TO CALL IT A BOOK OR DIARY THE
   AUTHOR DOES NOT CARE. IT IS THE HISTORY OF A
   CHALLENGING LIFE.
IF YOU DO BUY THE BOOK, YOU MAY BE WISHING YOU
   COULD HAVE LIVED THE SAME LIFE.
IF THE COMPUTER MISUNDERSTOOD WHAT I SAID
   AND MADE A BOO-BOO, AND I MISSED IT, FORGIVE
   ME WITH KINDNESS AND UNDERSTANDING.
 IF YOU BUY THE BOOK, I KNOW YOU WILL ENJOY IT.

THE AUTHOR *Howard Greiner*

FLYING HIGH IN IOWA
BY HOWARD W. GREINER

PUBLISHED BY:
> INDIAN HILLS PUBLISHING
> 100 HIGHWAY 34 EAST
> ALBIA IOWA 52531

Copyright © 1999
Printed in the United States of America
ISBN 0-9672141-0-6
Library of Congress Catalog Number 99-94314
Total pages 484

Publisher's Cataloging-in- Publication
(Provided by Quality Books, Inc.)

Greiner, Howard W.
> Flying High in Iowa / Howard W. Greiner. 2nd ed.
> p.cm.
> LCCN: 99-94314
> ISBN: 0-9672141-0-6

> 1. Greiner Howard W. 2. Agriculturists--Iowa
> --Biography. 3. Bomber pilots—United States—
> Biography. 4. World War, 1939-1945--Prisoners and
> Prisons, German. 5. World War, 1939-1945—
> Personal narratives, American. 6. United States.
> Army Air Forces—Biography. I. Title

> S417.G78A3 1999   630.92
>   QBI99-785

Printed in the United States by:
Morris Publishing
3212 East Highway 30 • Kearney, NE 68847 • 1-800-650-7888

Introduction

Part 1 of "Flying High In Iowa" is the history of a Iowa farm boy born on a farm in 1923 in Washington County , Iowa. These are the memories of what life was like for children growing up during that period of the depression, of the 1930's, of what a one room schoolhouse in Iowa was like, and what children did during that period of time. He lived for 52 years on this same farm .

Part 2 is the history of World War II and his entry into the Army Air Force for pilot training. He was trained to fly B-24 Liberator bombers. It is the history of all the various training periods and commands with all of the friends and girlfriends he made during that period. He was shot down over Magdeburg, Germany on a bombing run and was a prisoner of war and his liberation. The story of his stay in the hospitals until his discharge of Oct. 30,1945.

Part 3 is the history of an Iowa farm boy returning to the farm and marrying the love of his life. He met her in Casper Wyoming while stationed there with his crew during the war. He was a man who was always searching for a better way to improve farming. He was never satisfied with the old ways of doing it How he started various companies, importing cattle from Europe, and being successful with the farming operation. How He made a fatal mistake in a business venture in 1978 which made him start life all over. This is the story of his wonderful wife, Lois, and raising their six children until he lost her to breast-cancer in 1985.Howthey managed raising their special handicapped son. This was a true love story with the Lady he met in Casper Wyoming. His many civic projects during that time of his life, of trying to make his home areas a better place to live

Part 4 is the history of starting all over in the motel business after losing the love of his life. He is a man who never looks back. It tells of new friends he made and of the new things he took up in his life. He has traveled extensively and lived a very unusual life. Not a day-to-day- routine as is common to many. As Lois always said" Living with Howard has never been boring."

Dedication

I dedicate this book to my loving wife Lois, who stood by me not only as my wife but as the best friend that any man could have. There never was a time when she thought of herself before our six children or me. The worry she always had for our special son would also make a book. However God said he needed her before she had the opportunity to do that. I know she would be proud of me and given me encouragement in the effort to write the story of our life together. Those who knew her forever will love her.

Lois Greiner passed away April 2,1985 after a valiant three year fight with breast cancer. The family spread her ashes at Jenny Lake in the Grand Tetons, in Wyoming the state of her birth.

FOREWORD

Of all the clients I ever had Howard W. Greiner would exceed all others when it comes to being the most colorful, daring, and aggressive client I have ever had the privilege to serve. Whenever I saw Howard and asked "What's new with you?" There always was something new and usually most unexpected.

The war came along and his spirit of high adventure naturally directed his decisions. He wanted to be a pilot, knowing the minimum requirements for cadets to getting into pilot training was two years of college, Howard was able to pass the necessary entrance requirements to take pilot training.

Some of his training took place in Wyoming, where he met Lois Clare, who following the war, he married. He flew flights over Germany until his plane was shot down. He fractured his ankle and broke a leg while parachuting to the ground.

He was hospitalized in England and the United States for five months. He returned to farming after his discharge.

He was one of the first farmers to recognize the value of anhydrous ammonia and decided to sell it since it was so effective in making corn grow. He started Ke-Wash fertilizer Co. with a office in their home at their farm. This then grew to 30 anhydrous ammonia retail stations, 30 dry blending plants, 5 ready mix concrete plants, three propane plants, and an International Harvester dealership.

In 1966 he and his wife, Lois, made a trip to Russia, where he saw his first Simmentahl cattle. Howard started importing cattle from Europe.

Howard increased his farming operations to where it involved five thousand acres and then in 1976, he made what he calls the mistake of his life when he decided to build a meat packing plant at Sigourney Iowa. Needless to say it was a disaster. The timing and the period of high interest drove the plant into bankruptcy. Howard had personally endorsed the notes and his determination to keep on fighting to succeed" did him in". He could see that it was over. He had to liquidate his assets.

Howard and his wife, Lois, were able to buy a motel at Albia Iowa. He and his son Peter, have build it up to one of southern Iowa's finest motels.

Lois died of cancer on April second, 1985, and this had a profound effect upon his life. He has since taken up whitewater rafting and skiing at the age of 64 which he says he loves he has floated the Grand Canyon, and the River of No Return across Idaho. In 1990 he floated the Snake River, where he nearly drowned by being washed under a logjam. Howard does not know---- and neither do the Rangers---- how he survived that one.

Howard has been involved in many civic projects. He led the parish in building St. Joseph church in Wellman, chairman of the committee that built the Lagos Acres golf course in Keota Iowa. He was president of a nonprofit corporation that organized and build the Washington County Development Center in Washington Iowa for handicapped people and, after moving to Sigourney was the leader in building the Keokuk County Expo grounds for 4-H at Sigourney. Howard has been on the board of the Indian Hills College at a Ottumwa Iowa for 18 years and was chairman of the Board of Trustees eight years. He is probably the only person in the United States to be chairman of the Board of Trustees of a college with no high school education.

Our law firm has represented him for over 50 years and were involved with many of these projects. It has been most interesting working with Howard. As his wife, Lois, said," It wasn't dull living with him". I would agree. It has been our privilege to have know Howard, his wife Lois, and their family. They have not only been law clients but personal friends as well.

Very sincerely yours

Robert Day
Day Meeker Lamping & Schlegel

VII

TABLE OF CONTENTS
Part One 1923-1941

Chapter 1 Father Courting My Mother 6
Chapter 2 My First Memories 9
Chapter 3 Farm Surgery 13
Chapter 4 Eighth Grade In Country School 17
Chapter 5 That Old House 22
Chapter 6 The Old Homestead 26
Chapter 7 Growing Up 32
Chapter 8 My Mother 35
Chapter 9 Entertainment 38
Chapter 10 The Butchering Ring 40
Chapter 11 My Friend 42
Chapter 12 Hired Men 47
Chapter 13 The Bohr Family 49
Chapter 14 Another Close Call 52
Chapter 15 Milking On The Farm 54
Chapter 16 Another Narrow Escape 56
Chapter 17 A Tragedy In Our Family 58
Chapter 18 My Musical Career 60
Chapter 19 The Thrashing Ring 62
Chapter 20 The Grocery Wagon 65
Chapter 21 The Goose Pen Folly 67
Chapter 22 Entertainment In The Wintertime 68
Chapter 23 Dick "Old Reliable" 70
Chapter 24 Dick And The Runaway Truck 74
Chapter 25 Off To The Races 76
Chapter 26 Life On The Farm In 1938 78
Chapter 27 Trouble In The Family 86
Chapter 28 The Neighbors 89
Chapter 29 My First Trip To Texas 93

Part Two 1942-1945

Chapter 1 A Change In My Life 96
Chapter 2 My Air Force Career Begins 102
Chapter 3 University Of Missouri 108
Chapter 4 The Cadet Center 119
Chapter 5 Pre-Fight At The Cadet Center 122
Chapter 6 Primary Fight School 125

Part Two 1942-1945

Chapter 7   Basic Flying A Trying Experience 130
Chapter 8   Twin Engine At Ellington 133
Chapter 9   Fort Worth And The B-24 137
Chapter 10   Lincoln Nebraska Crew Pick-up 144
Chapter 11   Crew Training Casper Wyoming 147
Chapter 12   A Diary Leaving The U.S. 155
Chapter 13   466th Bomb Group 167
Chapter 14   Prisoner Of War Hospital 175
Chapter 15   94th General Hospital England 191
Chapter 16   Fort Logan Hospital Denver 201
Chapter 17   Santa Anna, California 202

Part Three 1946-1985

Chapter 1   Back To The Farm 206
Chapter 2   Home From The Honeymoon 212
Chapter 3   On The Farm 1947 218
Chapter 4   The Year 1948 221
Chapter 5   The Farm 1949 228
Chapter 6   On The Farm 1950 234
Chapter 7   On The Farm 1951 237
Chapter 8   On The Farm 1952 240
Chapter 9   On The Farm 1953 243
Chapter 10   Beginning of Ke-Wash Fertilizer 248
Chapter 11   Ke-Wash In 1955 251
Chapter 12   Ke-Wash In 1956 254
Chapter 13   Ke-Wash In 1957 257
Chapter 14   Ke-Wash In 1958 260
Chapter 15   Ke-Wash In 1959 264
Chapter 16   Ke-Wash In 1960 268
Chapter 17   1961 A Fateful Year 271
Chapter 18   Ke-Wash In 1962 280
Chapter 19   Ke-Wash In 1963 284
Chapter 20   Ke-Wash In 1964 287
Chapter 21   Ke-Wash In 1965 292
Chapter 22   Ke-Wash In 1966 296
Chapter 22A Russian Trip 1966 301
Chapter 23   The Greiners In 1967 314
Chapter 24   The Greiners In 1968 317

Part Three 1946-1985

Chapter 25 The Greiners In 1969 322
Chapter 26 The Greiners In 1970 325
Chapter 27 The Greiners In 1971 330
Chapter 28 The Greiners In 1972 335
Chapter 29 The Greiners In 1973 338
Chapter 30 On The Farm 1974 344
Chapter 31 The Greiners In 1975 353
Chapter 32 The Greiners In 1976 357
Chapter 33 The Greiners In 1977 364
Chapter 34 The Greiners In 1978 368
Chapter 35 The Greiners In 1979 372
Chapter 36 The Greiners In 1980 375
Chapter 37 The Greiners In 1981 379
Chapter 38 The Greiners In 1982 382
Chapter 39 The Greiners In 1983 389
Chapter 40 The Greiners In 1984 393
Chapter 41 The Greiners In 1985 396

Part Four 1986-1998

Chapter 1 Motel In 1986 407
Chapter 2 The Greiners In 1987 412
Chapter 3 The Greiners In 1988 420
Chapter 4 Motel In 1989 424
            Near My God To Thee 428
Chapter 5 Motel In 1990 431
Chapter 6 Motel In 1991 435
Chapter 7 Motel In 1992 444
Chapter 8 Motel In 1993 447
Chapter 9 Motel In 1994 453
Chapter 10 Motel In 1995 456
Chapter 11 Motel In 1996 459
Chapter 12 Motel In 1997 462
Chapter 13 Motel In 1998 464
            Memories 469

THE AUTHOR HOWARD W. GREINER

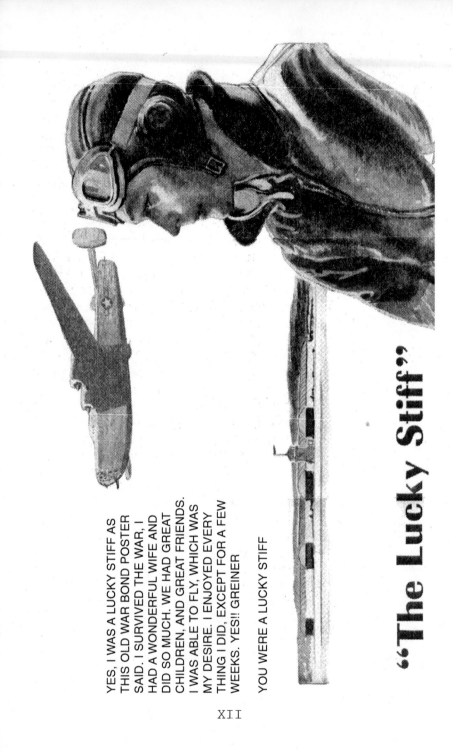

"The Lucky Stiff"

YES, I WAS A LUCKY STIFF AS THIS OLD WAR BOND POSTER SAID. I SURVIVED THE WAR, I HAD A WONDERFUL WIFE AND DID SO MUCH. WE HAD GREAT CHILDREN, AND GREAT FRIENDS. I WAS ABLE TO FLY, WHICH WAS MY DESIRE. I ENJOYED EVERY THING I DID, EXCEPT FOR A FEW WEEKS. YES!! GREINER

YOU WERE A LUCKY STIFF

XII

MY Fathers ancestors
Margretha Greiner

She was born in Overpearl, Germany on November 25,1840. She came with her parents Michael and Anna Herbaria by sailboat. Then to Burlington, Iowa which was the end of the railroad in 1855. Then they came by ox team to Keokuk, County, Iowa. Where they bought a farm southwest of Keota, Iowa. In May 1857 she married my great grandfather Peter Greiner who had been a steam boat captain on the Mississippi River. He left that trade after he contracted malaria. Peter was also from Germany. Peter preceded her in death on December 16th, 1884.

This union created nine sons and four daughters. In September 1864 the two oldest sons and the oldest daughter died from diphtheria within ten days of each other. They are buried one, beside the other, in Clear Creek Cemetery southwest of Keota, Iowa In July 1917, a son Joe was assassinated in Manitoba, Canada by an Indian he employed as an interpreter for his business.

When she died she was survived by nine children, six boys and three girls My grandfather John and his brothers Mike, Peter, George, Frank, and Henry and the three girls, Kate Conrad, Mary Horras, Margret Redlinger. They were all at her funeral when she died February 27, 1919. She had never moved and lived on the same farm for 64 years. She had to have been a strong woman.

It is quite apparent that my grandfather John came from a strong family. Each of these children had large families, and each of their children had large families. I have never had the privilege of knowing all of them. In looking at this picture of this woman it is not hard to see what a strong family this was

There does not seem to be much information about Peter Greiner except that he died at the age of 63.Margretha was supposedly with child when he died.

1

BACK ROW LEFT TO RIGHT-FRANK, HENRY, KATE, PETER, MARY, GEORGE, MAGGIE JOE. FRONT ROW LEFT TO RIGHT-JOHN,MY GRANDFATHER,MOTHER MARGRETHA GREINER MIKE.

2

My Mothers ancestors
My Grandfather and Grandmother

My grandfather, Conrad Aller, was born in Muscatine, Iowa September 6,1869. His father, Anton Aller, was born in the Republic of Germany, and his mother, Pauleyne Highberger, was born in Switzerland.

My grandmother, Mary Anna Klett , was born Nov. 30 in 1870 in Keokuk, County Iowa. Her father, Godfrey Klett, was born December 25 ,1843 at Garibaldi, Iowa which is in Keokuk, County Iowa. Her mother, Catherine Beiwin, I have no history of except she was born in Keokuk County. The history of Godfrey Klett shows that he was a Civil War veteran of many battles and hardships. His father was also a pioneer who laid out the town of Sigourney, Iowa and started the history of that area.

Casper Klett, who was Godfrey's father, was born April 13th ,1817, in Baden Wurttenburg, Republic of Germany. Both of his parents came from Prussia. Casper's mother, Sophia Wieland, was born Oct.4th, 1817, in the same Republic in Germany. I am enclosing the history of my great-grandfather and his father because it relates so well to my history. I know my mother never knew that her grandfather, Casper, was a Civil War veteran because I never ever heard her talk about it.

In the history of Keokuk County, Iowa in the year1880, Godfrey Klett was listed as living in Clear Creek Township, which is located just east of Sigourney. Godfrey is listed as a farmer residing on section 6 of the Township with a post office address of Harper.

Godfrey Klett, was a Civil War veteran, and fought in the 33rd infantry Regiment.

3

BACK ROW LEFT TO RIGHT.- MY MOTHER FRANCIS, WILLEY, CELIA,
FRONT ROW LEFT TO RIGHT--GRANDMOTHER MAUDE, GODFERY,CLARA,PAULINE, GRANDFATHER

I HAVE FOND MEMORIES OF MY MOTHERS PARENTS. THEY WERE LOVING GRANDPARENTS

Part 1
Chapter 1
Father courting my mother

My grandfather John bought 500 acres of what was called the prairie land, North East of keota Iowa in 1909. Now in 1909 most of the Prairie land in Iowa was very wet and had a lot of frog and duck ponds on it. The farmers had just beginning to learn how to tile the farmland and drain off excess water. Every town on the prairie had a tile factory. My father and his brothers had to haul tile from Wellman with horse and wagon so they could start tileing the prairie. At that time all of these tile ditches were dug by hand. And the tile were put every three rods so they could drain off the water so that the land could be farmed. Dad's brother, Omar, was 12 years old when he was driving a team of horses with a load of tile. He fell off the wagon and was run over and killed. All of the children in the family worked very hard and spent little time in school.

Now when my father became about 18, like all other young kids, he became interested in girls. Somewhere along the line at a barn dance he had met my mother. My mother lived about 13 miles south and west of keota and my father lived seven miles North East of Keota. Now remember it is 1913 and my father had at least a 20 mile drive, by horse and buggy, to get to where she lived. He became very infatuated with my mother and continued his pursuit of her. I can remember my father telling about how in the winter of 1914 he would get so sleepy going home, that he would wrap the reins of the horse around the buggy whip holder and go to sleep. An hour or so later he would wake up and the horse would be standing at the barn, waiting to get into its stall. Father, would also tell about the Times in the winter, when the snow was on the ground and it was really cold. He would go to see mother with the sleigh. He never said whether it had bell's on the sleigh or not . He would get so cold, that he would tie the horses reins to the sleigh and run behind it for a while to get warm. Of course he wore a coat made of Buffalo-hide, which was very warm but also very heavy. One night father had a new horse hitched to the sleigh. When father holler "Whoa" this horse would not stop and he could not get back into the sleigh. He said he was making 10 foot strides before he finally got the horse to stop and get back in the sleigh. It was fun to hear him tell of his experience. I can see that taking place.

After the winter was over, my father began pushing my mother to get married since he said it was too far and to cold to drive another winter. So on October 12, 1915, my parents were married at St. Elizabeth's church in Harper Iowa. My parents never talked too much about their wedding, so I do not have many memories of it. My father was 19 and my mother was 18 when they were married, but my mother became 19 just four days later on the 9th of October. My grandfather, in the meantime, had bought the farm that joined his called the" Old Jones Place", which was in the same section my grandfather already owned. This is where my father and mother moved to start farming and raise their family. This is the same farm that I lived on for 52 years.

WOW!! DON'T I LOOK TERRIFIC AT XMAS 1923

Part 1
Chapter 2
My first memories

I was born on a farm on April 24^{th,} 1923, to Albert and Francis Greiner. They lived five miles southwest of Wellman and eight miles northeast of Keota Iowa. This is in Lime Creek Township, Washington ,County Iowa.

I was a sickly baby, according to my mother. I spent considerable time in a hospital in Cedar Rapids, Iowa, while the doctors were trying to diagnose my problems. Mother had told me she was not sure that I would survive. In those years, mortality among children was considerably higher than it is today. I can recall my mother mentioning that friends would say," My goodness Francis, did you raise that child?" Evidently I was not a picture of health. However, the first three years of my life were quite ordinary.

Although my father went no farther in school than the third grade, he was very sharp with figures. He had a very good business head. Around 1925 he decided to operate a restaurant in Wellman Iowa. This lasted a little over a year. I remember my father saying "When it was time to go to bed is when people started coming". In the meantime he rented the farm and moved to Washington, Iowa. My grandfather Greiner had retired and moved to Washington some years earlier.

My grandparents lived in a huge brick home about a quarter of a mile south of where my father and mother bought a home with a small acreage. As I recall, father bought about 20 acres with the home. Grass covered the land and was never farmed. This was on the north end of Washington. We had a very adequate large house on the land.

Some of my first memories were going with my father to downtown Washington to the basement of a store, which had what was called "The bucket shop". A bucket shop was the name given to people who had a ticker tape so they could get the grain markets from the Board of Trade in Chicago. These were not very fancy places and usually had a bunch of chairs that didn't match.

In various places there were spittons and old coffee cans for those who chewed tobacco. That's where they got the name" bucket shop". This is where farmers came to catch up on the markets.

Now one of the good memories I have when we lived in Washington was the day my father took his three children (my two sisters and I) to a farm somewhere west of Washington, Iowa. On the this farm lived a gentleman who raised ponies. I can still remember when we walked into the barn that had a long shed on the side. There must have been 20 or 30 ponies in it. To this day, I can still recall seeing those ponies run out of the barn with their tails flying in the air. Some had spots, some were black, some were brown, and some were white. It was a beautiful sight for a child of about five years.

Most shetland ponies were usually quite short and dumpy and not built for speed. Now my father had a good eye for horse flesh. He picked out a black pony that was about three years old. Although at maturity, the pony only weighed about five hundred pounds. I can guarantee, that he could out run many horses weighing 1000 pounds or more. My father owned a Model A Ford pickup with a stock rack on the back. We loaded the pony and brought him back to town where our acreage was. My older sister picked out the name, " Dickey."

The next 10 to 12 years of my life were shared with this black pony. He and I were companions. It was a sad day when I came home and found that my father had sold him. However at the time my father sold Dickey, my life was changing as a teenager.

Eventually I attended parochial school in Washington. I do remember walking home from school with my older sisters. We had to cross the Rock Island railroad tracks and it was a challenge getting across the tracks. At least my older sister made it seem like one. The mainline of the Rock Island railroad went through Washington and the famous Golden State limited passenger train would go through twice a day. I took the same train to California several times during the war.

Now my father's adventure in trading with the board of trade turned out to be unsuccesful. In the spring of 1929 we moved back to the home farm southwest of Wellman Iowa. My father did a lot of what was called "scalping." This consisted of going out to a farm and buying any kind of an animal the farmer wanted to sell. To be a good scalper a person had to be a good negotiator. My father was excellent at this.

Before we left Washington, my good grandmother Greiner was suffering from stomach cancer. I can remember my father going down to grandmother's house. Where my grandmother would be setting on the back porch vomiting into a bucket. I can remember my father asking," Susan, what's the trouble?" She would reply "Oh, Albert, I'm so sick". This was just before we moved back to the farm at Wellman. My grandmother was taken to a Muscatine hospital which was operated by a gentleman named Norman Brinkley. He was a quack who was run out of the United States.

My Grandmother was a lady who knew only work and abuse. My grandfather Greiner and my mother never saw eye to eye. In my mother's opinion my grandfather physically abused my grandmother. My grandfather was a very successful businessman. However, he had a terrible temper, as do most Germans. He had the knowledge of having people do the work, and he spent a good share of his time in buying and trading real-estate all over Washington County.

Grandfather was very successful at this and had accumulated enough land so that he could give each of his children a 160 acre farm of their own. But my grandmother had to sew buttons on cards for the Pearl Button factory in Muscatine. She did this to get a little money to buy groceries and clothes. She had very few clothes and I know this did not set well with my mother. When grandmother died my grandfather had her buried wearing a silk dress in a coffin with a glass top. My mother thought this was terrible. My father never talked much about his mother, as he was very close to his father and he was the one my grandfather relied on.

In Grandfather's will he gave each one of his children a life use of a farm with the wife or husband of his child having the life use of the farm before it went to the grandchildren. This was true of all of his children but my father. My mother was not allowed this privilege because she would never take anything from my grandfather and did not like the way he treated my grandmother. My daughter Cathy and her husband John live on the home farm. today.

11

L TO R SISTER CORDELL, HOWARD ,MARJORIE GREINER 1926.

Part 1
Chapter 3
Farm surgery

In the 1930's when I was about seven years old I started to develop a rather large hernia. Times were extremely hard and money was very short. However, there never was a time when we didn't have good clothes to wear. We were fortunate also to live on a farm where we had lots of food. We always had milk and vegetables that my mother canned and plenty of meat. We never went hungry.

However, money for other things in life was short. We milked cows, providing cream, which was sold to pay bills. My parents had been told that I needed an operation to fix my hernia. We had no medical insurance. My parents knew if they took me to a hospital they would not be able to afford the bill. So the surgery was put off a couple more years until I was ten years old. This was the time when my father negotiated a deal with a doctor in Washington to come out to the farm, and do the surgery on the dining room table. The doctor agreed to do the surgery for one hundred dollars. I can remember it very plainly. They split the old dining room table, laid a couple of table boards length ways, layed a blanket and some sheets on it and pressto! they created an operating table in the dining room.

A neighboring farm lady, who was a very good friend of our family, and the mother of my best friend, was a registered nurse. She assisted in the operation, as well as the other nurse the doctor brought a long with him. Needless to say, I was in for an experience I would never forget.

This operation took place in 1932 when spinal anesthetics were first being used. But the Doctor started a procedure which he did not understand. He tried injecting me in the fetal position and every position he could think of but nothing worked. After what seemed like an hour he finally ended the torture by giving me an ether anesthetic. I can remember my head ,swimming and the roar in my ears and the horrible taste of the ether and how sick to my stomach I was. In those days, when people were

13

convalescing they were treated like invalids. I was forbidden to ride my pony, Dickey, for six months. I think I did stay off him for about six weeks. Eventually I was able to ride him some. My father soon decided I was able to herd cows along the road. In those days everybody who had cows ended up having them along the highway because pasture was a short commodity.

For a number of years after this operation, I had trouble with my back. If, for instance I went into the old barn to throw down hay for the horses and cows my back would catch. Our hay was not baled as it is to day. We used a three pronged pitch fork and had to pull the hay loose to throw it down the chute.

WHOPPEE!!! I AM BACK RIDING DICKEY AGAIN

14

OLD SMITH CREEK SCHOOL, SISTER MARJORIE, 2 FROM RIGHT BACK ROW I'M SECOND FROM RIGHT IN MIDDLE ROW. WE THOUGHT IT WAS WONDERFUL.

EDINA HENDRIX, TEACHER, SISTER MARJORIE EXTREME LEFT. SISTER CORDELL RIGHT OF THE TEACHER. I AM IN SECOND ROW IN FRONT OF MY SISTER CORDELL 1929

Part 1

Chapter 4

Eighth, grade in country school

My eight years in Smith Creek country school were among my best years. My longtime friends, Burell Jr. Foster and Delmer Bull, and the rest of us kids at Smith Creek School had our usual fall fun of playing softball and basketball. We played in the basement when it was raining outside. We could not wait for the snow to come in the wintertime. We then could take our sleds and head for the hills to do "our thing" on the slopes behind the schoolhouse.

Eighth grade was very easy for me. I love geography and history. Arithmetic was not hard, but I had a terrible time with English. To this day, I do not know how to phrase a sentence properly. I have always felt that I had one of the best educations's anyone could have for the first eight years of their life. In country school, it was easy to review past subjects because all classes were there together. Therefore, you could listen as each class had its period in front of the teacher.

Our school was in the middle of the section on land owned by Zeno Aller. On the south and west sides there was usually a pasture. Mr. Aller raised many sheep. In this flock of sheep there was a very large sheep buck. Our recess and dinnertime would regularly be spent antagonizing the old buck. When he saw us, he would come running to the fence to see if a fight was possible. Of course, we loved to torment him as he would back up and charge the old woven wire fence. This was not good for the fence, but we had a ball doing it.

There was no well at the school, we had to carry, water from Mr. Aller's well in the rain, snow, and the wind. Finally, the school board decided to drill us a well so we no longer had to carry water from Allers. We traveled a mud road to get there which in the wintertime was frequently full of snowdrifts. There were no maintainers in those days; however, nobody objected to this trip because it was a chance to get out of the school room.

The teacher for my last year of school was a lady whose

17

name was Marjorie Holt. Marjorie was raised in our school district and was one of the eight kids of Bert and Ada Godber, who farmed a half-mile north and a half-mile east of the school. I never seemed to have any problems with Marjorie in school. She was a good disciplinarian and we all respected her as the teacher. Her brother, Bill, was a good friend of mine during our school years and later worked for me after the war.

However, about three weeks before school was to be let out ,and the two of us in eighth grade were to graduate, an odd problem happened in Smith Creek School. Marjorie had a policy that when students worked long division problems, they were to use a full line for each set of numbers as they carried them out on the tablet. She did not want anyone to crowd the problem. I handed in a paper that had some long division problems on it. I put the last carry out at the bottom of the page on the last line, which was not a full space. It just happened that my problem worked out to where I had to use the last line on the tablet.

I remember very well Marjorie standing in front of the room and saying, "I thought I told you not to crowd a long division problem". I grew up in a very conservative household and I did not think that crowding the last problem on the last line of the tablet was too bad. It made her quite mad when I started giggling a little bit because I thought her reaction was ridiculous.

There were five rows of seats at our schoolhouse with the small seats in front for kindergarten kids and the last row for us older kids. There was a space behind the last section of seats. Marjorie walked back and berated me for laughing. I was having a terrible time containing my giggling when she really lost it. She stepped behind my seat, grabbed my hair, and pulled my head back. Then she doubled up her fist and proceeded to beat the hell out of me. I being a smart -assed kid, said to her " Go ahead I can take it". Then she really started pounding me. After her anger was exhausted or she did not have the strength to go on, she ordered me out of the school and sent me home.

I went out and got on my trusted pony, Dickey, and went for home. It was probably two o'clock in the afternoon and my folks were not home at the time. So nothing, much was said. My mother did remark that my eyes looked puffy, but they did not know that I was sent home from school. However the next morning when I got up, I could not see. Both eyes were swollen

18

shut , black and blue. Of course, my mother was very upset so I proceeded to tell her and Dad what had happened. My Father wanted to know if I had it coming. I replied I probably did.

At this time, it was close to the end of the school year. We country kids had to take a county examination to pass the eighth grade. After about a week of my staying home, my father got concerned that I might not pass the examination, and would not be able to help him on the farm the next year. By this time I still had the black shiners but I could see fine. (I never went to the doctor and nothing much was said about it). However, my father decided that I should go back to school. So I got on my pony and headed back to school ,about halfway I met Mr. Bull, who was one of the directors. He wanted to know where I was going. I told him that my father wanted me to go to school. " Well," he said" You go home and I will go talk to your father". My father and Mr. Bull decided to contact the county superintendent who was the director of the county rural school system. Then the superintendent and the three directors had a meeting at the school. By the time I was allowed to go back to school there were only two weeks left. I would just as well have stayed home because Marjorie Holt paid no attention to me. But this was fine with me. Then the date came for the eighth grade examinations and I passed them fine, proceeding to graduate from the eighth grade. Then as I said before, "I think I had one hell of an education."

Today if a teacher would do something like that, she might be sent to jail. However, to this day, I do not have resentment for Marjorie because of the discipline in the schoolhouse. We all knew what we were supposed to do which was get an education,

In later life after Lois and I were married, Lois was secretary of the school for several years. My older children, Clare, Cathy, and Doug attended the school for several years.

After the consolidation of our school district with Wellman, West Chester, and Kalona, our Smith Creek schoolhouse remained for several years. It is now a part of the Mid Prairie school district. It was moved to Wellman to become a country school house Museum.

THE OLD HOUSE THAT I LIVED IN 17 YEARS.

THE OLD BARN AND THE MUDDY BARN YARD
20

MOTHER AND DAD WITH THE FLOWERS SHE LOVED
21

Part 1
Chapter 5
That Old House

When people have a nice warm house to live in, they may not appreciate what their ancestors went through. Our old house was built in the days when money was very short. There was no insulation and making a house warm was a difficult job. On the outside walls of the house, were clapboards or sideing nailed there directly to the studs. The inside walls had the old-style plaster laths or little strips of wood with plaster on them. It is no wonder the house was cold. There was a draft along every wall in the house.

In the kitchen the walls were covered with white oil cloth. In the north east corner of the kitchen, which was the farthest from the stove, frost would accumulate on the oil cloth and stay when the temperature got below 25 degrees. Some winters the frost was there from fall to spring because of the cold. There was no basement under the main part of the house so people did not run around in their stocking feet in the wintertime. The same was true of the kitchen. We did have a small basement under the dining room which had a bin for storing potatoes and shelves for Mother's canned fruit and vegetables, as well as the meat that was processed. There was usually a 20 gallon crock of sauerkraut or mustard pickles which were so delicious.

If we had a blowing snowstorm, we would have to go up in the attic and remove the snow so that when it melted it would not come down through the ceiling. This would only be a couple times a year when we would have a terrible blowing snowstorm. The north door which we never used in the wintertime had a crack in it, so that when the wind blew, it would hum and make a beautiful little tune. It would have a high-pitched sound and as the wind changed ,so would the pitch and hum. There was no plastic to nail across the doors and windows as there is today. When Dad burnt wood in the stove, he was not laying out cash, but it just meant he had to cut some more wood.

One of the winters when my father took Mother to

Excelsior Springs Missouri, a lady came out from Keota, to stay with me and to cook for the hired man. I think I was about seven or eight years old. She and I slept in the room where the two beds were and where the two half windows on the north side were. It got terribly cold, way below zero, and the wind came up and it was blowing very hard. The lady, Mrs. Meyer, took a hot water bottle to bed with her. During the night one of the half windows blew out and leaned up against my bed. Well, the wind blew up over my bed and down on her. The hot water bottle frozen in bed with her. The next morning when she got out of bed, she was so cold she said", I'm not staying in a house like this!". She got in her old car and went back to Keota.

My father was always afraid of fire, when the stove would burn all night and on those cold, cold nights he would sleep in his sheepskin coat on the davenport and would keep a fire burning all night in the heating stove. He did it because it was the best choice for survival.

Another thing I remember about the old house is that behind the cook stove it was always nice and warm. A lot of the times my father would take a nap behind the stove on the floor and sometimes there was a 20 gallon crock behind the stove where Mother and Dad would be making a batch of home brew. I can remember Mother was always checking the thermometer to see that it was the right temperature. Despite all the close attention, neither Mother nor Dad drank much of the beer. They were always making it for the hired men or friends who would stop by.

One time I can remember Mother bottled a new batch of brew when it was a little too green and not through working. Our dear neighbor lady, Mae Durian, was a good Methodist and did not believe in drinking. She came up to visit Mother one afternoon and they were setting in the dining room above the basement. Suddenly they heard a loud bang in the basement and Mother said nothing. A bit later there was another loud bang in the basement. Mae wanted to know what was happening. Mother, of course, knew exactly what it was. But she said to Mae " My goodness, the cats must have gotten into the basement and knocked down some fruit jars!". As soon as Mae was gone the brew was removed from the basement.

I never cared for home brew and can't recall ever drinking

23

any of it. I was raised with hard liquor in the cupboard. My dad would say," If you want a drink, take it. Just don't make a damned fool of yourself". The challenge was gone.. It was the same with cigarettes. Dad always said, "If you want to be a fool and smoke, go ahead." My father never smoked. I never smoked and am so thankful that I never started the habit. Mother finally put a stop to the home brew because there were too many people stopping to get their drink of home brew.

MOTHER LOVED HER FLOWERS AND HAD BIG
FLOWER BEDS AT THE OLD HOUSE

MY GRANDPARENTS MARY AND CONRAD ALLER. THEY WERE
LOVING PEOPLE COMPARED TO MY OTHER GRANDFATHER.

SISTER MARJORIE AND BOOTS. THE OLD WASH HOUSE IN THE
BACK ALONG WITH THE MILK SEPERATOR IN THE BACK GROUND

Part 1
Chapter 6
The Old Homestead

       The home that we lived in was a typical Iowa farmhouse built in the 1860's. It was a one and one-half story house that had two chimneys, one to heat the living room, and one for the kitchen. Of course the kitchen was the most important room in the house. The kitchen was a room about sixteen feet square with the cook stove sitting off to one side. There was space between the wall and the cook stove where my father always managed to take a nap. Facing the stove to the right was a pantry where my mother stored the dishes, all her cooking ingredients, and occasionally the penny candy bars that were a treat for our school lunch.

       Off the left side of the stove in the kitchen was another room the same size as the pantry. In this room we hung our clothes, hanging our work clothes along the south wall. On the north wall of this little room was a little cabinet where a wash basin sat that was used to wash our hands and faces. There was also a medicine cabinet where items such as aspirin, extra razor blades, and face powder were kept. When farmers milk cows and feed hogs and are out slopping around in mud all day, they did not smell like a rose. Occasionally there would be such an aroma that Mother would insist the clothes be hung on the porch outdoors. There was no such thing as an automatic washing machine, It was on Monday morning that the old wringer washer was fired up in the wash house. Also in this room and hanging on the north wall was a razor strap about two feet long. It was not used to sharpen razors!. It was used to maintain discipline. It wasn't used very often on us children, but the mere thought of it hanging there was all that was needed.

       Off this kitchen was a screened back porch. The porch was about twenty feet long and six feet wide. But it was wonderful for two reasons, Under the porch was a cistern with a pump. It was wonderful to be able to go to the pump on a cold day and get a bucket of soft water to fill the reservoir on the cook stove. As soon as it got cold Dad would have a quarter of beef hanging there for fresh meat. We would then have hot water to wash the dishes and our bodies. Water didn't come out of a faucet. Most farms did not have running water.

From the kitchen into the dining room, around the corner to the right, set a safe where my father kept his personal papers. Incidentally that same safe is still being used here in our motel today. There was another big dining room table and a very old buffet that you see in antique shops today. My mother did not have many possessions at that time but what she did have, she was very proud of. Also in this old dining room set the pedal sewing machine that I can still see my mother using. She used it for making quilts and patching clothes.

As you left the kitchen and went into the dining room, if you turned left you would walk into the living room. The kitchen and the dining room were just one story. But when you walked into the living room you walked into the part of the house that was a story and a half. This part of the house did not have a basement under it. The dining room was the only part of the house that had a basement under it. You had to go outside to get into the basement. There was a bedroom downstairs, which was quite small, where my mother and father slept. There was also a very steep stairway that went up to the second floor where there was one small bedroom and one large bedroom with two beds. Up the old stairway there was a shelf sticking about four feet over the stairway. It was here that the full bags of flour and sugar were stored. I remember sugar came in hundred pound bags; there was always a supply. We always had one or two hired men who lived with us who usually slept in the large room with two beds. In the big room was a large wardrobe. Whoever stayed in that room could store some of their clothes. Of course there were a couple of dressers also.

There was no way to heat the upstairs in the wintertime, although the chimney did go between the two walls and there was a register cut in the floor. But my father never allowed this to be open as the downstairs was too hard to heat. However some heat went up the stairway. On each end of the upstairs was one window that would open on a double sash. And in the big room there were two windows about four feet tall that could be removed in the summertime to get a little air. However they let as much cold air in the wintertime as they did fresh air in the summertime.

27

I can't explain how cold it was in the wintertime, and how hot it was in the summer. But the heat and the cold were overshadowed by the good times that were had in that house. The neighbors were always playing cards with my parents, or neighbors who lived up the road always had hired men who would come and spend a couple of hours playing cards, making ice cream, or just visiting. It was not a lonely time as there was always something going on at the farm.

To try to make this house halfway warm in the wintertime my father would put bales of straw around the house trying to cover some of the cracks. But he always missed a few. Living on a farm we always had a lot of cats. Around the first of February, cats did their normal thing, and would always find a way under the house. So we could hear the old Tom cats fighting and knocking their heads on the joists. I think Father rather enjoyed this. Otherwise, he probably could have found a way to keep them out from under the house. Remember, we had only the radio in those days, so we looked for every bit of entertainment that there was.

When we moved back to the farm in 1929, the barn that had been on the farm had burned the previous year. My father had made a contract with an old friend from Harper to build a new barn. So that spring there was a lot of activity building the new barn, which was a very large one. It had stalls for six head of horses and my pony "Dickey." There was ample milking area with stanchions for ten cows plus a boxstall for three, and a shed with mangers where a person could throw down feed and hay to feed cattle.

All of the corn raised on the farm was picked in the ear by hand and had to be stored in a corn crib. A crib had a three quarter inch crack every six inches so that the corn could dry and would not spoil from too much moisture in it. This was a double corn crib with a big driveway in the middle. This was a really modern corn crib. It had an inside elevator that would take the corn to the top of the crib, and by gravity, it could flow to the bottom until each side was full. To power this elevator there was a big ten horse single cylinder gas engine with two enormous fly wheels. It created a terrible noise going " pop-up pop a pop-pop pop" so that you could not hear anything in the corn crib while it was running. For its day it was a really up-to-date building.

There were two chicken houses on the farm. The older

28

one was out by the corn crib, and my father had built a fairly new one east of our house. He had also constructed a two car garage that had a small shop and storage for machinery. It took very little room to store one's machinery. Of course, it was not built on to the house but was a fair walk from the garage to the house when the lots were muddy. The chicken houses were the domain of my mother. She was the one who raised the chickens so there was some money for groceries, and clothing, and other miscellaneous items.

The road in front of our house ran east and west. We were just 500 feet up the hill from a four way intersection. Turning into our yard, there was a row of huge old maple trees running west. I spent a lot of time there playing cops and robbers. At the west end of this grove was another group of young trees that my mother and father planted the day I was born.

On this farm we had a barn, corn crib, two chicken houses, a garage, a washhouse, and the house. Our farm buildings sat on 120 acres of land in Lime Creek Township. My father had another 120 acres, three and 1/2 miles south of where we lived. There was a big barn on this farm also. On this farm my father ran a lot of cattle since there was pasture on this land. We called this the Diehl place, I guess because a man named Diehl owned it at one time.

The fall of 1929 is when I started school 1/2 mile north of where we lived. It was a country schoolhouse with one room and a basement beneath it. It was a fairly new one room school, having the usual two hole outdoor toilets for boys and for girls, but no water. We had a stone water cooler in the basement where we all drank our water from the same cup. Isn't it strange that anybody rarely got sick. We usually had from 15 to 25 children in our school with one teacher who was teacher, janitor, fireman, nurse, and kept law and order.

By the time I was in the third grade, I would ride Dickey to school and feed him post hay. What in the world is post hay?. When a person tied a horse to a post so he could get nothing to eat, you called that post hay. My sister and I, when she was still in school, would ride him home to eat lunch at noon. Dickey only knew one thing when we headed home and that was to run as fast as he could. We would eat lunch and head back to school with Dickey for more post hay. When late fall came, it got too cold to ride Dickey to school, and there was no barn to put him in.

Our country school was a wonderful neighborhood school. One of my best friends Burrell Foster Jr, was one year of head of me. The school had a big old bell on top of the schoolhouse which the teacher would ring five minutes before it was time for us to come in. Burrell Foster and Delmar Bull and I were usually a gang of three. We were typical of all teenage boys, trying to see what went on in the girls toilet and trying to build up a head of steam to pee over the boys toilet. To my knowledge we never did get caught because if we stood in the right place,the teacher couldn't see us from the schoolhouse. When the weather got really bad we would play a rough form of basketball in the basement where we had an "x" mark between two joists, and that was our basketball hoop.

We had a great time twice a week. On Tuesdays and Thursday, we would have a hot lunch program where the parents would bring something hot to school for all the children. We had one family in our school who was quite poor, and the mother wasn't the best housekeeper, and like all stupid kids when it was their turn for the hot food, some turned up their noses. But all in all, it worked out very well and there weren't any government subsidies, and no special employees to feed us. We had some wonderful teachers at our school. One lady, Edna Hendrix, should be a saint in heaven for all the kids she taught and how she saw to it that they got their lessons, and did well in school.

THE FARM STEAD IN 1941. IT HAS CHANGED A LOT SINCE THIS PICTURE WAS TAKEN

Part 1
Chapter 7
Growing up

When my grandfather divided up the 500 acres of land he bought on the Prairie, my father Albert got the life use of 160 acres. His brothers Edward , John, Richard, and Alvina all got the life use of 160 acres of land. His sister Clara got the equivalent in money. Sometime after Father's brother Ed passed a way my father rented a 160 acres from Edward's children. Eighty acres of this land had a set of buildings that we called the"80". The farm had pasture on it and this meant that there were always chores to do. It was a mile and a half to those buildings. If the roads were muddy, that meant we rode Dickey to do the chores at the 80. He would never run very fast going over. But when the chores were done and you headed home, I had to hang on because he was headed for the barn! If the roads were not to bad, Dad had an old model a Ford pickup that we could drive. Back then when you were 10 or 12 years old, you would be driving even if you couldn't see over the steering wheel setting down. I love homegrown peaches. One day, when I was about 12 years old, I drove the pickup home from the 80. I was eating peaches and fell asleep at the wheel. When I woke up I was scared to death! I had just plain run in the ditch. The old truck was high centered and stuck, so I started walking home. Someone came down the road in a car, asked me if I knew who's pickup that was. I was too afraid, so I told them that I didn't know who owned it. But he knew and later told my father about it. They had a good laugh over it.

I walked on home, then Bud and I harnessed our old stallion, Dick, got a log chain, walked down, and pulled the old pickup out of the ditch. I was scared what my father would say, but he was thankful that I was not hurt. In 1930 when the depression was going full blast dad lifted our only car up on blocks to save the tires. We drove a team of horses to town when we needed to go. My Father decided we needed another riding horse. Broncos were selling at an auction in Sigourney Iowa. These were horses that had run on the range in the West. Some

32

were partly broke.

Father went to the sale and bought a dun colored horse for thirty dollars, but there was a problem. He didn't have thirty dollars! My mother's sister, Clara Horras, who ran a dairy in Sigourney had enough silver to pay for the horse. My father came home, the next day, put a load of first litter sows in a wagon. Then he took them by wagon to Keota. He got two cents a pound for them, which meant that the wagon load of sows just paid for the horse. The next day , Dad took Bud to pickup the horse and to pay Clara backed the thirty dollars. Bud then rode the horse thirty miles home. We drove cattle many miles with Cotton and Dickey. We always had cattle to drive somewhere. It would be impossible to do it today as most farms no longer have outside fences. I also liked to ride Cotton, because we had a saddle for him and not for Dickey, who I rode bareback. I just about wore out the Sears and Roebuck catalog wishing for a saddle. Dickey would always sweat so much that my pants would always be ringing wet.

I was tossed off of Dickey so often that my father thought it would be dangerous for me to have the saddle. I think the truth was he didn't want to spend the money for one. We often rode on the roadside and if Dickey saw a piece of paper or a tin can he would shy so fast you could not hang on. Then he would go down the road holding his head up in the air , so the reins did not drag on the ground, swinging his head from one side to the other as if to say" I got you again". Sometimes it was a game for us and while I was younger he usually won. As I grew older and bigger, he didn't throw me off as much.

During the summer of 1928 or 1929 a sad thing happened at our house. My Mother had contracted scarlet fever. Back then when a person had an infectious disease someone from the county would come out and post a quarantine sign on your house. While under quarantine I was not allowed to be with my Mother. The people responsible for those things came out and sealed off my Mother's bedroom from the rest of the house. There were three hired men working for us at the time and we would have to put a ladder against the house and crawl up the ladder through the window to get to the bedrooms upstairs. This would not have been so bad if my Mother had not been so sick. It turned into a tragedy for our family, particularly for my mother. This brought on a very severe case of rheumatoid arthritis. From that time on she

33

was a severely crippled woman. Before her sickness she loved to work outside, she had lots of flowers, milked cows, raised the chickens and had a huge garden and was always canning something or sewing.

DAD HOWARD MOTHER AND QUEENIE IN 1939

Part 1
Chapter 8
My mother

   I was very close to my mother. Of course, my older sisters always said she spoiled me, but she was my shining light. My father did not have the loving and caring way that mother did. I do not think I ever remember my father saying to me " I love you." Those words were just not in his vocabulary. Not that he didn't love his kids and mother. He just could not express himself. You have to appreciate that we always had hired men and that we ate three meals a day at the kitchen table. It seemed like about twice a week the hired men would start teasing me about something. Usually I didn't have the good sense to shut up. Invariably I would get a whack from my father. It seems I was what you would call a slow learner. I would leave the table crying and mother would always see to it that I got a little compassion. However it would not be too many days before the hired men would tease me again.

   As several years went by my mother became more crippled. She got to the point where she could not get out of a chair.   My folks had bought a willow rocking chair from an Amishman who was selling them in the community for five dollars. They were a comfortable chair. Someone would help my mother get up in the morning, get dressed, and put her in the rocking chair. She would stay there until someone came for her. Over the years she became very crippled and   deformed as she had arthritis in every joint in her body. I don't know how anyone could stand the pain.   Only those people with the severe crippling arthritis would understand. When people would say Francis " How are you", she would reply " I 'm fine" when they knew she wasn't.

   When I was about in the fifth or sixth-grade every morning before I went to school I would help her get up and dressed and put her in the rocking chair. We did not have a modern house. There was a closet in the downstairs bedroom under the stairway where we had a commode box with a chamber pot. It was my job to take it to our outdoor toilet and then rinse it out each morning. I didn't mind doing that. It was a ritual at our house that every evening before I went to bed my mother had me kneel at her rocking chair and say my prayers. My mother was a very religious person and believed strongly in her Catholic faith. I still know those prayers today.

My father was good to my mother in trying to find places to take her to try to get help for her pain. But we now know there is no cure. She went to Toronto Canada, to a doctor who was supposed to be able to cure arthritis. He was a total quack. She took gold shots in her joints and suffered pain tremendously from them with no relief. A lot of people went to Excelsior Springs Missouri, where they had mineral waters that were supposed to help. However, nothing helped. She had a life that was up-and-down. As time went along, she would get better for a while and would be able to get about. However, she still suffered the pain and the crippling of her body.

When mother passed away we found her driver's license issued in 1923 and she was five feet nine inches tall. However, when she passed on, she was barely five feet. No matter how sick she was she was always full of love for us children. She would always say" Thank God I have this instead of dad". The rest of the family knew that it was a blessing because Father could stand no pain. When I talk about mother in the rest of my writing, even though I don't mention it she was always suffering. I can remember she fell and broke her hip, broke her shoulders, her leg, but still would not give up. She would never get in a wheelchair because she was afraid she would never get out. From the time she got arthritis it was always my sisters and I who helped mother. Of course when we were not there, we always had help in the house to look after mother also. My dad was willing to help her, but he was always as awkward as a cub bear. He just didn't have the technique to help mother with out hurting her. I remember being in Iowa City at Mercy Hospital to see old Doctor Scanlon with mother and him saying" Francis when you die you should go straight to heaven, you have had your hell on earth".

I still have that willow rocking chair in my apartment that my Mother rocked a million miles in.

36

MOTHER AND DAD HOLDING KAREN SUE. MARJORIES CHILD.

THE HOUSE AND OLD WOODEN WINDMILL GIVES IT
A LOOK OF THE 1930'S. THE WINDMILL IS GONE

Part 1
Chapter 9
Entertainment

    I can recall having one birthday party in my childhood. I was about eight years old when my mother decided to have a party for me. She invited in a group of neighborhood children for this birthday party. I found it quite boring. I remember my Mother and Father had given me a new daisy air rifle. Nearly every farm boy had one in those days. My air rifle had a pump action which allowed the user to create pressure in the barrel before it would shoot a BB. Since the party was quite boring, I decided to take my air rifle and shoot Sparrows. When it was time for the ice cream and cake, I wasn't around. The rest of the children ate the ice cream and cake. When I did show up, I was not in good standing with my mother. So that might be the reason why I never had any more birthday parties as a child.

    Now I was doing quite well with my BB gun, having fun trying to kill Sparrows and occasionally breaking a window in the chicken house as that seemed to be where the Sparrows congregated. My Father didn't take too kindly to breaking windows, which were small pains of glass in the skylight of the chicken house. I was doing quite well with my BB gun until one day my sister. Cordell, and I had an argument about something. I can not exactly recall what we were arguing about but somehow I ended up shooting her in the chin. Of course, she howled and my BB gun went into quarantine for quite some time.

    When I was about nine years old my father decided I was old enough to start herding cows along the road to save our pasture. In those years the roads were narrow and all mud. There would be a lot of grass growing a long side the road and my father was one to take advantage of this. It was always the milk cows that we herded along the road. We had one old cow we called" Checkers". She was like the story you will remember, if you read Cowboy books about the Texas cattle drives, where a steer named "Old Blue" always led the way. Checkers was a red and white Holstein who, when I opened the gate, would lead the rest of the cows out to the road. By this time Dickey had turned into an excellent cattle horse. If a cow decided to go the wrong direction, I had to hold on, because he moved so quickly I would be dumped off!. Remember, I rode him bareback all the time. Taking the cows out on the road was usually from early spring, when the grass started to grow, until about the end of June. Of course during school time, I only took the cows out on Saturday

There were fences along all the roads and I would have to watch for open gates. I would let the cows go west one mile or south one-half mile and a half-mile west. It really was a fun time as this was before 2-4-D. Then we had wild strawberries, wild grapevines, wild roses, and various plants growing along the highway. I hardly could wait till wild strawberries got ripe. Although they were always very small, they were really tasty. We did not have fresh fruit as we do now.

The cars were mostly model A Ford's or Chevrolets. When it would rain and the mud roads would get rutted out, nobody could drive very fast. There was no danger in having cows on the road. There were no maintainers to grade and plane the roads. Different farmers were paid so much a mile by the county for dragging the road. Hank Foster and his old model G John Deere would drag the roads and fill the ruts. Then Dickey and I would really have fun. We would race with every car on the road. Usually the drivers never drove over 25 miles an hour and for a short distance Dickey and I would give a real chase. He was always ready to chase after cars coming down the road.

When it came time to take the cows home about 10:30 AM, I would start them down the road and old Checkers would lead them home. To a city boy this might have been a boring job, but I found it a lot of fun.

39

Part 1
Chapter 10
The Butchering Ring

Usually in February, four of our neighbors went together and had a neighborhood get together where the men would butcher all of the hogs that each family wanted for next year. This usually was a total of 20 to 25 hogs. The men would set up a scalding vat on the Durian place and build a fire under it to heat the water. They would then kill and slaughtered all of the hogs in one day and let them hang in the corncrib at the Durian place. Then one day they would go to the Fosters , cut up, and process all of their meat. Then go to the next neighbor.

My Father had a big black iron kettle that he would support between two barrels, and had a large lard press, and it was his job to render the lard. He was a real professional at it. It was always fun to help him press out the lard, as that left all of the cracklings, and they were so good to eat when they were fresh and hot. My mother always saved these and made lye soap out of these for washing clothes.

The rest of the people in the house would be cutting up and curing the hams and bacon, to get them ready for Fred Durian, to take to his smoke house, as he was the expert on smoking meat. The smoke house was their old outdoor toilet. The rest of them would be making sausage, when the lard press was finished, they would take the small intestines, that had been cleaned and scraped, and link the sausage. It was always fun to see the sausage come flying out of the press. We kids always liked to turn the handle on the press, to see the sausage fly out, and once in a while we would turn it too fast, on purpose of course, to see what would happen. That usually ended our turn at the press.

Some of the people would cook the pork chops ,and put them in big stone jars, then pour melted lard over them so that they would keep all summer long. Whenever you wanted pork chops you would go down and dig them out of the lard. And then smooth the lard back over, so they would not get air and spoil. They were wonderful.

At our house, my parents always cleaned all of the meat off of the pig heads. They cleaned the ears and my mother always made what we kids called "Pig Souse". She would make this in a type of gelatin, and it was always so good. If I could just have a piece of it now! When they butchered at our place my folks never smoked the meat, but always dry cured it. Then they would wrap it up in white cloth and hang it in the wash house to cure. There was always the chance of getting it too salty, but the folks had this down to a science.

It was always a fun time because it meant a week, of going to different houses and in the evening, wherever you cut up the meat you would have supper. Sometimes it was oysters stew and, sometimes fresh meat but it always was so good to eat. Sometimes our folks would play cards but usually they were tired and just go home to start all over tomorrow. Our neighbors were such good people and I was lucky to be raised in that neighborhood.

Whenever we needed beef to eat, Dad would select a steer and shoot it. Then take a block and tackle and pull it up under the fore shoot of the barn and dress it out. That usually meant we would have fresh liver for a couple of days and then mother would pickle the tongue and heart. How good it was. They would then hang the rear quarters on our back porch that was screened in. The front quarters mother would cut up, and cold pack it so we would have meat all summer. All you have to do is heat it up. I think my daughter Cathy,also does this. It was such a fun time for the kids and also for the older folks as they all had a great time and a lot of fun working together. We sure do not see that today we are all too busy doing nothing.

Part 1
Chapter 11
My friend

On the road east of our farm one half-mile lived Mr. and Mrs. Burrell Foster. Laura and Burrell had a son named Burrell Jr. He was one year older than I. We were together for eight years in the country school, however, he was one year ahead of me. My parents and the Fosters were together a lot. They liked having card parties and of course I got to go along. Burrell Jr. had a lot of toys that I didn't have. He had an electric train, boxing gloves, all kinds of building blocks, and lots of lead soldiers that we were always setting up to do battle. And of course our father's always liked to take us to the basement to put on the boxing gloves. I never won a fight because after the second punch in the nose, I would have a nose bleed. Therefore the fights never lasted very long.

North of the Fosters house was a big grove and a big pond. In the summer, we would try fishing. In the wintertime when the pond was frozen over there was always a group of kids trying to play hockey, but only a few had skates. We would take our sleds and go sledding because there were some big hills by the pond. Mr. Foster was a skeet and trap shooter and every year a big trap shoot was held back by the pond. This was a great day as people came from all over Iowa to participate. There was quantities of beer and whiskey consumed, but I never saw anybody out of line. The Fosters raised thousands of turkeys each year and they gave turkeys for prizes as well as shotguns and cash. All the neighbors worked and help serve the food. It was an event that the neighbors looked forward to every year. Burrell Jr. and I always had a great time..

As we've got a little older, we started thinking about girls. Burrell Jr. somehow met an attractive young lady in Dubuque. She had a friend who she made a date with for me. We talked our father's into letting us have the old 39 Ford and we headed for Dubuque 120 miles away. We got to Dubuque, and met our friends and had a good time. We stayed at the Julian Dubuque

42

Hotel which was hot stuff in those days. My date, a daughter of a policeman, was a very nice young lady. We had a good time for a couple of days. We would slip into east Dubuque and go to the nightclubs. I believe it was the Circle nightclub where slot machines were running wild. We really thought we were hot stuff. Now our friendship with these two girls lasted a couple of years, and we were just friends, until Burrell Jr. graduated from high school. Burrell Jr. was troubled with hay fever so he elected to go to the University of Arizona that fall. That was the fall of 1939.

That fall my parents decided to go to California a couple of weeks before Christmas. Burrell Jr. had a cousin living in Pasadena California.. He had a date arranged with her for me for New Year's Eve. I had made reservations at the Coconut Grove nightclub which was "thee" hot spot at that time in Hollywood. We drove my parents 1939 Ford car to San Francisco, then traveled down the coast to Los Angeles. Neither my parents nor I had ever been in California. We arrived at Los Angeles a couple of days before New Years and my parents stayed with some relatives in Los Angeles. New Years Eve, Virginia and I went to the Coconut Grove and had a delightful time. The next morning we were up early and went to the Rose Bowl parade. We Iowa farmers found it fascinating.

From California, we went to Tucson AZ so I could spend five days with Burrell Jr. We had a great time. We went to Mexico, I think the town was Nogales. We did the nightclubs, had a few drinks and went back to Tucson. The time I spent with Burrell Jr. was very precious. The following April, he and some friends went to Los Angeles to visit his cousin, Virginia. On the way back to Tucson, the convertible that they were driving rolled over and my friend Burrell Jr. was killed. This was a sad time for all of us in the neighborhood. In Tucson Burrell Jr. had a good friend named Norman O'Connell. We became friends and would see each other occasionally, when he came to visit the Fosters. When D-Day came during the war, Norman was killed in the first wave at Normandy. It always seemed, all of my good friends ended up being killed.

BURELL FOSTER AND I FISHING ON SKUNK RIVER IN 1940
44

IT WAS JANUARY 1941 WHEN I VISITED MY FRIEND AT THE U OF
ARIZONA .HE WAS KILLED IN AN AUTO ACCIDENT THE
FOLLOWING EASTER WEEK END.HE WAS MY BEST FRIEND.

BURELL FOSTER AND I WERE FRIENDS AND WERE ALWAYS
DOING SOMETHING. WE WERE GOOD AT CHASING GIRLS.

Part 1
Chapter 12
Hired Men

During my earlier years, my Father always had hired men who lived with us. During these years my Mother was terribly sick. We had a hired girl who also stayed at our house. The girl lived with us for several years. She and the hired men had a good time together. There was always something going on for excitement, with that many people around. Either they were going to ball games or to dances or making ice cream but it usually was something.

During all of these years, most of our farming was done with horses. Having many horses around and a stallion on the farm that we worked, my father arranged to see that all of our mares were bred to have foals. Usually we would have five foals, from the mares. This gave us a lot of extra horses to break, to sell or trade. I believe it was 1932, when my father traded six horses to an International Harvester dealer for a10-20 tractor that had been repossessed. This was not a row crop tractor, but one that we could pull the binder with, when we harvested oats, and did the plowing. It was also used to grind feed for the fat cattle my father fed. It was difficult to drive because it had steel wheels and there were was no power steering.

We had no portable hay balers so all of our hay was put up with a hay loader and horses. Usually, until I got older, it was my job to lead the hay horse. This is the horse that we used to pull the hay up into the barn. We always used old "Mays" for the job. However I always liked to drive the horses on the wagon with the loader, because I could listen to the hired men who usually were talking about sex. This is when my sex education began. After the first crop of hay was put up, it was time to start plowing corn. My Father didn't believe that two row corn plows were any good so we had three single row corn plows that we used to plow corn with. Cross ways the second time, and length ways the third time. The corn was always checked. In those days the corn was always planted with a wire so that you could cross plow the corn.

If the tension were right on the wire, when you planted, the buttons on the wire would place the corn in hills so that you could cross it.

The hired men were always looking for entertainment. They'd delighted in catching someone's Tom cat, sticking his head in a boot, and castrating it. One of the reasons they did this was because we had many female cats having kittens and stray male cats would kill the baby kittens. We always had sheep on the farm. Every time a stray dog came around we would do our best to shoot it. This may sound cruel, but knowing what stray dogs do to sheep, would make anyone feel less sorry for the dog.. It was an exciting life. There was a dance pavilion in Wellman that had a dance every Thursday night. Some of the hired men went to the dance. They always had good bands, and a lot of people had a headache the next morning from drinking to much beer. I went to the dances at Oakwood pavilion many times. Even Lawrence Welk played their at one time. We had a neighbor by the name of Henry Foster, who was Burrell juniors half brother. He would come to our house with his "Blue Bird" which was a car with the top cut off. We would load up the seine, and head for English River, which was about five miles north of us. We would set the seine in the River, strip off our clothes and try to scare the fish into the net. We never did have any big hauls but we drank a few bottles of beer. We never gave any thought to being caught by the game warden. We would go home with our clothes wet and muddy. When we got home we usually had ice cream. Our entertainment was cheap and enjoyable.

Part 1
Chapter 13
The Bohr Family

At the height of the 1930 depression, times were extremely hard. My father was just getting started farming again and was in need of a good hired men. A young man , Marvin Bohr came to my Father for a job in the spring of 1931 and my father gave him employment. This meant that Bud (his nickname) would live in our house and become part of the family. Bud fit well with our family. My Father paid him ten dollars a month. Bud bought a 1928 Chevrolet car and paid seven dollars a month on the car. In 1932, he started dating a young woman by the name of Christina Bayliss over by Keota.

On April 26, 1933 Bud and Christina were married. Although I was about ten years old, I then slept in the hired man's room upstairs. I was not going to let anybody by the name of Christina chase me out of my bed. However, I woke up the next morning in the bedroom where we had two beds to discover that I had lost my bed partner. By this time, my Mother was quite crippled and Christina worked and helped her in the house while Bud worked outside. That winter they had a son whom was named Howard Dean Bohr. This meant that there were two Howard's in the house so a nickname was used for Howard Dean. He was nicknamed " Boots". This is a name that he has carried all of his life and more people know him as Boots than any other name. In the spring of 1937 Bud and Christina moved to another farm which we called the 80. That fall in October, they had another son who they named Harold.

This meant that Boots and I had grown up together. It was about a mile and a half from the 80 to our place. Bud would do the chores on the 80 and then would come to our farm to help milk. My father usually milked from 12 to 13 cows, which meant he had to get up quite early. If it was muddy, he would have to ride Cotton, our saddle horse. Boots liked to go along with his father, anytime the horses was hitched, to do some work which was about every day. He was around many hired hands and picked up a bit of profanity. My father took him along whenever he went somewhere. He loved to ride Dickey as soon as he was able, which was when he was quite young. He and I would always ride Dickey bareback.

I had fixed up an old coaster wagon, that my uncle had thrown away, with Osage Orange, wheel bearings made from a hedge tree. I would put Boots in the wagon and tied a 20 foot rope to it. If the roads were not muddy, and somebody had drug them so they were smooth, we would take off down the road a flying. Dickey loved to run. I can see that tow headed four or five year old hollering, " God Dam'it , Howdy, slowdown!" Of course, I loved to hear him holler. And I admit, occasionally we would hit a rough spot in the road and Boots would go flying. However, he was a game little rascal and would climb right back in the wagon and away we would go. This usually took place when I was herding cows along the side of the road. I did not get too involved with Harold as he was smaller and younger and when he was two years old, Bud and Christina moved to her father's farm near Keota.

In 1940 Bud and Christina moved back to the 80 and started working with my father again. After I left for the Air Force a couple of years later, my father rented the farm to Bud and helped him get started farming. He later bought a farm a mile east of us and in 1964 Bud passed away with a heart attack. Boots and Harold took over the farmland and now Harold lives one-quarter mile north of the home farm and Boot's lives just down the road about a quarter of a mile east of the home farm.

I called Christina to verify some of these dates. Although she is 85 years old now, she gets around quite well and her mind is better than mine. This family has always been considered as part of our family and it is great to have known them. Later when I be came so involved, in the fertilizer plant, my father and I rented our farm to the Bohr boys. This gave them a good start in farming that I am sure they both appreciate it to this day.

50

BUD BOHR , GRANDMA ALLER AND MOTHER AND DAD 1938

BOOTS AND MY PONY "DICKEY" ONE OF THE FEW PICTURES
OF MY PONY. MY FOLKS NEVER OWNED A CAMERA

Part 1
Chapter 14
Another close call

In the winter of 1938 my Father decided to build a new house. He made plans for a square, basic house. As I recall it was 28 feet by 34 feet. This gave us big enough space so we could have the usually large family farm kitchen. There was no dining room and the living room extended clear across the house on the north side. There was a toilet and a lavatory downstairs. There was a small bedroom downstairs for my Mother. Upstairs there were two larger bedrooms and two small bedrooms. There was also a bathroom upstairs.

Plans had to be made to tear the old house down, and to have a place for us to live, while the new house was being built. South of our old house was the wash-house. There was room enough in the wash- house for two double beds on the east end. And another bed could be put where we've previously stored corn cobs. However, we still did the separating of the milk in the same building. Some years earlier my parents had built an addition on the old house for a large kitchen. This was separated from the old house and moved about 50 feet west of where the new house would be. This is where the cooking was done.

In 1938 there were no backhoes so the basement had to be dug with horses and a slip scraper. Most people probably don't know what a slip scraper is. It has two handles and a person was supposed to control the amount of bit in the dirt. If one had a fast pair of horses he would end up being thrown over the top of the scraper. It was a hard, hard, job to dig the basement.

My Father hired carpenters from the town of Wellman to build the house. I can remember that the cabinet maker, who was the highest-paid man on the crew, was paid 35 cents per hour. The rest of the carpenters all were paid 25 cents per hour. After the house was built the total cost was six thousand dollars. That included plumbing, cabinets, oil furnace, and everything in the house.

That spring about the first of April, I became sick with a

strep throat. It became more complicated because I have a blood disease called Thalessemia and I became very anemic.Then doctors didn't know that I had this disease. I was so bad and so anemic that my nose bled constantly. I didn't know about the disease nor did the Air Force ever find this. It wasn't found, until I was in Mercy hospital in Des Moines with my first heart trouble in 1984. I found I have passed it on to some of my children and my grandchildren. It is a disease of the red blood cells.

The folks ended up taking me to the Washington County hospital at Washington. My strep throat got worse. This was the time when sulfa drugs first came on the market. I was one of the first people in Washington County to get sulfa drugs. I feel that it saved my life. When I was well enough to come home, my folks didn't want to bring me back to the wash -house. That is when our good neighbors, the Fosters, stepped in and the folks took me to Laura and Burrell Fosters house. Laura had been a registered nurse. They put me in a room downstairs and I had excellent care for the next two or three weeks. I was a very lucky young man. When I met my wife Lois, her younger brother had gotten strep throat and died from the complications. Many people died from this as we didn't have the super drugs then to control it.

This didn't stop my nose bleeds, however, so that doctors decided to cauterize the inside of my nose. They burned a hole through the sternum in my nose. As I have been troubled with nose bleeds all of my life it was very frustrating after that because I could never tell which side of my nose was bleeding.(I could have worn a ring in my nose long before this so-called modern trend today). Just for fun after I was married, my wife would take a toothpick and stick it through my nose and I would look like someone out of the jungle.

That fall we moved into the new house. We all thought we had died and gone to heaven. After living in the old house so long, this was like a dream. I was 16 years old before, I knew you could go to the bathroom in the house. Joking of course. The summer of 1962 when our last son was born, Lois and I added a big addition and a two-car garage onto this house.

53

Part 1
Chapter 15
Milking time on the farm

My father always milked 12 to 13 cows so there would be income weekly to meet the salaries of the hired men and help to buy groceries. My dad was constantly buying and selling milk cows. He always made a little money on the transaction. He was a good trader. In the summertime we would feed the cows grain. They would be waiting at the barn door to get in. In the winter the cows were milked and were turned out to go to a water tank, then the barn had to be cleaned. There was a trench about10 inches deep and 18 inches wide behind the cows. Needless to say every morning this was full of manure. We had to take a scoop shovel to carry the manure out by hand. I always tried to find another job to do when this had to be done.

Father was fast at milking cows. But mostly milking was a job for the hired men. My Father was a good manager. He saw that the work was done properly, but I never saw him actually do a lot of the hard physical labor. The manure that was thrown out of the backside of the barn created a big pile. There were no tractor loaders in those times. Which meant, it all had to be loaded the second time into a manure spreader by hand, to be spread on the fields. There were no cement floors around the barn, and in the spring the mud would get so deep from the cattle stomping on it , you needed boots or five buckle overshoes. It usually was that way most of the winter. For that reason we would let the cows out for water, then put them back in the barn, close the stanchions around their neck, and feed them hay in the barn.

The milk had to be carried to the wash -house where the cream or butter fat was separated. Our wash house was at least 250 feet from where we hung the milk, on the wall behind the cows, when we finished milking in the barn. Now, when you have a lot of milk cows, you have a lot of baby calves that have to be fed on the bucket. Baby calves usually suck the cow for four or five days to get colostrum milk. The calves have to be taught to drink out of the bucket by letting them suck your fingers and sticking their heads into the bucket. A messy job, until they learn how to do it. We have always seen pictures of baby animals butting their mother's udder to stimulate the flow of milk. The baby calves would do the same thing to the bucket. It was necessary to hold onto the bucket or you would find milk all over you. This had to be done twice a day, which meant that the milk had to be carried back to the barn again. In addition the rest of the milk that was always fed to the hogs had to be carried back again to the feed lot. To this day I could never understand why my father didn't build a milk house beside the barn. They would have paid for itself in saved labor many times.

I hated milking with a passion. I would almost rather do any other job than milk cows. In the summertime when the cows were brought in from the pasture, and their bowels were loose from wet grass, they were put in the barn. The flies would bite them during milking and they would slap the milker, with their dirty tails. Believe me I would not have been a farmer if I had to milk cows. When we picked corn in the fall by hand and had corn pickers from Missouri staying at our house I would harness the horses and feed them while they helped milk the cows. I very much remember one morning when it was quite dark in the barn even though we had electricity. I walked behind old Babe then "BAM" she kicked me right on the knee. She knocked me up against the back wall and of course I started crying. Dad came over to see if I was seriously hurt, and seeing that I wasn't said "That is what you get for not speaking to her". No sympathy there. Even so it beat having to milk the cows. My sister also did a lot of milking and it usually was up to her to wash the separator and the milk buckets. If not, the hired girls would do it. Believe me my sister, Marjorie, did a lot of this also.

Part 1
Chapter 16
Another Narrow Escape

The 80 had several ditches running through it where the water dumped along its banks. Occasionally we would get droughts and the tile water would quit running. This meant that Dad had to find another source to water that cattle. He had heard that a man near Keota had a machine that he could drill a well with by hand. He went over to Mr. Kleins and borrowed the machine. This consisted of a tripod and an auger to drill a 14 in. hole that would allow for a 12 inch tile for a liner. This took a lot of work because the auger needed to be turned two or three revolutions, then would have to be pulled up full of dirt. This process would be repeated until the well was as deep as needed. After a lot of sweat and hard work, the well depth was about 26 feet.

My Father thought this would make a good well, and started putting down the 12 inch tile. After five tile were put down one of the tile fell over in the well. The question was what to do next. Now I was a skinny young kid about 10 years old, by holding my hands above my head over my shoulders, I would fit in the hole. My father and the hired man tied a rope around my feet, and with the winch put me in the hole, with my hands over my head. They lowered me into the hole, which was a tight fit. I proceeded to straighten up the tile. After I did they pulled me backup. It was then they heard a noise, and the well caved in down where I was. At this point my father realized what a silly, stupid, thing they had done. They would not have needed to dig a grave. Life came close to being over at that point and I was one happy young boy. The prayers that my mother had taught me paid off very well.

I was old enough to keep the wood box full of wood on the back porch for the kitchen stove, and to make sure there were chunks of wood on the east porch, for the heater in the living room. Each night when I come home from school it was my first job. The wood was split so it would go into the cook stove. I would hustle around and fill the wood box and get two baskets of cobs to start the fire with in the morning. If mother needed a real hot stove, she would use the cobs.

At that time of my life I listened to my favorite radio programs. Which were Jack Armstrong, the All-American Boy and Jimmy Allen and if I had time the Lone Ranger. There was no listening to the programs unless the wood box was full and my chores were done. Fortunately I was not quite old enough to milk cows yet when I was listening to the programs. That came a little later in life.

My favorite place to spend time was in my father's garage. My father never had many tools and he was not handy at fixing anything. He didn't like to get his hands greasy. Whenever he could not find a hammer, it's not hard to guess who got the blame. I was always making something. I never had any store bought toys, so I had to make my own, which was a form of entertainment for me. The neighboring kids had bicycles and wagons and all kinds of toys. I never had a wagon until I fixed up the one that I pulled Boots in with Dickey. Shows what you can do when you have to.We burned wood in our stoves, every winter my Father would go to a timber and cut wood. Now my father believed in making it easy to split logs, and I really think he liked to play with dynamite. Then any hardware store sold black powder or dynamite. To split big logs he would drill a two inch hole about halfway through the log and fill it with black powder, pack it with a fuse and a blasting cap. I liked to watch him do it. There would be a bang and the log would split in the middle making it much easier to handle. Now without my Father's knowledge, I decided to build a cannon. I found a piece of galvanized pipe about 12 inches long. I found a cap to put on one end ,Then I made a mount for the pipe to set on. I drilled a hole in the end of the cap on our old drill press, put a piece of dynamite fuse in it about a foot long. I took it out to our old grove of trees, poured it half full of blasting powder, set it up and lit the fuse. I hid behind another big tree and waited for it to go off. But I had forgotten, fortunately, to put a blasting cap in it. It burned until the fuse quit burning and then went out and nothing happened. Lucky for me, because I had built a bomb, and it probably would have blown shrapnel everywhere. Fortunately, I was smart enough to be afraid of it and left it there until the next day. I never did tell my father

Part 1
Chapter 17
A Tragedy In Our Family

This is a very difficult thing for me to write, but I feel you have a right to know about it. (to my older sister Cordell, I can only ask your forgiveness in writing about this). However, it is a fact of my life and part of my history.

Now when I was about six or seven years old, my parents had a hired man working for us. Like all hired men in those days he lived with our family. My older sister, Cordell, had graduated from the eighth grade. MY father didn't believe that anyone needed more education than the eighth grade. After Cordell graduated, my father would not let her go on to high school, but kept her home to help milk cows and help my mother. My father and mother didn't know that a relationship was developing between the hired man and my sister. As I recall he was about 15 years older than she. All of our good neighbors knew about the relationship and were afraid to tell my parents.

One morning when I got up and came downstairs, I found my mother and father in a state of anxiety. A few of my sisters clothes were gone and so was the hired man and my sister. It became evident that they both slipped out during the night. My parents were frantic and called the sheriff in Washington County. The search was then started for them. A couple weeks later they were found on a dairy farm near Davenport, Iowa. The hired man was put into jail. I do not know for sure whether my sister was or not. However, my parents and my grandmother went to try to talk her out of the foolish move she had made. She had lied about her age and they were already married. They could not talk her into coming home.

This was a real tragedy to my parents. My father didn't forgive my sister, Cordell, for many years and would not let her come home. It was a bigger tragedy for my mother because she would have forgiven Cordell, and did forgive her, but my father just wouldn't. However after a few years he did let Cordell come home. But he really never did forgive her for a longtime. In those days it

58

was a family disgrace for something like that to happen. I really did not grow up with my sister, Cordell, because she left when I was quite young.

One of the things I remember very plainly to this day was that the hired man sent his father out to pick up his clothes. Now the family of the hired man was always considered as being from " the other side of the tracks". The father of the hired man drove in with a car that was probably a 1924 Chevrolet. I can remember it being a square boxy car. He came to the door and my father met him there. After a few choice words, my father opened the door and took after him. The hired man's father ran for his car with my father right after him. We had two posts by our pump that a gate swung on. We always kept a corn knife stuck in the top of one of the posts. A corn knife is like a machete. My father grabbed the corn knife beating him on the back with the flat side of the knife. He had to crank the old car while my father was beating him and he was hollering "I'm going ,I'm going" and all the time my Mother was screaming "Don't kill him, don't kill him!!". This really made an impression on me because I can still see that scene today.

Fortunately time heals wounds. My sister ended up having a couple of children very young. It was not too many years later, after living in poverty, that my sister realized what a terrible mistake she had made. She ended up divorcing him and went on with her life. My sister had no choice but to leave the children with him. My Mother, who was badly crippled by this time was in no shape to take the children. And since my father would not let my sister, come home with them, she had no other choice. It was not easy for a single mother in those times.

Cordell, was a beautiful woman who educated herself.. She found a good husband and has had a happy marriage for the past years. I am very close to my sisters, Cordell, and, Marjorie. Both Margie and I have forgiven her many years ago. My father also forgot and forgave her.

Part 1
Chapter 18
My Musical Career

Many people dream of being a famous musician. When I was about ten years old I had one of those dreams. I thought it would be wonderful to learn how to play the guitar. The musical education that I got at old Smith Creek school was very short. We sang songs like "Froggy Would a Woo-ing Go" and "Farmer in the Dell", plus a few other favorites. We got a little training about sharps, flats, and notes. However for some reason or other it had no effect on me.

I would get the old Sears Roebuck catalog and start going through it, wishing for one of the guitars that were pictured there. Sears Roebuck had a special on guitars for learners. If I recall, I think it was about six dollars for that guitar which included a book of learning instructions and a few songs. I was finally able to talk my mother into sending for this guitar. When it came, I was really happy and proceeded to get out the instruction book. In the meantime I had learned the old Cowboys song "The Strawberry Roan". I think it is the only song that I ever memorized in my whole life. For about a month I worked very hard at trying to follow the instruction book. But when spring came I lost interest in the guitar. Then in the fall of the year, one day I decided I would like to practice on my guitar again. I'd looked all over the house and couldn't find it. Finally I asked my mother where it was. She hesitated a little and replied " You didn't practice anymore and I thought you had lost interest in it so I sent it back to Sears and Roebuck and traded it for the overalls you are wearing." What do you say. Well, there went my musical career. I knew from then on that I never would be a singing cowboy.

This was about the time in my life when every young boy dreams of becoming a cowboy. I was no exception. Now my father had an uncle who lived in Grass Range Montana, which was a real romantic name for a young boy who dreamed of becoming a cowboy. I had never seen uncle Henry, and I don't think my father had seen him for years. However, when things did not go right for me at home, I would write a letter to uncle Henry telling him I was coming to Montana.

Of course, my parents knew when I wrote the letter because I would have to ask mother for a stamp or the three cents to put on the letter. Then I would take it to the mailbox. At that point, one of my parents would go to the mailbox before the mail man came and retrieve the letter. I wondered why I never heard back from uncle Henry!.

In 1938 my father and mother decided to go to Yellowstone Park. On the way up to Yellowstone they went through Montana to Grass Range. My sister Marjorie and I both were on that trip. My father never believed in phoning anyone that he was coming for a visit. We found the old ranch and drove in. I can remember Henry's wife saying to my father "I would have baked a cake if there were eggs in the chicken house". My mother never forgot this. What I remember the most about this trip to uncle Henry's ranch was going up on some of the big hills and rolling down rocks to watch them bounce. It really was not a very big ranch, perhaps a couple hundred acres. It might have produced enough feed for a couple of Billy goats.

From there we went on to Yellowstone Park over the Cook City highway. It was a very beautiful drive for a flat lander from Iowa. Those were the days in Yellowstone when there were grizzly and black bears everywhere. I can remember us going to where the forest rangers would take the garbage out to feed the bears at night. They were waiting to be fed like a bunch of hogs. Later that policy was changed. Today's bears are seldom seen in Yellowstone as they try to keep them a way from the tourist. It just is not the same

However, on that trip to Grass Range I decided it would not be that much fun to be a cowboy on that ranch, so there went my dreams.

61

Part 1
Chapter 19
The Thrashing Ring

One of the things I remember very plainly during the 30s was the thrashing crew that came to our neighborhood every year. This was always fun for the children in the neighborhood area. It also was the time when friends visited your house the day the crew was at your farm. There were about ten farmers in our neighborhood who went together every year to form a thrashing ring. The ring would have a meeting at someone's house with treats of some form. The men would decided how many acres of oats were going to be thrashed by the neighbors. By knowing they would figure out how many men it took to run the ring. They would divide the number of men into the total acres of oats to find out how many men each neighbor would have to furnish to run a thrashing crew. They needed 8 bundle racks to haul the bundle's to the machine, They would need three wagons to haul away thrashed oats. Three spike scoop'rs were required to unload the thrashed grain . There would be five pitchers, whose job it was to toss the bundles of oats to the man on the wagon loading the bundles. After the oats were thrashed they were usually scooped into a small bin or the corner of some building. It was never an easy place to unload.

Charlie Brown was a character. It was Charley who owned the thrashing machine. He wore greasy overalls. He never came into dinner. He usually had a tub of ice with beer in it. However, he did run a very good thrashing machine. During the noon hour, he would always grease the old machine then set and drink beer. He also ran a sawmill and had a reputation of being one of the best operators in the country. He had to set and level the thrashing machine, and sometimes had to back it into a barn so he could blow the straw into a barn. It was not always easy to do. But where he really had a good eye was when it came time to back that tractor out and put on the long drive belt that would run the machine. The tractor would have to set about 100 feet from the threshing machine so there would be room for the bundle racks to drive their horses up alongside the machine. Charlie rarely ever missed lining up the tractor with one try. If the tractor was not lined up properly the drive belt would not stay on the pulley. The kids thought the thrashing ring that was just south of our farm would be more fun than ours. That was because they had a steam engine to power their machine and the kids always got to blow the steam whistle when they quit thrashing at night. It would belch black smoke that could be seen for several miles.

After the dew was off in the morning, the bundle racks and the pitchers would head for the oats field and start loading their wagons. After they had a load of bundles they would bring them to the thrashing machine. The men running the bundle wagons tried to see who could load the neatest square load without some of the bundles falling off. The bundles were slick, and if they were not loaded properly they would slide off the wagon. Two of the bundle wagons would pull up alongside the thrashing machine and the day would start. Sometimes the horses pulling the wagons would get quite excited at the noise of the machine. The thrashing machine had a long pipe on the straw blower that blew the straw into a barn or on a pile. The blower would rotate about 40 degrees from each side of the machine. Sometimes the farmers, including my father, stacked their straw. Others just blew it straight out into a big pile. We always used the straw for horse and hog bedding, and if the straw was stacked, it was easier to load and to haul it to the barn. It was an awful dirty job to stack straw. I'm sure that nobody would do that kind of work today.

Wherever the thrashing machine was working that day that farm would feed the crew. The neighboring women would come in and help prepare the meal. There always was a lot of fried chicken, different kinds of meat, salads, potatoes and gravy, desserts, iced tea, and lemonade made with real lemons. It was a real feed. There was always a wash basin under a tree with a couple of roller towels for the men to dry with and an old mirror so they could see how to comb their hair.

All of the bundles were tied with a twine string to hold them together. When the men would unload their wagons, they would toss the bundles on a conveyor that would take it to the thrashing machine. However there was a big set of rotating knives that ran real fast to cut the strings on the bundles. If the bundles went into the machine without being cut, it would make a big groan and

63

Charlie Brown would be on his feet immediately. The oats would go through a cylinder that would knock out the grain. That is where the oats were separated from the straw. The oats would go up a small elevator on the side of the thrashing machine and there was a little weigh hopper that would weigh 1/2 bushel of oats at a time with a counter on it. That is how Charlie Brown got paid. The oats were weighed at 32 pounds per bushel and not by volume. The hopper would dump into an auger that would take it out to a wagon by the machine.

At a lot of places I was the water boy. I would borrow a saddle for Dickey and take two stone jugs with burlap sacks tied around them. Then I would put a leather strap through the handles of the jug. They were wrapped in burlap because when the jugs were filled, the burlap bags would get wet and as the water evaporated it would cool the jugs. Since I hung them over the saddle horn, my pants were wet all-day. Dickey and I would be on the run all day. I would go out to the field where the wagons were loading, then back to the thrashing machine, then to the scoop'rs and by that time the jugs would be empty so it was time to start all over again. When night came both Dickey and I would be tired. I usually let the farmer decide how much to pay me. Some days I would make two dollars and some days only 50 cents.

Occasionally there would be a little excitement in the threshing ring. In my Fathers stable, we always worked old Dick, who was a stallion. He was a very good Percheron horse. Occasionally, out of all the horses on the ring, someone would have a mare who would be "in heat", as we called it on the farm. (Now I know there is a more technical name for it, but it was never used then). They would quickly unhook the stallion and take off his harness as well as the harness on the mare. After a lot of kicking and snorting it was time to watch the fun. Of course, this always took place out behind the barn. The children were chased away. It was just part of the fun at the threshing ring. I remember that I wore my bib overalls. Usually the toes were out of my shoes having kicked every rock I came to. There was always a clean red handkerchief in my pocket. My mother made sure that I had one. It was a great time in my life.

64

Part 1
Chapter 20
The Grocery Wagon

     During the years of the 1930s we were always blessed with the basics in food. That meant we always had plenty of meat and potatoes and Mother always had canned vegetables in the basement. We didn't have some of the finer things that we take for granted today. About six miles northwest of our farm was a town called Nira. This was located on the rock island railroad tracks which ran from Iowa City to Montezuma, Iowa. Nira had a stockyard for loading livestock that the farmers would take their cattle and hogs to ship to Chicago. There was one grocery store that was typical of stores in those days. It had canned groceries, some dry goods, and a poultry house where people could sell eggs and cream. The poultry house would sell some feed and a few supplies which was enough for them to make a living. There probably were two dozen houses besides the stockyard.

     Nira became famous during the first years of the Roosevelt administration when President Roosevelt started a new program called the National Recovery Act. This little village had a United States post office, which probably did not have over 40 or 50 customers. But the National Recovery Act was abbreviated to the letters NRA so all of its first check mailings were sent from this post office all over the United States, and the little village had its day of fame.

A Mr Yoder ran a grocery wagon from his store out into the country when the roads were good. He had something like a 1928 or 1929 truck with an enclosed box on the back. In this truck he would have various supplies like coffee, tea, baking supplies, and household items, as well as a few clothes. He would also have a supply of penny candy bars, and occasionally some fresh fruit. No matter where we were, if we were insight of the old grocery truck, we would come running. Mr.Yoder would go to the door to let Mother know what special things he had today. Mother would then go out to the truck and MrYoder would start pulling things out of the truck telling her the price. Then, of course, we kids would be encouraging her to buy this piece of candy or fruit. Usually we would get something to eat, but believe you me, Mother controlled the negotiating. One of the things Mother usually ended up buying was marshmallows. I was always eating them and trying to put the sack back like it was , but I was not fooling mother.

My father tells about driving cattle and walking to Nira to load them on a train to ship to Chicago when he was a young boy. That would have been when the old stockyard was still operating.

Unfortunately in this changing world nothing exists of the town of Nira today. Everything is gone including the railroad tracks, the stockyard and all the buildings.

I guess this is a sign that time changes everything.

SISTER CORDELL AND ME. I AM SO SKINNEY I CAN
NOT KEEP MY PANTS UP WITH OUT SUSPENDERS

Part 1
Chapter 21
The Goose Pen Folly

I have mentioned several times that my father was a " scalper". That means he would go out into the country and buy one or two head of cattle. I guess that term came about because whoever was doing the buying would always try to get the best of the seller. Dad was very successful at this and always managed to make a little money.

I remember one of the trips when dad took me along to a farm down by Richland, Iowa. We had the old model A Ford pickup which didn't have very good brakes. Fortunately the truck didn't have much speed either. Father and I went to a farm to look at a Jersey heifer. We ended up with dad buying the heifer. We loaded her into the back of the old pickup. The stock rack on the old pickup was not very tall. Father would always put a halter on the animal he was hauling to keep it from jumping out of the truck. On the way home it turns out that there was a farmhouse right at the end of the road, where it made a sharp turn father came over a hill to fast and could see he could not make the turn. It was apparent that we were going to go into the yard at the farm house. However, there was only one problem, there was a pen in the front yard with chicken wire around it. Now in the pen were a bunch of geese, some old ones and a lot of young ones. Well, we headed for the pen and ran over some feeders and the wire on the other side. The old geese were honking and the young geese were running everywhere. By this time, the old model A Ford had slowed down enough that my Father was able to turn back toward the road.

Father was able to look at the pen as we went back toward the road. His comment was "Well, we didn't kill any geese, but we sure raised heck with the Goose pen". After we got down the road a little ways Father said "Better not tell mother, cause I know if somebody ran over her geese, she would not like it". Well, the secret was too good for me to keep and Dad got a lot of razzing about running over the goose pen.

Part 1
Chapter 22
Entertainment in the Wintertime

When I was about 14 years old, I had saved up enough money to buy a 22 caliber automatic rifle. In those days the farmers would have rows of Osage Orange Hedge trees that our ancestors had planted back in the 1800s. These were a very tough tree full of hedge thorns. They were used as fences and all you had to do was poke a hole in the ground and drop in a seed and you would have a tree. As the trees grew they would spread out about 15 feet on each side and under the trees tall weeds and grass would grow. The trees made excellent cover for rabbits, pheasants, and wildlife. The rabbits were so thick you could easily shoot them by the dozens. In fact, people would hunt rabbits, freeze them, and ship them to Chicago in a barrel. People were so poor in Chicago they would buy the rabbits to eat. Now these rabbits were not cleaned at all. It does not seem possible that things like that were done, but they were.

I didn't shoot to many rabbits, because our family didn't like to eat them when we had good pork and beef to eat. My dad just didn't like the idea of eating rabbits. There were always a lot of crows in these hedge trees and I would try to shoot them, as well as a pheasant if I got the chance. I would usually rather take the pickup truck and go a mile and a half north to Smith Creek. There I could walk out in the timber for two miles if I wanted to, and just shoot anything that I felt like shooting. In those years every one raised chickens outside and the red tailed hawks were fair game to all hunters. Usually a person could find some chicken hawks flying a round in the timber sailing along the thermals, making loud screams. I wasn't trying to hunt game, I just wanted to get into the timber and be alone. I could spend a whole half a day or more just walking up Smith Creek. When I was growing up there were no deer on the prairie. If I had seen a deer, I would have thought it was the most fantastic view in the world. In 1999 they are so thick that they are almost a nuisance. In fact in some places they are.

There were no movies to go to, no television to watch. We

just got up on Sunday morning to do the chores and then we would go to church if the roads were passable   and if we had mass. We were a mission parish that only had mass every other Sunday. Therefore if it happened the roads were bad, sometimes we would only get to church once a month.

Another form of entertainment that I would do was to save all the burned-out light bulbs. Just at the bottom of our hill there was the beginning of a Creek were the tile ditches all drained which made quite a bit of water. I would take the light bulbs and small glass bottles down to the Creek, throw them in , and shoot them as they floated down the Creek. Not as easy as it sounds. I am sure that if Mr Durian were aware that I was shooting in his pasture and making broken glass in the bottom of the Creek he would not have been too happy. However, Fred was a very good neighbor and never minded my walking up and down the Creek seeing what I could find to shoot.

My dad had a 16 gauge "White Powder Wonder" single barrel shot gun. He was not a hunter and did very little shooting in his life. The main thing he used it for was to shoot stray dogs. I would use it sometimes to hunt with, but I really didn't like it and had always wanted a better shot gun. Christmas came, and because my folks knew I wanted a new shot gun, they thought they would play a trick on me. Christmas Eve we were opening presents, my sister Marjorie, got the old White Powder Wonder and held it behind her and walk out into the living room. I could just see the stock of the gun and hollered "I got a new gun". When I grabbed the gun from her and saw it was the old White Powder Wonder I was both humiliated and tearful. Marjorie then went and got my new gun, which was a double barrel 20 gauge single trigger. But my day was ruined. It turned out when you shot the new gun you never knew whether one barrel would go off or both barrels at the same time. When both barrels went off at the same time, it would about knock a person on his bottom.

While I was hunting on Smith Creek, little did I dream that in the years to come I would buy that same land and make the mistake of hiring a bulldozer, to push out all the trees, and straighten the Creek to get more farmland. At this point in my life, I do believe there was too much dozer work which has affected our country. I am as guilty of this as anyone else who felt that he had to farm every acre of land.

Part 1
Chapter 23
Dick "Old Reliable

I do not remember when my father bought old Dick for sure , but it would have been shortly after we came back to the farm. I know it had to be early because I do not remember our stable of horses with out Dick being in it. He was a very unusual horse, particularly because he was a stallion. Most stallions are very hard to control and have a very mean, high strung temper. Dick was a gentle horse to be around. He was a gray Percheron weighing about nineteen hundred pounds. While he was hell for stout, he was not a very fast horse. But on a heavy pulling job, he was still there when night came. Dad bought him from Mr. Adrian who lived south of Keota.

We always worked Dick, with his teammate, Fannny , who was also a gray Percheron. Fanny was a little bit lighter in weight than Dick was, but she was faster. When we wanted to move something extra heavy, Dick and Fanny were always the team we used. When they knew there was something heavy to start, Dick would be the anchor and Fanny, being faster, would jump into the collar. That's all it usually took to move the load. They were an excellent team except for one thing. I always hated to work Fanny, when it came time to unhook her tugs. She was what you would call a "switcher". Buy that I mean she would be constantly switching her tail, which was always rather short because of her constant switching. Now that was the good part. The bad part was that she usually ended up urinating on her tail and slapping you in the face with it. Lord, how I hated that!

Now one bad habit that Dick had was that he didn't like geldings. We could harness and hitch Dick and another male horse together and he would not bother the other horse. But if you pulled into the yard and unhitched Dick, and the male horse, Dick would immediately try to kill him. So we always had to make sure that if there were any geldings in the barn, that we did not turn Dick loose to go to the water tank or he would immediately run to the barn and start chewing on any geldings that were there.

This was also true if I happened to turn Dick into the lot where either Cotton or Dickey were. Although Dickey could out run him, he was so scared he would just stop and start urinating, afraid to run, Dick would start chewing on him. His teeth would leave big marks where he would scrape off the hair. It had to be very frightening. And then it was always a battle to get Dick back to his stall. It was exciting when this took place, and it was rather dangerous because the horse that was being chewed on would usually end up kicking. We didn't want to be in the way then.

We would turn Dick into the South lot with other horses, all mares of course, to get them out of the barn on days that we didn't work them. We had a white collie dog named Queenie. She would love to chase Dick and he hated her with passion. It was always a little entertainment to watch those two get at it. His mouth would be wide open but he was always just about a penny short of catching her. But they put on a terrific show. I think they both enjoyed it.

In the lot south of the barn my father had built a breeding stall, because when it came time to breed a mare it could be a little bit of a circus. This just consisted of a couple of very heavy planks fastened to two post that were far enough apart so we could lead the mare that was to be bred into it. It seemed that when we led old Dick out for this he could tell that there was a ritual for him to perform. If a mare was in heat he evidently could smell it. I of course was never involved in this when I was young, so we kids were in the hay mow looking out through the cracks. Usually when old Dick came charging out the mare would be scared and would start kicking, passing gas, and urinating. If she was ready, Dick would mount her, and my Father would guide him in. After it was over, he would just walk back to the barn as if to say "Well, that's taken care of". There would be days when Dick worked all-day .He would come in at night and have his harness taken off to find there was another job for him to do at the breeding chute. He would just sniff a little and go back to the barn as if to say "I'm too tired".

In 1938 when they were digging the basement for the new house, Dick and Fanny were the two main pair that were used on the scraper. Somehow or other in all the tough work, Dick injured one of his rear ankles. This bothered him and he never was as strong as he had been. He was a good horse.

OLD "DICK" AND QUEENIE WHO HE HATED

THREE OF OLDS DICK'S COLTS . THE LITTLE GUY IS ME

OLD "DICK" AND QUEENIE COULD NEVER MISS A CHANCE, TO HAVE A GO AT IT EVERY TIME THEY COULD FIND A PLACE TO DO IT.

Part 1
Chapter 24
Dick and the runaway truck

If you haven't lived in the time of the mud roads in Iowa, you have absolutely no idea of what it was like, because it is very difficult to describe the conditions that prevailed on Iowa's roads. At the east corner of our house there was an intersection of roads coming downhill from all directions. That meant that every time it rained the water from all four directions would concentrate at the bottom of the hill. Every vehicle that came on these roads had to go through the mud and water collected at the bottom of our hill. What a terrible mud hole their always was at that location.

In 1936 or 1937 I drove the pickup north to Smith Creek to do some hunting. When I came home, I got in the ruts and could not get out to make the turn up our hill. In other words, I high centered the pickup and got stuck. I knew the only solution was to wade through the mud and go to the barn and harness old Dick, so he could pull it out. After I'd put the harness on Dick and found a log chain and a single tree, I took him down to the truck.

I hooked Dick to the pickup, started the motor, and spoke to Dick to start pulling while I gave it gas. Now old Dick was good at putting on a show. He acted like he was pulling as hard as he could, but the tugs were so loose a person could have unhitched them. The more I shouted at him, the more he acted like he was really trying. By this time I was getting quite mad, so I climbed out of the truck and crawled across the fence to get a club from under one of the big old cottonwood trees by the Creek. Well, Dick saw me coming and knew what he was in for. So before I could cross the fence, he made a big lunge, pulled the pickup out and proceeded to run a way with it.

By this time I was hollering for him to stop, but all the "WHOA'S" I could shout had no effect! He was headed up the hill with the old pickup at his heels, going first to the left and then to the right every time he made a jump. I was following, trying to catch him. At the top of the hill, he turned into the barnyard with the runaway pickup careening behind him. There the barn door was wide open the way I had left it when I took him out.

Dick ran into the barn, but the pickup could not get through the door. When the spring steel bumper hit the barn, it bounced a foot in the air. Fortunately, he did not tear the side of the barn out, but it made one hell of a racket when he hit it. I ran a round through the hallway to get a hold of him, because he was still trying to pull the truck inside the barn. Finally I got him quieted down, unhooked, and put in his stall.

After everything had settled down and I got over being mad, I began to see the humor in this incident. I have had several good laughs over it throughout the years.

"DICK" THE OLD STALLION THAT WAS A REAL WORK HORSE

Part 1
Chapter 25
Off to the Races

Although Dickey only weighed 500 pounds he was a really fast pony. He could out run any cow and a lot of one thousand pound horses. Every year in Keota, they would have a celebration on the Fourth of July. This included pony races out on the county line Road. Dickey and I would always win those races. Every year at the Keokuk County fair at What Cheer there would also be pony races. One year dad promised to take Dickey, and me to the fair for the races. A couple of days before, I thought it would be a good idea to take Dickey out and run him around the section as fast as he could run. This was a total of four miles. What a mistake!. The next morning when we went to load Dickey to take him to What Cheer, he was so stiff that he could barely walk. My father let me know that I had done the wrong thing by running Dickey those four miles up and down hill as hard as he could run. But we loaded him in the model A pickup and set off for What Cheer, which was about 30 miles away. Uncle Godfrey, lived two miles north of the What Cheer, Fairgrounds so we went to his place. There we rubbed Dickey down with warm water, hoping he would be able to race. The next day I walked him the two miles to the Fairgrounds. He was still so stiff that he didn't walk properly. However, when we got there,and he saw the other horses and knew he was going to race, he forgot all about being stiff!

Now, of course, the people who had the pony who won the race every year were there. Their pony was a couple hundred pounds bigger than Dickey. They were friends of my uncle, and proceeded to tell him that I did not have a chance. We were to race a quarter mile. The fact was Dickey was raring to go. We won the race and I was one tickled young lad. The people who owned the horse that we beat had all kinds of excuses. The fact was Dickey just could run faster. I went to the fair than next year and won again

In the town of Wellman there was a racetrack. I rode Dickey the four miles to town and ran in those races. I always had to run against bigger horses. Sometimes I won sometimes I did not but we always put on a good show.

From the " Keota Eagle"(local papers in the 30's)

The pony race was one of the classics of the day. With seven entries weighing under the five hundred fifty pounds maximum the race was run on the county line Road from south of George Landers to the old Billy Mason corner. Howard Greiner on a chunky little black pony took the race from George Bonnarens by a neck with the others trailing. The race was so close between these two, that it was run over again. By the first three with the Greiner pony making a wonderful race under the handicap of bad position at the side of the road, and winning the race in the last hundred feet by at least one length. Howard is the son of Mr. and Mrs. Albert Greiner

From the" Wellman Advance"

" Last Saturday's races did not amount to a great deal. And there was only a small crowd. Some horses promised did not come. Jim Murphy's horse beat Lake Ayers horse, Sammy, in two races. A one thousand pound Iowa City horse nosed out Howard Greiners 500 pound pony twice but only by inches. The Greiner pony is a "Whiz" for its size. He was a wonderful pony.

There were 4-H programs for the country kids but since my father did not believe in them, and I was not allowed to participate in them, Dickey was my 4-H program.

Part 1
Chapter 26
Life on the Farm in 1938

After my recovery from strep throat in the spring of 1938, work proceeded on our new house at a brisk pace all summer long, and sometime in the fall we were able to move into the new house. It seemed like heaven to have a home with running water, with a furnace to heat it in the wintertime, a basement to hang up our dirty overalls and a place for our dirty boots. We had a shower in the basement, which was not fancy but practical. It was just a curved piece of galvanized pipe with a shower head on it. There was no fancy curtain or shower stall. The bather was just out there in the open. But it was still wonderful compared to a wash tub. All summer long, before we moved into the new house, we could not use the stove in the washhouse to heat the water to take baths with, because of the beds in the washhouse. So we would set a couple of wash tubs full of water out behind the building, and hope that the sun would shine enough to warm them up. We didn't think anything of going back where the tubs were, behind the wash house ,stripping off our clothes, and taking our baths. The water had to be pumped at the well and carried to the tubs.

After we moved into the new home the old kitchen had been moved away from the new house. This is where the cooking was done all summer. Now my father decided the old kitchen was too good to tear down so we hooked our tractor onto it and tried to move it. That F30 Farmall tractor that we had didn't have rubber tires on it. It spun its wheels about once and each steel wheel dug a hole about two feet deep. So we went to the neighbors and they came with a rubber tired tractor, and we hooked both tractors on to it. Well that maneuver was unsuccessful. So we got two more neighbors and had four tractors hooked on the old kitchen before we finally got it moved. It sure did not look very attractive but it serves the purpose of a garage for our tractor. The old pantry with its cupboards came in very handy for storing tools and farm supplies.

78

My Father had always said he would never have a rubber tired tractor because they just were not practical and would be too expensive to keep up. Of course, I can remember as a young boy when he said he would never have any tractor. But times, changes us all. So from the old 10-20, that today is a real antique, he traded for the steel wheel F-30. As he traded for the F-30 he negotiated with Mr. Wade, who owned the International Harvester dealership for the new F-30 and a 22-B two row mounted corn picker. Again, he traded in horses to Mr. Wade on the tractor and corn picker.

One of the hardest jobs on the farm was picking corn. Each ear of corn had to be picked by hand and thrown into a wagon pulled by a team of horses. Each wagon always had some high boards, about four foot high on the right side of the wagon. These were called bang boards, because when the person who was picking corn threw it at the wagon without looking, he knew it would hit the bang boards and fall into the wagon.

Until about 1934 or 35 before hybrid seed corn was developed all farmers grew open pollinated seed corn. This corn did not have very stiff stalks and it was not unusual for a wind storm to come and flatten the corn field.

It was very hard work to bend over all day long and husk corn after it had blown down. In 1934 Pioneer Hybrid seed corn company developed hybrid seed corn. A pioneer salesman came to our farm and sold my father two bushels of hybrid seed corn. My Mother thought he had lost his mind because money was so short. He gave, fifteen dollars per bushel for it. Up until that time we always went into the corn fields to select the big ears of corn and brought them into the barn. There my father hung them in corn racks to dry. That would become our seed corn for the next year. We had an old one hole corn Sheller that was turned with a crank. On the fly wheel there was an attachment that my father called a nubber. This was tapered and had rough edges so that when your corn was shelled in the spring you could nub all the small kernels from the ear that would not make good seed. The corn would not be uniformly graded as it is to day.

The next spring my father planted the two bushels of Pioneer seed corn and finished the field with our regular open pollinated corn. That fall we had a big wind storm and all the Pioneer seed corn was standing straight and the corn we had

79

been planting for years laid flat on the ground. This convinced my father from then on to plant nothing but hybrid seed corn. All of the neighbors around us, who thought my father had lost his mind, also planted hybrid seed corn from then on.

In the fall of 1936 my father and the hired man mounted the 22-B corn picker on the old F-30. It was a monstrous piece of equipment, but it worked. However, there were 220 zerks, that required greaseing every day and some had to be greased two or three times a day. They were very dangerous machines to operate and every fall in Iowa, numerous men would get caught in them losing their hands, their arms, and even their lives. So every fall, who ever operated the old-style corn picker's found that when the stocks got dry they would not pull the corn stalk through and would plug up, This is when the farmers would get hurt. When the ear snapped off it fell into a side elevator which would take it up to the husking bed that sat cross ways right behind the seat of the tractor. The noise made by this was a deafening sound of machinery rattling and banging.

The husking rolls that pulled the shucks off of the corn were within about 18 inches on the right side and the left side of the husking bed. When corn was picked to fast, it would not make the bend to turn and slide down the husking rolls. It was always a great temptation to reach in and try to unplug the corn. This is where many men lost their hands and fingers. It usually was in the front of the picker at the snapping rolls that men would get caught when they tried to pull corn stalks out of the machine while it was running. The rollers ran so fast that if someone grabbed a stalk of corn , which the machine started to pull through, the person couldn't let loose fast enough to keep from being pulled into the rollers. This is how most men got caught in these machines. I didn't run the corn picker in 1936 or 37 but did run the machine in 1938, and the years 1939 and 1940. However, I made it a practice to crawl under the machine, and of course, to leave it running to pull the corn stalks through from the bottom side. In the summer of 1938 my Father traded the F-30 to Mr. Wade for a rubber tired F-20 which was a smaller tractor. Because it had rubber tires it would pull as much as the steel wheel F-30. It was also much easier to ride and to drive.

In those years all the corn was picked in the ear. We usually didn't start picking corn until the first of November, because the corn had to dry in the field so it would not spoil in the corn cribs. This meant riding a machine, setting out in the open where you could not move because you were surrounded with machinery. I can remember being so cold that when I would get off the machine I could hardly walk. And then I knew that I had to grease that monster when evening came to get ready for the next day. Even so, it was much better and faster, than picking corn by hand. I sure would not want to ride one of those machines again because I can still remember the dust and the cold. It was always a treat when I would see somebody coming about 10:00 a.m. with hot coffee and food.

After the corn went through the husking bed, it went up a long elevator into a wagon that you pulled behind. Most farmers only had one tractor, which meant horses were used to pull the wagons to the cribs to unload them. During the years I ran the picker, my father or a hired hand pulled in the corn to unload it. The wagons we used were small compared to today. A standard farm wagon would hold one bushel of corn for every inch the wagon box was tall. The wagons were approximately three feet wide and ten feet long. If the wagon was 48 inches deep it would hold 48 bushels of corn. We were constantly hooking and unhooking wagons. We were just picking two rows at a time. Unlike the six and 12 row , picker shellers (combines) of today. I was young enough that I never did have to go out and pick corn by hand.

In the fall of the year when we were picking corn, we would usually quit about four o'clock in the afternoon. This was great because usually my father had the milking done when I got home. I loved that. It was great to come home to a warm house and to have a good meal that Mother and the hired girl would have prepared.

81

DAD AND I ON THE OLD 22B CORN PICKER IN 1938

L TO R CORDELL. MARJORIE, HOWARD MY MOTHER FRANCIS AND DAD 1940

TRYING TO MOVE THE OLD KITCHEN IN 1938 WHAT POWER!!!

DAD WAS GREAT WITH A HOE AND LOVED TO HARVEST ANYTHING.

THE OLD HORSE POWER TO UNLOAD CORN IN 1938

In Part 1
Chapter 27
Trouble in the Family

Grandfather Greiner, died around 1938. Before his death he was bedfast in Washington for several years. I would occasionally go with my father to see him. My father always had business to talk over with him. Their conversations would take place mostly in German. Since I could not understand German, I was not too interested in being there. I do remember that not too pleasant smell that goes with someone who is bedfast. There was not any kind of a warm relationship between my grandfather and me.

One of his granddaughters, Geraldine, usually drove him when he was able to get a round. One of the incidences that I recall is when my sister Cordell and I were at home on the farm indulging in what we called " coffee soup". This consisted of a bowl with a couple pieces of bread with sugar sprinkled on it and then coffee poured on top., I remember Cordell looking up the south road and screaming " Here comes Grandpa Greiner". Then she had us hide our coffee soup. I really don't know why because he would never come into our house. He was not welcomed there by my mother, nor would he come. He would crawl out of the old model A touring car with his cane and would say in a very loud heavy voice," Where is Albert?" After he and Dad would visit (in German of course), he and Geraldine would crank up the old model A touring car and leave. That would be the extent of his stay. With this type of relationship, close friends are not made. This is really about the only memory I have of him on the farm.

Before he died, we would go down to visit father's sister Clara and occasionally go over to dad's brother, John. My grandfather had appointed my father and his brother, John, as administrators of his estate. It is not clear in my mind exactly what happened. I was always under the impression that John went to Washington and had a severe argument with Grandfather Greiner. Now he was a man who took no talk from anyone. He called his attorney and removed John from his estate as an administrator. Needless to say from that point, things went downhill in that family. He then appointed his attorney to replace John. I remember a meeting that my father and his brother Johnny had a long side the road north of Keota where Johnny accused my father of having him removed as administrater. It was a real bang up meeting with two strong headed Germans going at each other. Fortunately, there were no blows struck, but this was the beginning of a family feud that lasted for years. All of it was unnecessary. As a young teenager, this made quite an impression on me.

Unfortunately, some years later Uncle Johnny went out behind his barn and committed suicide. By this time our family no longer had contact with his children. We grew up without really getting to know each other. The same is true for my aunt Clara and her family. However, in later years we did work at trying to get my Father and his sister Clara back to talking to each other. The feud was all so unnecessary and just meant that all the families suffered from and it all came about over money.

Dads, brother Richard had a lot of problems also. He was not a good financial manager and seemed to get into problems that my grandfather would help them with. After grandfather died, the problems became worse to the point where Richard was committed to a state institution. My father helped manage his family and finances while he was gone until he found out this was not appreciated. Then he washed his hands of it. My dads family was not an easy family to be around. It all was so unnecessary.

NORMAN O'CONELL AND I IN 1940. NORMAN WAS KILLED
IN THE FIRST WAVE ON D-DAY AT NORMANDY

Part 1
Chapter 28
The Neighbors

One of the nice things about living in a neighborhood a number of years is that friendships develop. This is something that is lacking in our country to day. There is not that friendly relationship that existed back in the '30s 40s and '50s. We had six families in our neighborhood that were close. These were all neighbors who would come and exchange labor for any job you had. We would make and bale hay together and any other job all year long.

Whenever you had wood to saw, everyone would find time to help. Another thing that we all exchanged labor on was shelling corn. Which is no longer done today. Back when we all harvested corn in the ear, and it came time to shell corn, we would make an appointment with Roy Yoder from Wellman or Leo Malley from Keota. They would bring their truck mounted sheller and set up the drag to start shelling corn. Of course there would always be corn cobs that everybody would want to supply their cook stoves with or to grind up and use for bedding for hogs. We never let them go to waste. We would roll out all the corn that would fall by gravity into the sheller. Then the real work started, because you would have to start scooping corn into the drag. This was always when the excitement would start, because ear corn was a natural shelter for rats. We would always try to have a good dog to help kill the rats. As we got down toward the end of the corn, the rats would come out everywhere. Then everybody would be hell for leather, trying to kill the rats with their scoop shovels. We did not have rat poison in those days and with all the corn the rats would not eat it if you had it.

I was down to Bud's place helping shell corn and a real circus took place. While I shoveling corn, a young rat about two-thirds grown ran up my pant leg. I was jumping up and down, screaming for the some one to help me get my pants opened because I had the rat by both hands fight below my crotch. I was squeezing it real tight and didn't want to let loose of it. I squeezed

89

it so hard that I ended up killing it. Everybody was laughing so hard that not one of them would open my pants. It was a real jumping and hollering time.

In those days we also had to vaccinate all of our hogs for cholera. When it was time to vaccinate them the neighbors would come and help catch hogs so that we could castrate and vaccinate at the same time. It was always a good time because we had dinner wherever we worked. This is what tied the neighborhood together.

Our neighbors to the east of us, the Foster's, raised about 15,000 turkeys a year. It seemed that they never sold turkeys until it was raining or snowing. The turkeys were raised outside and would be wet and muddy. Back then they did not have the power loaders like they do today. They would be flopping their wings and slapping you in the face. It was a tiresome dirty job, but nobody ever complained. It was just part of being a good neighbor.

MY FRIEND BURELL JR FOSTER. MY BEST FRIEND
AS A YOUNG BOY. WE WENT TO COUNTRY SCHOOL
TOGETHER EIGHT YEARS

A REAL DUDE ON THE STREET IN MC ALLEN TEXAS 1942

OUR NEW HOUSE IN 1939 AND OUR NEW F-20 FARMALL TRACTOR "WOW"   REAL POWER

Part 1
Chapter 29
My first trip to Texas

In the fall of 1940, my father made a trip to the Rio Grande Valley in Texas. He went with a gentleman from Wellman and three other people. The purpose of this trip was to try and talk my father and the other people into buying citrus groves in the Rio Grande Valley. By this time my sister, Cordell, and her husband were selling citrus groves in the Valley for Lloyd Bentsen. The Bentsen's would bring people down from the north, and then tell them all about citrus, and how much money they could make if they bought citrus groves. They had a big clubhouse located on Ware Road , between Mission and McAllen Texas. The Bentsen's bought thousands of acres of Mesquite and cactus west of Mission and were in the process of bulldozing this off in five and ten acre lots, and promising to bring irrigation to it. They would pitch a story about how much money could be made if a person bought this land. They would then plant citrus trees on it and plant vegetables between the rows. This would make you enough money to pay expenses and taxes until the citrus trees started bearing fruit. So they would say.

They would bring down retired schoolteacher's, farmers, and anyone who had a little money. They would take you to Mexico, to other citrus farms connected to their family, and keep you busy while you were there, not giving you a chance to talk to anyone else. Then the day before you left to come back north, they would put you in a room and try to sell you citrus land. They sold a lot of people land who could not afford to buy it. Buyers would pay for two or three years, and if they could not pay the Bentsen's would repossess the land and sell it again. My father bit on this. And until he sold his lots in 1946, the vegetables never once paid for the cost. The Bentsen's had a nice little racket. Other companies were doing the same thing. It was a perfectly legitimate business and the Bentsen made a fortune doing it. (This was the father of Sen. Lloyd Bentsen). I believe, if I remember correctly, my Father bought 12 acres of this land at that time.

93

In 1940 the valley was a beautiful place where they had not had a freeze for something like 40 years. The citrus trees were huge and beautiful, and loaded with fruit. The valley has gone so long without a freeze that no one ever thought it would ever freeze again. My father went back in 1941 and bought 20 acres of an old grove of citrus. During the following years, when the war was on and the government was buying citrus juice, the old groves made my father a lot of money. But he kept saying. after the war was over and the government quit buying juice there would not be a good market. So in the fall of 1946 he sold all of his citrus groves and got the money. That winter a hard freeze came to the valley, killing every one of the trees my father sold.. How lucky can you be, or maybe it was just being smart. The valley has not been the same since as there has been a freeze about every five years.

After my father bought his first citrus grove he had the gentleman from Wellman take me along on one of the trips to the valley, where we stayed at the Bentsen clubhouse. On this same trip another gentleman from Wellman went along down. Usually it one of the things that took place when you went to Mexico, providing no ladies were along, they would take you to a Mexican whore house, that was provided just for the Americans. This consisted of a tall fence around a good sized piece of ground and on the outside of the perimeter each one of the ladies who worked there had a little room of her own. In the center of this area was a dance hall where you could buy beer or a drink and there would be a little Mexican orchestra playing. In the center of the room was a wash tub full of hot coals to make some heat. Each one of the girls had a brand on her legs where they had backed into the wash tub. The Mexican government at that time kept soldiers at the gate so only Americans would get in.

As soon as a car pulled into the compound the girls would run out and grab someone they thought would be a prospect. We all went inside, and sat at a table, and of course a girl would climb on your lap and tried to talk you into going out to her little room on the perimeter. Needless to say Eddie and I had a good time. I can truthfully say that neither of us left to go to their room. That was not true of our escort who had a steady girl there. At this time in my life, my sex education had me scared to death of social diseases. I wasn't about to get involved at one of these places. But at the same time I can also say that a person could have fun

94

just dancing and being there. This was my first education into these kind of houses in Mexico. When I crossed the border in 1940 it was a different world. When I crossed the border at Reynosa, the streets were unpaved, there were no street lights, and it was a spooky world. It was quite an eye opener for a young kid from Iowa.

We stayed the usual four days in the Valley at the Bentsen clubhouse and then returned to Iowa. My parents and I did go to the Valley for several years before I went to the service. I met a nice young girl at the clubhouse from Minnesota by the name of Hazel Smith. Hazel wanted to go to the stockade in Mexico. So I told her I would take her but would not guarantee any thing. She and I had a date and we went to Mexico. We locked the car doors before we drove into the stockade. Just as the headlights shined on one of the rooms, a girl stepped out naked and emptied a wash pan full of water. Needless to say she was ready to leave and never asked again to go to Mexico.

HAZEL SMITH AND I .SHE WAS FROM MINNESOTA
95

Part 2
Chapter 1
The beginning of a change in my life

It was a beautiful Sunday afternoon and I was in the house listening to our radio when the first reports started coming in from Honolulu, Hawaii. The attack on Pearl Harbor had begun. I did not realize it at the time, but this was the beginning of a great change in my life. World War 2 had started. This was December 7, 1941. I remember walking out to the back porch and telling my mother and dad, who had just driven up in the car, that we were at war. There were no radios in the cars that we owned, because my father did not think it was necessary. I'm sure the thought went through dad and mother's minds as to what my position in the war would be. Being a young teenage lad, it never occurred to me that I would become involved.

That winter we went down to the Rio Grande Valley of Texas and stayed at the Bentsen clubhouse at McAllen, Texas. The war was just beginning so gasoline rationing had not yet started, and we were not yet feeling the effects of the war. The draft had been instigated and men were starting to go to the Army by the thousands. A lot of the young boys my age were enlisting in the Navy. The Navy would take enlisted men younger than the Army. We came home from the Valley along towards the end of February and prepared for the coming crop season. We were still planting corn with horses and I was the one who did that. I suppose I could have applied for a deferment because I was involved in agriculture. A lot of farm boys did. I guess however I must have been a true blood American. As the draft became more encompassing and was taking increasingly more people, I began to think about what branch of service would appeal to me.

My thoughts never went as far as believing that I could be a pilot, because I did not have a high school and college education. But I did think that I could be a mechanic. I started thinking about going to an aviation mechanics school. That way when I went into the service perhaps I could be an aviation mechanic. I do not know where I made that contact at this time, but there was an aviation mechanic's school advertised quite heavily in various magazines that I was reading. I settled on a school which was located in Glendale, California. I wrote to the school to get their program and then talked to dad and mother about going to California to the trade school. Dad could see that I would end up being drafted. In May of 1942, I sent my payment for tuition and was expected to begin in August.

I left Washington Iowa on the Golden State limited for Los Angeles. After arriving in Los Angeles, I went to Glendale and started looking for a place to live. I found a boarding house run by a lady who had four other borders staying with her. I can't recall what her name was, but she ran a pretty good house. I remember one of the borders at that time was a double for old Wallace Berry, who was in the movies. The land lady was a decent cook, but I did not eat all of my meals there. After I started my classes at this school, it was easy for me to see that it was about 20 years behind times. We were learning how to build fabric airplane wings, when all the planes at this time were being built out of aluminum. Unless it has been destroyed, the sample airplane wing that I made should be in the attic on the home farm at Wellman. I did get around to building an aluminum tool box at school which Peter is using today. I used it all the years I farmed.

I decided I needed to get a job to help get a little spending money, so I applied to Alexander's grocery store for a job. My job was to bag groceries and when I wasn't busy doing that, to stock shelves. The next thing I needed to do was to get some transportation. I found a Model A roadster that was in good condition for $125. dollars. By this time gasoline rationing was on, so I could only get four gallons of gasoline per week. I found that by mixing four gallons of kerosene, that was not rationed, and four gallons of gasoline, the old Ford would work fine. This gave me eight gallons per week which was sufficient for me. I drove the old Model A all over the Los Angeles area. Eventually I had a chance to get a job at a defense plant where they were manufacturing drop tanks for P38 airplanes. They were already stamped so we had to put them in a jig, and then take rawhide hammers and beat the edges down. After that they could be welded together. We did a lot of hammering. I'm sure today somebody could figure out a faster and easier way of doing it. I think I made five dollars per hour which were good wages then. However, I recently found a letter that shows my memory is faulty on the wages.

I have been going through some old records and books of my mother's for the writing of this book. And I found a notebook where I had taken notes at the aviation school. In this book I found a letter that I had written to my folks and did not get mailed. Here is the complete text of that letter and it will show you how far wrong I was.

Dear folks,
September, 1942
Well it is 20 after 10 and I have a few hours to go before I get to go home. In fact tomorrow morning at 8:00 I get to go home because I have a new job. I worked from 1:30 a.m. till 8 a.m. before I go home. I'm on that graveyard shift, so they call it out here. It sure makes a long day out of it. I'm working in a defense factory making auxiliary gas tanks for P38'S I get 66 cents per hour on weeknights and 99 cents an hour on Saturday and Sunday. I can make 42 dollars per week by working seven days if I wish. I don't know if I will work seven or not. I only work six hours a night and get paid for eight hours so I have a pretty good job anyway. It pays a lot more than my other job (sacking groceries at Alexander's supermarket) did so I'll try and keep it up. I've been doing cable splicing over the last three days. I might even send you a sample if you what one. I also have a few pictures and I'll send you one. I also am having some reprints made so everyone can have pictures if they want them. Love to you both. Your Son Howard

I had no idea my mother had saved the letter until I started going through boxes of clippings.

I continued going to the school through September, but I could see that I would need to get better training than the school was giving me. I wrote the folks and told them that I was going to enlist in the Air Force for pilot training, if I could pass the examination. The Air Force had removed the requirement that you had to have a college education. It was based on capability and if you proved that, you were in. I never telephoned my folks because we lived at the very end of the Keota telephone exchange. We had 10 people on our party line and they would all listen to our ring. So by that time no one could hear. My father was not very happy about my enlisting in the Air Force for pilot training because he was sure all pilots would die. He was not too far wrong.

In the first week of October, I went down to the old Pacific electric building in downtown Los Angeles and signed up for pilot training tests that were to be given the next week. I went down on the date of the exams and there were approximately two hundred fifty young men who had signed up for the tests. They sat us around tables alphabetically for the tests. You had certain time limits for each phase of the test. A lot of these test were things that would involve mechanical aptitude, arithmetic, problem solving, and general knowledge of various things. Because I was an Iowa farm boy and did a lot of reading I did not have any problems with this exam. In my whole career, I never ran a cross another pilot who did not have a high school education or a college degree. So I felt my chances were quite slim. I finished all the tests in the time period granted. We were then told to come back two days later.

I drove down to the Pacific Electric building with a heavy heart. I was sure that I had failed the tests and would be eliminated. We went to the floor that the Army Air Force had and waited for them to give us directions. A sergeant came out and announced that he would start reading the names of those people who did not pass the test. If you ever heard a couple hundred men be quiet, it was then. Everything as you know in the Army is done alphabetically he started reading the names beginning with the A's and then got down to the G's and he read off the Greens. Then the next thing I knew he was in the H's before I realized he had not called off my name. This was a group of men who all wanted to fly and some of them were very disappointed and some were crying. I almost was in a state of shock. I just found it so wonderful that I had passed when so many college graduates had failed. How great life was.

Two days later we were to come back to the Pacific electric building for medical and psychological tests. It was here that I ran into some problems that I did not expect. When it came time for my heart examination, I was so excited and happy that my heart beat was way too fast. The sergeant running the tests said, "You are too excited, go out in the hall and relax, I will call you back". Well, he called me back and my heart had slowed down so I passed the physical tests. I could not believe what was happening to me. An Iowa farm boy with no education was playing with the big boys who had education.

We were instructed to go to our homes and await orders to active duty. I went back to Glendale and informed the school that I was leaving. I then had to find a buyer for the Model A which I did. I got back the one hundred twenty-five dollars that I gave for it. I then made my" Good bye's", to my land lady and got a ticket on the Golden State limited back to Washington, Iowa and home. I had the month of November and December at home. We had a good Christmas as I was waiting for my orders to come. It seemed like a dream to me. I just could not imagine the great experience that lay ahead of me.

IN GLENDALE CALIFORNIA IN 1942 WHEN I ENLISTED IN THE US ARMY AIR FORCE

I came home from California in November and helped with the harvest that fall. We did not harvest as early in those days as is done today. Usually we started picking corn about the first of November. Bud and Christina Bohr had come back and moved to the 80. Father had made up his mind that he was going to retire from farming. He was 45 years old. He arranged to lease the farmland to Bud and set up a farm sale for the first week in January of 1943.

I helped father and Bud prepare for the farm sale. This was not a very big job because a farmer in those days did not have a lot of machinery and the livestock consisted mostly of breeding sows and stock cows. Dad had been selling off some of the livestock before the sale. Of course, there was hay to sell, as well as corn. The most important part of the machinery that was to sell was the 22-B corn picker and the F20 rubber tired tractor. My father did not own a combine. There was also a harrow and the disk, a two bottom plow and a two row corn planter. In addition there were the usual small items on a hayrack that every farm sale has.

What I hated to see sold the most was old Dick and Fanny plus Babe and Mays. They were old standbys that had done so much work for my father and I had driven them so much over the years. Not that I would want to keep them, if I were to farm, I really did not like to work horses. And I'm sure I would never have been a farmer if this were the only way I could farm. It was too slow and too much work to take care of horses. The tractor had no manure to be hauled, did not have to be curried, have to be harnessed up every morning, given feed and water every morning and evening as well as to be unhitched and given a drink of water at noon. All you had to do was fill it with gas and oil and drive it.

The sale was a good sale for those days and Bud bought most of the machinery because he was going to start farming. My father financed part of the machinery for him, as I remember.

Part 2
Chapter 2
My Air Force career begins

  In January 1943, I received special orders to report to Des Moines Iowa, to the Army recruiting station. There probably were a couple of hundred of us who had to report at the same time. The Air Force had a big backlog of young man who had enlisted and were waiting for training. However, the Army Air Force was starting to get a lot of complaints because young men like myself had not been called to duty, but men who were close to forty years old, with families were being called. Therefore under political pressure, the Air Force called the younger men to active duty.

  I reported today to Des Moines and like all the rest of the man there had a physical examination. We bent over and spread ,our cheeks, and had the usual short arm inspection that was always required in the service. They then placed us in various hotels for the night. The next day we were loaded onto a train and left for Jefferson Barracks Missouri. Jefferson Barracks is one of the old Army bases that was established before the West was settled. We arrived at Jefferson Barracks along with about 5000 other men. They were totally unprepared for this many men to show up at one time. It was the end of January, and on the banks of the Mississippi it was mighty cold. We were put in huts that were about 20 feet square with 12 men to a hut. There were six double deck beds in each hut. That meant there were 12 man living in these huts that were placed about three feet off the ground. The sides of the hut were about six feet tall and then had a canvas top over the rest of the hut. In the center of each hut sat, a coal fired stove.

  Upon arrival at Jefferson Barracks, we assembled off the train still in civilian clothes and they marched us to general mess for dinner. The general mess was a huge building where cooks could serve 5,000 men meals three times a day. We then were marched back to our huts and found that we were issued two GI blankets for our sleeping. However these bunks had springs but no mattresses. So we really were sleeping on springs with two GI blankets. We would spread one GI blanket on the springs and cover-up with the other one. But the cold would penetrate from the bottom because there was no mattress. The stove could be red hot and you could not feel the heat three feet away from it. Black troops were used to fire the stove at night. The first night we had not been issued our G.I clothes so we all slept in everything that we wore on the train coming down. The next day we were issued clothes,shoes, plus an overcoat and a raincoat. Unfortunately I had long skinny feet and wore a size 12I/2AAAA shoe. Since there were no shoe's this size I was issued a pair of 11B shoes to wear. I could almost turn around in them and go the other direction. It took about two months before 12AAA became available for me. In the meantime with all the marching, those 11B shoes did not help my feet.

The first few days we were busy taking our immunization shots, our physicals, getting our GI insurance and all the other paperwork completed. The 12 men in our hut got along very well, except for the second night when my friend Charlie Horstman, woke up to find his bunk mate, who slept on the upper springs, covering him up with his raincoat. It turned out that he was a bed wetter and had just soaked himself and because there was no mattress it was dripping down on Charlie, so he was putting his raincoat over Charlie. He was immediately discharged from the service as this was an automatic way to get out. We do not know if he did this intentionally or if he was a true wetter. Anyhow, we had a good laugh about it.

When you have 5,000 men in one place basically killing time, you have to find something for them to do. Jefferson Barracks has a large parade ground and we spent hours and hours on this parade ground doing calisthenics and marching. We marched in formation to general mess, equipped to feed a lot of men very quickly. When we were there about a week we were given a special Army Air Force test. We did not know what the test was for when we took it. It later turned out that this test determined whether you would be in A ,B.,C,D,E squadron. All of us were to be sent to a college training detachments somewhere but we had no idea where. If you were in A squadron you would stay one month,B you would stay two months,C for three months and so on. It ended up that I was to be in B. squadron and would stay two months somewhere. I felt good about this.

After being there about a week, people started getting sick. We were constantly cold and could not get any medical attention. The nickname of the place became " Pneumonia Gulch". The ambulances were constantly picking men up and taking them to the hospitals until the hospitals became full. The second week we were there a man in our hut from , Webster, Iowa became sick with spinal meningitis. He was taken from our hut by ambulance. Our hut was put under quarantine. A guard was posted at our hut 24 hours a day. A medic would come by and give us all sulfa pills and take our temperature. If we had to go to the latrine, a military police soldier would accompany us. We were then marched separately to general mess after all the other troops had eaten. I became sicker every day and kept asking to go to the hospital, but my request was refused. By now almost all of the men were sick. Some of them even died. When we marched to general mess, lined up in formation, to go in the men would all be coughing up phlegm in big gobs. We called them "J B Oysters". You can imagine the mess, when 5000 men, all sick lined up to go into general mess, all spitting. We would have to march about a mile and a half, by that time you were warm and you started coughing this up.

After ten days the guards were removed from our hut. I still tried to get on sick call, but was refused because there were too many sick people. By this time, we were all thinking the Air Force was a hell of a place. We had been promised mattresses for our beds, but they never showed up. We slept on the springs the whole month we were in Jefferson Barracks. After we were there about a month 200 of us were taken down and given orders to ship out the next day. They took our temperature and if you were breathing you were ready to go. They loaded us on the train the next morning.We found we were headed for the University of Missouri. I had no idea where that was. We got to Columbia, unloaded off the train, and marched to the campus of the University of Missouri. We found we were to stay in fraternity houses for the two months we were there. I was sick and looked like a walking zombie. We were assigned to our fraternity house. They did not have the bunk beds yet, so we slept on Army cots.

There were many bad repercussions from the treatment that was given at Jefferson Barracks. A lot of hell was raised and some of the top brass received a lot of criticism for what happened there. Men had died unnecessarily from poor planning and every collage detachment that was shipped out early were sick. We were one happy group of men to get out of that place .

We could see our surroundings were going to be delightful at the University of Missouri. To the east of our fraternity house was a golf course, which is no longer there. To the West was a sorority house and to the North was another sorority house, all full of girls. We thought we had landed in heaven!

CHARLEY HORSTMAN AND I WERE IN JEFFERSON BARRACKS
UNIVERSITY OF MO. AND SAN ANTONIO CADET CENTER

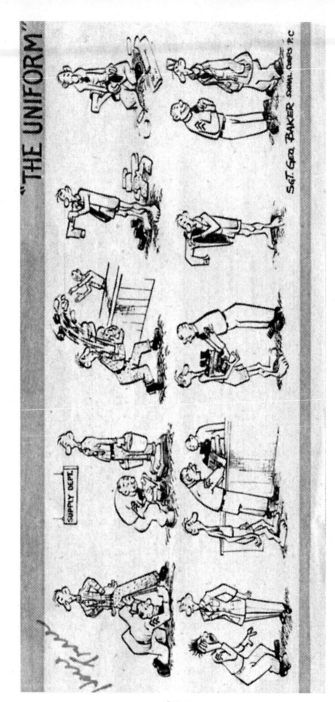

106

"TEN-SHUN!"

—Cpl. Bill Newcombe, Fort Knox, Ky.

Part 2
Chapter 3
The University of Missouri

After we left Jefferson Barracks, Missouri, we were told where we were headed and that was to be the University of Missouri at Columbia Missouri. When we arrived at the train station, we were organized into platoons and marched to the basement of the Methodist church, downtown, and were informed we would be eating there each day. We were then assigned to various fraternity houses at the Campus for our quarters during our stay at the University, I stayed at the Sigma Epsilon fraternity house, a very nice house. However all the furniture owned by the fraternity had been removed. It was then refurbished with the GI furniture. We were supposed to sleep in bunk beds but they had not arrived. So we slept on Army cots till the bunk beds arrived. We settled in for the night as most of us were sick and tired. About midnight we were awakened by the medical officer. The medical staff was going through the house taking temperatures of the cadets and sending them to the hospital, including me. I was in the hospital about one week. By the next day about half of the detachment were in the hospital. After being in Jefferson Barracks, Missouri, we could not believe that this was the Army Air Force and that we were getting medical treatment. Every detachment that shipped to other colleges had the same problem we did

We were to be called the 307th College Training Detachment. And since we were in B Squadron we were to be there for eight weeks. While there we were to get 10 hours of flying time in Piper Cub airplanes. However, the 14 Piper Cub airplanes that were to be there were snowed In and did not arrived from Boston for another two or three weeks. The first week was just spent in getting organized. We were all assigned various courses that we were to take according to the test that we had taken at Jefferson Barracks, Missouri. We were to spend one hour a day at the airport learning to fly, one hour a day taking calisthenics which was taught by the University of Missouri football coach, Don Fraught. He was a very famous football coach and the University of Missouri football stadium is named after him. I was assigned and hour for physics, English, mathematics, and an hour on the theory of flight.

We were supposed to be eating our meals at Crowder Hall which was very close to the fraternity house where we were living. However, this was not to be so we had to march about a mile and a half to the basement of the Methodist church in downtown Columbia. This really did not hurt us as it gave us a lot of practice in marching formation. Later on after we left, Crowder Hall, was used as the dining room but it was for cadets that came later in the training program. One of the things I will always remember was that we had beef tongue for lunch and for dinner every day. Beef tongue must have been a surplus meat because we sure ate our share.

Our day schedule went something like this: Reveille was at 5;30 a.m. in the morning and we assembled in the street outside of the fraternity house rain or shine. After roll call we were then marched downtown for breakfast and were back to the house at about 730 a.m. Classes began at 8:00 o'clock and ran until 5:00pm with our usual march to the Methodist church for lunch. Then we would assemble at 5:30 p.m. and march downtown for our evening meal. On week nights we had a one hour study period and then lights were out at 10 p.m. Saturday nights we were allowed to go downtown until 11:45 p.m.

Most of our classes were held in Jesse Hall, the trademark center of the University of Missouri. But since we were there, there has been so much building at the University Campus I am not even sure if the old landmark is still standing. I found my classes very interesting and enjoyed them very much. They were taught rapidly with the instructor having chalk in one hand and an eraser in the other. I always enjoyed the trip to the municipal airport where we were flying the Piper Cub airplane's. Each student flew for a total of 10 hours. The days went very fast

One incident that I can remember was when we would have a break in classes at Jesse Hall we would congregate outside. There was a large St. Bernard dog that was kind of a mascot at Jesse Hall. Most of the boys would pet the dog and he was a very social individual. Unfortunately, he came down with rabies. All of the cadets who had touched the dog had to take rabies shots which were very, painful. Fortunately, I had never petted the dog.

The company from Boston, Massachusetts who were furnishing the Cub airplane's brought a total of 36 to Columbia for the program. However, only ten had arrived when we were there. One incident that I remember at the municipal airport was that a couple of hotshot pilots landed a B25 bomber. They taxied to the line shack and turned the airplane so that it was just in front of the line shack. The line shack had a big plate glass window in the front of it and this is where the dispatcher of the Cub airplanes had his office. The asphalt on the runway at that time was not thick enough for airplanes of that weight. The next morning when the crew came out to take off, they found the B25 had settled into the asphalt about 10 inches. These two hotshots crawled into the B25 and fired up both engines, but of course the airplane did not move as it had to lift its self out of the holes. They then threw full power on the big engines trying to lift the airplane out of the holes. They did not consider what was behind them. The big window blew out of the line shack and the gentleman inside hid under a table and was scared to death. There were two Cub airplane's tied down behind the line shack and both of the these broke from their anchors and were damaged. People in charge of the airport were waving their arms and screaming but the noise of the two big engines drowned out their efforts. The pilot finally realized his mistake and shut his engines down, crawled back down and got a wrecker to pull the airplane out. I'm sure their commanding officer gave these two fellows a little bit of trouble. It was an exciting time for us cadets at the airport.

There were three colleges in Columbia, Stevens college and Christian college both all girls school, and the University of Missouri which was co-ed. There was always someone wanting to have a social program with the cadets and the servicemen at the University. We were not the only servicemen at the University as there was a contingent of sailors there who were taking an eight weeks course on diesel mechanics. However, the Air Force cadets seem to have the most parties and dances. I think this was partly because we were really killing time until we could get into the Air Force for serious flight training. The Navy people were serious about getting their trainees ready for service in the Navy. But for a country boy who did not have a high school education and so had not attended high school functions, it was a great time

110

for me. Quite a few of our cadets were married and had more serious things to think about. It was a fun time, and besides I didn't have any cows to milk. With sorority houses on each side of our barracks, we had ample opportunity to make friends with different girls. I made friends with a Mary Brown who was called "Brownie" for short. I also made friends with another young lady who worked the chow line at the church. My good friend Charlie Horstman, and his wife and I spend a lot of time together whenever it was possible. I recall one Saturday night while we were downtown we found a fifth of Jack Daniel's Black label. Good whiskey was hard to buy during the war. Charlie had this in his coat but he dropped and broke it. Did you ever see two grown men cry? We were two very unhappy cadets. We never did have an overnight pass and in fact I was in the service for a year and a half before I had an overnight pass. Even the married men did not get overnight passes. My first overnight pass was when I graduated from Ellington field in Texas as a twin engine pilot.

Sometime in early April, plans were made for us to ship to San Antonio, Texas where the Central Training Command cadet center was located. I let my parents know that we were shipping out, and Mother and Dad drove to Columbia before I left. We had a great visit and I was very glad to see my parents.

When it came time to leave, 200 of us, each with two big barracks bags, were loaded onto three of the oldest railroad cars that I think they could find. We were packed in like sardines. Of course there was no air conditioning. However, the toilets did work because they just used the side of the tracks. We would stop at various towns and usually a group of Red Cross workers would feed us. It was so hot in the cars that all the windows were opened and the dust and soot from the steam engine came into the cars. You can imagine how dirty we were, when we arrived in San Antonio Texas, three days later. We were certainly glad to get off of that train and it was not a deluxe trip. After getting a shower and new quarters, we were anxious to start our next phase, which we would find out would be more waiting. I had my taste of college life and enjoyed it very much.

MOTHER AND DAD ON A VISIT TO UNIVERSITY OF MISSOURI
AT COLUMBIA IN APRIL 1943

MY GOOD FRIEND "BROWNIE" WHILE AT THE U.OF MISSOURI

STUDENT WAR BOARD OF
WAR ACTIVITIES PROMOTIONS

MARY ETHELYN BROWN
ROBERT SMITH
CO-CHAIRMEN

Howard, it was really great fun knowing
you as the Old State U. — and I'll always
remember the night we talked till 8 — those
Saturdays at the Coronado — and a million
other things — I miss all of that a great deal
already. Really, you made my senior year
quite happy — Thanks for everything

And, write me ———

Love,
Brownie

UNIVERSITY OF MISSOURI

"BROWNIE" AND I .SHE WAS A GOOD FRIEND AND WE ENJOYED
EACH OTHERS COMPANY. IT WAS GREAT TO HAVE FRIENDS.

CHARLES HORSTMAN AND I AT THE UNIVERSITY OF MISSOURI
CHARLES FLEW 25 MISSIONS OVER GERMANY, HOWEVER
HE WAS KILLED IN A B-52 CRASH AFTER THE WAR

ONE OF MY GREATEST FANS MY MOTHER IN JUNE
1943 AT FRATERNITY HOUSE WHERE WE LIVED.
WHILE IN COLLEGE TRAINING DETACHMENT.

117

THIS IS SO TRUE AS WE HAD SORORITY HOUSES ON
EACH SIDE OF OUR FRATERNITY HOUSE. THE GIRLS
ALWAYS GAVE US SOMETHING TO WATCH

Part 2
Chapter 4
The cadet center

When we arrived at the cadet center in San Antonio we had visions that we would be going directly into pre-flight. This was not quite true. We did not unload where the cadet center was but across the road from it in another large camp. This was the holding camp for cadets waiting to get into the cadet center. We received the news that we would be in the holding center for approximately two months. It was a camp that did not make very good use of all the men waiting.We had a couple of hours of calisthenics everyday, and would go out on various work details to just try and keep everybody busy. I found out that if you volunteered to work in the garbage house every other day, you could get a pass to go into downtown San Antonio. Lot of the cadets drew K. P. duty. I spent three years in the Air Force and never once drew K. P. duty. How lucky can you be. It did not take me long to find out in the service to shut up and not let the orderly room know who you were. It saved a lot of problems. Volunteer only when it was something you wanted.

Well, the garbage detail worked just fine for me as my sister, Cordell, was spending a lot of time in San Antonio and besides it was more fun to be in San Antonio than it was at the cadet center. The cadets all hung out at the Gunter Hotel. It was a beautiful old hotel and where every one met and took their dates. I would go into San Antonio on the bus to kill the day. But, of course, the next day I was back into the garbage hut. It was a good job because I just had to tell the cadets drawing K. P. for that day to separate the garbage into various containers. The garbage good for hog feed, was kept separate from the rest. At that time there was no prohibition against feeding raw garbage to hogs.

Somewhere along the line I met a girl by the name of Jean Jones and spent some time with her. I just cannot recall how I met Jean, or where. But I did manage to have a girl in every port. My folks never came to San Antonio ,while I was at the cadet center.It was in the summertime, and of course Dad had his yard

119

to mow. They did come to San Antonio, then on down to the Rio Grande Valley in the winter. Dad had to look after the business of his citrus groves.

It was not an exciting two months while we were waiting to cross the road into pre-flight. We were becoming quite physically tuned as we were doing a lot of marching and exercising. The food was good and the cadets picked up a lot of rocks. The labor was cheap, as I recall we were getting forty dollars per month. As cadets we were sort of in a separate category. We were neither officers nor privates. Finally the day came to move across the road. We got into serious training to become Air Force flying officers, whether as a pilot, navigator, or bombardier.

"YOU TOO CAN BE AN AVIATION CADET AND FLY FOR UNCLE SAM . . . !

JEAN JONES AND I IN SAN ANTONIO IN JULY 1943

121

Part 2
Chapter 5
Pre-flight at the Cadet Center

The time had arrived and this is what we have been waiting for ever since we entered service. This was the serious beginning of our officer training. We moved across the road into the cadet center for two months of intensive training, which involves the theory of flight. We were to take training in radio by Morris code, and we would have to take and receive 10 words per minute. A lot of cadets including myself,had trouble with this but I finally got the hang of doing it. We had aircraft recognition classes, navigation classes and other subjects plus an hour of close order drill everyday and an hour of calisthenics classes. There were other classes that I cannot recall just now. Discipline was very rigid. It was " Yes Sir" and " No Sir" at every command. If you screwed up, you would be walking your demerits off in white gloves under a boiling Texas sun. Inspections were held every day and each barracks had to pass inspection. There was no time for foolishness ,as there was more waiting cadets, and if you fouled up you were out. This was not a place where you could get by with anything

We were required to wear name tags at all times. If you failed to salute an officer, you could expect to be called to your day room. This is when I really found out for sure that you volunteered for nothing and kept your mouth shut. At the time we went through the cadet center, Hazing by the upper class had been outlawed. It made it a little easier for us due to the fact they had outlawed hazing. In the PT program I found I was a fairly good runner so 1 volunteered to run the four mile cross-country everyday. This allowed me to get back to the barracks before the group playing baseball, volleyball, or basketball. This way I could be alone in the shower. Each barracks had at least eighty men and there were eight shower outlets. Confusion reigns when all these men tried to get into the showers at once. That was the reason I would run the cross-country so I would not be involved in " dropping the soap ". We were allowed to go to the cadet center's for shows and for soft drinks. To my knowledge or memory, I do not believe there was any hard liquor or beer served on the cadet center except in the officers clubs and of course, we were not allowed to go there.

Time went very fast for me because we were so busy and were always preparing for inspections. The beds had to be made just so, and shoe's had to be polished to a shine that would show your face. The brass belt buckles and your insignia all had to be in perfect shape. It sounds like a lot of knit picking, but it is the overall program that makes an officer and a gentleman. Things always seemed to go well because we had discipline and everyone knew what he was supposed to do.

We would fallout at 6:00 a.m. in the morning in the street for roll call. Anyone missing roll call would walk his demerits off when the rest of the cadets were going to town for the weekend. Although we could go to town on Saturday and Sunday we could not get overnight passes. Even married men with children, could not get an overnight pass. Again this was part of the discipline. Even where a man had children who got in after 12 p.m. or later could expect to get demerits. None of this bothered me as I knew what my limits were so I had no problem going through training. Not once did I have to walk off demerits.

When we were finished at the cadet center. We could head for primary flight school. We were all like kids with the new toys and even though we had no idea where we were going. We loaded up in buses with all of our barracks bags and left.

123

PT-19'S IN FORMATION AT STAMFORD TEXAS

Part 2
Chapter 6
Primary flight school, flying at last

We found our orders were to go to Stamford Texas. None of us had any idea where Stamford, Texas was. We rode all-night and the next morning we were north of Abilene, Texas headed for Stamford which is about 40 miles north of Abilene. We were in the high plains of West Texas and it didn't look too good. Stamford was a town of about 4000 people and not very impressive. We got out to the airfield and found that it was a very adequate small base. It was a base that was operated by civilians under contract to the Air Force. It had a very nice mess hall and classrooms and the barracks were one-story but very adequate. But what really caught our eyes were the PT 19 airplanes waiting for us, a bunch of over eager cadets.

The previous class had left a week before we came in so everything was in ship shape condition waiting for us to arrive. It was very easy for us single cadets to move from base to base, but some of the married men who had children had problems finding places for their families to live. Some of the wives did follow the men from base to base.

We were assigned to our bunk and got settled in the first day. The next morning we received our ground school schedule which included getting familiar with the PT 19. We then were assigned our civilian instructors. This is the only air base using civilian instructors that we would have. I drew a man by the name of J. Kelly. He was addressed as Mr. Kelly. Mr. Kelly was from Boston and was an old barn storming, pilot who had been in several airplane crashes and had scars on his face. He had been a policeman in Boston and was a typical Irish man and talked with an Irish brogue. However, he was a very good pilot and I was fortunate to have him as an instructor.

After our ground school courses with the PT 19 were over, we were prepared to start flying. We could hardly wait for the PT 19 which was a low wing monoplane with six cylinder, 300 horsepower, inverted Franklin engine. It flew about 120 mph and

125

was a reasonably good acrobatic airplane. There were no radio communications in the airplane so there was a pair of rubber tubes fastened to each side of our helmet running back to the instructor in the rear cockpit. He would talk into this rubber tube and we could hear surprisingly well.

After having 10 hours flying time in the Piper Cubs at the University of Missouri, we all had an idea how to taxi the PT 19 as it was a tail dragger like the Piper Cubs. It is much more difficult to fly a tail dragger then to fly a tricycle landing gear. There were three or four auxiliary fields scattered around Stamford, Texas. We all had to learn where those fields were and were assigned to a certain field for the day that we flew. We flew every other day, which meant there were about a hundred airplanes in the air around Stamford all the time. The days we did not fly we had ground school. There was PT everyday and again I ran the cross-country to beat the rest of the cadets to the showers.

A typical flying schedule was like this: we would go out and find an area where there were no other airplanes. Mr. Kelly would show me how to stall the airplane, how to recover from the stall, and then put the airplane into a spin and show me how to recover from a spin. Plus all of the other acrobatic maneuvers that we could do. It is easy to recover from a spin. But when pilots first started flying airplanes, many were killed before the art of recovering from a spin was learned. I enjoyed the acrobatics and Mr. Kelly did a good job of teaching them to me. All of my experience on the farm handling machinery, tractors, served me well in my flying. After about eight hours, Mr. Kelly had me taxi up to the line shack and crawled out. He said " You know what to do". I was ready to solo. What a wonderful feeling it was to taxi out and solo on my own. I circled the traffic pattern, made my approach, and did a good job on my first landing. I got praise from Mr. Kelly. I was stepping about 10 feet high. This was not the case with all of the cadets as some of them made terrible landings, but the PT 19 was a forgivable airplane. Because they primarily were made of wood and cloth, the center section of the airplanes would crack and sometimes break if the plane landed too hard. Every time a class soloed there would be a few airplanes with broken center sections. Our instructor continued to ride with us about every other day, and when we went solo, we would go practice stalls and spins and all kinds of maneuvers and general control of the airplanes.

I had a couple of incidents with Mr. Kelly that has remained with me through all of my flying days. We were up doing acrobatics and I crossed controls in the airplane doing a maneuver. Now this is a no -no when you are flying or trying to recover. My ear's started ringing as Mr. Kelly was saying " Greiner take me back to the field ". I could tell that he was quite upset. I landed and crawled out of the airplane and started filling out the A-1 forms (where you wrote in the hours flown and any mechanical problems with the plane) and as I did so Mr. Kelly had his arm draped over the back of the airplane waiting for me to finish. Then in his Irish brogue he said " Greiner, the factory that made this damn thing is still making them, but the one that made me closed down." I have thought of that so many times when I was flying and it is a very true statement.

Another incident happened to me in primary while I was flying solo doing acrobatics. One of the things a pilot must always do was to make sure that area was clear of other airplanes and that your seat belt was securely fastened before doing acrobatics. Because these were open cockpit airplanes a person could fall out. I was going to do some inverted flight and cleared the area. The seat belts were the Army type that had a long latch that you snapped down. I checked my seat belt and it was fastened and I proceeded to roll the airplane over which takes some maneuvering with the stick. I suddenly found myself starting to fallout of my seat! I hung onto the stick and the airplane went into a dive so I fell back into the seat and recovered the airplane. My thought was " Gee whiz, my seat belt is sure too lose". I look down and found that it was unhooked! This scared me nearly to death because I knew if I had fallen out I probably would have been washed out of cadets as a result of the airplane being lost. Of course, I had a parachute on but my fear was of being eliminated for carelessness. I was so nervous that all I did the rest of the flying time was to fly straight and level and try and recover my composure. These were the only two incidents that I had in primary flying. We all flew our first cross-country northwest to Spur Texas and we thought this was a big deal. Along towards the end of our flying, Kelly and I did some low flying where we chased a few Hereford cows. But I never did this alone for fear of being caught as this was a no-no.

I made some very dear friends at Stamford Texas. I am not sure exactly how I got acquainted with Mrs. Andrews, who loved to ride horses. She turned out to be a very dear friend and she and I would ride horses together on weekends. She and her husband, who was an attorney, would invite me to dinner at their house and I enjoyed it very much. She was a very gracious lady. Another lady that I met at the cadet club was Mrs. Robert Hall. Now Mrs. Hall was always my favorite because she always said I looked like Gregory Peck. Why wouldn't you like a lady like this. Lois and I stayed in touch with these people for many years and the last letter I had from Mrs. Andrews was in 1977 telling me that her husband had passed away. .Several years previous to that when I was in West Texas, I visited Mrs. Andrews and Mrs. Hall. They were still the same lovely people. I was lucky to have their friendship while I was at Stamford

There was not much social life in Stamford. Sunday morning found the sidewalk in front of the drugstore setting full of cadets. It was a dry county in Texas, meaning there was no liquor to be sold. If a person wanted liquor (and this was no problem for me) you would have to take a taxi to Abilene. There were a few dances, at a cadet club downtown, but most of the social life I had was with Mrs. Andrews riding horses on the weekend. It was a very memorable time in my life because I love the people. Both those at the base,and the ones I met downtown. They made me feel welcome.

We had the usual military marches and formations. The military never let us forget we were in the Army Air Corps. There was the lowering of the flag and the usual formations that go with it. We would fallout for formations every morning, but by now this was all becoming routine. I enjoyed Stamford Texas and was ready to move on to the next phase of my training. I did not know what was in store for me or I would have been a little more anxious. Thus ended my career at primary, it was a great time.

I last heard from Mrs Andrews in 1977 when her husband died. Since writing this I started wondering about these dear friends. I called Stamford, Texas and found both are deceased. They were such wonderful people and I have many fond memories of them.

Three-point
Landing

This is the way I made all my landings pop.
ass-end first. Ha.

Part 2
CHAPTER 7
Basic flying a trying experience.

Class 44 D. which meant we were to graduate on the fourth month of 1944 left Stamford Texas, and headed for Perrin field at Sherman Texas, for flight training in the BT 13. This was an airplane that had a 450 horsepower engine that had a nine cylinder radial engine. It also was a monoplane with an enclosed canopy and built totally of aluminum. Moreover very rugged fixed landing-gear wheels.

The Vultee Aircraft Corp, built it to take a lot of rugged abuse. It had a nickname as the Vultee Vibrator.Our arrival at Perrin field was much the same as any arrival at an air base. Get assigned to your barracks and do the medical checks and all the other assignments needed to prepare for flying. We were assigned our flying instructors, started our ground school on the airplane, took our aircraft recognition courses, and the usual PT and we were ready to go to the flight line.

The first three weeks at basic went very fast and I was very happy with my progress when things started going wrong. I started getting sick and would wake up in the morning with my throat so sore I could hardly swallow. I went on sick call and was given sulfa and penicillin and was told to report back in about three days. My throat had improved some but I was far from feeling well. I then had to report to the flight surgeon where I was told in no certain terms that I had to take a thirty day leave. I started protesting immediately, as this would let me fall behind my class 44 D. and throw me into class 44 E. the flight surgeon minced no words. He replied "Cadet Greiner you will take a thirty day leave or I will ground you permanently". There was no arguing with the flight surgeon as his decision was like God.

My Mother and Dad were in San Antonio at this time. I called them and told them I would have to take a thirty day sick leave and go home. They got on the old train and came to Sherman Texas where we then continued onto Kansas City on a train so crowded you could not find a seat. At Kansas City we

130

caught the Golden State Ltd. and went to Washington IA where I began my months leave at home. My blood had broken down again.I was anemic and had to take medicine for that, but my throat had gotten better, and I could not wait to go back to start flying. After being back home about three weeks I made my plans to return to Sherman, Texas and Perrin Field. Nothing eventful happened at home as most of the young boys and friends were in the service or gone.

I reported back to the flight surgeon.. I was approved for flight duty which made me very happy. I reported to my squadron and now was assigned to class 44 E. All of these cadets were strangers to me so I lost the comrade ship that had been built up previously. I reported to Capt. Greene. now since I was an extra, he assigned me to a Lieutenant Moore. Lieutenant Moore was a check pilot who had only two students instead of five or six like the other officers had. The two students he had were both infantry officers who were taking flight training. My troubles were just beginning. I was scheduled to fly the next day with Lieutenant Moore and met him at the squadron room. He did not say good morning, go to hell, or anything except in a gruff voice meet "me at the airplane". I met Lieutenant Moore at the airplane assigned, saluted him as is normal. I started the airplane and taxied out for take off. We were out for approximately 45 minutes when he said," Take me back to the field" which I did. He got out of the airplane never said a word and walked into the squadron room. I came in figuring he would talk to me, but he did not. In about 10 minutes, I found that he had put me up for an elimination ride which would have washed me out of cadets. I was dumb struck and humiliated. Capt. Greene called me into his office and told me that he would give me my elimination ride in two days. These were two dismal days.

I reported to Capt. Greene on the designated day and we walked out to the airplane. I did the usual preflight, crawled in called the tower and proceeded to take off. We climbed up to altitude. I cleared the area and did the maneuvers that Capt. Greene wanted me to do. I did stalls, spins, and snap rolls, then Capt. Greene told me to go back to the base. After we landed Capt. Greene told me to report to him in the Squadron room. I reported to Capt. Greene, saluted him as is customary ,and waited for his verdict. He asked me if I knew anything I did wrong and I

131

told him a couple things that I knew were not quite right. He then said "Cadet Greiner report to the the orderly room on your regular schedule and I will give you a new instructor". I saluted him and only God and I knew how happy I was. I walked out of their stepping 10 feet high. I knew I could fly that thing as good as anyone.

When the next day came I reported to Capt. Greene to find out who my new instructor was. He replied" I'm sorry Mr. but I'm short of instructors and you will have to keep Lieutenant Moore". According to Air Force regulations he was not allowed to do this but I knew I was in no position to argue with him. I was supposed to have another instructor. Again, Lt. Moore would not talk to me. We would go up to fly and he would do everything possible to irritate me hoping I would do something that would give him grounds to eliminate me. He would grab the stick and try and beat my knee's with it. He was evidently passed over for a promotion. He was taking it out on me and the two lieutenants that he had for instruction. However my being just a cadet I was the one who caught the most of the anger that this man carried. I was just like the runt pig trying to survive. All of the instructors would take their cadets and do blackboard work with them explaining things they did not understand. I had none of this. I made the mistake of asking one lieutenant, who was an instructor, a question and he quickly said to me "go ask your own instructor". So from there on I was like that runt pig running from teat to teat. I would listen to what an instructor would say to his students but could never ask a question. Then I would go to another instructor and listen to him. The two lieutenants who were of equal rank could ask questions of any instructor but I could not.

This went on the entire five weeks that I was flying with lieutenant Moore. Later years I met a fellow flyer from Perrin field and he too agreed that this was the most miserable man he had ever met. For years I could have spit in his eye if he were laying dead at my feet. Now I would like to spit in his eye but would hate to see him dead. Although this man had done all of the things I mentioned above, when it came time to graduate and move to my next base, he graded me AA's or above average in every one of the categories. For that I thank him but those five weeks were the most miserable in my entire training period. From there on my flying career was a piece of cake.

132

Part 2
Chapter 8
Twin engine training at Ellington

About March 20, 1944 we had graduated from the PT 13 and were headed for Ellington field at Houston Texas. For twin engine training, in the AT–10. Which was an airplane with two 300 horsepower engines, made of mostly plywood, but a pretty stable airplane for training.

I cannot remember how we went from Perrin field to Ellington field whether it was by bus or by train. We checked into Ellington with the same procedures that by now were pretty standard at each air base. We had our usual physical, bending over parting our cheeks, that went with every transfer. Ellington was an old, adequate base. We had excellent barracks and a good mess hall. We were organized for our usual ground school, and athletics. We were assigned our instructors and I cannot recall who my instructor was. However I flew with him about eight or 10 hours and he pronounced me ready to solo. Because there were two pilots in an AT-10, students soloed with another student pilot acting as co-pilot with with you.

Ellington was a piece of cake for me. I had a very good time flying and our social life was very good. Somewhere along the line, I met a young lady by the name of Doris Pokluda. Doris and I had quite a few dates while I was stationed at Ellington and I became very good friends with her mother. In fact Mrs.Pokluda, and Lois and I exchanged Christmas cards for years and years. They were wonderful people. As we got closer to graduation, we were allowed to go to Houston to order our new army officer uniforms. This was such a treat because we knew we were getting close. We had been wearing these old khakis for so long that we were ready for something different. The officer uniforms that we were able to get were really sharp.

There was a large hotel in Houston that was the center for the cadets and every time a class graduated, a graduation dance was held at the hotel. I think it was called the Roosevelt hotel. It has long since been torn down. When graduation day came we had a fancy graduation exercise just like you were graduating from college. Doris was there and pined my wings on which was a tradition for your girl to pin on your wings. It was a real grind but yet other than the trouble I had at Perrin field I went through the Air Force training program like a whiz. I have always said this was my high school and my college wrapped into one. I was now a Lieutenant in the Army Air Corps.

I did not have very many memorable times at Ellington rather than just the usual flying however there was an incident that happened that I feel compelled tell about. We were due to take a long night cross-country trip. I and another student were scheduled to fly from Houston up to Lufkin Texas then over to Palestine then Back to Houston. We took off and flew north to Lufkin, and then headed northwest toward Palestine. Found Palestine and our map showed a rotating Beacon on the airport which was our auxiliary airport. We always had to select an auxiliary airport for emergencies. We got about halfway back to Houston when we received a call on the radio, that Houston was socked in with fog. We were ordered back to Palestine to land and report in when on the ground. As we passed over Palestine and saw the rotating Beacon, we saw many bright lights that looked like the perimeter of the airport.

So we thought " Gee, this will be a snap the airport is brightly lit and we will just have to land". Well we turned around and went back to Palestine lost our altitude and tried to reach the airport by radio with no results. We did not think too much about this as it was past midnight and we just figured the field office was closed. The rotating Beacon was shown as being in the center of the airport. But when we dropped down low and flew over the lights we saw that it was some kind of a prison camp. The rest of the area was totally dark. The question is" What do we do now". Because the rotating Beacon was working and in the middle of the airfield we started flying magnetic headings with our landing lights on across where the field should be. We finally found some markers that showed where a runway would be. When we let down and left our wheels down to slow down and fly across the field, a bunch of cows were looking up at us every time we flew over and they did not run away. We were flying around this town making so much noise that we awakened the whole town. Soon the fellow who managed the airport guessed that we were trying to

134

land. We saw a car come out and chased the cows off of the runway. We then came in, making a damn good landing. We found out the lights we saw was a German prisoner of war camp.

The airport manager took us into town, got us a hotel room where we then phoned Ellington at Houston and told them we were on the ground. Our instructions were to wait till tomorrow and some body would fly up and clear us to fly home. We went out to the airfield and finally saw an airplane come and he circled and circled until we called him on the radio as he could not find the field in the daytime. It was a unique experience and a tale that I have told several times over the years.

After my graduation I got a ten day leave and then went home and was transferred to first pilot training on B-24 liberator bombers at Fort Worth Texas another new phase was to start. Ellington was a great place to be I had a lot of fun there. And the people I met were great people. They liked me and I liked them and I know Mrs.Pokluda is with the Lord. She was a very wonderful religous lady. I will not forget her kindness.

I HAVE MY WINGS!! I HAVE MY WINGS!! I HAVE MY WINGS!!

DORIS POKLUDA, MY GIRL FRIEND AT ELLINGTON FIELD WHO
PINNED ON MY WINGS. DORIS AND HER MOTHER WERE
WONDERFUL TO ME.LOIS AND I HEARD FROM MRS POKLUDA
FOR YEARS. THEY WERE GREAT FREINDS

PART 2
Chapter 9
Fort Worth and the B-24

We arrived at Fort Worth, Texas and went to the airfield that was named Tarrant field. It was a nice airfield and was located west of Fort Worth. The officers quarters were nice and we each had a private room. We went through the usual procedure with the flight surgeons, and then got down to the serious business of learning how to fly the B-24. We were first assigned our ground school schedule, which included the engineering of the plane, also the engine's, and anything mechanical on the airplane.

We went out for our first look at the B-24 and thought "wow"!!! Are we going to learn to fly this thing. It was so much larger than anything we had flown. By todays standards it was small. But believe me it was a harder airplane to fly than what the new airplanes are today. It is like comparing a new automobile you would buy today against one that you bought in 1940.

We had a week of ground school and familiarization on the airplane before we went out for our first ride. Two students were sent with an instructor for the first familiarization ride. One rode in the co-pilot seat and the other one stood behind the pilot and observed everything that went on. We then spent numerous hours just sitting in the cockpit and learning where all the instrumentation and all the levers and handles were so that we could find them blindfolded. This was very important because in case of engine failure Pilots would need to be able to immediately know where the fire extinguishers for the engine were and how you feather the propeller, and how to do other procedures. The procedures were pretty well nailed. It was a wonderful challenge that every pilot had to learn to fly these airplanes.

We had to have 50 hours of flying time, before we could solo, with an instructor shooting landings and doing traffic pattern work. There were a lot of things that everyone had to do before they could solo the airplane. We learned all kinds of emergency procedures. Such as the loss of one or two engines, the loss of

137

your hydraulics, fire procedures, fuel transfer procedures, landing gear procedures, flying traffic patterns on three engines just a host of things had to be learned before you were allowed to solo. It was all very interesting and a great challenge. However I had no problems learning to fly the Liberator. I found it to be challenging and enjoyed the training that went with it.

While we were learning to fly the Liberator there was a good side in being at Fort Worth. This was an old cow town where you could still have fun and believe me I did have a lot of fun at Fort Worth. I was lucky in finding another good 29 model A Ford Roadster. It was in excellent shape, it had a canvas top with a rumble seat. However there was no seat, in the rumble seat, so I went to a junkyard and found a good used seat for five dollars. I had good transportation except the brakes were not the greatest. I had already learned in California when I had a car just like this one that I could burn half kerosene and half gasoline and it did not know the difference. A short time after I was in Fort Worth I met a lady by the name of Betty Forbes. I do not know at this time exactly how I met Betty or where but it was a short time after I arrived in Fort Worth.

She was a very lovely young lady who had an unfortunate marriage. She also had a little daughter named Beverly. She was a very good young mother and did an excellent job of taking care of little Beverly. Beverly had never been baptized and I was honored to be her godfather at her baptism. Of course she would now be a lady 55 years old who has no idea who her godfather was. We had a great time in Fort Worth. I was allowed four gallon of gasoline per week. However Betty's boss was president of the Fort Worth bank and got an unlimited amount of C rations for gasoline and he gave some to Betty. By buying high-test gasoline and mixing it with kerosene, I had never to worry about having enough fuel to run the old Ford wherever we wanted to go.

One of the favorite places that Betty and I would go to was a place at that time called Eagle Lake. It was hot in Fort Worth and the inside of the old B-24 would get up to a hundred and twenty five degrees with the sun shining on them. They would be almost too hot to touch so after flying in one of those it was always fun to go to the lake. At that time in my life I really did not know how to swim at all. So Betty taught me how to swim and although I am not a good swimmer and could only save my own life if I did

138

not have to far too go. We had a great time swimming at Eagle Lake. It was always cold watermelon after swimming.

Charlie Horstman and his wife Evelyn visited Betty and I in Fort Worth. I can remember the old model A took a fit, and as near as I could figure out the carburetor float was hanging up from burning the kerosene. By beating on the carburetor you could get it to run. Then maybe it would run for a few days with no problems and then you would have to beat on the carburetor again. We were in downtown Fort Worth when the old model A threw a fit so Charlie stepped out on the running board, lifted the engine hood and started beating on the carburetor. We made quite a sight in downtown Fort Worth. A lieutenant, hanging on the front of an old model A Ford, beating on a carburetor laughing and having a ball. It was a fun time. I am sorry to say my dear friend Charlie was killed flying a B-52 after the war when it crashed after takeoff from Minneapolis, MN.

In the meantime, my flying out of the air base was doing very well and I was enjoying it. I felt very comfortable with Betty. Always the same smile on her face and just a lot of fun. She fell in love with me and wanted to marry me. I must admit that I thought about it several times and gave it serious consideration. But there was the fact that she had been married and had a lovely child but all the problems just did not fit for me. There was the religious problems and whether or not it is not proper to say it now, but at that time a young lady like that was considered used goods. That's a terrible thing to say, but it's just the way it was. I would see Betty again later on before I went overseas and then she later came to the farm in Iowa. After the war every Christmas Betty would write a letter keeping Lois and I informed about her life and Beverly's. Lois and I sent Betty our Christmas" Farm News" for at least 20 years and then one year the letters quit coming. I would very much like to know where Beverly is but have no idea how to try and find her. It would be fun to talk about her life and her mother's. It is just one's stories of life.

My flying at the air base progressed very well. I spent more time having fun as I remember than I did working. However we did everything that we were supposed to do. Along towards the end of my time at Tarrant field the brakes on the old model A were getting to the point where they were no good. When I would drive up to the field the guard shack was on a slight incline, the personnel on duty would see me coming and just wave me on through. We had most of our flying time that was required. However one day I will remember another officer and I took a B-24 up to an auxiliary field at Gainesville Texas. We spent eight hours shooting landings at Gainesville. We landed and took off 29 times that day. It was a lot of work but that is how you learn to fly airplanes. We had a great time doing it and don't I wish I could do it again..

The time came to leave Fort Worth and I sold my model A to a student in the next class for the same one hundred twenty-five dollars that I paid for it. It did a very good job for me and I had a lot of fun. I gave Betty my good bye's and we went out for dinner one more time and then it was off to Lincoln Nebraska to pick up my air crew. I do not remember now how I went to Lincoln whether we flew commercial or went on the train.

JOSEPHINE MY TRANSPORTATION AT FORT WORTH.
A 1929 MODEL A FORD COUPE. PRICE $125.00 WOW!!

MY FRIEND BETTY FORBES IN FORT WORTH TEXAS WHILE TAKING
FIRST PILOT TRAINING. MY FAVORITE AIR BASE FOR FUN.

PROFICIENCY RATING

Proficiency	Ratings: AA-Above Average; A-Average; BA-Below Average	Preflight	Elementary	Basic	Advanced	Transition	Pilot Observer	Navigator	Bombardier	Flexible Gunnery
Military	Bearing and Neatness	A	A	A	AA	A				
	Attention to Duty	AA	A	A	AA	A				
	Cooperation	AA	AA	A	AA	A				
	Judgment and Common Sense	A	AA	A	AA	A				
	Leadership	A	A	A	AA	A				
Academic	Average (End 3151 st weeks)	A	AA	AA	A	A				
Pilot	Spins and Stalls		AA	AA	A					
	Accuracies			A						
	Instrument		A	A	A	A				
	Night Flying			A	A	A				
	Formation			AA	AA	AA				
	Navigation			A	A	AA				
	Gunnery									
	General Pilot Ability		AA	AA	AA	A				
Bombardier	General Bombardier Ability									
Navigator	Pilotage									
	DR									
	Celestial									
	Radio									
Gunnery	Flexible Gunnery									
Accidents (See Code Below)										

MY ENTIRE FLYING RECORD UNTIL I GRADUATED. I LIKE ALL THE DOUBLE A'S OR ABOVE AVERAGE. I LOVED TO FLY AIRPLANES AND FORMATION

142

QUESTIONS TO BE ANSWERED BY INSTRUCTOR:

1. Does Student handle airplane with confidence? / Yes ____ No
2. Does Student show excessive nervousness? ____ Yes __/__ No
3. Does Student show any indications that he has developed a fear of flying? ____ Yes __/__ No
4. Does Student seem eager to go to combat? ____ Yes ____ No ____ Indifferent
5. Are you aware of any domestic or financial difficulties which might keep him unsettled? ____ Yes __/__ No
6. Would you want this officer for a wing man in combat? ____ Very Much ____ Yes ____ No
7. Has this man repeatedly complained of physical ailments during his training period? ____ Yes __/__ No

Note below any further explanations of above answers if desired.

REMARKS: (Give brief estimate of student's flying ability listing any flying or command deficiencies)

I think this student is above average in general flying ability. He flies accurate traffic patterns and good formations, both low and high altitude. He has always been ready and willing to fly and he seems to know the B-24 well. He has always been prompt and courteous. He should be a good plane commander.

John M. Cennick A. 2Nd Pc.

Training Squadron Commander

MY REPORT FROM B-24 FIRST PILOT TRAINING AT FORT WORTH TEXAS. IT WAS FUN.

Part 2
Chapter10
Lincoln Nebraska Crew Pickup

On September the seventh 1944 I was to report to the Lincoln Army air base at Lincoln Nebraska.It was at this base where we would be assigned our crew and be sent on to another air base for further crew training. There were not a lot of things to do at Lincoln except to be assigned the crew, issued flying clothes, and sent on to our next base which was to be Casper Army Air Force base at.Casper WY.

The following members were assigned to my crew No. 8783.
Lieutenant Howard W.. Greiner 020057277
F/O Edmund B. Knoll T131306
F/O Francis H. Balensiefer T7080
C/PL Frank J. Korycanek 36686074
CPL John G. Spissinger 32987582
CPL Robert E. Shaddy37483851
PFC Richard G. Maki16087877
PFC Ernest H. Ratliff 34792971
PFC Andrew L. Swartz 33843958

I had a very diverse crew and they were a good bunch of boys. We made our acquaintance at Lincoln and then the usual things in building up a comrade ship amongst the crew. They were all anxious to proceed on to the next air base to do some flying.

I spent some time in downtown Lincoln with some of the other fly boys. The Corn Husker hotel was the hangout for a lot of the Air Force people. I remember one night meeting a young lady from York, Nebraska whose husband was overseas and she very frankly told me she wanted to party. Now I was a young red blooded American Air Force pilot who was willing to help her have a good time. At 12:00 p.m. I took her to the train station and put her on the train for York Nebraska. She thanked me for a nice evening and said I probably will never ever see you again but we've had fun. This is the way it was during that time.

As I recall I think Lincoln was a dry County at that time. But they had a mighty powerful ALE that they sold called Gluck Stite or something like that. It was very easy to get your self into a state of being just a little bit towards having too much to drink. This only happened to me once at Lincoln but I do recall the time as I was totally embarrassed while rideing back to the air base in a cab and I lost it. I guess the reason I remember it I was so embarrassed because the cabbie would have had to cleanup the mess. I never let that happen again but I always remember it.We then made plans to leave for Casper Wyoming as transportaion was provided.We were looking forward to flying.

IT ALL STARTED WITH THIS PT-19 AIRPLANE IN STAMFORD TX

HOWARD SECOND FROM LEFT FRONT ROW. FOUR OF MY CREW PERISHED

146

PART 2
CHAPTER 11
Crew Training at Casper Wyoming

Our assignment, after getting our crews at Lincoln, Nebraska was to go to Casper Wyoming for B-24 crew training. Twenty air crews consisting of 10 men on each crew were loaded onto a train at Lincoln Nebraska and started on our trip to Casper Wyoming. I do not believe that there was hardly one man who knew where or what Casper Wyoming was about. We left Lincoln Nebraska in the evening after we had our meal. The officers were all in one car and the enlisted man were two cars.

The next morning we awoke after a miserable night in old chair cars. I do not know where the railroads found all of the old cars they used. Anyhow we woke up in Scotts Bluff, Nebraska where we were served a breakfast and then proceeded on to Casper Wyoming. This farm boy who was always raised in the midwest and used to the green corn fields was not used to seeing the sand and sage brush in Wyoming. To me it did not look to good. We followed the Platte River mostly and sometime in the afternoon we arrived at Casper, Wyoming. We sat in the railroad yard a couple of hours and another switch engine took us out eight miles west of Casper to the Casper Army Air Base.

After seeing all of the nice air bases in Texas that had two-story barracks and looked very nice we were not prepared for the dismal look of the Casper Air Base. All of the buildings were tar paper shacks which meant they were all-black and rather dismal looking. There were two wooden barracks for a WAC detachment or enlisted women. The only good-looking buildings were the four main repair hangers on the flight line. All of the buildings were heated with coal and there was a detachment of black troops who done nothing but fire the old pot bellies stoves in all of the buildings and our living quarters. None of us were very impressed with what we saw. We were assigned to living quarters with four men living in a room with a pot bellied stove, and a couple of places to hang up our clothes. You had to go outside to a central building for the shower and latrine. They were not very clean as there was always coal dust from firing the stoves. Occasionally at

147

night when a soldier would come in and throw coal in the stoves they would explode blow open the door and have coal dust and smoke everywhere.

Politics always enter into everything including the war. One of the senators from Wyoming who got the air base located at Casper was from Northeast Wyoming where the coal fields were. He insisted they use coal to heat the buildings when there was natural gas on the base as you children know Wyoming has a lot of oil and gas. But we got used to it. Our first impression was that the air base was not very well-run. That proved to be true on the first day we went to fly airplanes.

We done all the preliminary things that you have to do when you report to a new air base and get ready to start flying. The first morning we were assigned to the flight line we were given the number on an airplane. I took my crew to the airplane and we proceeded to do our first pre- flight. The first airplane I was assigned had so many mechanical problems that I refused to take it up in the air. So I requested the second airplane it was the same way, then I requested the third airplane and it was the same way and then I requested the fourth airplane and it also had a lot of mechanical problems. By this time the officer in charge of the airplanes came out and started chewing on me for not taking the fourth airplane. I explained to him why I would not take it and that it was my choice as airplane commander to refuse it. I then got my fifth airplane which we left on for an eight hour training mission.

That evening when we came back to the air base two of the runways were blocked with B-24 crashes. On one a nose will collapsed and I do not recall what happened to the other one. The airplanes were a bunch of wrecks. We even were flying the old B-24 Jack Ass Mail which had been in the raid at Polatsie in Romania. There was no discipline at the air base and when you have no discipline the job is not done well. The same thing applies to our schools today when you do not have discipline you have nothing.

About two weeks later we had a new commanding officer at Casper air base. His name was Col. Scott who was one of the flying Tigers in China. In a week you would not know it was the same air base. Where before the mechanics would come to the flight line one by one he had them marching and would have hot food and coffee on the flight line and things really started to change. I was assigned a plane for a night bombing missions towards Gillette, Wyoming where our practice range was. We made our bombing runs over the target and could not see where the bombs hit. We had cameras to take pictures of the bomb when it exploded with just a couple of pounds of powder in it. I turned the plane over to my co-pilot and went back and watched through the open bomb bay doors and could see we were missing the bomb target by at least two miles. This was from 24,000 feet. After two or three runs we were missing the target each time by the same distance. I called into the air base and reported a malfunctioning bomb sight and returned at 3 a.m. in the morning. We know more landed than Col. Scott met my airplane and wanted to know why we returned. This was a real commanding officer and that is why things changed at the air base. We were lucky we did not kill some ranchers sheep.

We were free to go into Casper on the nights we did not fly. Casper was not too large of a town at that time. There were plenty of bars and the Sand Bar was still operating. The Sand Bar was where the houses of prostitution were. The old nightclub the Riverside had gambling slot machines and was running wide open. So there was a lot going on in downtown Casper. One of the reasons for the Sand Bar at that time Wyoming had a lot of sheep herders and they would come into town after being out for two three months at a time and this was their relaxation. It was just not looked at by the city fathers as something immoral but as something needed.

After I was there a couple weeks another lieutenant friend of mine by the name of Hefner had a date with a girl downtown and wanted to know if I wanted a date also. I said sure and his date Elaine made a date for me with a girl named Lois. Well we caught the taxi downtown and picked up our dates and headed for the "Riverside". My date was a very nice young lady and of course when we got to the Riverside we got a table an ordered dinner. During the conversation like all Air Force wolves I mention that I was married because I did not know yet what I was into. My date immediately started crying and said "Take me home I won't be out with a married man". It took a lot of persuasion but I finally convinced her that I was not married. I'm beginning to think this is a mighty nice girl. The rest of the evening went very well and I got

149

a taxi to take her home to 426 East 11th Street. I took her up to the door and was going to give her a midnight kiss when she started to resist. I said "well they make them like that" reached up and grabbed her pertty white scarf and wrapped it around my neck and got into the taxi. I had already thanked her for a very nice evening. She went in and wrote my name down before she forgot it. Now she worked at the air base in the Transportation Department. So the next morning she went and called her friend who worked in personnel to verify that I was not married. For some reason she just did not trust me. I called her for a date the next day and she said she would be downtown and that I was to meet her at 2:00 at a certain storefront. Well I got downtown about noon and I saw her walking down the street with another officer. I casually walked by and said" I will see you at two o'clock". I embarrassed her and she ended her other date and we were together till I shipped out of Casper on Dec. 28.

As you children know this was to be your mother who I had the privilege of living with for 38 years. This is how we met on a blind date in 1944.

That Saturday afternoon we walked up to 426 East 11th and I met the rest of the Clare family Lois's brother Jim was at that time in the invasion of Iwo Jima and his wife Alice and there boy Brian were living with mother and dad Clare. Mother and dad Clare both took a liking to me. I felt like I was at home back in Iowa.It was a wonderful beginning with my in-laws to be The Clares were a very social family and Lois and I were invited to a lot of their friends Christmas parties and it was really a wonderful time. Lois and I and her friends played a lot of bridge and had various dinner parties. At this time cigarettes were hard to buy and ketchup and such items were also in short supply. I would bring the folks cigarettes and occasionally stick a bottle of ketchup in my trench coat pocket. I really became a part of their family. This would be to long if I tried to tell you of the wonderful treatment I got from the Clares. Lois had a sister, Mary, who had married, previous to my coming, an Air Force pilot by the name of Jack Compton. Jack was one of the pilots flying a B17 into Pearl Harbor the day the Japanese attacked. Her sister Marjorie was 12 years old at the time. We have been a very close family ever since. I have tears in my eyes as I write this. Christmas day came and I was invited to the Clares for a wonderful Christmas dinner. I really was not anxious to be leaving but we knew that I would be going overseas. The same 20 crews left Casper on Dec. 28 by train for Topeka, KS where we would be assigned to overseas duty. We were called filler crews. Of course that meant we were taking place of those shot down on the raids over Germany. We arrived at Topeka KS air base and were granted a 10 day leave. I was able to get air transportation to Fort Worth TX and spent four days with Betty Forbes. Then I spent the rest of my leave in San Antonio with my folks and some time with Jean Jones. There's nothing like having a girl in every port. Of course mother and dad knew that I was going overseas and mother was very distressed about it but she put on a good show. So after my leave was over I flew back to Topeka to join my crew and get our orders for overseas. We did not know what was coming.

LOIS CLARE MY NEW GIRL FRIEND IN CASPER,WYOMING

LOI'S GRADUATION PICTURE FROM HIGH SCHOOL
WHO WOULD NOT LOVE A GIRL LIKE THIS.

"THEY SHALL MOUNT UP WITH WINGS LIKE EAGLES,THEY SHALL
RUN AND NOT BE WEARY,THEY SHALL WALK AND NOT FAINT"

B-24 LIBERATOR BOMBERTHAT I FLEW OVER GERMANY.
THERE WERE MORE B-24 BOMBERS MFG THAN ANY OTHER
AIRPLANE. THERE WERE OVER 17,000 PRODUCED
153

LOIS'S PARENTS, EMILY AND HAROLD CLARE. THEY WERE LOVING AND FUN TO BE WITH.

Part 2
CHAPTER 12
A Diary from leaving the U S to capture

The following is a diary that was started some time in January 1944 while in a convoy crossing the Atlantic ocean. This will be an exact copy of what was written at that time. It does not seem possible that I wrote this 56 years ago. I find myself having trouble believing some of the things I wrote but they were all true at the time. The diary is as follows, There are things in this I cannot recall today. I have no memory of being in Stone England, yet I know I was there.

  This is word for word.

  I really don't know a more opportune time to start a diary than right now. Riding a boat somewhere in the mid Atlantic, bobbing up-and-down, in the middle of a large convoy headed for the destiny of war which we hope will be as pleasant as our passage is now and has been. To start off with I will try and tax my memory to go back when we left the phase training at Casper Wyoming and headed for Topeka KS that was the staging area. I believe it was Dec. 29 -- 44 when we headed for the trains. The officer club at Casper was built to accommodate a lot of men but on this last night at Casper it was filled to capacity. It seems as though KS is a dry state and everyone we knew took advantage of their last day in Casper. Well at 1930 we fell out and proceeded to the designated areas and loaded on trucks and went to the train. We loaded aboard with the officers on the sleepers of which there were three. We pulled out of the station and started to roll and about 2100. We, the peaceful ones, tried to go to sleep but everyone was very drunk. You no sooner fell asleep and some one would wake you up,to ask if you were President Roosevelt or who ever came to there mind. Well little by little the evening past when about midnight lieutenant Dye came back drunk as a pig and tried toget into bed. He made it after a little assistance from his navigator and he like all drunks proceeded to get sick.I being on the same level with him did quite all right. However,my copilotunder me and flight officer Pierce shoes received the full benefit.What a mess. The next day Dec,30 found us in Hastings, Nebraska,about nine in the morning and nothing much happened. We poked along about 20 mile per hour all-day and arrived in Lincoln Nebraska at 7:20 p.m.. I sneaked over to a restaurant and obtained a couple hamburgers and just caught the train in time. Something a few did not do. They ended up taking a bus and getting to Topeka anyway they could. The morning of the 31st found us rolling out of the Kansas City MO towards Topeka. We rolled into Topeka Army air base at about 9:30 unloaded and headed for a lecture in preparation to going on a ten day a leave

Knowing this I started calling for plane seats and through the transportation office finally obtained a seat on Braniff Airways. Well at 10:30 a.m. I left the base and went into town at 11:15 went to Jayhawk hotel, shaved and washed and then went to have dinner after which I went to Topeka airport and waited on the plane. Was there at 1:30 and left on a plane at 5:00 for Fort Worth. I arrived at Fort Worth at 10:00 and was to meet my friend Betty at 10:30 at the hotel still the same sweet gal as always.. Found out I could get no hotel room so ended up going out to Helen Harkriders for that night and a joyous night it was. New Year's Eve of 1945. Not too much celebrating at all but had a good time. January 1st 1945. Found me a phone and tried to call mother at San Antonio. Talked to her and she wanted me to come to San Antonio right away so I called and changed my plans and went back down to San Antonio that evening of January 1st. Arrived about 5:00 and was greeted by the family and was glad to see them. We went back to the park motel where we stayed and talked a while to the folks and, Cordell, and Sid. Could not wait to call the skipper .(Jean Jones) and did so. Wouldn't tell her who I was at all and finally she guessed who it was. Well she had a date but told me to come out at 11 p.m. which I did and was greeted by her old man who was not too happy with me (he did not like Catholics) but I could care less. Well I met the skipper as was planned at 11:00 and we sort of talked it out so I made a date for the next evening. January 2nd found me up late and went to breakfast with the folks and the next few days we were very happily spent. I had a date with the skipper every night from the second through the eighth except Thursday the fourth when she had another date. We got along splendid and patched up our troubles. I can't deny that I love the girl very much to say the least but I'm sure of this. She will be a big pack of trouble and etc but I do love her. I know my father would be very unhappy with it if I were to marry her because there is so much between us, religion, type of life and all, but still I love her and think a lot of my old friend Betty in Fort Worth. True she's been married, and has a cute little girl, but she loves me very much I know but the disadvantages after being weighed lean to word Jean so we sort of planned on big things if I came back from the wars. Well that evening I didn't spend with Jean I spent with the folks and we toured all of San Antonio and went to Kelly and Randolph fields and had a wonderful time. Was unhappy with Mother's health but nothing I can do at all. Well the morning of the ninth rolled around and it was time for me to leave. We got up quite early and went out to the airport and at 6:30 a.m. I bordered the plane and left for Fort Worth.

Arrived at the Fort Worth airport and at 8:30 a.m. and was met by Mary and Betty. We ate breakfast at the airport and then went down to the Worth Hotel where Betty had a room for me. Betty and I were their till about 11;30 when we decided to go to Dallas and see Beverly who was Betty's little girl. We got to Dallas about 1:00 and saw the little girl who had changed a lot and came back to Fort Worth in the if evening then Betty and I had dinner. And we started to make the rounds. Went to the Clover club which was very dead. After some time Betty went home or rather I took her and then came back to the hotel. The morning of the 10th, I was awakened by a telephone ringing and it was Braniff Airways telling me I had been put off of the plane. Well that put me an awful fix so I didn't know what to do but about 10 minutes later they called and said I was back on. It was difficult to get a seat if you did not have a priority. Well Mary and Betty came after me and we went to the airport and I left about nine o'clock. Mary went to Dallas but Betty was left behind. The trip to Topeka was uneventful helped the hostess in the best way I could and arrived in Topeka at 1:00. Well I went out to the field and then signed in and waited for my crew to come after they did I went back to town and picked up some lady by the name of Vicki something .. Well the 11th was the usual things of processing, drawing equipment and etc. the 12th came and more of the same. Took the crew to" garden acres " or some snake Ranch for dinner. Like most parties

157

there was a lot of liquor but I did not drink very much. At 10;30 I brought by engineer co-pilot and also my navigator back to base. The 13th, 14th, 15,th, were all about the same I didn't go to town because I knew why, so stayed home and called the folks and Marjorie my sister on the 15th.

The 16th came up and in the p.m. we left. They had a troop train there and we left Topeka on the train at 3 p.m. we sailed right along and at noon on the 17th. We were in Chicago and had a delay. We left the morning of the 18th and we were in Pennsylvania and on the train till 5 p.m. when we pulled into camp Kilmer New Jersey. Our train ride wasn't bad my navigator and I had a drawing room and it was a very nice ride. Not like the troop train's usually are, noisy, dirty, this one was very quiet due to our private drawing room. If only the infantry could see us now. Well camp Kilmer was a hell of a place. They didn't like the air Corps at all and I liked it less. The food was awful and treatment was worse. I had no use for it at all. The 19th, 20 and, and 21st were all alike and we went here there and elsewhere. Met a little gal at the officers club dance on Saturday evening and she sold to me my overseas supply of candy and etc. Sunday a large group of men came in from Fort Meade Maryland and I thought perhaps Bud ,my brother in law, was along but he wasn't. Well we were all disappointed because we weren't going to see New York. We left camp Kilmer on the 22nd at 1 p.m. in a convoy to go to the pier. We were about out of Kilmer on the way to New York when it started raining and on the slick road our convoy sailed over a hill and on the other side was a couple of civilian trucks that had cracked up. It so happened nobody could stop at all. So truck by truck that convoy crashed , banged, and run wild. Of course the traffic jam put four of our trucks out of commission and lucky no one was hurt but at the best, I thought there would be a dozen or so dead.

After the wreck was over we were all on our way to New York pier. We arrived at the pier at about 5 p.m. and were ready to board the boat. Well it was a banana boat as we had expected all right. Her name was " S.S.Santa Marta" she was 380 feet long and a boat of about 5,000 tons. Built in 1909 in Ireland and a sea worthy old tub at that. We were very lucky to be a board the ship as it was used as a passenger boat between north and South America. We were the only men aboard the boat. Twenty one air

158

crews and that made 63 officers and 126 enlisted men. We officers had state rooms of which there were four to a room very nice indeed. We had nice bunk beds our own latrine and wash bowl. It was as far as we were concerned very nice. After we settled in we ate dinner a board and I volunteered for guard duty to see the ship sail.. This was a refrigerated vessel that was loaded with frozen meat. My tour of duty ended at 1 a.m. and the ship sailed at 3 a.m.. I went to bed and did not see the ship sail. The morning of the 23rd found us out to sea. We were with a convoy of some size I could count 32 ships the first day and later I could count 70. It was nice aboard ship but even so time will hang long on our hands. I was on the late meal schedule to eat and what a meal. Just like eating in a big hotel with white tablecloths.(the government was paying cost-plus for us to eat) and a waiter at each table. All of the officers ate in the ships dining room and we really had the food to eat. We had a choice of entrees.

Didn't do much on board the first day and the day was passed by playing cards and so forth. As yet no one was sea sick and all was well. The second day at sea we awoke at the usual hour of 7:30 and about 10:00 had breakfast and at 1030 an inspection was pulled. My being state room commander I forgot about the inspection and had a dirty state room. This drew me the detail of taking some enlisted men and cleaning the latrine in the p.m.. However I had about five fellow officers and we just watched the men do the work. We didn't have a boat drill at all as one was expected so the evening meal came, we ate, passed the evening and about 9:30 I hit the sack.

The morning of the 25th was a different day altogether. During the night we hit a terrific storm. I awoke when I heard a large wave hit the side of the ship and heard it crash as it busted out two port holes and the sea poured into the enlisted man's quarters about drowning them. After all the water was soaked up we dressed and let the enlisted men in our state room's. It was a rough day and sea sickness is now taking its toll. At officers breakfast this morning one by one they got up to leave with various excuses when flight officer Pierce finally jumped up and shouted " I'm going upstairs and puke my God Damn brains out" which was what everyone had in mind. The old tub is really rocking like hell. The front end goes under the wave and the back

159

end comes out. We are sailing in the convoy which now has over 60 ships-counted which isn't near all of them. The convoy is moving at one knot per hour with weather like this " Fritz" (German subs) has a rough time to give us any trouble at all. All day today one can hear the China breaking in the gallery as dishes slide off the tables and etc. I am much in favor of quiet sea's. I am not sick but I have felt a hell of a lot better. Well the last few days have been like one would imagine all cruises to be on a boat that is boring as hell. The day of the 26 and the 27th didn't bring up very much at all. Same old stuff and the sea was still awfully rough as usual. I passed time by reading books and playing bridge.

The morning of the 28th came and it was Sunday I drew guard duty from 8:00 am till 4:00 p.m. and didn't like it much at all. And that p.m. we had a boat drill and Capt. Greene is highly P. off at the men and I don't say as I blame him. I got my crew together and passed the buck. Give them hell in a slight mild way so to speak to just be a little military. Really can't say much about my boys. They have been awful good. In the evening I read the book -- Destry rides again, and hit the sack ready and willing at 12 p.m. the next day was the 29th and we haven't done much at all. Cleaned up the room ready for inspection and the enlisted men are to have a full field pack inspection at 2:00 p.m. Ugly rumor that we will have reveille at 6 a.m. tomorrow and a field inspection. Guess they are really turning chicken shit to be honest. So guess another day on the seas won't hurt but God I'm glad I'm not a sailor. All days at sea are about the same. The 30th came along and we had the usual inspections and so forth and then came the 31st. Today seem to be passing pretty fast. We don't get up until 9:00 and have breakfast and play a few cards or lay on the deck a while and before we know it the day is passed .

February first has found us still, and for how long God and the skipper only knows, at sea. But it is the most beautiful day at sea we have had yet. The ocean was calm and it was warm and nice. Our little friends the sea gulls were still with us as they have been since we left New York. In the p.m. they had gunnery practice in the convoy and some racket it was to.. The old tub shook with each belch of the four inch gun on the stern but she is still a good old boat. The p.m. was spent as usual playing cards and reading. The Chow is still wonderful and all in all it is Damn near like a pleasure cruise minus one thing "women.. With all these hungry men all women should thank their lucky stars they are not aboard. February second was like all days at sea so far we got up and had inspection. We loafed a round and took P. T. during inspection. The afternoon was usually quite quiet. The seas were smooth and quiet and all was well. We then had several submarine alerts and we slept with our clothes on that night. February 3rd was the same had inspection and went back to bed at usual. Laid in the sack all-day, evening came and we passed time writing letters and wishing we had some mail.

There is little excitement going on today, we didn't get up early at all. It is now Sunday February the fourth and there is little activity. Played bridge with the signal man from the Navy a very nice fellow. They had a little variety show in the p.m. but nothing much happened. February 5th found us close to England and happy we are. It's about time to get off this old tub we have been on two weeks now and that is quite awhile. Just wonder if I'll be able to walk when I get on solid ground if it isn't pitching and rolling. We had an inspection and passed the time playing bridge with the signal man in the p.m. the only excitement on board was a submarine alert. They dropped eggs (depth charges) left and right and it makes me happy to think I'm so close to England. Could swim if we had to. Just joking of course. We can see the English Coast at about 4 p.m. rumor is we will dock at 10:30 tomorrow morning guess time will tell that.

Feb. 6 we sailed into England and came into Southampton and pulled in then dropped anchor. Everyone one wanted off the boat but we stayed on that night and passed the day the best we could by playing bridge and etc. sure had an awful anxious day on board as everyone was ready to get off. February 7th we got up late and laid around until 12:00 when we pulled anchor and started to go into dock. What a mess of ships were there. There is everything possible however all were bearing the flag of the good old USA. After we docked we left the good old faithful S.S.Santa Marta and piled ashore. Seemed good even if it was England. Finally we were organized and they started us out walking. We walked a hell of a way under full pack and the air Corps is not used to that at all. Finally we pulled into a place that the infantry had in Southampton. God what a hell of a place it was. Mud up to your ass and cold as Billy hell. We got wet walking in making it worse. Finally we had a tent appointed and

161

such a tent it was. Holes all over and half burnt up. Well we had Chow call and had C rations which were the first I ever ate and care less if I eat no more. After drawing blankets tried to go to bed but Damn near froze to death. Everyone was cold as hell and couldn't sleep. Dam England. Morning of the eighth found us half froze to death and it was raining making more mud. God but it was nasty. Worked up enough energy to go eat breakfast came back and crawled into bed. With my trench coat,B10, jacket my wool cap, long underwear, wool pants, wool shirt and finally got warm enough to sleep. Slept the whole night through with all that on except the trench coat and still froze with four blankets. Well about 11:30 we ate and got ready to leave when we went to turn in blankets we were 12 short and had a hell of a time finding them. Finally left camp at 2;45 PM walked and I mean walked to the train . And that night we spent traveling through beautiful England. I wonder

February the ninth found us at Stone England about six hours north of London and headed for camp with a bus this time. Good old air Corps, we processed for about 10 minutes came back and ate breakfast and took a shower the first in 17 days and then hit the sack. Up and moved ate and went to shave spent evening writing letters and catching up on my diary. February 10th found out that around 9:00 were to finish our processing. Did that in one day and was very little to do. The place is quite small and a lot of the men. Saw a show how to get along in England. February 11th was Sunday got up and went to communion and mass at 9:00 at Howard Hall. Came back playing cards until about 12:30 when we found our bagage had to be out by 1:00 p.m. spent the p.m. in a show and clearing the field. Also played bridge in evening with Lt. Bush from Los Angeles CA.
February 12th was up at 7 and went and ate breakfast at Stone. Then we went to formation at 8:15 boarded bus and went to station. Got to train and rode till 5:30 when we came to Norwich England and unloaded came out to field and moved into this pig pen and tried to eat. Went to eat came home and hit the sack. February 13th up at 7 went and ate and reported to the adjutant Then toured the field signing up and etc. at noon ate and spent the p.m. roaming over the field and went to a show in the evening and wrote my first mail.. Home to bed. February 14th up late and went to adjutant and then to squadron operations in the afternoon.

162

I flew for the first time. I got checked out on runway localizer and spent the evening playing bridge and walked into Johnson in the club. Meet with Johnson and glad to see him, took transition with him at Fort Worth Texas.

February 15th up at 7 and spent the day going to ground school and did not learn much at all. Wrote a few letters in the evening and to bed early a very dull day in England but the sun did shine in the afternoon. February 16 Friday and not much doing at all went to ground school all-day and spent the p.m. at the officers club the 17th was about the same and I worked a pass and went into Norwich for the evening. Oh what a town, black and dark, wooden heels on the women and etc. give me the old USA please. Sunday the 18th didn't do much came home from my liberty and went to formation at 1:00 p.m. and meeting at the chapel then went to the club and laid around all-day but went to mass in p.m.. The 19th day came we went to ground school all-day had an engineering class that day, Got a haircut and in the evening went to the Red Cross Gal and gave her 30 pounds or, $120 dollars for a bicycle. Came home and hit the sack well February 20 came and we went to ground school again. This was the last day of ground school and not much else to do so came home early and went to bed. February 21 came and we laid in the sack and went to formation at 11:00 and didn't do much. When to club in evening and came home early flew the first time . 22nd went to a formation came back to the club and ate dinner went to a show in the p.m. and then picked up my bicycle at the club. Went to mass and communion and got sick and spent the night in the hospital. What a spell I had. February 23rd didn't do much laid around and went to formation and loafed the day away February 24th up to 11:00 formation and went to fly in the p.m. flew one hour and 25 minutes and bounced in a couple of landings. To the show in evening and home to eat cheese one lad had. Dance at the club but didn't go. February 26 was about the same not much doing at all loafed around in the evening. February 27 came and we went to fly and to the 11:00 formation and was to fly in p.m. but didn't fly until evening when we flew a couple hours. February 28 was a good day weather was nice went to formation at 11 and got an airplane to fly. Flew" Dixie" for about four hours and came back spent the evening at the club. What a life. I am alerted for a mission tomorrow. March first well up at 5:00 and to briefing at

6:30 for misson. What a haul it was. Nine hours to southern Germany circled and bombed INGOLSTADT close to the Munich rail road yards . Very uneventful. Went to meet the enemy, but no enemy.. Airplanes galore the sky was full like blackbirds in the fall, never saw so many but nothing happened no flak no fighters know nothing. Am alerted for tomorrow.

Well this is the end of the diary that I started after I left New York by boat for England. I left on my second mission with my crew and some of us never returned. It has been a terrible thing for me all these years I will cover some of that in my next story. As I read this 56 years later I laugh at my love life because it was not at all like I wrote in this diary. It was the young lady from Wyoming who stole my heart. Who I had the privilege of living with 38 years, and raising six children, before we lost her to breast cancer in 1985 I did not know this diary was still around. At the bottom of this diary in pencil some one has written March second-shot down over Magdeburg Germany and was taken prisoner.It could be my mothers writing.

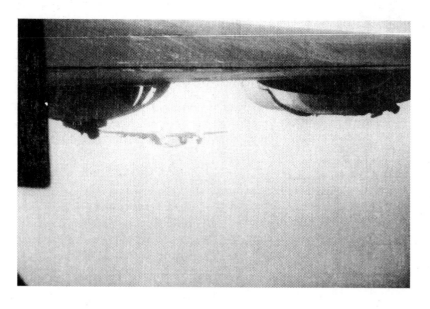

THIS IS THE CAPTAIN "TIGHTEN UP THAT FORMATION NOW"

GETTING IN FORMATION TO HEAD FOR GERMANY I LOVED TO FLY FORMATION.

165

GETTING IN POSITION FOR THE TRIP TO GERMANY IN MARCH 1945

Part 2
Chapter 13
466th Bomb Group ,England

Norwich England at the base of the 466 bomb group 785 bomb squadron. Yesterday March 1 1945 we flew our first bomb mission. It was a nine hour run and we never saw a burst of flak or any German fighters. We thought it was a piece of cake. The morning of March 2 we were alerted at 5:00 for the 6:00 briefing for a bombing run to Magdeburg Germany.

Our bombing run was to be a tiger tank factory. It sounded very simple and we anticipated a bombing run like we had yesterday. We were to find out it was not to be. We were scheduled for a 7 a.m. take off and all of the planes that were able were on the bombing run. There were 12 B.24s in our squadron. At the briefing we found our position was to be the one that no one liked to have. There were two names applied to this location one was" Tail end Charlie" and the other was "Coffin Corner". When you are assigned a location you fly it to the best of your ability. The lead plane of your squadron was usually a Major or a lieutenant colonel in the lead airplane. There would be an airplane on his right and on his left. To his right would be three more airplanes and on his left an additional three airplanes our three airplanes would fly on the right side of the right plane from the lead plane for a total of 12 airplanes.

The lead plane would take off first and circle the field climbing to a designated altitude to assemble the formation. The lead plane would shoot a designated color flare and you would then start catching up and falling into formation that you were assigned to. Our take off went well as our squadron assembled and took our position behind all the other airplanes. All of the bases were putting planes in the air and the sky looked like a bunch of blackbirds in the fall getting ready to go south. On March the 2nd 1945 the U.S. Eighth Air Force put 1200 heavy bombers and 800 fighter escorts in the air that morning. Can you visualize 2000 airplanes being assembled at one time. It was almost unbelievable.

Our bomb squadron climbed to altitude which was to be. 24,000 feet, for our journey to Magdeburg. We did not fly straight to Magdeburg but had a route that varied south east till we were about 50 miles from Magdeburg and then turned and started our bombing run to Magdeburg. When we were about ten mile from Magdeburg the sky suddenly turned black with bursts of flack from the German 88 anti-aircraft guns. They were a very superior gun that out shined anything we had in the American Army. They could use it for anti-aircraft protection ,they could use it for artillery, or any other use. You will need to ask any American soldier who fought against the Germans, how good the German 88 was

It was easy to see that the Germans had our altitude correctly and they would do this by having a German fighter sending information to the anti-aircraft guns. BY now there radar had improved also. The American fighters would lower or raise their altitude to get out of the flack. We poor" Devils" in the bombers had to hold a steady course and fly directly into those beautiful black puffs of smoke that you knew had hard centers. You also knew that every black burst of flack was a shell exploding sending out thousands of pieces of hard steel to do damage to you.

We tightened up our formation on orders from our lead plane, were given orders to open the bomb bay doors and when the lead plane dropped its bombs our bombardiers would toggle our bombs. We were carrying

one hundred pound bombs. We had just dropped our bombs and made our turn to head home and we closed our bomb bay doors.

This was when we picked up our first burst of flack. A huge explosion shook our plane and I'm sure we were lifted a hundred and fifty feet in the air. It sounded like rocks in a tin can when you would shake it as the flack tore through the plane. Then there were three more just like that in a row and we were on top of each burst of flack with that huge orange explosion. We immediately lost the oxygen, the radios, the intercom system and three engines as well as the hydraulic system which let the main gear fall down. Since we had lost the oxygen and three engines we could not hold the airplane at 24,000 feet we started rapidly losing altitude and got down to about 14,000 feet and the plane was struggling to hold that altitude. Because we had no intercom there was no way I could communicate with the waist gunners and the engineer. The P. 51 who stayed with us for a few minutes gave us a signal and pulled out and left us.

It was then the engineer came up and told me there was a fire on the plane. He was very excited. I turned the flying over to the co-pilot and left my seat and crawled down into the bomb bay. Looking up into the wing I could see a fire burning up by the fuel tanks. On a B. 24 you have a whole group of transfer hoses above the bomb bay and these had been cut and there was gasoline in the bottom of the bomb bay doors. It was easy to see that this thing could explode anytime. I shouted at the engineer to go to the waist and abandon ship and have them all bailout. I gave him the order and then I went to the flight deck grabbed the co-pilot arm and told him to abandon ship. I went down to the nose and got the nose gunner and we jettisoned the nose wheel door and the two of us bailed out. I assumed the co-pilot was right behind us as I had given him the order also to abandon ship. After the nose gunner and my chute opened I started looking for chutes and could not believe that I saw none. I found out later that the engineer never gave the waist the order that I gave him. They were in the waist when the airplane exploded, which I knew was going to happen. I was sick about this for years and always felt like I should have gone to the waist and threw them out. But yet when you give an order you expected it to be carried out and this was not. I have finally after all these years excepted this as the fate of war but it has not been easy to know that some of your people lost their lives because the order given to them was not carried out.

As I came floating down I could see that I was drifting over a canal. Over the canal was a railroad with a high-grade and a electric line across that. I could see that if I drifted into that and went into the canal I knew I would drown because I am not a good swimmer and having all the flight suits and sheep skin boots made swimming impossible. I was trying to get my chute to drift away from the canal when suddenly it seemed that the ground came up and I hit the ground terribly hard. We had on backpack chutes that were only 24 feet in diameter and were designed to get you down fast so that German fighters would have less time to shoot at you. I really do not know, in my effort to slip away from the canal, whether, I had my chute partially collapsed, but I know when I hit the ground it was a terrible collision. However on the way down I saw seven German soldiers running across the field to intercept me. I was stunned and tried to get up and couldn't because I broke my leg and my ankle. However I do not know where this German civilian came from, but I felt a gun poked in my back with the words" You Schwine a Houndt my house kaupt" and after he poked me a couple more times I struggled to my feet.

By this time the seven German soldiers had come up to where I was. They had me put my arms around two of them and we started walking and hobbling towards the Berger Meisters home or office of the little village we were in. It is funny what you remember but this building has such a musty smell that I think I could tell you yet to day if I smelled that smell today. They took my rings my watch the candy bars in my flight pocket then made me strip naked and stood me in a corner of the room. I could only stand on one leg as the other one hurt so bad. After what seemed about a half an hour I thought one of then said something to me and I turned around and was rewarded with a punch to the chest. I was beginning to get the message that I was in trouble. It was then I heard the old crank telephone just like the one in Hogans Hero's. They make that terrible odd sound. The Berger Meister was talking to someone in a heavy German voice and in about 15 more minutes they had me put my clothes back on. I was glad because by this time I was starting to get quite cold.

In about a half-hour a German staff car came. Again the type you saw in Hogans Hero's, and loaded me up in the back and hauled me down to downtown Minden. They took me up to what I gathered to be City Hall, anyway, there were a whole bunch of steps for me to hobble up and took me in for what they called interrogation. I can remember it like it was yesterday. The German gentleman who was to interrogate me had on a pair of small gold rim glasses and I thought he was probably sixty or older. Anyway at my youthful age I thought he was an old man. He started out asking me for information and our instructions were to give our name our rank and our serial number. When he found out that my name was Greiner he almost threw a tizzey. His reply was"ACH such a good German name why you not fight for the FATHERLAND" he could not understand that I was an American of German descent and not a German citizen. I was an American.

After he was finished with me they took me out and I started hobbling down the steps when they were bringing my

170

nose gunner up. I said to my nose gunner "Well they got you to" when the soldier behind me hauled off and hit me which speeded up by descent down the stairs. They then took me out into the middle of the street and started toward what I assumed was the local city jail.

The civilians on the street were shaking their fist and shouting at you but at this point I paid them no heed as I was having enough trouble trying to walk. We finally got to the jail and it was exactly like those in the movies. The cobble stone floor with the thick wooden doors. A jailer opened one of the doors and showed me into a cell. The room was about five feet wide with a wooden bunk that had an old straw mat laying on it. In the corner set a bucket that was full of feces and urine that had not been emptied for some time. It's smelled terrible. I went over and lifted up the straw mat and the lice and crabs were under it by the thousands. There was one very small light bulb about ten feet high and a small window so small that you could not possibly reach it or crawl through it if you wanted to. I sat down on the bunk after they shut that big thick door and it was then that I went to pieces.

I knew that I was alive and I knew that my Mother and Dad would get word that I was missing. I knew that I was all right but they would not. I knew what this would do to my mother. Isn't it peculiar what people think about in times like this. You lay on the bunk knowing that you are going to become infested with lice and crabs and you can hear the cobble stone boots walking down the hall, stopping and opening the little peep hole and then continuing to the next cell. That evening they opened the door and handed me a slice of black bread. And a cup of coffee made from oak bark. I bit into the piece of bread and it was like biting into it piece of plywood. I thought I could not eat it and tried to drink the liquid they gave me and it almost turned my stomach. The next day I wanted water very bad and tried to show them with motions that I wanted something to drink so they bought me more coffee. My leg was hurting so bad I think I was running a little fever when finally one of the guards after my motions said Yaah wasser!!! How easy it was with my folks talking German and it to took two days to get a drink of water.

The next day they took me to what I gathered to be was a hospital. In fairness to the Germans they took an x-ray of my leg.

171

There were no windows in the hospital if that is what it was. There was blood all over the floor.It looked like a slaughter house. The man who took the x-ray said "YAH Kaput!". Put on an apparatus of some kind, wrapped it with paper bandages and back to the cell. There was no such thing as pain medicine or anything else because they had nothing ether, it was so apparent. The next day the paper bandages stretched and the apparatus fell off. So be it. By this time they had gathered up about eight American crew members. A German sergeant who was a man of about 60 years old and was in the home guard, and two young German soldiers started us on a trip to Frankfurt Germany, to Stalag headquarters, where all Air Force prisoners were taken.

I remember this as being a terrible trip from the start. I do not remember all of it but I remember certain parts of it. I had no idea where we were or where we were going. Several things that I can recall that stick in my mind we were traveling at night ,walking for some reason and I had been hanging onto the shoulders of several of the other prisoners. I can remember tearing a board from a fence and using it as a crutch until my shoulder and arm pit got so sore that I no longer could use it. I remember the night when we slept in a barn and this German farmer had this huge mean dog who would have liked to have eaten us all. However after a while he settled down and we did get some rest and some sleep in the barn.

One of the things I really remember and if it were not for the old German soldier I would not be writing this book today. We were in a little village in a little depot waiting for the train to back into the village. This was at night I have no idea of what the time was. They ran the train at night and in the daytime they would camouflage it so the American fighter planes would not shoot it up. The depot started filling up with people. Every body was on the move carrying what few possessions they had either on their back or pulling a baby carriage or wagon. It was not too long before the depot became full and the civilians realized there were eight American Air Force men laying in the corner. Suddenly the place erupted in a mad frenzy. There was a young Jewish boy who was a gunner and he could understand German but could not talk it. All of a sudden he said
"Oh my GOD they want to hang us." At that same time the older German soldier jumped up and all of the civilians had us

172

surrounded in the corner shaking their fist at us and screaming. Our older German soldier was poking his rifle under the chin of some of the civilians and at the same time he barked orders to the two young German soldiers to get us out and take us down the railroad track which is what we done. As far as the two young soldiers were concerned they could of had us. That's how close it was and a lot of the American airmen were killed that way. I have never forgotten that night however I must say that if our homes were bombed, our families killed, nothing to eat, and someone bailed out over town we would probably do the same thing.

Another instance I remember we were riding in the back of an old truck with a charcoal burner on it and every time we came to a hill the driver would stop shakes the grates to get enough fuel or fumes to get over the hill. Somehow the charcoal produced a gas that the engine could run on. We picked up two German soldiers along the road that had just came back from the American front. We were all ridding in the back of this German truck colder than hell, as there was no top on the truck. Again our little gunner who could understand German said the soldiers would like to shoot us as the Americans were taking German prisoners and shooting them. Believe me, in spite of the censorship, our army did do this. People become so hardened to war that you do things like this. Fortunately, our older German soldier would not allow something like this to happen.

Another instance I recall we were getting on a train and the German trains had compartments on them. We filled up a compartment. Some German civilians a couple of them women were trying to get in to our compartment. The old sergeant threatened to kick them in the face and would not let anyone else in. Another time we were on a train and we had to lay in the aisle and people were tramping on my leg all the time which was almost unbearable. By this time my leg was swollen so bad and so black and blue that I thought I would surely lose my leg but there is nothing that you can do about it. I remember us arriving in Kassel by train shortly after a bombing raid that night. I remember the destruction in the railroad yards with engines standing on end and rails twisted like pretzels and all the buildings damaged or destroyed the devastation that was caused by the bombing was unbelievable. We were underground in some kind of a walkway and there were large numbers of displaced persons waiting to go

173

back to work to get a rail line through Kassel again.I was becoming so miserable and sick that I do not remember too much a bout how we got to Frankfurt.

When we got to Frankfurt and I do not remember too much about this except that I recall laying in a cell and hurting so bad that I screamed and screamed and screamed until they gave me a shot of morphine. All the time, after the first night that I was a prisoner, I was covered with lice and crabs. I was constantly taking crabs out of my hair, out of my pubic area, and under my arms when I had a chance. The lice did not bit as bad as the crabs. I assumed the shot they gave me at Stalag No. 1 was morphine but it could have been something else Anyway it knocked me out..

The next morning I was loaded into a staff car, and was taken about 10 miles northwest of Frankfurt. There in a little village called, Holte Mark located near ,Ober Ursula, was the holding place for all of the burned airmen and those with broken legs and any other medical problems. This is all that I can handle on this today and will take up the rest of my stay tomorrow.

Part 2
Chapter 14
Prisoner of war Hospital

My stay at Ober Ursel the hospital for American prisoners. I arrived at the German hospital for prisoners of war in a not too good of state. My leg was as green as grass in the spring as was my ankle. Because I was constantly having to hobble and walk I constantly agitated it and it was worse for wear. I was crawling with crabs and lice and never had a chance anywhere to clean up. There was not any toilet paper, so you can imagine how filthy I was.

This was not really a hospital but was the third-floor of some kind of a Lutheran church affiliated home. There were always German soldiers in part of it recuperating. There were a lot of Lutheran nuns wearing their big white head dresses. It really was in a beautiful setting back up a long Lane. There were beautiful pine trees and trails through the area where you could take a pleasant walk if you were a resident.

When I arrived the Scottish medic who was captured on D-Day by the Germans was in charge of anyone who needed medical attention and I needed it. They removed all my clothes gave me a shower and a treatment to get rid of the lice and crabs on my body. I think they boiled my clothes to get rid of the lice and eggs in my B-10 jacket. They gave me pajamas furnished by the Red Cross and a sweater and put me to bed . How wonderful it was and after four or five days of being off of my leg the swelling went down. The Scottish medic then put a cast on my leg and I was finally given a pair of crutches that I still have to this day, and have used several times since. In fact I used them three years a go when I got a new artificial knee.

There was a German sergeant in charge of this operation. He had a son in the American army and he and his wife owned a clothing store in Miami FL. He went back to Germany in 1938 to settle his father's estate, and the German government would not allow him to go back to the United States. I never got to visit with him but it was through his efforts of delay that we were not moved

175

as the American troops got closer. After I got a cast on my leg I was able to move around however again I became anemic and started having problems of getting light headed when I would stand up. However all of this was not very pleasant but was tolerable and I was very lucky to be at this place.My arrival here was not any to soon.I had lost a lot of weight and it was an experince I DO NOT CARE TO DO AGAIN.

It was not too long after I got to the hospital that we could hear the American artillery in the distance across the Maine river. It was shortly after this that the German sergeant disappeared. He left the hospital and went through the German lines and surrendered to the Americans. He then informed them where we were. The American fifth calvary, which was part of Patton's army, sent a armored spearhead through to surround our place. It was an exciting time as all of the German soldiers were surrendering their rifles and all of their dress swords in piles. We were the first prisoners liberated. I selected a couple of nice German swords and a German rifle. I still have the rifle today but the swords were stolen when I came through the port of New York.

The soldiers who liberated us were glad to have a place to take a bath and we shared our Red Cross parcels with them. These boys had a hard dirty job to do and no one wants to take any credit away from the infantry.   They lived a tough life everyday. They stayed at the hospital all-night and they were on guard duty all night. There were news photographers with this spearhead and they took pictures and there was a story written up about this liberation in a magazine and I cannot remember which magazine. My mother had the pictures and the story and I had forgotten completely about it until I started looking through papers to write this event in my life. It's a bit of history that's not important to many people but it is to the 50 some people that were prisoners at this place. The majority of the people who were prisoners had broken legs and ankles some were burned cases. There was a Scottish pilot who flew mosquitoes and this was his second time to be a prisoner. The first time he would shot down in Yugoslavia and walked out with Tito's partisans.   This time he got badly burned and lost and eye ,a very funny chap.

176

When the soldiers who liberated us a arrived they notified their headquarters by radio and the next day about 20 ambulances showed up and we were all loaded into ambulances and taken to an evacuation hospital behind the American lines. We were at the evacuation hospital one night and the next day we were loaded onto C. 47 transport airplanes and we were in England and sent to hospitals. I was sent to the 94th general hospital southwest of London on the six of April 1945. I was glad to be back amongst Americans again..

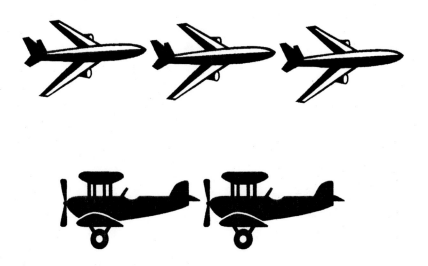

GERMAN MEDIC LEADS RESCUERS TO U. S. FLYERS

Hospital Staff Stays with 59 Allied Airmen

BY ROBERT CROMIE
[Chicago Tribune Press Service]

WITH THE 5TH DIVISION RECONNAISSANCE TROOP BEYOND FRANKFURT, March 29 [Delayed] —A hospital with 58 wounded allied aviators—the majority of them Americans—was reached this afternoon by the United States 3d army's 5th division reconnaissance troop after a German medic slipped thru Nazi lines two days ago with word that the patients were still there.

As the first armored cars and jeeps—two of the latter filled with war correspondents—rolled up the drive, patients able to walk came pouring outdoors. Some were on crutches, others limping, some with arms in casts, some one-legged, but all grabbed eagerly for hands to shake or enthusiastically pounded their rescuers on the back.

One British flyer said simply: " I've been waiting three years for this."

178

Medical Staff Remains

The entire German medical staff had remained with the patients. They seemed almost as glad to see the rescue party led by Capt. Donald Robinson of Detroit, Mich., as were the convalescent flyers. The Germans brought out drinks, passed them around, and promptly surrendered the weapons of all security guards.

The flyers unanimously agreed they had been well treated during their confinement in this particular prison hospital at Hohe Mark located in woods near Ober-Ursel, about 10 miles northwest of Frankfurt. They ranged from an American pilot shot down only nine days ago to a British flyer who would have been a prisoner three years next June 1. One was shot down in Italy, another in Hungary, some were bomber pilots, some fighter pilots.

They were loud in their praise of the German medic who kept them informed of the latest war news, and finally offered to sneak thru the German lines when it became apparent the Americans were near. The flyers said higher authorities had ordered their removal elsewhere, but the medic managed to invent excuses and delays until it was too late.

Foreigners Liberated

When he brought in the news to 5th division headquarters, the reconnaissance troop was ordered to try to reach the hospital. Some distance behind Capt. Robinson's rescue party, we passed thru the town of Oberhochstadt, in which the burgomeister was summoning citizens by ringing a bell and reading them a warning that any soldiers known to be in town would have to be surrendered or the Americans would shoot up the town. We also passed happy gangs of liberated workers—Poles, Russians, French. When we caught up with the lead vehicles, we found they had halted a German bus and taken off about 25 Germans, including one medical officer and two nurses.

The officer bore a dueling scar on his left cheek, which caused some one to wonder aloud if he were a Heidelberg man. He grinned and replied in excellent English that he was.

The armored cars and peeps waited at the crossroads a few minutes, also netting a frightened little baker in a sedan, who was en route from one town to the next, a pretty girl on a bicycle, and a truck from which a German mailman emerged, mail sacks on back, and continued afoot down the road, seemingly without the slightest surprise at the interruption.

Guides Commandeered

Finally another medical officer on a bicycle, accompanied by a woman on a second bike, carrying a bunch of flowers, came up and were halted.

The bikes were hoisted on armored cars, and both the man and woman taken along as guides. The hospital soon was reached.

We could hear loud cheers as the patients caught their first glimpse of the Yank convoy.

All who could walk or hobble poured out into the front yard, while one man with two broken legs said later he had managed to crawl across the bed next to his on his hands and sit on a stool, looking out the window.

Wait to Shake Hands

Inside the building—which was light and airy—the bed patients waited impatiently for some one to come in so they could shake hands, grin, and try to say how happy they were.

They were well supplied with cigarets and reading matter, and said they were fed as well as the Germans, but were a little tired of potatoes, cabbage, and black bread.

All, of course, are eager to have their folks notified as quickly as possible, but because of censorship rules it is impossible to give names or home towns of men seen today until their next of kin have been notified thru official channels. There are a handful of midwesterners among them, however, as well as at least one Australian, one New Zealander, a Canadian, several Englishmen, and one Irishman.

181

A Hundred Handshakes Greet the Prisoners' Rescuers

American troops storm into a village near Frankfort. The Nazi prison stands just by. On crutches, bandaged, limping, prisoners of war hobble from their prison to greet their rescuers.

182

THE GREATEST DAY
IN THE LIFE OF A P.O.W.

He had borne the privations and indignities of the prison camp for years. Now the Allied advance brings him the tonics he needs—liberty and the sight of his captors being defeated.

A German Guard Sees the Liberation Scene

On the left is one of the German attendants who has stayed behind. He sees his former charges behave like boys let out of school. They invite their liberators inside.

12

Almost Too Happy to Talk
He grasps his rescuer's hand and shakes it as if he
could never stop.

BRITISH prisoners of war, liberated by the
Allies in their rush across Germany, are
arriving back in England in great numbers, by
sea and air. On one day recently, for instance, 915
were brought to British airfields by Dakota transport aircraft. It was a great moment for these men,
who had been cooped up for years in German
prison camps, when the wheels of the transports
touched down on the soil of England. But will the
memory of even that first instant of homecoming
eclipse that other dramatic memory of the day when

"Where Are Our Chaps Now?"
There are eager questions about news of the advance and of home.

British or American troops burst into their prison camps?

The great pace of the Allied advance is creating some very special problems for the military authorities responsible for dealing with liberated prisoners. Their motto is "get the prisoners from their prison camps to their homes in Britain in the shortest possible time." As soon as a batch of prisoners is freed, accommodation has to be found for them and they have to be fed. There is no hard and fast rule about the accommodation. Suppose, for instance, that roads are still heavily crowded with our own advancing troops, it may be found advisable to hold the men for the moment in the camp where they have been imprisoned, always provided the quarters are good enough. Food has to be found at once—far better and more ample rations than they have had for many years. This food is drawn from the general supplies which the advancing troops have with them. Food, and, above all, tobacco, are just

185

about the first consideration. Next comes the question of transport to a rear area. In the early stage of any advance there are very strict priorities on all transport. But a very high priority is reserved for getting our released men back to transit camps in the rear. Here they receive essentials for the journey home.

In the transit camp the men, waiting until transport to England can be arranged, rest and are entertained. Travelling "movie" shows play a big part here. There are canteens and other general welfare arrangements. The Red Cross takes a hand

The Guard is Changed
In place of the Nazi sentries, an American
tank keeps watch.

in the welfare work by distributing various comforts, especially shaving gear and other toilet articles, to men who are without them.

The journey to England ends at another transit camp. The men are given new kit, provided with temporary food cards and sufficient money for their 42 days' leave. It has been noticed, that the one thing the men hate more than anything is fuss. They don't want flags or reception committees. They don't want to be looked on as prisoners of war. They want to resume their ordinary lives quietly—but quickly.

Something to Take Home
This German rifle once threatened the prisoners. Now it's a prize of war.

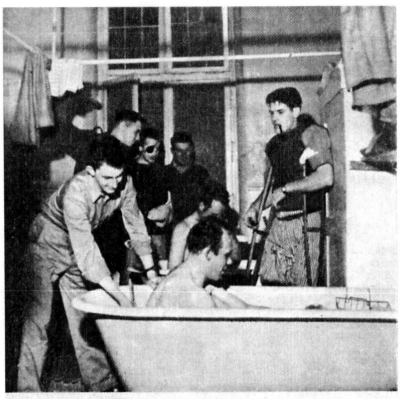

HOW THE RESCUED MEN TREAT THEIR LIBERATORS:
The relieving troops are war-grimed so the prisoners fill hot baths for them, the first they've had for many days.

They Throw a Party With Their Red Cross Rations

The prisoners insist that their rescuers must eat. They insist and won't be refused. The embarrassed G.I.s eventually accept.

190

Part 2
Chapter 15
94TH General Hospital SW England

I was flown to the 94th General Hospital, southwest of London, and put to bed. I was mostly skin and bones as I weighed under130 lb.(Just 100 lbs. less than I weigh today) Not much for a fellow six foot two inches tall. I had lost a lot of weight because I was anemic. I was given liver shots. In addition my old cast was removed. I started to feel better gaining a little weight and my leg no longer hurt. I had sent cablegrams to my parents letting them know I was okay. It was a happy day for them also, because my Father had gotten the missing telegram on his birthday. We were treated like royalty. I was awarded the Purple Heart so belong to the special group of veterans.

I usually liked to make friends everywhere I went. The 94th was no different and I started a great friendship with Annie Usa who was one of the American nurses at the hospital. Annie was from some .where in Missouri but I can't recall now the town. We had a lot of fun even if I was on crutches. There was a large old English Castle very close to the hospital, in fact the hospital was on the grounds of the Castle, that I liked to hobble over to. I would have thought they were the coldest most unlivable places that any one could build. These huge rooms with huge fireplaces would have been very uncomfortable. Of course the people who lived in these had a battery of servants to take care of the nobility. In fact I remember talking to an old gentleman who was trimming the hedge in front of the Castle and he said he had been working there for 35 years. As an old servant, he could not have had much enjoyment in life.

There were a couple country Tavern's not too far away but we did have to walk across fields to get there. We would frequent these and had a very nice time. I remember one night the commanding officer went with us to a Tavern and it was then that he told us that we paid the British one dollar a gallon for all the water we used at the hospital and this was considered lend lease and was the way Britain paid some of it's war debt. Uncle Sam paid again. One night at the evacuation hospital Annie and I were laying out under an apple tree at night as were a bunch of other people when somebody hollered" President Roosevelt died" the grass came alive with soldiers and nurses. Everybody thought it would be the end of the world. But the sun came up the next morning shining as brightly as ever. Annie and I were just good friends and we traded Christmas cards for a long time after I was married. My wife Lois never minded. She knew we were just friends.

After I was able to get around a little better I had a couple days leave in London and then went up to some place north of London where all of our personal effects were sent and held after we were shot down. It was here that I first learned from an intelligence report that a German jet fighter ME262 was also involved in shooting us up the day we were shot down. However, we never saw that airplane.

A few days later I was put on a schedule to fly by ambulance plane to New York City. I remember flying across the Atlantic and thinking how much different it was from the 17 days we spent on the Convoy going to England. In a matter of a few hours we were in New York City and then by ambulance to camp Kilmer New Jersey. Back to that camp that we did not like. However this time I was in the hospital and things were not that bad.

I went to downtown New York several days and one day was in front of the Rockefeller Theater when they came out and got me to be an honored guest to see the Rocket's quite a treat for the country kid. Also met a nice student nurse and we had several dates and several nice evenings while I was at camp Kilmer.

I then got orders to be transferred to Shicke General Hospital at, Clinton Iowa. I do not remember how I got from camp Kilmer to ,Clinton Iowa. So I was ready to start another phase of my life. Now this hospital was only about 120 miles from my home and of course that is what the service tried to do and that is put service personnel close to your home. Again my leg was x-rayed and had a new cast on it. When I bailed out by parachute it was such a shock on my system that I had a reoccurrence of the rupture that I had fixed when I was 11 years old. So the doctor scheduled me for an operation to fix the hernia. This is when I had a knock down drag out with the doctor about a spinal anesthetic. However true to the Army I lost. I could still remember

192

the terrible time that I had when I was being operated on at the age of 11 when the doctor did not know what he was doing. However this anesthesiologist gave me the spinal and I did not even know when he gave it to me and I have had several since with no problems whatsoever.

In Clinton was the uncle of my good friend Burell Jr. Foster. His uncle lived in Clinton. He was a doctor and he invited me to their house several times while I was in Clinton. I had fun at the Clinton hospital. I had met another nurse who I had a very good time with. It was not anything but a friendship but we did have fun.

While I was recuperating from my hernia operation and in those days you stayed in bed for ten days. I had the pleasure of having Dinah Shore come through the hospital and sing a song to me from the foot of my bed. Diana was never shown with a side profile and I know why. But she sang a beautiful song and I really enjoyed it. I was at the Shicke hospital about six weeks when they gave me a 30 day leave and then transferred me to Fort Logan convalescent hospital at Fort Logan Colorado which is just south of Denver.

I went home and spent the 30 days just relaxing and not doing much of anything. I had a very good gal who was an army nurse while at Schick. She wrote to me for quite awhile. I was still on crutches had gained some weight and was feeling very good. But with gas rationing on there was not a lot to do. Most of the girls I had dated had left the area and were working elsewhere so I just did not get involved with anyone while I was home. I know my mother appreciated having me home. When it came time to go to Fort Logan I went by train from Iowa City on the Rock Island Rocket. I was ready for my next venture.

WESTERN UNION

A. N. WILLIAMS
PRESIDENT

1204

The filing time shown in the date line on telegrams and day letters is STANDARD TIME at point of origin. Time of receipt is STANDARD TIME at point of destination.

MR Intl

CD Sans Origine   via WU Cables

EAM Mr Albert Greiner
      Wellman Iowa.

All well and safe. Illness is not serious. Please dont worry.

Howard V Greiner.

450 PM

194

LT. HOWARD GREINER MISSING ON MARCH 2

22-YEAR-OLD PILOT WAS ON SECOND MISSION OVER GERMANY

First Lieut. Howard Greiner, 21, son of Mr. and Mrs. Albert Greiner of northwest of Keota on a Wellman route, is reported missing over Germany since March 2 on his second flight as pilot of a Liberator bomber based in England.

The last letter his parents had from him was dated March 1 on his return from his first mission. The official telegram was received by them late last Thursday afternoon. His parents have the names and addresses of his nine crewmates and have communicated with them. To date they have heard from the families of the co-pilot and the engineer and they, too, are missing since the same date.

Howard was last at home in October, 1944, and served with the Legion at a memorial service for a local soldier killed in action. His parents last saw him while they were wintering in Texas and he flew that way enroute from Wyoming to Topeka, Kansas, and spent several days with them.

He enlisted in the air forces in October, 1942, and was called to duty Jan. 9, 1943. He took his college training at Columbia, Mo., was commissioned May 23, 1944, at Ellington Field, Houston, Texas, and took further training at Casper, Wyo. He joined his crew at Lincoln, Nebr., and went overseas from Ft. Meade, Md., about Jan. 20th of this year.

He is the only son of Mr. and Mrs. Greiner and has two sisters, Mrs. S. D. Harrison of San Antonio, Texas, and Mrs. Paul Blumenstein, now at the parental home and whose husband is fighting in Germany.

5,000 PLANES RIP NAZI LINES

LONDON, ENGLAND (AP)—Fleets of U. S. and British bombers and fighters, 5,000 strong, ripped German communications feeding the entire western front Thursday and the German radio said strong Allied air forces were raiding Berlin and southwestern Germany in the evening.

The U. S. 8th Air Force announced that nine bombers and five fighters were missing from its sweeps, which destroyed two jet-propelled planes in the air and nine other enemy planes on the ground.

The R.A.F. sent its heavies against industrial Mannheim in an attempt to choke off new equipment being fed to German armies on the front. The target area was left aflame.

About 1,200 Flying Fortresses and Liberators and 450 escorting Mustangs struck rail choke points in Heilbronn, Bruchsal, Goppingen, Reutlingen, Neckarsulm, Ingolstadt, Ulm and Augsburg.

WE WERE ONE OF THE NINE PLANES LOST THIS DAY. ONE OF THE GERMAN JETS HIT US HOWEVER WE DID NOT KNOW IT UNTIL LIBERATED. IT WAS A BAD DAY BUT IT WAS WAR AND MANY GOOD AMERICANS MET THE SAME FATE.

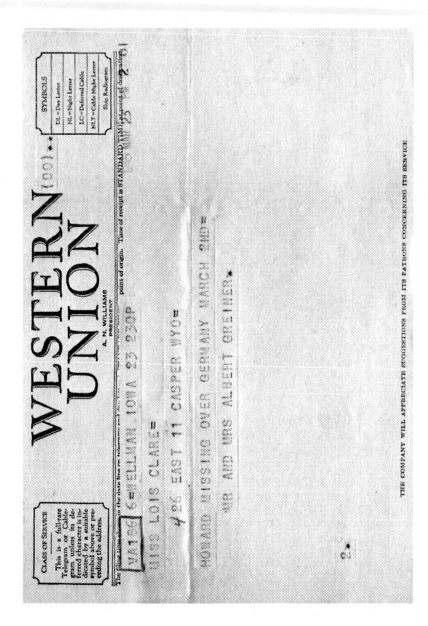

WESTERN UNION (00)..

A. N. WILLIAMS
PRESIDENT

The filing time as shown in the date line on telegrams and day letters is STANDARD TIME at point of origin. Time of receipt is STANDARD TIME at point of destination.

VA186 6=HELLMAN IOWA 23 230P

MISS LOIS CLARE=

426 EAST 11 CASPER WYO=

HOWARD MISSING OVER GERMANY MARCH 2ND=

MR AND MRS ALBERT GREINER.=

2.

Lt. Howard Greiner Writes From Hospital

Mr. and Mrs. Albert Greiner of northeast of Keota have had a second cablegram and two letters from their son Lieut. Howard W. Greiner, bomber pilot who was reported missing over Germany as of March 2 and was with prisoners released in Germany by advancing American troops approximately 27 days later. It is evident from his letter, printed below, that the crew bailed out of the plane. Details cannot, of course, be released yet. The letter follows:

April 2, 1945.
In England.

Dear Mother and Dad:

Well, I wrote you a letter last night from the lines in Germany, and here I am in England in a hospital today waiting for further developments. Sure would give a lot to hear from you. Cable back as soon as possible to my address on this letter. I'm so anxious to know if you are all O. K. or not. Am so afraid you have let yourselves worry too much. However I know it was something to worry about.

As for being in the hospital, I'm O. K. Nothing wrong. I'm in good shape and will hold my own with any of them. Ha! But in case you did get a notice from the War Dept. I am injured, to ease your worry, I have sprained ankles from my jump. Being a prisoner of war just a month, I know you are wondering about the treatment I got. Well, it's bearable and I'll tell you more about it when I get back. As it is I can't say much here anyway. Sure were glad to see those Yanks roll up that day. Had all kinds of newspaper correspondents there that day, including Life Magazine. One was from the Chicago Tribune. Watch it from March 29 on for a while!

I'm really hungry for mail from home. It's really a good way to express it if you know what I mean. Hope you send me a cable as soon as you get this or can do it.

Well, it's springtime back home. Wish I were there for a while. I seem to have spring fever. Can't wait to get where it's quiet. I'm kind of nervous and would like a good quiet rest. But I'm still ready for action. I've

een awfully lucky, folks. I figure God has been good to me in more ways than one.

Mother, when you get this, make your cable long enough to give me a little news. I surely hope you are all well, and give my love to all.

Lovingly, your son,
Howard.

P. S.—"God Bless the Red Cross!" If it hadn't been for that we would have starved to death. I'm writing this with a borrowed pen. When I was captured they took everything I had, including my pen, watch, ring, etc.

197

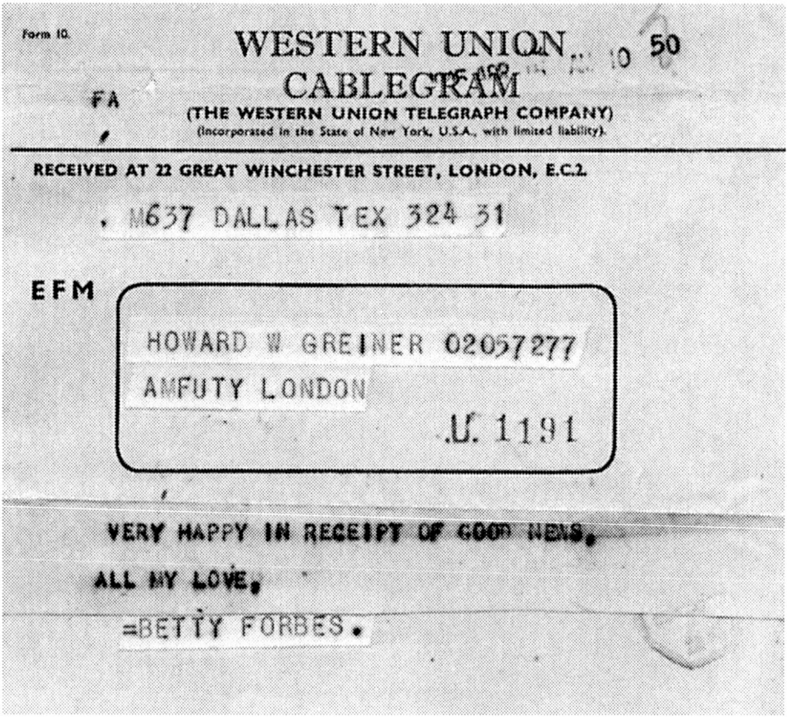

WESTERN UNION
CABLEGRAM
(THE WESTERN UNION TELEGRAPH COMPANY)
(Incorporated in the State of New York, U.S.A., with limited liability).

FA

10 50

RECEIVED AT 22 GREAT WINCHESTER STREET, LONDON, E.C.2.

. M637 DALLAS TEX 324 31

EFM

HOWARD W GREINER 02057277

AMFUTY LONDON

U. 1191

VERY HAPPY IN RECEIPT OF GOOD NEWS,

ALL MY LOVE,

=BETTY FORBES.

MY GIRL FRIENDS WERE WORRIED ABOUT ME TO.

198

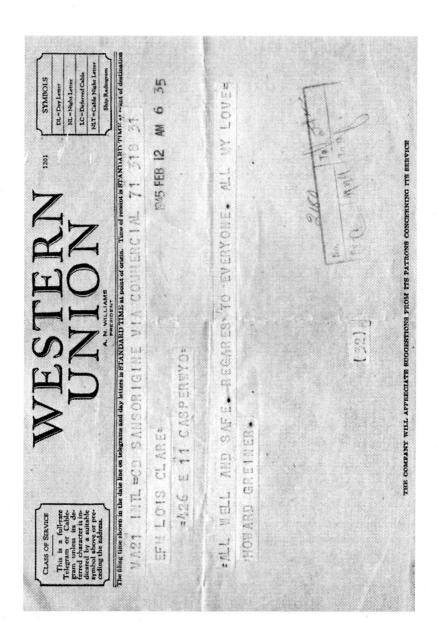

WESTERN UNION

1201

A. N. WILLIAMS
PRESIDENT

CLASS OF SERVICE

This is a full-rate Telegram or Cablegram unless its deferred character is indicated by a suitable symbol above or preceding the address.

SYMBOLS

DL=Day Letter
NL=Night Letter
LC=Deferred Cable
NLT=Cable Night Letter
Ship Radiogram

The filing time shown in the date line on telegrams and day letters is STANDARD TIME at point of origin. Time of receipt is STANDARD TIME at point of destination

VA21 INTL =CD SAHSORIGINE VIA COMMERCIAL 71 318 31

1945 FEB 12 AM 6 35

EFM LOIS CLARE=

=A26 E 11 CASPERWYO=

=ALL WELL AND SAFE- REGARDS TO EVERYONE- ALL MY LOVE=

HOWARD GREINER.

(32)

THE COMPANY WILL APPRECIATE SUGGESTIONS FROM ITS PATRONS CONCERNING ITS SERVICE

199

I AM GLAD TO BE HERE. THE 94TH GENERAL HOSPITAL SOUTHWEST OF LONDON

Part 2
Chapter 16
Fort Logan Hospital Denver

Fort Logan convalescent hospital was an ancient old Fort but a very beautiful place to spend time recuperating .Located in the south part of the Denver area. My medical records were checked, my leg was again x-rayed, the decision was made to remove my cast. From here on it was a blast.

I had absolutely nothing to do so every evening that meant going to downtown Denver and spending the evening at the Brown Palace hotel. In the historical Brown Palace Hotel was the Ships Tavern and a great place to spend an evening .Someone was always wanting to buy you a drink. It really was a fun time. I have many fond memories of the Ships Tavern and I do believe it is still operating today in that old historic Hotel.

At the base, in the daytime, there were a few miscellaneous duties that were required but nothing of importance. It was exactly what the name implied, a convalescent hospital. I met a fellow lieutenant, can't recall his name today, who had a motorcycle. I would ride a round Denver with him but it did take away my desire, to ever own a motorcycle.

After I was at Fort Logan about ten days my thoughts turned to Casper Wyoming and the lady friend and family that I had in Casper while I was taking crew training. I thought it would be appropriate to go back up to Casper and spend some time with Lois. I applied to headquarters for a week's leave to Casper and to my surprise it was approved. I had first called Lois and talked to her and she said that would be fine and was glad to have me come. However they were having a family reunion up at her Uncle Johnny's cabin which was located on Ten Sleep Creek on top of the Bighorn mountains west of Sheridan. I thought that would just be wonderful and was able to get airline tickets from Denver to Casper. I flew to Casper in a DC-3.They were the workhorse of all airlines at that time. Lois met me at the airport and then I went with her up to Ten Sleep Creek and the cabin at Meadow Lark in the Big Horn Mountains.

We had a great time up in the mountains at ,Ten Sleep. I had my first training at fly fishing, on the creek, which ran right below the cabin. Lois's uncle Johnny was a wonderful teacher and a wonderful man to be around. I thoroughly enjoyed him as he was a typical Irishman, liked a good drink, and liked to have fun. The fish we caught were little brook trout.They were just great for the frying pan. Johnny's wife, Lela was a wonderful hostess and a very good cook. I always remembered the vacation at Johnny's cabin. (in later years after Lois and I were married we spend a lot of time at the cabin and I spent a lot time at the cabin hunting. But that was much later) I started to really appreciate what a nice family and what a nice girl Lois was. But I had not reached the point yet where I thought I was ready to settle down.

The week went awful fast and we went back to Casper for a couple of days and it was time to get on the old DC-3 and head back to Fort Logan. It was now nearing the end of September. The war was over in Germany and peace had been declared in Japan. I received a leave to go home and then to proceed to Santa Ana California for discharge from the Air Force. Went back to the farm at Wellman and of course the folks were glad that the war was over and I was going to get a discharge. Father agreed to let me take the car,a 1942 Ford and drive to Califonia so that I would have something to drive when I got my discharge.

ON LEAVE READY TO GO TO SANTA ANNA CALIFORNIA

Part 2
Chapter 17
Santa Anna California

I arrived at Santa Anna CA in the latter part of August to begin my processing for discharge from the United States Air Force. Upon arriving at Santa Ana I found there were thousands of men there for the same purpose that I was. I checked into the base and reported to the squadron that I was assigned to. I found out that we had no duties and I only had to check in and sign the duty roster once a day to see if my name was on the list to get into the funnel for discharge. They were just gearing up good to start releasing the thousands of men that had to be discharged from the Air Force.

I then found out that I had a big advantage for getting into the pipeline quicker. The base had established a policy of putting prisoners of war on a priority basis. This not only got me my discharge much quicker, but also proved to be a big advantage for me when I arrived back home and started preparing to farm.

I was a young man 21 years old and was ready to have a good time. I had run across another lieutenant that I was in training with and the two of us proceeded to do Hollywood. We would wait until the daily roster was posted ,and if our name were not on the list we were off for downtown Los Angeles and didn't care if we got back that night or not just so we could read the latest list. If our name was not on it we were off for another day. During that period, the most famous corner in town was Hollywood and Vine. I am sure if you stood on that corner long enough the world would have came by. My friend, Felber and I were standing on the corner of Hollywood and Vine one night when a big Chrysler convertible with two gals came around the corner twice. On the second time around we got into their car. Now it is hard to judge a gal setting in the seat of a big Chrysler convertible. Both of these gals were a little on the heavy side but we both thought what the heck.

They wanted to know if we would want to go out to their home. We were game for anything and said " Why not". We ended up in a very very exclusive neighborhood with a huge Spanish style home. For a couple of country kids we were both quite impressed. One of the things I remember very plain, this was in the time when meat was rationed and a lot of groceries were also rationed. This home had a huge walk-in freezer and cooler with quarters of beef and a lot of grocery items that were rationed. It was quite apparent that this was not an ordinary family. It turned out that their father was in the wine business and had vineyards in the San Francisco area. I do not know if it was a Mafia family or not but if it wasn't it could have been mighty close. Both of these young ladies had a couple of problems that did not impress two Air Force wolves on the prowl. One they both were overweight and two they must have been eating a lot of garlic because they had a little bit of a problem that way. Although we were impressed with their money we elected not to get involved and after a couple hours we came up with an excuse that we had to go back to the base and had them take us back to Hollywood and Vine. So ended our chance with a pair of young ladies with a lot of money.

A couple of nights later we were standing in line waiting to get into a club that was just off the corner of Hollywood and Vine when we made contact with a couple gals in line just ahead of us. This began one of the wildest two weeks that I think either of us had ever lived. The big band area was still on and there were dances at various beach towns and we just had a wild time. Neither one of these ladies would have been gals that we would have been interested in getting serious with but we were just out for a good time.

On the third week of September my name came up for discharge on the list at the orderly room.This meant that I had to stay at the base and the running around was over so on September 27th 1945 special orders No. 231 contained my name where I was attached unassigned to squadron H 1040 Louisville KY for record purposes only came through. I was granted travel time and 23 days leave so that my effective date of inactive service was the 31st of October 1945.

I really don't know whether I was glad to get out of the service or not at that time. I had a great three years. There were some times of trauma but they were so far outweighed by the experiences I had that I think it was one of the greatest times in my young life. I have always said and I still say today that the war was the greatest thing that ever happened to me. It got me off the farm and out into the world more than I had been before. I got to do things that I never would have experienced any other way. How could a young farm boy with no high school or college education be able to learn to fly four engine airplanes? Without this kind of training I am sure I would not of had the same outlook on life that I have had and it has been a wonderful life.

I bid farewell to my friend got into the Ford car that had served me so well and headed back to Iowa. I was ready to start a new life again. I willed my lady friend to Felber and in a couple weeks I received a card from him and all is said was" She was more than you said" thus ended my stay at Santa Ana Air Force Base and the end of my flying for the Army Air Force.

I AM BACK HOME WITH QUEENIE AND HAVE HAD A GREAT TIME, AND AM GLAD TO HAVE THE EXPERIENCE.

205

Part 3
Chapter 1
Back to the farm

I arrived back in Iowa at the farm on about October 1st 1945. My father had already given Bud Bohr the necessary notification by mail on September 1st that he no longer would be renting the farm as I was coming home. At that time my father owned 315 acres of land. If my memory serves me correct Bud then rented the 160 acres that my father had been renting that we called the 80.

One of the big problems after the war was that farm machinery was in very short supply. There had developed a black market in farm machinery and you could not just go in and buy a piece of farm machinery because the machinery was given out on a priority basis by a board of some kind. I do not remember what the board was called.. However,. Because I was a prisoner of war and one of the first people in the community to get discharged, I was able to get priority for a whole line of new machinery. What a lucky break this was! I got permits for a new International M tractor, a new three bottom plow, a new 10 ft. tandem disk, a new four row and corn planter, a new 2M corn picker, a two row cultivator and a new four section harrow. Not only did I get the permits,but most important part I was first in line to the machinery because tractors was scarce.. Now it was a matter of waiting until the equipment came during the winter.

I remember my M tractor with rubber tires cost $1515.00 dollars. I had that tractor the entire time that I farmed and was on the farm sale. It was a great piece of equipment. Of course there is a great difference between what this tractor had on it for equipment, and what the new tractors have today.

My father and I had an agreement that we would farm the farm on a 50/50 basis. That meant that father would furnish the land and I would furnish the machinery and the labor to farm the farm. It all the years that this agreement took affect we never had a written contract. There never was in the entire time I farmed any disagreements over the basis of our 50/50 agreement.

206

That fall Bud had to finish harvesting his crop and I helped him with his harvest wherever he needed me. I knew that I would like to raise cattle and hogs as my father had always raised hogs before I went to the service. I spent some of my time going to farm sales and bought some used equipment but most of what I bought was new. My father had bought some livestock and had some cattle that he ran on the grass at the Deal place. This was a 120 acre farm three and one-half miles south of the home farm. There always was about 70 acre's of permanent pasture on this farm at that time. That is why when I was growing up we always had cattle to drive the three and one-half miles back and forth between the farm's. That is when I used , Dickey, so much when I was a young lad.

I made arrangements to hire a friend of mine to work for me on the farm the next spring. His name was LaVon Klein. He had been in the Marine Corps and was about my age. My other male friends had either been killed or moved out of the area. So we started chasing girls together and were quite successful. We spent a lot of time chasing girls in Iowa City and any other place we could find. We also drank a little good whiskey on some of these trips but although we had a lot of fun we still got our work done in good order.And we never got into trouble.

Spring came and by then we were farrowing a lot of pig's and the labor to take care of them was very intensive. When spring plowing season came, and my father and I decided to break up 30 acres of the permanent pasture at the Deal place as the pasture was not very productive. To do this required it to be plowed. There are hills on this land and farmers up to that time were just plowing up-and-down the hills, which allowed for a lot of ground erosion. That spring , I had enrolled all of our land into the conservation program. My father was not exactly thrilled with this. When I started plowing those first hills I first had the conservation commission come out and survey the land so that I could plow it on the contour. The soil conservation commission advertised this as a demonstration plot as very little of it had been done at that time. Quite a bunch of farmers showed up and at least half of them thought I had lost my mind by plowing around the hills rather than over them.. Now people who grew up seeing this type of farming do not realize what a change it was for old farmers to make this kind of a change.

207

During that spring my good friend Betty, had came up from Fort Worth, to visit me. She stayed a week and we had a good time. I was living of with my mother and dad and Betty stayed at the house with us. There were no motels in those days for people visiting. The plain simple fact was my father thought that I was going to get serious with Betty ,and he did not like the idea of her having been married and having a young daughter. It was not in my mind to consider marrying Betty at that time any way even though I liked her a lot.

After my visit to Lois in August of 1945 we had continued to write to each other. The telephone system in those days was not very good. We would probably write to each other a couple times a week and then I invited Lois to come out to the farm and visit with us for a week. She agreed to come in June. She was no longer working for the Army air base as it had closed, and she was now secretary for her father in the savings and loan company that he operated.

So she came by bus which was about a two-day trip. We had a delightful time even thought it was in the middle of corn plowing time. I recall I came in at noon with the tractor and plow and pulled up to the gas pump before going into dinner. After dinner Lois and I came out and I had some work to do in the shop, something to fix, and she asked me if there was anything she could do. I replied " yes you can fill the tractor with gas" pretty soon I heard this voice say" Honey it will not hold much it is full." I thought that is strange because I plowed all morning and that meant almost a full tank of gas. So I went out and started laughing because she had filled the radiator full of gasoline instead of the gas tank. Jokingly I said" Lois if you and I ever were to get married I think you should do the housework and I will do the work outside." I never dreamed at that time that it would turn out that way.

My father took an immediate liking to Lois as did my mother. They thought she was a very sweet girl and I was beginning to think the same thing. I think now about the diary I found that I had written when I went overseas about the girlfriend in San Antonio ,Texas, who I never gave the second thought to, and I get a good laugh out of it now. Lois spent the week and then I took her back to Iowa City where she got on the bus and went back to Casper, Wyoming. We wrote to each other a couple

208

times a week and occasionally I would go into town and telephone her and call her from the telephone exchange. That way we could hear who we were talking to. Aug. came and I decided I would like to go back to Casper and see Lois. I was tired of chasing other girls which I had been doing all the time I was writing to Lois ,and she was also having dates. But down deep we were thinking of each other.

I drove out to Casper and was welcomed with open arms by Lois and her family. Lois and I had a good time and one night when we pulled up in front of 426 East 11th Street we sat in the car talking and I asked her if she would marry me. She did not hesitate and we were a pair of happy kids. I was old-fashioned and asked her father and mother the next day for her hand. I was welcomed into her family with open arms. I can truthfully say that in the coming years no one had a better relationship with their Mother-in-law and Father-in- law than I did. I will alway's remember how they accepted me when I was a young officer at the air base. It was exceptional.

After the news broke that Lois and I were going to get married we went down to the Jewelry store on the corner of second Street next to where Lois worked and we picked out the engagement ring and the wedding band. After a lot of discussion we decided to get married in December after the corn was harvested. So when I left Casper that was our plans. I got back to Iowa and told my folks that we were going to get married. My father was extremely happy because he had visions of my hooking up with some" floozy" The only problem was housing was almost impossible to find. We had no solution except to move in with my parents in the house on the farm. Lois and I had talked about this before I left Casper and she understood the problem. Now I know that this usually failed anytime two women tried to live in the same house. I had promised Lois that we would do our best to try to get our own house as soon as it was possible.

After I got home I got to thinking why should we wait till December so I tried to call Lois for several days and could not get anyone to answer. Then when I did I found that she had been up to Johnny's cabin in the big horn mountains were they had taken the husband of aunt Nellie for a little vacation because he was dying of cancer. This was sister Pat's father. I raised the question to Lois so she agreed to take it up with her mother to see if they

209

could get everything ready. Lois called me back and we had set the date as September 23rd 1946. It took a lot of hurrying and scurrying for Mother Clare and Lois to plan the wedding and get everything finished, but it all worked out. I had chosen Bud Blumenstein (my brother in-law) to be best man. and Lois picked out her brides maids.

I drove out to Casper four days before the wedding and my parents , Bud, and my sister, Marjorie, came out just a couple days before the wedding. It was a fun time and the Clare family always believed in having a good time. Dad Clare never believed in drinking cheap Scotch. The more I was with the family the more I knew I was one lucky young man to find such a wonderful woman and such fine people. Their friends were all wonderful also. The people I got to know in Casper were wonderful people.

We had a beautiful wedding at St. Anthony's church and Father O' Riley got us married off and our reception was held at the Townsend Hotel in downtown Casper. We had a great party. In the afternoon after the reception was over with we loaded up the Ford full of beautiful wedding presents. Lois bid her good bye to her parents and we started off on our trip or honeymoon back home to the farm.

THE START OF 38 WONDERFUL YEARS WITH A WONDERFUL LADY
210

LOIS,ON HER VISIT TO IOWA IN JUNE 1946
I HAD A NEW M TACTOR AND ONLY 4 ROW
CORN PLOW IN THE COUNTRY.

Part 3
Chapter 2
Home from the honeymoon

The first night of our married life was spent in Lusk,Wyoming. We left from there and went up into the Black Hills and spent a day. Then on up to ,.Spear Fish ,South Dakota,next north to the Roosevelt national Park,stopping at Minot ND for our third night. We then left and went to Grand Forks, North Dakota and then onto Bemidji Minnesota, where we looked for the big ox. We drop down to St. Cloud,then on down to Mankato and back to the farm at Wellman. It really was not an exciting honeymoon, except we just had a good time being together for our first few days of married life. Making a trip like that was a lot different than doing it today. I can recall we traveled on a lot of gravel roads which were state highways. The roads in those days were very narrow and crooked and you really could not make a lot of time, it was not like traveling on the interstate highways that are used today. But it was still fun and we did not know any better.

After arriving at the farm Lois and I took possession of the north bedroom upstairs and started unloading the Ford car that we had driven home from Casper. We took possession of the two big closets off of our bedroom for all of our clothes and our wedding presents as there was no other place for them.

In 1946 there was absolutely no housing available anywhere to rent or to buy as all of the soldiers coming home from the service were getting married. Since each couple wanted their own house and were getting married right and left. A housing shortage developed. Lois and I were both aware that we had to share the house for the time being with my parents. One of the first things Lois and I dId was to buy a new bedroom suite. This made it our room and we felt very comfortable with that. When Lois was in college, she took home economics, and learned to become an excellent seamstress. The next thing we bought was a new Singer sewing machine that she loved dearly. She spent many hours over the years at this machine.

21.2

As most people are aware, a house is usually not big enough for two women. It is a rare instance when this works, but I can truthfully say to you that I cannot ever recall one time that my Mother and Lois ever had any kind of an argument or any disagreement over anything. It was absolutely a great relationship that grew over the years. Lois was of a temperament that could get along with anyone. My Father too was able to get along with Lois and I can never recall them two ever having any words. It was an unusual relationship, for a young girl coming from the city who had never lived on a farm, leaving that life and coming to Iowa where it was a whole different life.

There were a lot of things for Lois to get used to. This was back in the days when the neighbors exchanged a lot of labor back and forth and I may come in and tell Lois there would be six men for dinner at 10:00 in the morning. Maybe we were shelling corn or vaccinating hogs or baling hay but that is the way life on the farm was. The women would have to have dinner ready at 12:00 because that is when we ate dinner, not 11:00 not 1:00 but 12:00. This was true on all the farms in our neighborhood that we exchanged labor with.

This really wasn't anything for my mother but it was rather shocking to Lois at first and then, it to became just another chore. When I brought Lois back to the farm she really couldn't boil water. She was a great secretary could take short hand and type up a storm but she did not know very much about cooking. I knew that before I married her. During the war Dad Clare had raised a bunch of chickens in his garage for meat as meat was rationed. Mother Clare had dressed a couple chickens and Lois decided to have a little dinner party so we fried the two chickens. Mother Clare said "Okay, you can use the chickens but replace them". I think she really was checking to see if I knew how to dress a chicken as I'm sure she knew Lois did not know how. So I said "Okay". I got a bucket and hot water and went out and killed a couple chickens. I scalded them, and took off their feathers, rolled up some newspapers, set them on fire, and singed, them and took them in the house to finish dressing them. I opened one, put my hand inside to pull out the entrails. Lois watched me do that and said " You mean you put your hands inside that". I knew right then, I had a lovely girl but she really didn't know very much about cooking at that time

My mother was an excellent cook and Lois was a very fast learner. It was not long before she became a very wonderful cook. My mother was one of the old-style cooks who hardly ever used a recipe book but could make things that would make your mouth water. Lois was a little different kind of cook in the fact that she enjoyed making things from the cookbook and could do an excellent job. Because my Mother was terribly crippled and could not do so many things, my Dad would often bring in outside help, when we had a big job to do. In those years we would raise a couple hundred chickens for laying hens and a hundred roosters to eat. When we would dress 60 or 70 of these chickens at one time usually, Christina Bohr, or, Lula Redlinger, would come and help do it. This would make short work of a big job. By this time we had two big deep freezers in the basement to keep full. It was always a busy time.

In late October of 1946 we started picking corn. We picked all of our corn in the ear. It was not easy to handle like it is today where everything is handled mechanically. I always ran the corn picker then and it was a cold miserable job. On the old corn pickers that were mounted on the tractor the operator sat down a round all the machinery and were right in the middle of all the dust and the noise. That noise is one of the reasons I'm wearing a hearing aid today. It usually was quite cold and because I could not move around very much, I became very stiff and cold setting in one place. And unless we had a damp morning, the dust was terrible and irritated your eyes and nose. Every farmer expected his wife or someone to bring him hot coffee and a snack about 10:00 in the morning. It was always such a good feeling to see the car coming with hot coffee. I usually was so cold and stiff when I got off that I could hardly walk.

In between times I was trying to get the home farm somewhat modernized. There was no running water anywhere on the farm for livestock. There were two water tanks that we pumped water to and these watered all of our livestock. I started on a program of laying new water pipes so we could have some running water. You didn't call a trencher to come dig your ditch, as there was only one way to do it ,that was with a shovel and spade. We did not think anything of it and just went ahead and did it but believe me digging through those old feed lots, which were full rock was not an easy task.

214

We finished harvesting corn about the first week of December and then there was some other surprisingly good news as Lois informed me she was sure she was pregnant. Like all couples we were very happy about this. Laura Foster our good neighbor was very good to Lois and they became very good friends. Laura, being a nurse, advised Lois to go to the University Iowa Hospitals to a Doctor Kettle who was a specialist. Years later we often asked each other why we did that when we had a very good local doctor named Dr. J. Miller at Wellman.

Like all new brides Lois wanted to go home for Christmas to be with her family. She had an aunt in Omaha who I had never met. Aunt Nellie Sullivan had lost her husband and we were going to stop and stay overnight with them on our way to Casper. On the way to Omaha, Lois said I could meet cousin Pat who was going to go be a nun. We got to Omaha about 8:00 clock at night. Found aunt Nellie's house and found that Pat was having a party. She and her friends were playing poker, drinking whiskey, smoking cigarettes, and like all young folks were having a great time. As Lois and I retired for the night I made the remark" Pat is going to be our nun" and Lois merely replied "Of course." Later Pat left for Chicago to the convent. A couple of months later Lois got a call from aunt Nellie to met her and Pat at the Iowa City (the Rock Island Rocket was still running)depot. We did and aunt Nellie and Pat stayed at the farm a couple of days and then went back to Omaha..I, in my great wisdom said to Lois "See what did I tell you". To which Lois replied "Just wait" How right she was. After a couple of months Pat went back to the convent, after satisfying herself, to become Sister Patricia Clare Sullivan and devoted her life to God and taking care of the sick. She was administrator of Mercy Hospital in Des Monies until she retired. She was so good to Lois in her sickness.

We went on to Casper and as usual had a great time. Mother and dad Clare were glad to see their daughter and had some very good parties lined up for us. Lois got to see her friends and we just had a great time and after about a week in Casper we headed back to Iowa.

215

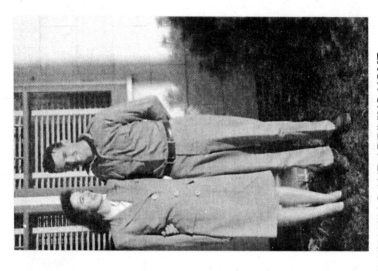

TWO HAPPY KIDS ON OUR TRIP TO BLACK HILLS AND ARRIVING HOME

216

SAINT ANTHONEYS CHURCH IN CASPER. NO LONGER TWO BUT NOW ONE

217

Part 3
Chapter 3
On the farm 1947

After coming home from the service and spending the first-year farming I could say that, I would not be satisfied with raising hogs the way my father did. First of all it was far too much work trying to raise hogs in little two stall farrowing sheds. Ever other day I cleaned these out, it was all stoop labor. I was too tall to work in the small farrowing sheds. I just knew that there had to be a better way and of course, I did not let any grass grow under my feet planning for it.

My good friend Kay Statler would come over to our house every Sunday morning for coffee and a visit. I could sure set my clock, look up, and there would be Kay. Once in a while he would come when it was time to go to church, but with a smile on his face he would always come back later. He was more than welcome because we always had a good time visiting and planning various things. On one of the January morning's of 1947, Kay knew a farm where we could get a bunch of free lumber if we wanted to do it. A farmer northwest of Keota about four miles had 40 acres of timber that he would give to us if we would cut it down. I immediately had visions of a new hog house and said" Let's go look" That afternoon we went over to the timber and walked around it, I could see that there would be a lot of lumber in this timber. Kay was wanting to build a grain elevator so between the two of us we could use all the lumber. There was a fellow at Wellman who was in the logging business with a chain saw. They were new then, and we hired him to go over and start cutting down all the timber and sawing out the logs. Now old Charlie Brown who used to run the threshing machine had a sawmill. He agreed to move his sawmill over to this timber and do all of our sawing. Things were starting to add up. We were getting into the lumber business. By this time both Kay and I had been able to buy a Ford tractor each. We took both machines over to the timber and started dragging up the logs. We must have spent a month doing this at least. When we finished pulling up the logs we had a real pile.

I had been dreaming about this hog house for quite some time. I had drawn the plans for a 40 sow farrowing house that would allow the second floor to be used for baled straw and feed with room for a feed mixer. It really looked more like a large barn then it did a hog house. After figuring out the lumber bill I knew I would have all the lumber I needed for the building except the siding and the shingles. This took a little persuasion to get my father to agree to build the building. I was willing to do the work and pay for all the labor if he would furnish what we had to buy. He finally agreed and the project was on. So of course the first thing was to prepare the site and to make preparations to dig the water lines from the well to the hog house.

Living north of us was the neighbor, Zeno Aller, who lived on a small farm and was a pretty good carpenter. I made arrangements to hire Zeno to help when he could after getting his own crops in. In fact, I even planted his corn so that he could help build this hog house. We mixed all the concrete with a two horsepower Briggs and Stratton gasoline engine on a very small concrete mixer. Now remember we would do this in between times when we were sowing oats, and planting corn, and doing the plowing. We were having a terrible time hiring labor This work continued all summer in between the other jobs shooting for the deadline December first when I had 40 sow's ready to farrow.

We were in such a short supply for labor that I was almost desperate. A carnival came to Keota and I ended up and hired a carnival worker who appeared to be very hungry. He wasn't too great. So you can imagine what Lois thought of me bringing a carnival worker home and putting him in the upstairs bedroom next to where Lois planned to have our new baby were expecting.. Well, the way it worked out the carnival worker only lasted a couple weeks. He decided it was too much work for him and the hours were too long so he hiked down the road for greener pastures. I had been advertising for a man and I got an application from a man from Brighton, Iowa by the name of Eugene. Now poor Eugene was a bachelor who had a frustrated love life who when his girlfriend refused to marry him he decided to commit suicide. Well he stuck the gun in his mouth, but didn't have the angle right. Instead of killing him it really messed up the left side of his face and his left eye. This left Eugene with a terrible problem when he ate his meals. Because he had lost some control of his face when he chewed his food he made a terrible noise. Now, of course, Eugene moved in our house and slept in the upstairs bedroom where the carnival worker had. We had to board the hired men as the second house on the farm had not been built.

Mother and Dad and all of us ate our meals at the same time at the same table. Mother Greiner had Lois put a bowl of pickled peaches on the table for dinner. Pickled peaches are something you may take one peach and eat it as they are sour. Lois handed the bowl to Eugene and said" Would you like a peach, Eugene" he replied," I don't mind if I do". He sat the whole bowl on his plate, reached over and got the pitcher of cream setting on the table for coffee, and poured it on the pickled peaches. Of course, the cream immediately curdled, but it didn't bother Eugene. He ate the whole bowl of peaches. The rest of us were so astounded we couldn't say a word. What a joy our hired men were.

Our baby was due in the latter part of August. This was the same time as the Iowa State Fair, which was an event that every farmer tried to go to. On Saturday my sister Marjorie and Bud had came up from Geneso, Ill so that Bud and I could go to the state fair in Des Moines, Sunday morning. It was August 24th and Lois awoke me about 1:30 a.m. I thought I was going to the races, but instead we headed for the university hospital in Iowa City. At 3:30 a.m. we had our first baby boy who we named Clare. Lois was in University of Iowa Hospital about eight or ten days as were all women in those days. I remember the hospital bill was a couple hundred dollars. Dr.Kettle for all the prenatal work and the delivery was one hundred dollars. The summer moved along, work on the hog house continued at a strong pace, It looked like we were going to get it finished in time for the farrowing in December. It was absolutely necessary to have the hog house done by December first.

When December came we were having pigs before all the inside pens were done. It was a big job however, we accomplished it on time.

That fall we had a very poor corn harvest because of a cold, wet summer. Corn prices went up to three dollars a bushel. This was an unheard of corn price. As I recall now I think our corn made about 65 to 70 bushels per acre. Prices of hogs that summer were very good. We had a lot of good feeder shoats weighing about 45 pounds apiece that my father sold for 90 cents a pound. A really good price for young pigs. The rest of the year went along very well. Our new baby grew and prospered. By the to time Christmas came the new hog house was full of those cute baby pigs and we were getting ready for the year,1948.

This was the year that I got my education about playing the board of trade in Chicago. That summer with the short corn crop and the price of corn starting to go up, I started playing the board. Everybody was saying corn was going to go higher and maybe to three dollars a bushel. And of course Dad said" Who ever heard of corn going to three dollars a bushel" Short the markets some more. In other words we were betting that corn would not go that high. I was involved with one -fourth as much as dad. But every few days we would short some more as the market kept going up. By the time our contracts were to come due in Chicago Lois and I had lost $4000.00 and Dad had lost$12,000.00. Needless to say, this was a good lesson to me. It was a long time before I ever played the board of trade again. Lois and I did not have that money to lose. What really drove the message home to me was Dad was in Chicago for an operation. Our neighbors had a friend who had a seat on the Board of Trade in Chicago. His name was Beach Wickham. They wanted me to go see him so I did. He was a very old man then.(probably as old as I am today). He wanted to know if I wanted to go down to the pit. I told him "yes" and on the way down in the elevator he said" Young man one day I traded a million bushels of wheat and made 10 dollars. I immediately thought one-man can do that and I am out in Iowa trying to out guess what these guys are all doing. I never played the board of trade again, The lesson was well learned.

OUR WEDDING DAY IN CASPER,WYOMING. SEPT. 23 1946

Part 3
Chapter 4
The year 1948

We finished our Christmas and new years with great joy. We had our new son, Clare and the preceding year had been a good one. Our crops and the prices allowed us to have a good year financially.

We had finished the new hog house and it was bristling with the new crop of pigs, Everything looked like it was a go. But American agriculture was starting to change. It was about February 15th when big headlines hit the farm news papers. Pfizer chemical Co. announced they had made new synthetic milk that would allow farmers to wean baby pigs in one week. It was apparent to me, that if this was as advertised, it could change the entire hog industry. I became very interested as I thought if this would work, we could raise pigs in batteries as they do baby chickens. I could triple my hog production. I jumped into this idea with both feet. There was a company in Mount Vernon, Illinois that manufactured chicken equipment, by the name of Hawking Million Dollar Hen. The company was a leader in the field. I contacted them and they became interested immediately. They proposed making some experimental equipment. I went over to Mount Vernon Illinois and spent about four or five days at their factory. We designed a device to put baby pigs in and a system to pump and circulate the synthetic milk. Just to look at the equipment it really looked great. The beautiful part of this was that it did not cost me any money except my time.

I brought the equipment home,and set it up in the new hog house, and filled it with about 100 baby pigs. We sat back, rubbed our hands together, to watch it work. We mixed up the new synthetic formula and started circulating it through the various feed troughs. At first, the baby pigs did not take to it. W hen they got really hugry they started drinking it. ,When they started drinking the formula, of course, they would get their mouth's wet and then immediately start trying to suck on anything they could find, including the closest pigs ears. It did not take a rocket scientist to figure out that this was going to be a problem that was inherent to the pig. Then in about two days, there was the start of diarrhea, in the baby pigs. This then turned into a horrible smelly mess. The pans under the pigs had to be cleaned everyday, and this was a job that was not too pleasant. It is easy to see that putting the pigs in the Million Dollar Hen was not going to be very successful. The product that Pfizer chemical Co. came out with was just not ready for the market. The people from Mount Vernon Illinois drove up to the farm to see what was happening. After a couple good looks at the pigs, decided they had better stick with chickens. I agreed with them because all I had done was signed the death warrant for 100 pigs. My first experience with confining pigs was a failure. It would not be my last attempt. I removed the equipment and confined it to the scrap yard, although wiser from the experience.

I started trying to figure out how to save some of the baby pigs, that were a week or ten days old, that had been nursing the sows an had a good start in life. I built a pen above one of the sows pen and put a floor in it of quarter inch rat wire. This was so any liquid would drain out and keep them dry. There were some good, dry, baby pigs feed at that time and the pigs dID quite well for about two weeks. Then their feet started getting sore from being on the wire. Isn't it strange how long it takes someone to figure things out. If I had used wider slats this would have worked, but I gave up on that because of the sore feet, and also because as the pigs became heavier the wire was not strong enough. So this was my first experience with confining hogs, of course, everyone said you'll never be able to confine hogs and we know what history had shown us. It just takes a few people with imagination to change the way anything is done. Of course, an awful lot of that change is done by trial and error.

Our home farm had very few cement floors. In the spring of the year, the mud was, as the saying goes, up to the ass of a big elephant!. We had one small concrete floor west of the old corn crib. Kay, was over one Sunday morning complaining about having no concrete floors, as he was trying to raise hogs. At that time my Dad was managing some land down close to Kalona and the English River ran through it. In the river were some very big sand bars. Therefore, we got the wild idea that we would go down to Carver pump Co, in Muscatine and buy a sand pump. We would pump the sand from the river. Well we went to Muscatine, and I think we talked to the wrong person, because the pump that they sold us would sure pump a hell a lot of water. After the crops planted Kay and I started setting up our sand pump. We used steel pipe, and I had a 30 horse Wisconsin engine to power it with. We had everything started and were pumping water and sand up onto shore. We had set up a steel wagon box to hold the sand and let the waterflow back to the river. We filled the sand box and emptied in about twice. We started noticing the volume of water was starting to reduce, and the sand was not coming as fast. After a couple more hours the pump almost quite pumping water completely. We tore the pump down, and to our surprise, the entire inside of the pump was ground out from pumping sand. Well, we were a couple of mad characters, as they had told us this would pump sand. Kay had his old jeep there, we loaded the pump in the jeep, and headed for Muscatine. By the time we got to Muscatine, it was almost evening. Carver pump denied they had told us this pump would pump sand. In other words you bought the pump and we deny any responsibility. It was hot when we left the River, to go to Muscatine,and we then started back home. I think this was the second coldest night I had ever experienced, in riding in that old open top jeep. We did not take any sweaters or coats and by the time we got home I had darn near froze to death. I remember curling up in the back of the jeep, on the floor, trying to pick up some heat from the muffler. I can still see Kay hunkered down over the steering wheel driving that jeep home. What an experience!

Although our pump experience was a complete disaster I did not give up on on trying to use the sand. I wanted to pour concrete floors and having a limited amount of capital, could see that by getting the sand it would save a lot of money. Eventually as I did in many other projects I substituted labor for capital. We then just took the wagons and pushed them down into the river, and scooped them full of sand by hand. The only flaw was the sand was not as clean as it should have been. Although some of the floors poured did not last quite as well, it got us out of the mud. That old hand concrete mixer with the two horsepower Briggs Stratton engine mixed a lot of concrete.

Lois and I ,at this point, were still living with Mother and Dad Greiner. Our baby boy ,Clare, was starting to crawl. It was

224

convenient having them living with us, as we had built in baby sitters. Lois and I went to Iowa City one-day and Mother and Dad volunteered to take care of Clare. When we returned that evening, we found a terrible thing had happened. Mother Greiner was crippled quite badly in her feet and whole body with arthritis. Baby Clare, had crawled in front of her somehow and in trying to keep from stepping on him, she lost her balance, and fell breaking her hip. When we got home we felt just terrible that this had happened. Dad rented a hospital bed after mother came home from the hospital and set it up in the living room. Laura Foster our good neighbor would come down and help Mother, and give her, her bath. Mother Greiner was one determined woman, and she would not give up, and after a couple of months she was up moving around, and overcame this accident.

Around June, Lois and I had a pleasent surprise. Lois informed me that she was pregnant again. We were delighted. I think my parents began to get the message, that we may move them out of the house, by filling it with children. They really didn't think that at all, but knew they needed to do something. It was about this time that one of the livestock buyers in Keota, Ray Stewart died, who had a large home on the very East end of Main Street. Mrs. Stewart believed in the finer things in life. She had a daughter living in Chicago and decided that she would sell her home, and move in with her. Now most people when they sell a home do just that. They take there pesonal things with them. However her daughter had fine things in Chicago. Mrs. Stewart decided she would sell her home and all she would take was her clothes. This meant she would leave her fine china, her sterling silverware, all of her antique furniture, the grand piano and anything else in the house. It was unbelievable that anyone would do this, but she did. There also were 17 acres of land along the Rock Island railroad track that went with it. My father bought the house and the land and antiques, and everything in the house, including things you cannot imagine anyone leaving. The house the land and everything sold for forty thousand dollars.

This took place in the fall the year, and it was wonderful for Lois and me, because when my folks moved, all they did was take their clothes, and move to the new house they had bought in Keota. This meant that Lois and I had a house full of furniture and everything we needed to start housekeeping on our own. If I remember correctly I gave my Father $500.00 for everything that was in the house on the farm. It indeed was a lucky break for us. Although Lois understood why we did not have a house of our own, she was like all new brides, and would have loved to had her own home. She was a dear for understanding the problem.

I had made plans to take Dr. Peterson, who was our veterinarian from Washington, to Wyoming to go antelope hunting that fall. Dad Clare had a good friend who had a large ranch north of Douglas Wyoming about 50 mile. This was a gravel and mud road to the old Bear Creek Post Office. That is where Jack Alamand had his mailbox. Then the ranch house was 10 miles from the mailbox. I remember Dad Clare had a Nash automobile that we drove to the ranch, and plowed mud about half the way. Dad Clare always said, the car was never the same, after that.. I remember Dad Clare always called that mud" ape shit" and I think that was a good description. Dr. Peterson was a trophy hunter, and the antelope on the ranch were thick as flies, and he could have shot a hundred antelope that day. He was so particular to get a good head that he didn't shoot an antelope till just before the season closed for the day. This frustrated Dad Clare, as he wanted to get back to Casper. However nothing would do, we had to stay for supper. That evening going back to Casper, the roads were much better, as they had dried a lot during the day. It was a fun hunt. However, to me there is much better meat than antelope. It tastes too much like goat for me. We would always bring the meat home and Lois, would figure out a way to serve it so that it tasted pretty good.

The year 1948 was a very busy year. We did a lot of different things on the farm that year. I was always trying new ideas and new things that frustrated my Father. Dad was of the old school, and that is "do it the way everyone else does it". I think, the reason that I was always looking for new things, was that farming was not a real challenge to me. I always felt that anybody could set on a tractor seat, and go back and forth across the field. I always loved a challenge. We had fairly good crops that year and as Christmas drew near, we again made our way to Casper for the Christmas holidays. The roads were certainly not like today and it was always a strenuous trip, but we loved being in Casper. So good by 1948 and welcome 1949.

226

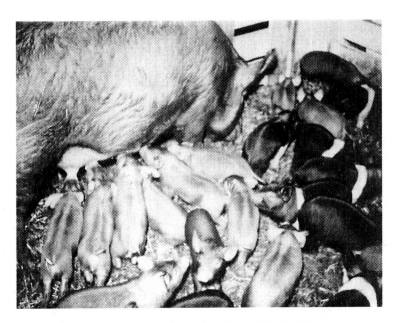

THE END RESULTS. BABY PIGS ARE CUTE

THE NEW HOG HOUSE BUILT IN1948

Part 3
Chapter 5
The farm 1949

This year started off with a big event for our farm operation. When I was a small child, we used to have to drive a team and wagon down to the Diehl place, to feed cattle in the spring., when the roads were so terribly muddy. We used to drive by a farm that was owned by an old bachelor and his two old maid sisters. It was a beautiful farm and had a big evergreen grove and a fruit orchard. The barns were old but well kept and there were two good houses on the farm. I can remember we used to talk about someday this farm would be sold. I always thought it would be nice to own that farm. I can remember my father saying be patient and someday it will come up for sale. In the fall of 1948 Bert Wilson, who owned the farm died. His two sisters had preceded him in death. They had no heirs. His estate left money to their church in Keota and because his sisters liked to read and I think were retired schoolteacher's they left the balance of their estate to the town of Keota for a new public library. The farm was to be sold at a private telephone auction.

The day of the auction came in January. Dad and I were at our lawyers office in Washington, Our good attorney, Bob Day, would do the telephoning as the auction progressed. The biding started at two hundred dollars per acre and went in five and ten dollar increments. It got up to $265 per acre, which was our bid. We were sitting on pins and needles and then the bid came that somebody had bid $270 per acre. Now I know this may not sound alike a lot of money, but it was a lot of money then. So just before the auction was to end, Dad and I placed a bid of $275 per acre and we ended up with the two hundred and forty acres that I had wanted ever since I was a young child. When March 1-1949 came we settled for the farm and I was now farming 555 acres.I was having so much trouble getting hired hands to work for us that I talked Dad into building a small house on the farm east of our big house.This was the time when there were a lot of displaced persons from the European war were being brought to the United

228

States. Our Catholic Messenger the newspaper for our diocese explained how to get a displaced person for your farm. I made application and was granted the right to have the church send us a family. That spring, Brownie Bronislaw, and his wife, Janina, arrived at the farm. The new house was not completed so they had to live with us until the house was finished. Janina was pregnant, and expecting a baby that fall. Both of these people had been prisoners of the Germans. All Brownie did was pour concrete day after day. His wife, Janina, was given 15 minutes by the Germans to leave her home and go work in Germany as a housekeeper. They never saw their parents again. This family was Polish. Brownie was a willing worker but had to be showed how to do everything, as he had no experience on the farm.

The most important thing that happened to us that year was on February the second Lois gave birth to a daughter who we named Mary Catherine. She was a pretty baby as all parents think. She too was born at the University hospital in Iowa City with the same Dr. Kettle doing the delivery. Lois stayed her usual number of days and when she came home Cathy took off like a beautiful baby. Now that is a proud father talking.

Needing another hired man, I contacted the diocese again They had a family who had to been moved to a farm down in and Lee County Iowa, and the housing was not livable. They wanted to know if I would like to take that family. This family had four children, three boys and one girl. I drove down to Lee County and found the farm, which was in a terrible place. I talked to Mary and Joe and told them I had a good house if they wanted to come. I drove the new truck I had down, and loaded them up and moved them, to what we now called the Wilson farm. Mary and Joe were good people. They were with our family for seven years. We saw their children grow up to be good Americans and go through the Keota school system. When Mary and Joe got to the United States Mary said "We are in America now and we will talk English" and that is exactly what they did.. Of course they still talked some Polish among themselves but they learned English quite well. Over the years Mary helped Lois, and worked for other neighbors as well. She too had been taken as a German laborer to Germany to work. Joe also worked for the Germans as slave labor ,mostly pouring concrete for air raid shelters.

That summer I got the flying bug and went up to Cedar

Rapids and Lois and I bought a four passenger Stinson Voyager airplane. This was a very good airplane and at that time it was all fabric. It had a 150 horsepower engine with an aeromatic propeller. And of course it was a tail dragger. Lois and I went over to Keota to tell the folks that I bought an airplane. This did not go over too well, his main remark was "You will kill yourself in that damn thing". He wasn't very happy about it at all but mother didn't say a word. I don't know for sure what she thought. We had a strip of land in alfalfa, down at what we called the box cars, (which were later destroyed in a tornado) and I used that as a landing strip and built a portable hanger down there.

In August Lois and I loaded Clare and Cathy and headed to Wyoming for a week's vacation with mother and Dad Clare. We were between North Platte, Nebraska heading for Scoots Bluff when we hit a stationary front, without a cloud in the sky. However the air was as rough as it usually ever gets. I would have the nose of the airplane pointed towards the ground and we would be going up at four or out five thousand feet a minute. Then we would hit the reverse, where we would have the nose pointed up and we would be going down. Lois had just fed Cathy a bottle of milk and she gave her to me, so I had Cathy on my lap trying to fly the airplane. Clare was standing up in the back seat, and he suddenly turned green as grass. Lois said "He is going to get sick" at which he promptly threw up all over the back seat of the airplane. Lois at the same time threw up all over the front seat. Then baby Cathy, who I was holding on my lap, opened her mouth, and poured out the whole bottle between my legs. Now I have never been air sick in my life, but believe me, that was as close as I ever came, smelling that airplane. After we got through the front and came to Scotts Bluff, We had to land, change all of our clothes, and wash out the inside of the airplane. At this point I really did not know if an airplane, was such a good idea. We had many a good laugh about this over the years.

After we arrived in Casper and all of our greetings were over, mother Clare and a couple of her friends decided they would like to have an airplane ride over Casper. I volunteered to take them. When we came to Casper there was an airport just on the east end of Casper that had dirt runways and of course it was very close to town so that is where we landed. So we went out to the airport Mother Clare, and Dick Davis and his wife. Dick was a pretty good-sized man and the four of us got into the Stinson and proceeded to take off. To make a long story short ,I had the living hell scared out of me. The Stinson I had bought had an aeromatic propeller on it. Which was set for lower altitudes. Where the propeller should have been turning 2500 revolutions per minute I could only get it to turn about 2000 rpm. Before I realized what was happening, it was too late to stop and barely fast enough to fly. It was one of those stupid things that one will do, that causes airplane accidents. I got the airplane just over the fence at the end of the runway and it was literally hanging from the propeller. If you talk about a nervous pilot this was one. I made a circle of the town with full power and came back and landed. I did not mentioned to them about how close we had came to an accident. They thought the ride was wonderful. I almost had to put on clean underwear. It was sometimes later that the same kind of airplane with an aeromatic propeller crashed in Denver killing all four people. The aromatic propeller's were dangerous to have on an airplane and were only used for a short time.

Now that I had two hired men I started increasing hog production and we also started feeding some cattle. The crop that year was good and it was nice to have some help even if there was a problem with language communication.

In the years since Lois and I were married we had made many friends. There was Mary and Baxter Freese and Lyle and Margaret Palmer who we were very close to and lived right in our neighborhood. We would go to Iowa City to our favorite spot the "Lark" for dinner and a big steak. Then there was a whole bunch of people in the Keota area who would party together and just have a good time. Our social life at that time was very good. We were all having children and so we had a lot in common.

Our crops that year were very good and I was looking for more things to do. It was a great time in our life.

The crop that year was good and it was nice to have some help even if there was a problem with the language in communication.

In the years since Lois and I were married we had made many friends. There was Mary and Baxter Fresse and Lyle and Margret Palmer who we were very close to. We would go to Iowa City to our favorite spot the" Lark" for dinner and a big steak. That fall I had planned an antelope hunt and had asked John

231

Romoser, who lived a mile and a half south of our farm. John was a veteran of world war two who had the misfortune to drive a truck over a land mine in Germany. The explosion left him totally deaf. John handled the handicap very well., and learned to lip read so well that you would not notice he was deaf. John and I loaded the Stinson and went to Casper for the hunt. We stayed with Mother and Dad Clare while we where there .Dad Clare loaned us transportation to get out to the Alamand ranch. We had a successful hunt and shipped the meat home, We were there three days when John said" Would you call my wife and tell her we are all right. Mother Clare, looked at him and asked "Why don't you call." They did not realize he was deaf. That is how good he was reading lips. One time I had been teasing John's father, Theodore about taking an airplane ride. Theodore was a real character with long white wavy hair who usually had his shoe strings flapping. I stopped one Sunday and said "Come on Theodore , We will go for a ride". He replied that he would, but his wife hollered and said "Theodore, you're not going" I can see it like yesterday. Theodore came out of the porch with his hair blowing and his shoe laces flopping saying, "By God, Elma I'm a'going". As we flew around ,Theodore kept looking around, looking out saying "Where's them damn cows" I never will forget giving Theodore that ride. He was at least 75 years old and was hard of hearing, but he always said that airplane ride ruined his hearing. Theodore played the violin and Elma played the piano at all the dances when I grew up .
In the winter time when the roads were bad we would go to different neighbors have an excellent pot luck meal After the meal was over they would roll up the rugs and have a great dance. Theodore would play the fiddle and if there was a piano Elma would play that .Shorty Dill would play the banjo and every one would have a great time while the kids would sleep after a while. We did not think we were deprived of any thing and we were not.

OUR FIRST AIRPLANE A STINSON VORAGER 150. A FOUR PLACE PLANE.

Part 3
Chapter 6
On the farm 1950

The year 1950 started out with a bang because it became evident that Lois was pregnant again. We were beginning to wonder what we had started. The farm operated in a good fashion and the two Polish families that we had working for us were turning out to be very satisfactory employees. They seemed to be happy with their lives. Our hog operation was running full bore and I was very happy with the way our new hog house was working. There were people coming constantly to see it .We were not as strict about disease as operators are now with hog operations.

The crops went in without much trouble and it appeared that there would be another good crop. By this time we had a sizable cow herd, that were having calves and things were really rolling along. I cannot think of too many things that we were doing on the farm except pouring concrete and the digging new water mains at the Wilson farm. It really is amazing that these farms had such a limited way to water live stock. I have never been able to figure out whether they could not afford to put water lines in or whether they would rather pay for cheap labor to do the watering. It still baffles me to this day .As I mentioned earlier, when I was a kid where we had to drag the milk clear to the house when a milk shed beside the barn would have saved so much labor. I always detested doing labor that I thought could be made easier.

It was in 1950 that a young salesman from the Kinross lumberyard called on me to sell me the first dry commercial fertilizer for the corn crop that year. A company by the name of Spencer chemical Co. had started manufacturing ammonia nitrate for fertilizer to be used on corn. This was one of the war surplus anhydrous ammonia plants that made gun powder for the war effort. I used this fertilizer on second year corn and had a tremendous corn crop. It was better than the crop of corn that I had following clover ,which was supposed to replenish our nitrogen for the next crop. This is when I got the idea that you could grow continuous corn ,which our agriculture college at Ames said you could not do. Of course now we all know better.

We always made a lot of hay ,as we had to have so much land in clover and alfalfa to replenish the nitrogen for our corn land. This was about the time that Minneapolis Moline Machinery Co. came out with a new wire tie baler. Bud Bohr and I bought one of these in partnership. It took a genius to keep the thing running, but we still baled for ourselves, and for the neighbors. It brought in extra spending money for Lois and I to take trips with. It was what we always called our hush money.

We were still growing a lot of oats because it required a nurse crop to get our clover started. However it was never a profitable crop. We of course always baled the straw as we needed this bedding for livestock.

Early in the year during February, Lois wanted to go home, so we piled in the Stinson Voyager and went to Casper. We had a delightful week. It was always fun to go to the Clare home. We were always treated royally. The weather was good both coming and going. While in Wyoming, I always when out to the ranch with Milt Kauffman who had a big sheep ranch. It was interesting and got me out onto the ranch to see how they done it in Wyoming.

In September, I made my usual flight to Wyoming for my annual antelope hunt. It was always a chance to get out on the ranch in Wyoming because I liked these people very much. I believe this was the year that I bagged a big bobcat ,the only one I have ever seen in the wild. The ranchers did not like them especially if they raised sheep.

A few days before I left to go to Wyoming Lois added another bouncing boy to our family. On Sept. eighth Douglas Albert Greiner was born in Iowa City, again at the University hospital. This was starting to be a habit.

We did not have television yet on the farm however Clare was old enough that he liked to go into Keota and watch television at my parents house. My mother so loved her television and it was great entertainment for her. She and Clare would spend a lot of time watching Hoppe on the television.

Lois and I made several trips this summer to Kansas City, St. Louis, to Chicago, and other places with the Stinson. We were enjoying the plane while we could. It was another good year .

235

A REAL IOWA FARMER WHO WOULD TACKLE ANYTHIING

236

Part 3
Chapter 7
On the farm 1951

Nineteen fifty one did not start out very well. Our hog operation had been running at for several years at full speed. However one morning in January, I think it was about the end of the month I went up to the farrowing house at 5 o'clock in the morning, opened the door and the smell almost overwhelmed me. I couldn't figure out what the problem was until I went in and saw that every baby pig had terrible diarrhea. This, was a new disease that had hit the country and was called Acute Gastro Entiritis. When baby pigs became sick they would be dead within 24 hours time. If a new letter of pigs were born they would be dead the next day. Even the sows that were nursing the baby pigs got the disease also.

There was no cure for this disease or vaccination. It just had to run its course through all of your breeding stock until they developed an immunity to the disease. We lost over 600 pigs and had no choice but to just let the sows build up an immunity to the disease. For a couple of years it really put us out of the hog business. We saw no alternative except to follow that kind of a program.

In the meantime my father always liked sheep so somewhere he found a group of 500 ewes, and we now found ourselves in the sheep business. However, we did not buy the sheep until fall.

My father was managing some land NE of, Wellman , which had always been considered very, poor land and the summer before I talked him into letting me farm it for 1951. He was not too anxious to have me do this as the tenant who had been on the land never raised a crop on the farm. We put all of our crops in that spring and I planted the whole farm NE of Wellman into soybeans. Remember ,in 1951 we did not have any weed control for soybeans. When fall came I had an excellent crop of 50 percent soybeans and 50 percent weeds. It made a little money but not very much. In addition to all the other problems that year 1951 turned into a very poor crop year because it was so wet..

We now had three children and were getting busier all the time and Lois and I decided to sell our Stinson airplane. We just did not have the time to fly. Besides now that we had three children it would not hold us all, so good by Stinson. We hated to see it go but you do the things you have to do. During the summer, one of our Polish families decided to move to Pittsburgh where there were more Polish people. We hated to see them leave but yet we were happy for them. We then made application to the diocese and had another family come that were Hungarians. This was really not a satisfactory couple, as the man was older, had no experience driving tractors, and just was not very handy. They had a boy about six years old . Whom we sent to the country school and Lois would pack him a lunch every day. He would bring it home and would eat none of it. Finally in desperation between Lois and his mother and sign language she packed his lunch and put plain lard on bread and sprinkled it with paprika. He loved this as that was what he was eating in the displaced person camps in Europe. They were not with us very long before I decided I would have to send them on and find new help.

I doubled my use of nitrogen fertilizer for the year and could see better results were I used it. It was becoming apparent to me that this was going to become something that every farmer would be using. This year I used it on land that was third year corn and when we harvested, it was as good as first year corn off of clover. Usually when you had three crops of corn the third crop was quite poor because of lack of nitrogen. I was starting to get the message.

We got the 500 ewes bred so that they would start lambing in January of 1952. We would have early lambs to sell for the Easter market, which was important at that time. Since we knew we would have no hogs in the hog house, we planed to lamb the sheep in the hog house.

We got the bean crop harvested after fighting the weeds and they average about 25 bushel per acre, which was not too bad considering the land. However, I knew that next year I would put the whole farm in corn, with some kind of a fertilizer program.

I made our annual antelope and deer hunt to Wyoming in

238

October. This time I took; along our neighbors, Richard Durian and Boots Bohr. We went out to Allemandes ranch for our antelope and then drove up to Uncle Johnny's cabin, in the bighorn mountains at Meadow Lark on Ten Sleep Creek for our deer hunting. We got our deer and had a good time doing it. Both men enjoyed it and so did I. It was always fun to be with Uncle Johnny Clare. He made every one feel welcome every time you went to the cabin.

We loaded the children up and went out to Grandma Clare for Christmas and had a good time. We don't know what happened, but we had no deliveries from the stork this year.

LOIS LOVED HER PLANTS

Part 3
Chapter 8

On the farm 1952

January and February were hectic months as the 500 ewes started having lambs. They had to be watched almost continuously. However, once I got the lambs dry they could stand a lot of cold. I had moved a portable building up by the hog house and slept in it so that I could be close to where the sheep were lambing. I think I was begining to smell like a Wyoming sheep herder before spring came. We would fill the whole building full of sheep. Of course, the ventilation system would not handle that much in the building, so the ammonia smell would get a little strong. However, we struggled through the spring. We had the usual number of baby lambs to feed on the bottle, which the kids were enjoying. Lois was not only fixing baby bottles, but bottles for the lambs as well. After we made it through the spring, we started losing lambs. Come to find out this group of sheep, also had a strange new disease, that required us to get rid of them in the fall. Disease is always such a problem with livestock but it goes with the territory.

We got the crops planted in good shape and everything was going along fine. We were way down on the number of hogs that we had to farrow but were building backup now that we had some immunity in our breeding stock. Hogs are just like people, you do have to buildup a certain amount of immunity. This is what happened to the American Indians when the Europeans came and exposed them to smallpox and other diseases. We had to do the same thing for our hog operation.

Well what do you know!. Lois is pregnant again and our fourth baby was day due to arrive July first. Lois and I had gone tolowa City to buy grocires and do some shopping. buy She suddenly started to have some pains and decided that I had bettre take her to the Hospital. She was put in a wheelchair and left setting out in a hallway. She said to me" I can feel this baby coming". I went into the delivery area and told them "This woman

240

is going to have this baby in the hall if you don't do something".
They just assumed me, I was an over eager father. However, one
did come out to see Lois and then things started happening. Our
regular Doctor was on the golf course, not wanting to be
disturbed. Some intern on the staff at the University of Iowa
delivered Beverly. She weighed five pounds 13 ounces and was a
month premature. She had a lot of black hair and was a good-
looking baby even if she was a month early.

In a couple of days Lois was telling our Doctor, this baby
does not want to feed like the other babies did. They told her that
she was just a worried mother and there was nothing wrong with
the baby. Beverly started losing weight, and Lois kept insisting
that there was something wrong, so they called the specialist in
from the Children's Department at the University and he was
convinced, there was something seriously wrong with the baby.
By this time to get food into her they had shaved her head, and
were keeping her alive, by feeding her through the veins in her
head. They had her taped to a one inch by twelve inch barn
board, so that she could not move. They had shaved her with a"
Mohawk" hair cut so that they could alternate the needles on each
side of her head. By this time they had moved her over to the
children's pediatric section at the University hospital. This was
during one of the polio epidemics and they had a heavy staff of
nurses on hand so she did get good care. We would ask the
doctor if she was going to be all right, and of course, we were
worried about the mental side of it. His answer was maybe she
will and maybe she won't. We honestly didn't know whether we
wanted Beverly to live or to die, In fact my mother saw her and
prayed that she would die because she looked so terrible. We
were very unhappy at this time about how she was delivered, and
the care we got, when we came to the University the day she was
born. We called in Dr. Foster from Cedar Rapids for consultation
and he asked Dr. McQueen if she ever had diarrhea?. Dr.
McQueen said "No she hasn't". Then Dr. Foster picked up her
little legs, and she squirted out, with a severe case of diarrhea.
Dr. Foster did not tell us immediately, but told Dr. McQueen that
he would give her 24 hours to live. But in a few days she started
improving and started gaining weight and low and behold in a
month we were able to bring home our fourth child, Beverly. Like
our other three children she turned out to be a joy to us and there

241

was absolutely nothing wrong. We were so relieved.

We had a lot of visitors to the farm that summer and it was always a pleasure to have people come. We enjoyed them very much as it made a lot of joy around the farm. Mother Clare came and stayed a couple weeks to help Lois with the baby and it was greatly appreciated.Mary the Polish lady was also working for Lois and helping out. She was a good person.

Clare was five in August and started to school at the same country school that I went to. He really liked to go to school, as it was a fun time for him.

We didn't get to do any traveling this year as we were just too busy. I did not even go on my usual antelope hunt as I had more important things to do.

I had put the old farm northeast of Wellman in corn and had a fair crop on it. Made a little money on it as I was paying cash rent for it. I had made up my mind I would farm it one more year and that was the end of it. The rest of our crops were very good and all in all we had a good year. The land that I had put in to continuous corn was actually increasing in yield. This was starting to open my eyes to what could be done with fertilizer. We did not make our usual trip to Casper this Christmas, but closed out the year at home, and had Christmas with my folks in Keota. So ended 1952. It was a good year. By this time Beverly was doing fine and we could tell she was going to be all right. Thank you Lord for your blessings.

242

Part 3
Chapter 9
On the farm 1953

We were getting back into the hog business, and I had rearranged the hog house. I then built the nursery on the west side of the farrowing barn, where we could move our weaned pigs. This worked out very well and saved a lot of labor, and was the beginning of the confinement raising of hogs. I had made quite a few trips to various hog operations, some with liquid feeding setups. that just did not look good to me. It later proved out that all of these were unsatisfactory. By this time we were building up a herd of Hereford cattle also.

I had been starting to read about the cotton farmers in the South, who were starting to use a new nitrogen fertilizer, called anhdryous ammonia on their cotton crop. It was a cheap form of nitrogen, and was working very good. I could hardly say the name, let alone know anything about it. When I found there was a convention in St. Louis, of ammonia people, I made arrangements to go to that convention to see what I could learn. Everything I learned I brought home with me and decided that this year I would use the product if I could find it. All of the application equipment for ammonia was made in the South. So any the ammonia equipment needed would have to be bought from companies in Mississippi, Alabama and Louisiana who were the leaders in using direct application of anhydrous ammonia. I found a company in Belle Plaine, Iowa and I made arrangements for them to apply 45 pounds per acre of anhydrous ammonia. When spring came, we planted the crops. At that time anhydrous ammonia was put on after the corn was up, which we called, side dressing. We did not know whether a person could put on pre-plant or in the fall at that time. To make a long story, short that amount of anhydrous ammonia turned that old farm northeast of Wellman into a beautiful carpet of green. Nobody in that area could believe what had happened to make that farm turn out such a beautiful crop. Before there would be yellow spots all over the corn fields where it was short of nitrogen, but here we had 200 acres of perfectly green corn. Before I had the nitrogen put on with a Ford tractor, and a three row applicator, my father thought I had absolutely lost my mind because he did not believe anyone could make corn grow with gas. He did not understand that 82 percent of that gas was nitrogen. He had managed the farm 20 some years, he had never seen a crop like that. In fact the people who owned the farm lived in Washington state. They came back and saw this beautiful crop and thought my father had been robbing them, for what he charged the other tenants and I for rent. They never saw this farm when all it raised was weeds and cocklburs. Because of this beautiful crop I did not get to farm it the next year.

This was the beginning of a new adventure for me, as I decided that anything that could make corn grow that good out of soil that poor that I should be selling it. Most people now know that anhydrous ammonia is a product of manufacturing nitrogen. It is a liquid that must be kept under pressure in pressurized tanks. This meant if I was to get in the business I would have to buy a 30,000 gallon storage tank, as all anhydrous ammonia had to come in by railroad tank car then.

When my father bought the house in Keota the property joined the Rock Island railroad track. At that time there was a side track that allowed me to unload ammonia. My supplier was Olin Mathesion from Huntington, West Virginia.

The young salesman from Kinross, Don Fosdick who sold me my first fertilizer wanted to get in fertilizer sales. Don was a good salesman and I hired him to be sales manager for the new company I was starting. Because my folks property was located on the county line between Washington and Keokuk County we would call the company Ke-Wash Fertilizer Co.. At the same time I had undertaken to build a 60 by 100 ft. quonset building on the Wilson farm ,a good project itself because to save money, I built the rafters for this building. This required the gluing and nailing of 24,000 lineal feet of one by threes, to build the curved rafters for the building. We completed that ,filling that building full of Smith Douglas fertilizer, to be sold the following spring. All of this fertilizer came in 20 tons at a time and had to be unloaded one bag at a time in 80 pound bags. The 50 pound bags had not been developed . We opened an office in our downstairs bedroom at the farm. Lois started keeping the books and records for the company and doing all the correspondence. I had to order the new storage tank , get it shipped in by rail and installed, as well as buy the application equipment from the John blue manufacture in Alabama and another company in Louisiana. Nobody was equipped to apply anhydrous ammonia, so I had to buy tractors to mount the equipment on   ,so we could do the application of the product. How do you do all of this without any money? I forget how I'd did it, but I did. Sales were going good as Don was an excellent sales man ,and could sell ice boxes to Eskimos. By this time word was starting to spread in the state of Iowa about this new gas, that would grow corn. Most farmers at that time could not even pronounce the name and called it gas. They would come in and say can I buy some of that gas. We were starting to look for elevators who were in the business of selling dry bagged fertilizer, to sell anhydrous ammonia for us and I started talking to some about installing tanks the next year.

My dad was not happy with what I was doing as he thought the only way you could make any money was with your hands. In addition he really did not understand. Zeno Aller was running the picker sheller for me over at the farm northeast of Wellman ,and running the tractor and auger box to load the corn on the truck. Dad came very close to getting severely injured if not killed. He had the power takeoff running on the auger wagon and stepped up onto the wagon, when a pin in the power takeoff shaft caught his pants leg. He felt it and grabbed a hold of the top of the wagon and held on as hard as he could. It pulled his overalls completely off and pulled the socks out of both shoes and off of his feet. Zeno was close at hand and stopped the tractor and brought him back to the farm. His legs were skinned up quite bad, and he was mentally shook up, other wise he escaped uninjured. He was very lucky indeed.

We had a very good corn crop that year and our livestock operation was doing very well.. The corn crops were nothing like the crops we are growing now. Our yield per acre was more in the hundred and twenty bushel per acre range. Agriculture has come a long way.

On July 5th we had a hail storm come through and did considerable damage to our crop. This was just the crop on the home farm. But it still recovered enough to have a pretty decent yield. The kids were growing up and Lois was doing a bang up job of keeping the books for the new company. It was an exciting time and I was in the height of my glory getting everything organized. We found time to take another trip to Casper so that Lois could be home with her folks, this was in August, and we then went up to Uncle Johnny's cabin on Ten Sleep Creek in the Big Horn Mountains. We had a great time and I love to fly fish for those little brook trout. They make delicious eating. We always enjoyed going to the mountains and so did the children.

The year was drawing to a close and Don Fosdick was there selling fertilizer and ammonia like crazy. There were a lot of farmers who were pre-paying their fertilizer bills for the next year. This was great for us as it helped solve some of our capital problems. However it did not take nearly so much money to operate then as it does now. So 1953 grew to a close and we were excited about what the next year would bring.

THE CLARE FAMILY L TO R JIM, LOIS, MARJORIE, MARY
MOTHER CLARE EMILY, ALICE, JIM'S WIFE

L TO R BEVERLEY, DOUGLAS , CATHY, AND CLARE READY FOR CHURCH.

247

Part 3
Chapter 10
Beginning of Ke- Wash Fertilizer

We started 1954 with a bang. Our fertilizer sales had exceeded our expectation and now it is a question of just getting the personnel hired and trained to deliver what we had sold. At this time our office was still out on the farm in the downstairs bedroom. We still had the old style telephone line with the magneto telephone that could not be heard whenever anyone tried to call you and transact some business. That was a real handicap. Today we can not even imagine that type of service. Don Fosdick had done a good job in selling product and now it was just a question of getting people trained in how to apply anhydrous ammonia. This product as everyone knows today is a very dangerous product to handle. However people in 1954 had no idea of how dangerous it was. Many people have been blinded and severely burned with this product. I had purchased a new heavy-duty truck that would hold two 1,000 gallon anhydrous ammonia tanks. It could serve as a nurse tank supplier for the commercial applicators that we had. We were able to talk some people into applying anhydrous ammonia before they planted their corn and of course as we know now, it is almost 100 percent done that way.

We started applying anhydrous ammonia early in the spring. We ran two five row applicators that we pulled with Super M tractors. I can remember I had one character who was applying anhydrous for me by the name of Pickle's Romine. I took ammonia over to him northeast of Wellman on a cold blustery day and Pickles was shivering and shaking up a storm. I said "Pickles are you cold" his answer was "By God I'm not nervous" I never ever forgot that. But in between keeping the fertilizer equipment running and the anhydrous equipment going, I still had to get the crops planted and oversee that. I had hired a new man that year that had experience showing cattle and we decided to hit the road with a show string.

It was on the last Friday in April when one of those roaring thunderstorms that Iowa is so famous for hit the farm. However, this one turned into a tornado. It came down from the South and hit our hog barn, turned down towards our big cattle barn, and then went out between the two houses. We were very, very, lucky all though it twisted the houses on the foundation, it did not do serious damge to either one however, it did do damage to the trees. Some of the smaller buildings were damaged.It took down the old wooden windmill and did other strange things. It hit our box cars down South and destroyed that building. We had an eight-foot round water tank south of the windmill that we burned our trash in. The storm brought a piece of roofing from the box cars, a half a mile south. It picked up the water tank, turned it over dumped out the ashes and the paper and garbage in a pile. Put the piece of tin inside the water tank and wrapped it around a tree to where we had to take a tractor to pull it off of the tree. Strange things happen in tornadoes. I came home from delivering anhydrous ammonia shortly after it happened and could not drive into our yard because of all the trees and damage. While the storm was going on Lois and Mary were down trying to close the basement door that opened to the South. When the funnel went through. It was a strange thing. The funnel lifted, right after taking the top half off of the chicken house that sets between the two house's. That was the end of the tornado. It had blown out the North door of the hog house and we never did find that door.

The year 1954 was a dry year and it did not rain as much as it normally does. The fields that we applied anhydrous ammonia to gave a tremendous yield and everybody was looking forward to using that gas next year. We thought "WOW" next year will be terrific and we had better get some more storage tanks installed at different locations around the country.

We had a pretty decent show string put together for our Hereford cattle. We showed the cattle at the state fair in Des Moines, Cedar Rapids, Davenport, West Liberty, and Oskaloosa. We did pretty well.. We had a grand champion bull and female. It was a lot of work to show cattle, Other than getting a few ribbons I decided that this was not something that we would continue doing even if it was fun.

Up until this time Iowa State College at Ames had an agronomy department that did all the soil testing for the state of Iowa. The college had the 99 counties in the state convinced that their researcher's were the only one, who were smart enough to do this. There were a couple of us who challenged them and just plain refused to submit to that idea. There was one other private soil testing laboratory in the state of Iowa and that was located at Quimby, Iowa. Doyle Simonson and his brothers manufactured dry fertilizers spreader's and I had bought one from them. I made a trip to Quimby, Iowa picked their brain got all of the information that they had and came back and proceeded to set up a soil testing laboratory in Keota. The problem with the state laboratory was they had so much to do that it would take months to get a sample back. The soil conservation districts at that time paid a portion of limestone application, if a person's soil test indicated that your ground needed it. However we soon had the soil conservation districts approving our soil tests, however, with some of them it was not easy to get done. I hired a lady from, Keota, Ellen Krause, to take charge of the laboratory and trained her in how to run the PH test and the nitrogen, phosphorus, and potash tests. We eventually ran thousands of these kind of soil tests that we were able to use in selling fertilizer. It was an excellent sales tool and of course any soil test is merely a guide. However, it was a very successful operation along with our fertilizer sales.

There was another national anhydrous ammonia convention in the month of December that I went to. These were really wild conventions at that time because this was a new and exciting business and I was in on the ground floor. I thoroughly enjoyed going to the conventions and learning everything I could about equipment and selling fertilizer. The equipment part was really changing rapidly and was something that one had to keep up with for safety reasons. The reason there was so much anhydrous ammonia available, was that the World War II surplus manufacturing plants that had been making gun powder for the war effort, now were converted to selling anhydrous ammonia for crop production. Their sales force, all of them, had big budgets to woo and dine prospective customers. I liked to take advantage of their generosity.

We made plans to go to Casper on December 23 for Xmas on the City of Portland, which left Cedar Rapids Iowa, and went through, Ratlines, Wyoming where the folks from Casper would pick us up. It was a good year, exciting things were happening and we were eagerly looking forward to next year.

Part 3

Chapter 11
Ke-Wash in 1955

After the successful year of 1954 things were looking up for the New Year. It was easy to see that farmers were becoming more attuned to a fertilizer program and was much easier to sell anhydrous ammonia " That Gas". Our bookings for 1955 were almost double from what they were in 1954 at the same time. Our soil testing laboratory was doing very well and it was helping us in setting up fertilizer programs for the farmers. Most of the counties were now accepting our tests, and in fact were sending soil samples to our laboratory for testing. Originally we had one person working in the lab and now we were up two full-time people just testing soil.We were still handling bag fertilizer and this was a lot of work.

I had decided to start handling bulk fertilizer, because it required so much less labor. So we started making plans to build a building for bulk fertilizer in the fall. There was only a couple of dry blending plans in the state and I started making trips to these places and picking their brains for information. I knew we had to get into the dry fertilizer business as soon as I could scare up the capital to do it.

After the ammonia season was finished ,I saw the opportunity for a propane gas retail operation. There was none in, Keota so I made arrangements to buy three 6000 gallons propane storage tanks and set up a retail operation. I went to a propane convention in Kansas City and made arrangements to buy a propane delivery truck. We had purchased a pickup from international Harvester, and just by chance we bought a pink pickup with black fenders. It made a pretty outstanding truck. We settled on this color for all of our future trucks, propane tanks, buildings, and anything else that needed to be painted. Everybody else used white trucks. Our propane delivery truck was painted pink with black fenders. I hired a young man to work sales and another man to install gas appliances.

The farming operations were coming along just fine, but it was beginning to be harder and harder for me to stay on top of it. I was starting to grow continuous corn on our flat land and it seemed to be getting better every year. I remember distinctly when one of the college professors from the agronomy department came down to the farm to talk to me about why I could not run the soil testing laboratory. They still thought they were the only ones who were smart enough to do it. I told this professor about the continuous corn I was growing and he became so interested that he really forgot about the soil testing laboratory. He was telling me I could not grow continuous corn because I could not keep up the organic matter in the soil. So I said "Okay" we will go down and I will show you that it can be done. I think this had been the fifth year that this field had been in straight corn. He was amazed and forgot all about the laboratory and it was just a year later that the college decided that farmers could grow continuous corn. There was, however, a problem with corn root worm but that was being taken care of by a new chemical that we used at the rate of one pound per acre.

We were very short of rain during the summer of 1954 so the corn that we grew that year we grew on the sub soil moisture. During the spring of 1955, we did not get heavy rains to replenish our sub soil moisture. So the sub soil was still very dry. The corn that we applied anhydrous ammonia to in 1955 grew to be very lush and was a couple weeks ahead of the corn that was not fertilized. It started shooting ears just at the driest time of the summer. The fertilized corn suffered from lack of moisture. Corn that was not fertilized was about two weeks later, and then we started getting rains. It did very well and out yielded the corn that the farmer had put anhydrous ammonia on. This was a low blow to the ammonia business but at that time nobody understood why the yields were less. Today we know if the same conditions existed the same result would occur but we have not had that kind of a situation since.

Our family was growing up during all this time and we now had three children in Smith Creek school. Our old country schoolhouse was still serving its intended purpose. Clare, was in third-grade, Cathy, was in first and Doug, was in kindergarten. Lois was spending three days a week at least doing office work in the downstairs bedroom. However, she did have help with the house and with the children.

In July we got on the Union Pacific train and went on a vacation to Rawlins, Wyoming, where mother and Dad Clare picked us up. We went up to Uncle Johnny's cabin in the Bighorn Mountains and had a great-time catching mountain trout. Doug tried his hand at fishing, and when he wasn't looking, I hooked a fish on his line. He was so excited that he caught a fish we did not have the heart to tell him what had happened.

We finally got our new telephone system this summer and how wonderful it is to have a private telephone line to do business with. It really was a pain in "The you know what" department all of these last year's. Cathy spent six weeks with Grandma Clare, and flew home on an airplane alone, quite an experience for a little girl.

The year 1955 was another exciting year with so many things going on. It's hard to believe that time could be going so fast. We were enjoying our friends in the neighborhood and it was just a good time in our country. There was not the turmoil that there is today. We spent Christmas with my parents because my mother lived for the children. She was a great grandmother, as you older children know. Granddad enjoyed Clare and Doug and was taking them fishing which was something I'd never had time to do. I suppose if there are any regrets in my life, it was that I was so busy during the years the children were growing up. But I loved the challenge and Lois always said that living with me" Was never boring". There was something new all the time.

Part 1
Chapter 12
Ke-Wash in 1956

It seemed impossible that I had been farming for 10 years since leaving the Air Force. Time goes so fast and so many things have happened. I can see that I was just beginning to get into a really busy and interesting life. So many things were happening to agriculture that were new and I loved every minute of it. In the fall of 1955 I started building the warehouse for a new blending plant at Keota. I got the building completed and although it was a awkward way to handle fertilizer, poor people do poor things. We would ship a car load of dry fertilizer to the unloading ramp that was located by the depot in downtown Keota. We would then take an end loader, what everybody knows as a Bobcat today, and load our truck and haul it to the warehouse in the East end of town. Awkward, but it worked for the first year. We sold a lot of fertilizer in bulk, handling it that way.

Our anhydrous ammonia sales dropped drastically because of what happened last summer. We knew it would happen so we geared up to sell more dry fertilizer. Early in the spring, I decided there was a need for a ready mix concrete plant in Keota, so I went to the state convention and bought a couple power takeoff driven concrete mixers. They were small three cubic yard mixers, and I bought to used trucks to mount them on. In terms of today's equipment they were really" Mickey Mouse" but they worked. We used one of the trucks to blend our dry fertilizer with in the spring. We had to" poor boy" the operation as we were growing faster than we produced capital.

In the spring it was easy to see that we needed a new office building in Keota. It was just too difficult having the office eight miles from town and trying to run a business in Keota. Therefore, I laid out the plans for an office building, and as soon as the fertilizer season was over, all of our employees were put to work building an office building. By late August we had this building completed and we moved the office into Keota. Lois reluctantly, I'm kidding, of course, surrendered her bookkeeping duties to a very dedicated lady named Margie Sellman. She was a very loyal and dedicated employee. Margie is still living and is in the nursing home at Keota at this time.

In the fall the International Harvester dealership was closing in Keota. The gentleman, Al Mess, wanted me to take it over, and of course, the people from International Harvester also were pushing for me to do it. I could see some advantage for it, in that it would bring more people into our fertilizer and propane and concrete business. The problem was management for sales, as I did not have time to do that. Danny O'sweiler who had been working with Mr. Mess agreed to come and work for me and manage the business. Danny ,was a great guy, he was always fun to be around him. He did a great job managing the international Harvester business for me. We made arrangements to move the parts department into one end of our office building and then we started building a long building for parts and for service and for the manufacturing business that I would start later. As I look back now, I often wonder how did I get it all done. I had a lot of dedicated employees who put their hard work together to accomplish the things we did.

The actual farming operation was becoming such a burden for me that I was having to start neglecting around the edges, and of course, my father did not like this .Neither did I. So in the fall of 1955, I sold most of my machinery to Howard and Harold Bohr to take over the actual farming operation, This was a great relief to me. Lois and I would continue living on the farm as this was home. In the new partnership, Dad and I had 50 percent and the Bohr Brothers had 50 percent. This worked out quite well for me and Lois. I was much happier making the fertilizer company grow than I was farming. It always frustrated me then and it still frustrates me now that a farmer always has to take what someone offers him for his product. I felt that by working at building up a company, it was what I did that determined my success or failure and not what somebody offered me for my labors. Unfortunately forty years later the same thing is still happening to farmers.

We had another dry year but this year the fertilized corn did well. I got the crop harvested and was ready to turn the farming operation over to the Bohr Brothers and put my full-time to work in what I was doing in, Keota. In the spring my father had sold the big house on the end of Main Street to my salesman, Don

255

Fosdick. Dad and mother needed to have a house that was all on one floor as it was so difficult for mother to get up-and-down stairs. So in the spring Dad started building a new house just north of the one he sold. He did not sell any of the land, only the big house. All summer long, I was also helping dad with the building of this house. They built a new ranch style home and moved into it in the fall. Mother had her television set to watch, and she spent many hours watching television with the grandchildren, and they love to come to her house as she spoiled them.

Clare, was in the fourth grade and Cathy, was in the second grade and Doug, in the first at the old country schoolhouse. They were growing up. We had made plans to go to Grandma Clare's for Christmas. The children always looked forward to this so they could play with their cousins in Casper. We had a lot of company this year and always enjoyed everyone. Lois and I decided to take square dancing lessons this year and I had trouble telling my left foot for my right, but we still had fun doing it. It was a great busy year and we were looking forward to another year.

DON FOSDICK AND I IN THE SOIL TESTING LABORATORY

Part 3
Chapter 13
Ke-Wash in 1957

During the summer of 1956 I started making plans to build a hot mix fertilizer plant which involved a lot of machinery including rotating drums six feet in diameter by 50 feet long plus a Tennessee Valley ammoniation mixer. This was a mixer which you mixed super phosphate with anhydrous ammonia and other solutions and then added potash to make a chemical reaction. When the product came out of the TVA granulator, the product would be in pellets that would have to be heated and dried, and then into a rotary cooler to be cooled, and then run over a screening system to select out the proper size fertilizer. The oversize would have to go through a hammer mill to be broken and what was too small went back in the system again. If it sounds like a complicated system, it was. We built a large fertilizer warehouse of 18,000 square feet. I had found a source of used lumber in Chicago where they were tearing down a lot of old buildings and we would haul load after load of used lumber from Chicago to build this building.

In the meantime, we had to build a new railroad spur to make it easy to unload fertilizer into our manufacturing facility. We worked on this building all fall in 1956 and through the winter of 1957. I had purchased a lot of this equipment used from various dealers of machinery and adapted it for fertilizer use. I remember I went to a sale down along the Platte River east of Lincoln, Nebraska and purchased a lot of machinery and conveyors at a quarry sale. We all worked our butts off to get this put together and to start production in the spring of 1957. We did get it accomplished and manufactured quite a bit of product and had it sacked for spring use. However, things were not all great as some of the fertilizer went through a chemical reaction that made in set up in the bags. If there is anything a farmer does not like, its fertilizer that has set up in the bag. We went the whole spring in getting over some of these problems, plus getting all the bugs out of this equipment. I was beginning to see that the building was great as we needed it for storage, but I was becoming convinced I made a mistake in putting in the ammoniation equipment. Dry blending that we dld the year before was so much simpler and easier that I could see that was the way to be go. I could see that I had a "monster by the tail" and knew that any new plants I would put in would be dry blending plants. One of the the reasons that I built this plant was that the basic fertilizer producers did not want to sell to blending plants. However, it only took a couple of years until they changed their program and would sell blending plants as competition increased.

We had put anhydrous ammonia tanks in Crawfordsville, Amana,and Riverside. We were also looking at other locations. I could see a lot of growth for the fertilizer industry. International Mineral and Chemical Co. from Skokie IL became my major supplier of product. Their company treasurer was a man named Fred Kachline who over the years became a very good friend of Lois and mine.

The international Harvester business was selling a lot of tractors and Danny had won a trip to Los Angeles for Lois and me which we took in October for ten days. We had a lot of fun on that trip.

In 1956 school reorganization was being planed where we were merging Kalona. West Chester, and Wellman into one school district to be called Mid-Prairie Community School. I was on that committee in 1956 and in 1957 we succeeded in getting it done. It was easy to see that the State of Iowa was going to force consolidation of our schools whether we liked that or not. We were very happy with the education our children were getting in the country school but knew that change had to come. The spring of 1957 was the last year that good old Smith Creek School was to operate.

Clare, turned ten years old in August and was able to join the 4-H club and bought his first steer who he named Pedro. We made several business trips that year as well as visiting Mary and Jack at Wichita With our friends Mary and Baxter Freese and Lyle and Margret Palmer we went out for dinner off and on during the year. One incident I remember, I was welding on the inside of one of the drums putting in flights that would distribute the fertilizer as it dried.We went outfor dinner somewhere in Moline,Illinois to some fancy restaurant I started to complain about smoke in the building. Nobody else thought it was bad but I made a teribble scene about it. To make a long story short I had severely burned my eyes welding in that drum from the reflection of the welder. By the time we got home that night I was one uncomfortable person. It took about four days to recover from the burnt eyes. It hurt like hell.

There were enough retailers of anhydrous ammonia in the state that we formed a state association I was elected President this year. Trying to over come the year of 55.

We had a good crop on the farm this year and Granddad was having a good time making the sales buying cattle for the Bohr boys to feed. Dad and the boys got along fine. I was willing to let them do the farming as I was enjoying what I was doing.

HOWARD AT A CATTLE MEETING IN DENVER
259

Part 3
Chapter 14
Ke-WASH 1958

The year 1958 was a good year for the new fertilizer manufacturing plant. Our sales were great , we were finding that it took a lot of labor to operate the plant. There also was a problem with dust from the manufacturing facility affecting the electrical lines in the area. I was beginning to see that the dry blending process would soon eliminate manufacturing plants of this kind. So even before the year was out, we were making plans to convert the plant into a dry mixing operation. Fortunately most of the equipment that I had installed I purchased used, so there was not a big monetary loss when we eliminated this portion of the plant.

We were getting more involved in the chemical spraying of crops and had became a distributor for Hahn High Boys which were a tricycle sprayer that were manufactured in Evansville IN. We did a lot of commercial spraying for weeds and com borers at different locations, wherever we had salespeople. Our operation was becoming more of a complete farm service operation. Chemical sales were a big part of our business and each year new chemicals were coming in. I attended chemical meetings at various areas in our trade area so we were becoming quite busy with that type of operation.

This year we were up to 16 full-time employees and each year we seemed to be growing considerably. However the need for capital was starting to drive me crazy as we were out growing our means to finance the operation at a local bank. We were successful in getting an SBA loan which helped us tremendously. It was necessary to keep all of our employees because as soon as the fertilizer season ended, the ready mix concrete business would start and run until cold weather stopped that operation. Then it would be time to start on fertilizer sales again. I would have to say that 1958 was a catch-up year and that winter we started converting the plant at Keota to a dry blending operation.

The most important event of 1958 was our fifth child was

born. On December 18th we found something new under the Christmas tree and his name was Thomas Francis Greiner . The whole family agreed he was the best Christmas gift we could get.

We had taken several vacation trips in 1958 and one was to the Badlands in South Dakota where we went to the passion play. We then went on up to Devils Tower and then spent three wonderful days in the Bighorn Mountains at uncle Johnny's cabin on Ten Sleep Creek west of Buffalo Wyoming. What a beautiful relaxing place to spend a few days trout fishing. We then went on to Yellowstone Park and ,Jackson ,Wyoming, and on to Casper to visit Grandma and Grandpa Clare. We took three weeks and the children enjoyed it thoroughly.

We had a wonderful time going to the Alamand ranch for the round up. It was a real cowboy round up. The Allemande's had their neighbors come in and help round up all the cows and there calves by horse back. No, three wheelers on this job. I did the vaccination for Blackleg and Brucellosis. Jack Alamand done the castrating and his son did the branding. There were two women and one man doing the roping and dragging up the calves. We probably did something close to three hundred head of calves. It was a hot dirty job but lot of fun. After the round up was finished we went back to the Ranch Headquarters and had a great picnic. What a great day for the family. The Alamand's were great people and showed there old fashioned hospitality.

The kids had a busy year with Cathy and Doug starting piano lessons in January. In February Lois and I had a nice weekend in Chicago. Clare showed his Hereford steer at the county fair and won a blue ribbon for rate of gain. In September, we spent a weekend in Clear Lake with the Freese's and the kids really loved it. That following November we had a Clare family reunion in Lincoln Nebraska and all of Lois's brother and sisters were in attendance along with Mother and Dad Clare. We had a wonderful time.

The kids are growing up and Clare, will be in the sixth grade Cathy, in the fourth, Douglas, will be in third and Beverly, will be in the first. It's a busy time for Lois who was hauling kids back and forth to school for all of the various things they need to do. Clare is feeding two 4-H calves for the coming year.

As 1958 draws to a close the machinery business has

been good for the year and we have been selling and promoting LP gas tractors which is helping the propane business. We are in the midst of construction at the fertilizer plant converting it to dry blending operation for the spring of 1959.

THE FARM AT WELLMAN WITH THE PLANE IN THE HANGER

MERCHANTS NATIONAL BANK

CEDAR RAPIDS, IOWA

July 7, 1958

Mr. Howard W. Greiner
President
Ke-Wash Fertilizer Company
Keota, Iowa

Dear Howard:

   Congratulations, Celebrity! I read with
a great deal of interest the fine write-up in
yesterdays Des Moines Register under the
title Iowa Business Personalities.

   You are certainly to be congratulated on
the progress that you have made in your operation and the respect that you have gained throughout your business associations with people in
Southern Iowa.

   Best wishes for your continued growth and
progress and may your hard earned "good
fortune" continue.

Very truly yours,

John

John E. Mangold
Assistant Cashier

JEM/nhg

263

Part 3
Chapter 15
Ke-Wash in 1959

The year of 1959 was a very happy year for the Greiners. We had many things going on for the family as well as for the growth of the company. Our business in Keota, was continuing to grow and expand. We now had 30 full-time employees and this was starting to be quite a family. I had made plans to install a ready mix concrete plant at Farmington, Iowa and in the spring we started on construction of that plant. It was during the winter that I also purchased the old Chicago and Northwestern railroad round house at Belle Plaine, Iowa and started constructing a dry blending plant at that location. This was a different plant than was the hot mix plant at Keota. In dry blending you take nitrogen, Di-ammonium phosphate [which is 18 -- 46 -- 0] and straight 0-46-0 which is phosphate ,and 0-0-60 which is potash and mixed in various weights. Then you come up with the formulation that you need, according to the soil test that you made for the farmer. We dID this mixing by buying old concrete mixers and mounting an electric motor on them. They worked excellent and it was not long before the industry started copying these ideas. They are now are at all fertilizer locations. It is only specialty fertilizers such as garden, and golf course mixtures, that are hot mixed today. I thought I should give you just a little history of the difference between what we would be doing in Keota and doing at Bell Plaine and Farmington. However, we were preparing to change the operation at Keota also.

I got the bug to buy an airplane which as I felt I could use in doing a lot of flying from location to location where I was installing new fertilizer plants. We had our own private air strip that I could fly into an out of any time I felt like it. It was very convenient as I could get in the airplane and be down to Farmington in about 35 minutes. It took most of the month of April to get the ready mix plant completed. The plant at Belle Plaine had been completed in time for the spring fertilizer season, Things were really rolling along quite well however it was a very busy time. I was usually gone when the children got up and they were asleep when I got home. This was true in the spring of the year during the fertilizer season. We also added a bulk fertilizer mixing plant at Farmington at the same time we put in the ready mix concrete plant.

Don Fosdick and I flew to Oklahoma City and hired Bob Deeds as a production superintendent in July for the coming year. There were getting to be several plants and it was difficult for one person to be in charge of the ready mix concrete, the propane plant, the fertilizer plants and the international Harvester dealership. We had to get more personnel.

As far as our fertilizer operation for the year, it was continuing to grow We held our annual dealer meeting at Iowa City where we had 120 dealers present .It was a fun time in the fertilizer and chemical business.

My dear wife Lois had her hands full as in June all five of the children had measles. This was before there was a vaccine All of the children had them very hard with the exception of Tom who had a real difficult time. He ran a fever of a hundred and five and hundred and six degrees for several days. Lois did everything possible to hold down his fever but nothing seemed to work. All he wanted to eat was ice cream. Doug broke his left arm in July on the teeter, totter and Beverly broke her left arm in the same place on the same teeter totter. Thank God for Blue Cross. Lois had an Amish girl Barbara to help us when Tom arrived last year and she has came back to help Lois through some of this.

Lois and I flew with some of the children to Clear Lake in August for a few days with the Freese's. We always had a good time boating and eating on the trips. Our families loved getting together and we were very good friends. Lois and I flew to Illinois in August to be with some salespeople for a weekend and had a great time doing it. In October of that year Lois and I flew to Philadelphia and New York on a 10 day trip with International Harvester Co. We were able to see my sister, Cordell, in New York for a few days. We had a great time. How wonderful it was that Lois and I were able to do all of these things at that time in our life. It was really wonderful and as I think about it today I find it hard to believe that it all happened.

On October 1st, Father Manning and Baxter Freese and I

flew to Jackson Hole, Wyoming where we had made reservations to hunt for elk and deer in the high country north east of Moose, Wyoming on the headwaters of the Yellowstone River. This was a trip of 50 miles by horseback that took two days to get to the high camp. But what a beautiful country it was. Anybody who has the pleasure of making that trip can really see what is beautiful and pristine in that part of our beautiful country. We were successful in getting both elk and deer. We packed up into this country with Kenny Heart who was a famous Wyoming University basketball player. He was an excellent guide who in later years went to Alaska and started a hunting camp in Alaska.

We were privileged to have Mother and Dad Clare fly in on a trip they were making to New York and Canada, and Dad Clare got to see his favorite Notre Dame football team play Iowa at Iowa City. He was one happy Irishman.

The winner of 1959 was a really cold winter and we had some heavy snow storms so three different times during that winter we were snow bound for three days at a time. When that happens I was fit to be tied, but there is nothing you can do until the roads were plowed. The boys always dID a good job of getting up winter and summer to take care of their steers. Their Dad never gave them help as it was their responsibility. They never failed, rain, snow, or cold.

This year we had our office party at the VFW hall in Keota and we served elk and deer steaks for everyone. I was beginning to need a cure for ulcers and a mint of my own.

In April when I was flying the airplane all the time to Farmington I had forgot that my birthday on April 24 came and went. I was so busy I failed to check my driver's license to find that they had expired. I went down to Washington in July when I discovered my license had expired, and took the test. I zipped right through it without taking any time and low-and behold I failed the tests. I came home and had to eat crow as Lois and my kids had a ball teasing me because Dad failed the test. I could not believe I did that, but I did. I had to go take it again, but this time I passed.

That fall in November Lois and Shirley Bohr went to Cedar Rapids to shop. Lois always had a special way that she went to park when she wanted to shop at her favorite spot, Killians Department Store. From the last time she had been there, the city had installed a red light. Because she was not used to it she drove through the red light right into the arms of a cop. So he said "Okay lady, follow me down to the police station". She humbly did, and had to appear in front of the magistrate, who fined her thirty dollars for running the red light. Then he said to her " Lady do you know your drivers license has expired". Then fined her another thirty dollars. She did not have that much cash with her, and they would not accept a check. She had been hoarding two fifty, dollar travelers checks that she had to give the judge to pay her fine. I had a lot of fun getting even .This was one time that Lois was very humble, but we had many good laughs over this. She could not even drive home and it was a good thing that she had someone to do the driving. What fun.

LOIS WITH TROUBLE. L TO R DOUG, BEVELEY, CLARE, AND CATHY
WHAT A HANDFUL. LOIS COULD HANDLE THEM LIKE A CHARM

267

Part 3
Chapter 16
Ke Wash in 1960

The winter of 1960 and the spring as well turned out to be a real rascal as we were snow bound in January and February . The school buses did not run for approximately two months because the roads were so bad and then in the spring it rained continuously and the bottom fell out of the roads everywhere all over Iowa. It really turned into a disastrous spring for the fertilizer business as our spreader trucks and delivery trucks could just not get the job done. The corn was planted very late and fertilizer applications were all messed up and we'd never really were able to catch up. It was not one of our better springs for fertilizer and the company. However after the spring was over the weather did turn very nice and the corn turned out to be better than expected crop and the corn on the home farm averaged 135 bushels per acre which is not to bad.

This summer plans were made for a new propane retail operation at our operation in Farmington Iowa. So at that location we now had ready mix concrete, a propane plant, and a dry fertilizer blending plant. The business was doing quite well we had a good manager and things were moving along at a satisfactory clip. The fertilizer and the concrete business in a farming community work very well with each other. The farmers did not do much building in the spring when the fertilizer was busy and in the summer and fall the concrete business was very good. Now if you buy a cubic yard of concrete you pay about 62 dollars per cubic yard and we sold thousands of cubic yards of concrete for 14 and 15 dollars per cubic yard. What a difference. But it was still a good business if you could get enough cubic yards of concrete for the year. There was not very much exciting news in the fertilizer business this year and it was mostly a year of catch up.

As far as the family was concerned we made a big switch with our children in the fall of 1960 by sending them to Saint Mary's parochial school in Keota. This meant Lois had to do a lot of driving but she changed off with another neighboring family so she only had to drive half of the time. We felt it was important for them to get their religious instruction and it worked out very well.

We decided to take a vacation in July so Lois and I took the two girls for a wonderful long July 4th weekend with mother and Dad Clare in Casper Wyoming. Tom was such a rambunctious young child that we left him home with the two older boys and a babysitter. In August we repeated the same trip only this time we took the two boys and the girls stayed home with, Tom and a babysitter. All of the kids were taking swimming lessons which meant more running for Lois that poor lady found herself on the road all the time taking children here and there. Beverly was in Brownie camp, and all of the children were in Bible school, and Clare and Cathy were in 4-H camp. Clare showed is Hereford steer at the county fair and had champion Hereford.. In the fall Doug bought a short horn steer for next year. Cathy was to give a demonstration on yeast roll making at the county fair so we had rolls all summer long. She did win purple ribbon with her demonstration.

Father Manning and Baxter Freese and I flew again out to Jackson Hole Wyoming for another wonderful hunt in the high country at the headwaters of the Yellowstone. However I decided a touch of pneumonia was in order and ended up with a week in the Jackson Hole hospital. Normally we took two days to ride and pack the 50 miles into the high country. However our guide Kenny Saliors picked me up at the hospital when I was discharged and we left early in the morning for the high country. We got to the halfway camp a bout 2 o'clock in the afternoon and he wondered if I felt like riding the rest of the way and I felt fairly good so said sure I can make it. We rode till 9:00 that night and when we got to the high camp I literally fell off of the horse. The last three hours were in the dark and frankly the guide knew where he was going but I was totally lost and just hung onto my horse with the rest of the pack string following. After a good night's rest I felt pretty good the next day and succeeded in bagging a bear and an elk. We had a great time but I always will remember that trip. After I shot the elk I looked at it and said what the hell did I shoot that for when I had two big deep freezer's in the basement at home full of good beef and pork. So I then had to gut out the elk and pack it into camp for the 50 mile ride back. Although it was so beautiful in the high country I never went back elk hunting again. I always called the bear meat preacher meat as I could barely stand to eat it so we gave a lot of it away and took a lot of it to parties were people thought it was wonderful. However Lois had learned how to cook it and that is remove every bit of fat that is on the meat to be cooked. I remember when we had the bear skinned and hanging up in camp it looked like a human hanging there. This may be one of the reasons I never cared for bear meat and would not walk across the road to shoot one again. But we did have a lot of fun on these trips. We would go into Jackson hole and like all hunters do a little celebrating. It was a great time in my life.

We belong to the St. Joseph's Catholic Church in Wellman which was a very old church and we only had about 20 families but desperately needed a new church. And some of the parishioners had been trying to organize but it seems like nobody could get things put together. I had been going to mass a couple of times in Cahokia, Missouri where I was building another ready mix concrete plant and saw this nice church that they had built there and saw no reason why we could not do that at Wellman. So I loaded up Father Manning and two other church members in the airplane and took them to look at this church in Kahoka. I organized the design of the church at Wellman and started preparing an asking for donations to start building the church in the summer of 1961. Dr. J. Miller had donated a couple of lots in a nice subdivision in Wellman for us to build the church on. So that fall and into the spring of 1961 I was organizing getting companies to donate material and hiring the necessary contractors for the brick work and electrical work to be available in the summer of 1961 to build the church.

Our son,Tom was two years old and absolutely ruled the roost at home. He was very hyperactive and was like he was jet propelled all the time but he had a wonderful way of winning you over with his smile. Our Christmas was with grandfather Albert and grandmother Francis at their home in Keota. My sister Marjorie and her family were usually there also and we had a great meal always at gandmother Greiner's house.

270

Part 3
Chapter 17
1961 A Fateful Year

     Nineteen sixty one was a year when Lois and I had some things happen that we often wished we could have erased from our memory. However we are never given that choice and must exempt things as they come to us. It is with the faith of the Lord and many friends that help you get through times of stress. 1961 was one of those years.

     We sort of consolidated our position in the fertilizer business. However we could start to see a very competitive period coming into this business as there was a campaign on nationwide, among those in higher echelons, who think they have the answer to the world problems. That campaign was" we cannot feed the world and we all will be hungry in the next century ". This brought attention to all of the major corporations that may be the fertilizer business was the new business to get into two help feed the world. All of the major corporations in the oil business who had the product to start manufacturing nitrogen or anhydrous ammonia were to get into the business of feeding the world. So they all decided to get into the retail business as well as the manufacturing business and we could see down the road that we would be facing them as competitors. That started to concern me as to how I would be able to compete against major oil companies who could produce the product and finance the farmer. There never was any truth to the slogan a bout feeding the world and here we are in 1999 and we still have more food products than the farmer can be paid a decent price for his survival. But there was no choice but to see what was to come .

     Our fertilizer operation and chemical sales went very well for the spring of 1961 I had some excellent employees at various locations who were doing a good job for the company. I really had a great bunch of people who I think done their best to produce. We tried to operate as sort of a family operation and it worked very well.

     As soon as the fertilizer season was under control I begin

spending most of my time with the beginning construction of St. Joseph's church in Wellman. Being in the ready mix business we had a semi load of concrete forms where we could form and pour the basement for the church. The usual construction such as digging the basement was all under my supervision as well as the total construction of the church. The men of the parish always showed up when we needed them and everyone worked very hard and nobody ever questioned what we were building. This was not a project were people came from outside the parish to help with the building but was done with the few people who were the parish. The project moved right along and by midsummer the brick layer and the one carpenter and the one electrician who were hired were able to work on the building for their designated job. By this time the parish had the church up and the roof was on and things were moving along great. Our groundbreaking ceremony for the church was June 18th and to have the church completed by fall was the work of many dedicated people. I spent a tremendous amount of time on this project until October at which time the church was almost finished.

My flying bug was still going strong and we were doing a lot of flying. I felt I needed a bigger airplane so in August I traded the Cessna 180 off for a Cessna 185 with a cargo pod and six passengers seats. This was a 300 horsepower airplane that is used as the workhorse of the Cessna line for floats and rough field operation. The radio equipment was now so far superior to the old airplane and the extra horsepower I felt was a safety factor for the family. It was quite a different airplane from the 180 that I had been flying because of the extra horsepower.

My lovely wife Lois was starting to talk to me about Tom. She was concerned about his hyperactivity that he was always on the go and often falling and injuring himself. It also was apparent that he was not talking the way the rest of the children were doing at that same age. She kept telling me there is something wrong and of course my reply was" everything is all right he is just slower than the other children". How wrong I was. As the summer wore on and Tommy was not improving in his speech Lois asked me what I thought about taking him to the University of Iowa Child Evaluation Clinic. Knowing she was concerned I agreed that we should do it. We made the appointments and we had one of the first evaluations of Tom at the clinic. They confirmed what LOIS had been suspecting. There was a problem of brain damage probably due to the terribly high fever Tom had run when he had the German measles. It was a devastating blow to us but we were determined that we would accept what the Lord had given us,for Tom and then we started counting our blessings. Although Tom was a good-looking young boy and looked as normal as any other child We thanked the Lord for that. There are so many people who are given children who are not blessed this way that we knew it would all work out.

We flew our two girls down to Lois's sister at the Altus, OK Air Force Base were Jack was commanding officer. We left our two girls and brought their two boys home with us for a couple of weeks. Then Mary and Jack brought the girls back a couple of weeks later and picked up their boys. They all loved the exchange.

The first of September all seven of us flew to Casper Wyoming for a vacation over Labor Day weekend to visit mother and dad Clare. Our children really enjoyed going to Wyoming as they could play with Lois's brother's children. They always had fun and enjoyed each other. Jim's children were about the same age as our children and they had a great time.

The county fair was held in August and the children were deeply involved in 4-H. Cathy had five exhibits that brought her six blue ribbons. Doug won short horn breed champion which was very good for a ten-year old boy who had been taking care of his steer all winter and summer. They never received any help from their father for their projects. They were learning what responsibility was. The two older boys also raised three hundred and fifty chickens as a special project to make a little money for themselves. We never had to worry what our children were doing as they were always busy on the farm and by this time it was Clare's responsibility to keep the airport strip mowed. There were never any complaints from any of the children about their responsibilities or their jobs. Maybe it was just the old German way that I was raised. However both Lois and I agreed on all the decisions we made about the children. In all of our decisions to me, Lois came first and for Lois, I came first and then came the children. Maybe that is what made Lois and I so close.

On the night of October 6 Lois and I had gone to Cedar Rapids hospital to visit and employee who was hurt in an accident at our Belle Plaine fertilizer plant. We were south of Iowa City on Highway 1 about 10 o'clock at night on our way home from Cedar Rapids, Iowa. Lois was always tired and she had laid down and put her head in my lap to sleep which she often did.. This of course was before seat belts were known to be a safety factor. We came around a curve and met a whole string of traffic coming back to Iowa City from our Mid-Praire school football game. A load of kids pulled out to pass a whole string of cars and met us head-on into the curve. It was a terrible crash and I drove Lois's face into the dash of our 59 Oldsmobile so hard that it caved the dash in. Of course it threw me into the windshield and rammed my right knee into the dash. However it was Lois who was severely injured and had her whole face broken from slamming into the dash. Someone called the ambulance and the ambulance got lost and never did show up. Someone loaded us up and took us to Mercy hospital in Iowa City where Lois was found to have everything above her lower jaw through her eyes broken and crushed. Of course we were admitted and Lois was scheduled for surgery the next morning and was in surgery for about eight hours having her whole face rebuilt. We were very fortunate that the doctor from the University of Iowa hospital who was a specialist in dental surgery was available as well as the specialist in eye ,ear, nose and throat for the rebuilding of her face. The day after the surgery which would've been a Sunday they took me down to see Lois. They warned me ahead of time of what I would see. There lay my beautiful wife with a black and blue bruised face with her mouth wired shut completely unable to talk, but the most wonderful thing was she was alive.

This accident happened on a Friday night and Lois had a period due on Saturday. This did not show up and the doctors said this was due to shock and trauma due to the accident and surgery. However this was not the case and it ended up that Lois was pregnant with our sixth child. It was a terribly depressing time as here she was with her mouth wired shut and a new face and pregnant. When Lois was a young girl she had a front tooth knocked out in an accident and because this tooth was also knocked out she had a place where she could suck on a straw for water and liquid food. After two weeks in the hospital they were ready to release Lois and me and at that time Dr. Simpson came in and talked to us. He told Lois that last week he had another accident where the woman was injured the same as Lois except a small sliver of bone was driven into her brain which ended up and killed her. From that point on we both were thankful that we had escaped alive. This would have been much easier for a man to except that a woman who now had a new profile whose looks would be changed for the rest of her life. It is very difficult for a woman who had found out before the accident that our son, Tom had a problem. Now she was pregnant again and she knew that this baby would not be all right. Neither I nor the doctors could talk her out of it. When we got home she would set in front of the mirror and cry. I assured her her that she was as beautiful to me as ever. Because she could not eat, she lost a lot of weight and it was a terribly depressing time for her. In a couple of months we went back up to have her jaws and all the other wires removed. She was unable to open her mouth which was a normal thing that happened with this type of surgery but gradually she was able to get it opened far enough to be able to eat. However her sinuses were completely crushed and always gave her trouble. But she never complained about it. Although her profile had been very much changed, in my eyes she was still the same beautiful woman that she always was. It was about this time that the hospitals in Iowa City had announced that they had used the terribly crippling drug that deformed so many children in Europe. She was convinced that she had gotten some of these drugs and I could not talk her out of it. But as time went on she started returning to be the same loving person.

Of course my injuries were not so serious. They sewed up my nose but my knee was giving me a lot of trouble and I spent many hours sitting on the table with weights on my foot trying to strengthen my knee. They did surgery on it but it just never was the same. Now in 1999 as I write this I sit here with an artificial knee but I can walk so I have no complaints and thank God for technology.

Both cars in the accident were totally demolished and we were lucky that we were not killed. The four boys riding in the car that hit us were thrown out. Had their car rolled over after hitting us it would probably have killed all four of them. When their car hit ours it sprung their car to where both right side doors flew open, throwing them all in the ditch. However none of them were hurt. However, I hope they learned a good lesson from it, as we were the ones who paid.

In September I flew my father and two other hunters out to Casper Wyoming for our annual antelope hunt. We got both are deer and antelope for a successful hunt. I also bagged a big bobcat. My father however did not hunt but just went a long for the ride which he thoroughly enjoyed .

In February of this year we also flew out to Casper on Feb. 11 to the wedding of Lois younger sister to Gene Sweeney. It was a gala time as the Clares always put on tremendous weddings. Dad Clare was in rare form.

The church project was about completed when we had our accident except for finishing the painting. It turned out to be a beautiful and practical church. I was proud to have had a hand in getting that done for our parish.

As Christmas approached Mother and Dad Greiner had their Christmas a week before so that we could all seven pile into the 185 and head for Casper for Christmas. It was a fun time when we went to Casper as there was always Christmas parties and we just always enjoyed making the trip and we were always welcomed with open arms.

LOIS ON A TRIP BACK TO CASPER FOR XMAS 1961

276

BEVERLEY JEAN, CLARE EUGENE, MARY CATHERINE, DOUGLAS ALBERT IN 1955

277

ADDITION BUILT TO OUR HOUSE AT WELLMAN IN 1962

SAINT JOSEPH CHURCH I DESIGNED AND LED THE PARISH
IN CONSTRUCTING AT WELLMAN IOWA IN1962

MOTHER AND HER CRIPPLED HANDS. GOD LOVE HER

DAD WITH ONE OF LOIS'S FAMOUS ANGEL FOOD CAKES.

Part 3
Chapter18
Ke Wash in 1962

      The winter and spring of 1962 was spent organizing fertilizer sales and dealer meetings over our sales area, which was expanding quite rapidly. During the winter we had built two more dry fertilizer blending plants. One located south of Cedar Rapids at Koinngingsmark, which was just east of the Cedar Rapids airport, and the other located at Drakesville, Iowa, down in the southern part of the state. We also were in the process of installing five more anhydrous ammonia installations in South East Iowa at various locations. Although competition seems to be increasing, we were holding our own and still expanding. Sales for the year of 1962 looked very promising. The chemical business was increasing every year as companies were developing new weed control products. As more continuous corn is being grown, the need for root worm control is expanding also. These chemicals were quite toxic, but they really did the job in controlling corn root worm.

      All of those years, I had been dealing with a good fertilizer salesman by the name of John Hatfield. John came to me with with a proposal that he had been talking to some other people about, which was building a 100 ton a day anhydrous ammonia production plant at Creston ,Iowa. He wanted to know what I thought about the independent fertilizer dealers building the production facility and operating it as a production cooperative where you would take a ton of anhydrous ammonia for each share of stock you own. This was the way for the private individuals to compete with the major oil companies, who were moving in everywhere in the anhydrous ammonia and dry fertilizer business.

      I asked John if he had any investors who had actually given him any money and he said he hadn't, but he had a lot of retailers who were interested. I gave him a check for twenty-five thousand dollars which was what he needed to really get the program rolling. We would have to borrow two million five hundred thousand dollars and raise another million. This was a pipe dream that was going to take a lot of work and time. Creston was an ideal location because the operation required a lot of water which we could get from Green Valley Lake. The electric cooperative was located next door so all the electricity and the natural gas needed was close at hand. It would take about two years to get it put together. We had to hire a money finder, whose sole job was to call on insurance companies and various lending institutions to borrow the two million five hundred thousand dollars. He found the money. Because of being independent producers, we had to make contact with somebody who could give us credibility for our project. First Mississippi Company, in Mississippi was a producing cooperative manufacturing anhydrous ammonia and dry fertilizer. We must give the Southerners credit because they were ahead of the mid west on using anhydrous ammonia. This development started late in the fall of 1962 and it would take several years to put it together. But the seeds were planted.

In April during the middle of the fertilizer season, Lois got a call that her beloved Dad had a severe heart attack in Phoenix, Arizona and died very suddenly. He was 69 years old and enjoyed life every day. He just came in from playing a round of golf which he dearly loved to do, laid down on the couch, and went to sleep. What a wonderful way to go. We did not take the children to the funeral as I remember, but got in the airplane and were there the next day. This was a sad day for everyone.

Lois was doing very well with the pregnancy of our sixth child who was due about the end of June. She still did not feel right about the baby and was depressed over that as well as losing her father. During the night of June 13th, Lois woke me and said we had better go to the hospital. This was 2:00 AM so I called Dr. Jay Miller at Wellman and I grabbed a handful of towels. Then we left for Iowa City which is 30 miles from home. We were about halfway between Wellman, and Kalona, when Lois said " What are we going to do? I think the baby is coming!!" I replied," Well, we will just stop and have a baby". Which is exactly what we did. For some crazy reason, the dome light in the car would not work so it was darker than blazes, except for the speedometer light under the dash. I had the baby by its head and by its feet and he cried just once. Lois was saying "Is it all right!!?" "Is it all right!!?. So I held it up under the dash and the baby was looking

281

around and was okay. I wrapped him up in a towel, gave him to Lois, and headed on to Iowa City. We caught Dr. Jay Miller before we got to Iowa City. When I stopped him, he came up and said," Everything is fine. Let's go on to the hospital". So that is how Peter entered our lives!!

When we got to the hospital, they put Lois and the baby in the room together. She loved that because all of our other children were kept in a nursery, and Peter was contaminated so they said. And of course, in those days the father was kept as far away, as possible. I had always wanted to see one of my children born and was never allowed to do so. So I fooled them and delivered the last one myself. As soon as Lois found out the baby was all right, her mental depression disappeared overnight. What a wonderful relief that was. Peters birth certificate states that he was born on Highway 22 between Wellman and Kalona, Iowa. I always made a joke that we had just crossed English River when I delivered him and I had missed a good opportunity.!! We were extremely happy to know that all was well. Lois and I were both 40 years old and we decided that surely God did not have another one planned for us.

With six children in our house, it was starting to become a little crowded. Lois and I had been talking about adding on to the house. We had drawn up various plans. Finally, before we got a divorce, we decided on a big two car garage and a large 18 by 42 foot room that would double as the living room and a family room , plus a mud room and another half bath. As I look back over our wonderful marriage this was the only time Lois and I ever had any kind of an argument. I was looking for a plan that would be easy constructed. We compromised and after it was completed she loved it. We planned a fireplace for it, so on a nice Sunday morning after mass, Lois and I took the truck to the rock quarry for a load of limestone to build the fireplace. I built the fireplace, and must say I enjoyed doing it as it is the only stone work I have ever done. It is still standing without a single crack in it. I could have been a stone Mason also. Maybe I missed my calling.!!

Lois had so many clothes to wash that I bought her a commercial washer and a 30 pound clothes dryer like you see in laundromats. This was a real help for her. After Peter was born, we had an Amish girl, Mabel Bender, helping in the house and freeing Lois for the endless chauffeuring that was needed. She was very good with the children and was a friend of ours for years.

On June 26, we had the dedication of our new church by Bishop Hayes. It was a great day for our parish and our son Peter, who was born on June 14th and was the first baby baptized in the new church. It was great satisfaction for the work done, it was a joy for the parish. It had a full basement for Sunday school, dinners, and wedding receptions.

Our farm crops were good that year and we had an excellent fall harvest. The Bohr boys were doing a great job and everything was going great.

Our children were still going to St. Mary's in Keota, except Clare who was doing his first year of high school at Keota public school., Tom was now four and we were still having tests done and knew that he would start to school next fall. He would be going to Wellman for school. We were thankful for the help we were receiving from the child development clinic at Iowa City. Tom was now talking very well and although most people did not recognize a problem we knew it was there. We were searching everywhere for help but the answers were always the same.

All in all it had been a very busy and exciting year we were ready for 1963 to come. Time was going so fast.,

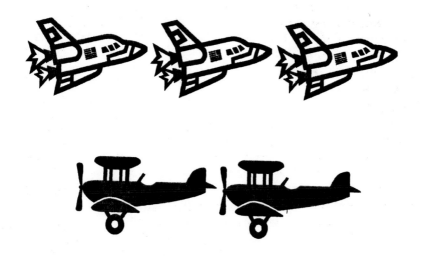

Part 3
Chapter 19
Ke Wash in 1963

Everything was moving along well at the company. Fertilizer sales were increasing and we had built the new concrete ready mix plant at Kahoka , Missouri and a new propane plant at Hedrick, Iowa. Sometimes I met myself coming and going, but competition was really increasing in the fertilizer business. We were trying to compete with the major oil companies like Standard Oil, Sinclair Petroleum and all the rest. They had unlimited resources for capital and it was difficult for an individual to meet all the programs they were coming out with. My main supplier of fertilizer and anhydrous ammonia was International Minerals and Chemical Company of Skokie, Illinois. Their treasure, Mr. Fred Kachline, had taken a liking to me and was doing everything his company could do to help me compete with the major oil companies. Fred and his wife, Pearl, remained friends of Lois and I until Fred passed away while hunting pheasants in Illinois. This was some years after I was out of the fertilizer business. He always enjoyed coming to the farm and hunting pheasants. We had made plans for four more fertilizer plants and at each plant we were installing a anhydrous ammonia storage tank and retail operation. It was a very exciting time in this business connected with agriculture. What fun.

My friends plans for green Valley chemical at Creston Iowa, were slowly taking shape and it looked like we may be putting together our own manufacturing plant for anhydrous ammonia. But it was still too early to know for sure whether or not, we would get a commitment from someone for the $2,500,000 we needed to borrow as the total plant would cost at least four million dollars. If we were looking at that project to day, it would cost 15 to 20 million dollars to build an identical plant.

In January the anhydrous ammonia convention was held at Phoenix, Arizona and we had made plans to show and displaying our Grizzly Anhydrous Ammonia applicator. In later years applicators were no longer used that carried a tank, because

284

ammonia is put on with toolbars pulling a thousand gallon tank pre-plant. Faster and easier. We had sent one of our salesmen out earlier. The weather was so bad we could not fly our airplane out. Lois and I took the Santa Fe train to Phoenix. We spent ten days and had a wonderful time because after the convention it was just the two of us. It was great for Lois to get a break from the children. Conventions were always a learning experience for me, and I thoroughly enjoyed them.

In the summer we had sent Cathy out to Grandmother Clares and she spent seven weeks, almost becoming a native of Wyoming. However we were glad to get our girl back home.

We finished the new addition to our home and were proud of the way it came together. Lois did a lot of the finishing work such as varnishing, etc. We know more than had it finished when our son Doug, started a fire in the fireplace. We were not home and he did not open the damper. You can imagine the mess that made !! Lois, had the urge to kill, but somehow or other was able to control it. However, all of the ceilings had to be washed and scrubbed. Never a dull moment with six children around.

This year we started all of our children back to Mid Prairie school in Wellman. After driving to Keota for three years and with a new baby, Lois decided that was enough. She had her hands full with Tom and Peter.

We had a lot of visitors to the farm in 1963 and we enjoyed them all. It seemed like Lois was running a motel and a restaurant combined with all of the people she was always having to feed, but she enjoyed every moment of it. She was a terrific cook. By now we had three deep freezers in the basement so there was always plenty to eat.

We had the usual aches ,and pains, and runs on broken bones. Doug nearly sawed off three fingers in the power saw downstairs. However, the doctors were able to stitch him up so he could retain full use of his fingers. Tom was running at usual, fell, and broke his shoulder in September and Clare broke his arm the next day. I was installing a 60 ft. long truck scale at the office in Keota and was down in the pit when I lifted on a steel beam and threw my back out. I was down for a week. The only strong people in our family were the women.

In August, Lois, Clare, Doug, Beverly, and I flew to Red Lake Ontario, Canada for a week's fishing trip on a house boat. I will always remember that Lois caught a walleye and was so excited. After getting it on board, I made the stupid statement " We will catch bigger fish" and threw it back into the Lake. What a mistake, we never caught another fish. The family was on my neck all week, but we still had a great time being together.

The boys did not win any great prizes with their calves this year, but bought 16 for next years 4-H. So they would have their work cut out for them all winter long. It had been a good year.

Part 3
Chapter 20
Ke Wash in 1964

      Things were humming with the fertilizer company and we had made plans for four more fertilizer plants. Sales just kept increasing and we also had taken on a line of livestock feed for a company out of Des Monies. I was having trouble with my knee that was injured in the auto accident in 1961 and the doctor recommended surgery, so I was in the hospital about 10 days in January. After I came home I must have been out of my mind, because I took on another project. And this was the kind that never made any money.

      There were a group of people in Keota who had been talking about trying to get a golf course built for the town. But nothing was ever done except talk. Their always comes a time for action. I went downtown and talked to Don Fagen who was the operator of the local grain elevator and my competitor in the fertilizer business locally. I told him we were going to build a golf course and a swimming pool for Keota and he was going to help. He did. I started down the street calling on every business and getting pledges to buy a share of stock for this project. Many were enthusiastic and some laughed. I'm sure when they said "No",, and I walked out the door they would say" What is that crazy guy up to now". At the east end of Main Street was an 80 acre farm owned by a retired livestock dealer. It had a large house that I figured would make the clubhouse and my father had 15 acres of land that he would sell. That gave us enough land for a 9 hole golf course with grass greens and room for a swimming pool. The land was arranged so we could build a large pond that would furnish water to irrigate the greens, which would solve the water problem. We had enough plans made so that we made a good presentation to the Farm and Home Administration, who had just come out with a program to help rural towns do these kind of projects. We worked out an agreement with the town to rent the swimming pool to them for the summer for three thousand dollars, as I recall. This was far cheaper than the city owning a swimming

287

pool. My attorney, Bob Day volunteered his services to help, but at no charge. We succeeded in getting the loan to build the golf course, it took a lot of work and time and many people volunteered and helped. It is a beautiful course today and I'm sure if you ask most people who are playing there how the golf course was built, they would have no idea. But I know, and it was great satisfaction to see it accomplished and see how much good it has done for that community. It has been a very good project for the area. I was president of this for several years.

By this time I had built the company up to where we had one hundred sixty employees in the spring of 1964. The fertilizer industry was building plants similar to mine in every corner in the state. We had a good spring. I never will forget the 8th day of May, when friend Kachline, who was treasuer, called me from Chicago and asked me if I had any idea how much money I owed International Mineral and Chemical Company. We had five semis hauling anhydrous ammonia around the clock from their plant in Illinois plus carload after carload of fertilizer for which we had no invoices. My reply to Fred was "I know it's a lot of money but I don't know how much". Fred replied "Well, it just went over a million dollars".(which in 1999 dollars would be five million or more) I owed IMC over a million dollars on open account and had somewhere around $1,350,000 in receivable's. After I hung up, I leaned back in my chair and said to myself "Greiner, you damn fool, what are you trying to prove!!

That same afternoon a man came into my office by the name of Dale Chapman and said "My company would like to buy you out because you have distribution and people." my reply was "I am not sure I'm for sale". But to myself I thought you make me any kind of a profitable offer and I will be most happy to sell. It took six months before we finally had all the details worked out and Southern Nitrogen of Savannah GA was now the owner of Ke Wash fertilizer company. I had plants all over the southeastern quarter of Iowa from State Center to Farmington, to Melrose, Cedar Rapids, and all points in between. I was hired to stay with the company which I did for two years. What a relief to be rid of the financial burden of running a company which had grown so large, but what a challenge and a joy it was to put it all together. I had some wonderful people working for me who are still great friends of mind today.

Three years after Southern Nitrogen bought me out, they were forced to sell to Kaiser Agriculture Chemicals. That is how competitive the fertilizer business became.

You never take the farmer out of the boy raised on a farm. After I sold the company, I started looking for land to purchase and found 1400 acres between Milton and Pulaski, Iowa. This was a farm that was owned by Craig Schaefer of the Schaefer Pen Co. of Fort Madison. Mr. Schaefer had committed suicide and the farm was put up for sale. It was a hobby farm for him and he had installed a lot of conservation projects for wildlife. It was a very nice Southern Iowa farm. By fall I had one hundred fifty cows running on the farm. We decided on the name of the farm and it was called Rawhide Ranch.

In January Lois and I cranked up the airplane and flew to New Orleans for the anhydrous ammonia convention. We then went on to Misson, Texas where Col. Jack Compton and Mary had retired to raise citrus. Jack, being an old Indiana farm boy, got in the business of taking care of citrus groves for retired military. The Bensons were now selling to the retired military instead of Iowa farmers. We then flew on down to Monterey Mexico and just had a wonderful time.

The plans with green Valley chemical company were materialized and we had found financing for the company with an insurance company in Canada and in Omaha. In September Hatfield, Paul Downing, Carl Reed, and I loaded an 18 horsepower motor in the back seat of the Cessna 185 and took off for Lynn Lake up close to the Yukon Territory. It was a wild trip, but we had a great time, and it was the beginning of a long relationship with these people. We landed on a Sunday morning in a wheat field at Dauphein, Canada, where the Canadians were having a fly-in. We had breakfast and then to take off we had to use a wheat field as there was no landing field. I still remember how the 185 struggled to get into the air. There was a Greek Orthodox church with the onion fixtures on top at the end of the field and a they were getting bigger and bigger, but we finally struggled into the air and headed on North. Some of the pictures of that trip are in the lounge downstairs.

Tom started kindergarten in Wellman. Of course, kindergarten was never a class where you could really tell what was going to happen later on, but he had a good teacher who had a lot of patience with his hyperactivity. We would have to see what the next year would bring.

The other children had a great year at 4-H and showed a lot of cattle and had a busy year. We again had a lot of visitors and the time when quickly. We made a flying trip to Casper for the Fourth of July to visit Mother Clare. Doug and Clare had to stay home to take care of their livestock for the upcoming 4-H show. Some of the children were going to Kalona, to school as well as Wellman, and Lois met herself coming and going. I, of course was always 8 miles southwest in Keota. The golf course was built and was ready for playing next year. It was quite a year and as I look back I wonder how I did it all. I would not have accomplished all of this had it not been for my loyal loving wife, Lois, who really did all the work raising the children. She was a gem.

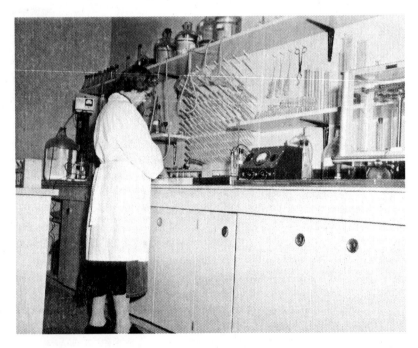

ELLEN KRAUSE AT WORK IN THE SOIL TESTING LABORATORY

ALBERT AND FRANCIS GREINER'S 50TH WEDDING CELEBRATION OCT.1965
L TO R IN BACK SISTER MARJORIE,YOURS TRULY,AND SISTER CORDELL

Part 3
Chapter 21
Ke Wash in 1965

The new year was very busy in the spring of 1965 as we were preparing for the coming fertilizer season. I had made several trips to Savannah , Georgia and was hiring assistant managers for the company. We had taken a lot of the management from two fertilizer plants in northern Iowa and Minnesota. I had hired a local fellow to work as assistant manager for the company. The year of 1965 was not too exciting. We did start a couple new fertilizer plants. The feed business was growing and we had started a line of hybrid seed corn that was private labeled for us. That was coming along well.

It was starting to appear that the company who bought us out had also overextended itself. They were not too anxious to do any more expansion than what we had done in the spring of 1965. We were handling a lot of chemicals, liquid nitrogen and anhydrous ammonia. However, the fertilizer business was becoming very competitive.

The company that purchased me had put no restrictions on my buyout and I continued with my investment in green Valley chemical Company in Creston, Iowa. I was elected treasure of the company and served on the board. We had succeeded in getting everything in order, as far as are financing was concerned, and for the sale of stock to other private anhydrous ammonia dealers and various Co-op elevators. You made no money from this stock unless you took your share of anhydrous ammonia and retailed, or wholesaled it to other dealers. A share of stock cost $50 and entitled you to one ton of anhydrous ammonia. We made a contract with Pritchard Construction Co., who urge specialists in building anhydrous ammonia installations. It would take a year to get the plant built, so we were looking for production to begin in 1966. This has been an education for us Iowa farm boys on how high finance is arranged and done. The insurance company put a man on our Board of Directors to watch out for their interests. It's a whole different world when you get into borrowing large amounts of money from insurance companies. The money we borrowed in 1965 would be like borrowing 12 to 15 million dollars today.

In January, I took Beverly to high school in Wellman, and then headed north for the interstate to go to Des Monies for a fertilizer meeting. Then I was going on to Denver for the western livestock show. I was on a black top road north of Wellman when I saw a car coming down the road with its windshield all frosted over. The car had tried to make a right turn into a farmer's yard but did not do it. Just before I met her, she made a left turn in front of me. I hit the car doing about 55 mile per hour, but this time I had on a seat belt. What a difference that made. I remember seeing the woman's body come out of the right side of her car and then go back into the car. A farmer sitting in his house saw the accident and immediately called an ambulance from Iowa City. This made a firm believer out of me for wearing seat belts both of the cars were totaled. I was driving a leased car and I called the company and they brought me over another car

I went on to Des Moines to the fertilizer meeting and just felt terrible, because I did not know if the woman was alive or dead. I called the hospital at Iowa City and found out that she was alive. They thought she would live, but she had many broken bones. I went into the Red Cross station where the meeting was being held, took some aspirin, and laid down for about an hour. I had lost interest in the fertilizer meeting so I got in the car and took off for Denver. I got to Hastings, Nebraska, checked into a motel and slept for 24 hours. I could not believe it, but it happened. I was so sore and stiff that it took me a couple days to get over it. I escaped again! The Lord said, " It's not quite time".

Our children were growing up and each had their special thing in school. Lois was busy going from place to place, trying to take in all the projects with the children.

We started Tom at Prairie Flower School, which is Washington's County's special school. He had a very good teacher who was trained to work with brain damaged children, so his progress was good.. We prayed for good things to happen.

My parents celebrated their 50th wedding anniversary and my sisters from Florida and Illinois were home for it. It was held at St. Mary's church in Keota and they had a very good day for it. Mother Clare visited us twice from Wyoming and we always enjoyed having her stay with us.

Construction was started at Rawhide on a new farrowing house and we had a very good corn crop for the first year. I did have to construct 50,000 bushels of corn storage and a complete dryer set up with elevator leg to handle the crop.

Lois, Tom, Beverly and I flew to Casper, Wyoming for Lois's 25th class reunion. We had a great time. We also flew to Biloxi MS and the Ozarks for vacations. What a short summer it was.

We received terribly bad news in December. My good friend Danny O'sweiler who had managed the International Harvester for me, was on his way to Keota and was involved in a automobile accident and was taken to the university hospital in Iowa City. Danny pulled through a stop sign in front of another car. We got word that Danny passed away that night from brain injury. I think I mentioned before that two of my key men Don Fosdick, and Danny were reckless drivers and I would not ride with either one of them, unless I was driving. Now they are both gone. Danny was such a wonderful person and always fun to be around. He learned to fly an airplane and kept it at our farm. He was missed by everyone. One of the things I always remember about Danny when he worked for me if things got slow he would say, "It's about time for me to go downtown and start a new rumor". Sure enough he would get the job done. He was a great guy and a good friend.

CABIN AT TEN SLEEP CREEK IN THE BIG HORN MTS

DINNER AT THE CABIN ON TEN SLEEP CREEK

Part 3
Chapter 22
Ke Wash in 1966

My job working for the company was certainly all right but my heart was not in it. When someone grows up making all the decisions, trying new ideas, and then finds himself in a position where he cannot make a decision without permission from someone higher up who has never done what he has done, is frustrating. The company was moving along. However, there were no expansion plans and everything seemed to be on hold. The ready mix concrete plants were sold, and of course, those employees were terminated from the company. If it sounds like my enthusiasm is not so great, that would be correct. However, this was only my personal feeling, and I was still doing my job for the company as far as sales were concerned. But I knew down deep, that this was not something that I wanted to keep doing.

The new golf course and swimming pool had a terrific year, but I was unable to play very much golf because my knee gave me a lot of problems. However it was in top shape for the coming year and it gave me a lot of pleasure to just see all the people who are enjoying it. There are a lot of people who had laughed at me, who were now out there playing golf. It just tickled me when I saw them. I know a lot of them think "This was a good idea we had". But that is human nature, always has been, always will be. The world is full of users and doers, which is a good balance.

News got to me somehow that there were a group going to Europe for a feed and grain trip. They were to leave in July and I thought it would be a great trip for Lois and I to take. I mentioned it to Lois and she was not sure if she could leave the children. We settled that real quick by notifying the Iowa feed and Grain association that we would go on the trip. We were to go to Belgium, East Berlin, West Berlin, Switzerland, Italy, and Holland, but what I was most interested in was Russia. We were to be going from July 19 until August 10th, which was a nice long trip.

Lois was an excellent secretary and kept an excellent record of everything along the trip. Her record of what she wrote about Russia was included in this year's report on the Greiners. This trip was in the height of the Cold War, when Khrushchev was in power. There were many people in Russia who would only talk to you when you were alone. They would not talk to you if there were more than one person. It was a terrible society and would have been a terrible depressing place to have to live and raise the family. A trip like this really makes you appreciate what we have in this country. May we never lose the opportunity we have here.

We started building a new hog confinement building at Rawhide and we had finished the farrowing house. Our corn crop is in great shape so things look promising on the ranch.

Things were progressing very well at green Valley chemical. At the end of February, the plant was about 90 percent complete. There was some production for the spring of 1966. But when starting a plant of this kind there are always bugs to work out before the production can begin. However, there were a lot of meetings to attend during the year and my share of the production for the year 1966 was sold to other people needing ammonia. I had placed anhydrous tanks on the home farm and on Rawhide. These were 12,000 gallons self-contained storage tanks that set on skids. You no longer had to worry about being on railroad sideings, as truck shipments were now available. It looks like green Valley will be a good investment.

This year I became a founder of Hawkeye National life Insurance Company of Des Moines. I thought it would be a good investment, but as things turned out six years later it was merged into another company. Starting a new life insurance company, is a struggle to get enough premium to support the company. My investment would have made as much money if I would have invested in certificates of deposit at a local bank. But that experience was worthwhile, as it gave me a look at the inside of life insurance companies.

Tom was still in school, Loved it and was doing quite well. It seemed that things he was interested in he excelled at. We would see what developed. Peter is four and has never seen a stranger. Everbody is spoiling him and we are all guilty. Beverly spent the summer in Casper at Grandma Clares. Clare was a freshman in college at Iowa Falls, Cathy and Doug are in high school, and Beverly is in junior high. They are growing up.

In January Lois and I flew to Dallas, Texas for the

anhydrous ammonia convention. We then went on to Mission, Texas and took a four day drive into Mexico. We came home with a load of Texas grapefruit from Jack's groves.

I had a big decision to make, and I did decide that this would be the last year working for the company. My heart was just not in it. So we notified the Bohr Brothers before the first of September that I would be taking over the farming operation again. I now had two thousand acres of land to farm. I was happy to be with the family and not have to put up with all the corporate baloney that goes with working for a company. The decision was not hard for me after working 13 years building up the company, I was ready to leave and face a new challenge. Lois was glad also, because it meant that I would be home with her and the children much more.

After being in Russia and Switzerland and seeing breeds of cattle, particularly the Simmentahl, that we did not have in this country my interest was aroused as to how we could get them. I felt there was an opportunity there, but with restrictions of our U.S. government on hoof and mouth disease, I knew it was impossible to get live animals from Europe.

While we were in Switzerland I wanted to get a big Cow Bell, but I did not want to buy it in a tourist shop. I wanted one from a farm, or one that had something unique about it. We were in Frieburg where Emmentahl cheese (Swiss) is made. The guide came and said to me "Follow me, I think I found your Bell". A professional Swiss wrestler had a trophy case full of bells that he had won wrestling. I asked him if he would sell one of the big bells, and he said he would. I asked him how much money and he said "One hundred sixty marks" which was 40 dollars American. I said "Okay" and he took it down, then looked at it like he was sorry he said he would sell it. I saw that and said "Okay, I understand", but yet he had made a deal and he did not want to back out. Then he said "May be if you give me 20 more marks" which was five dollars. I said "Okay" and I bought the bell. It has hung in our house until we moved to Albia and it now hangs in our lounge. It is engraved where he won it and the year 1959. It is a nice trophy.

GREINER FARM NEWS

18TH ISSUE ✶ CHRISTMAS – 1966

A Blessed Christmas to You

St. Basil's Cathedral on Red Square

OUR WONDERFUL TRIP...
Howard and Lois took a
dream trip, a People-
to People 22-day Good-
will Tour of Europe,
sponsored by Iowa State
Grain and Feed Dealers,
52 in the group. Left on
July 19 & home August 9
visiting Belgium, USSR,
East & West Berlin,
Switzerland, Italy and
Netherlands. This was an
agriculture-oriented
flying tour..in each
country we saw the big
cities and also took
wonderful bus trips in farm areas and met agri-
cultural leaders. Each country was fascinating,
the Northern ones so clean, busy and friendly,
full of marvelous history. Switzerland is our
favorite spot, beautiful fairyland. Italy, another world, the Vatican's magnificent art treas-
ures overwhelming. Russia, unforgettable (P.4)

Editors---
Howard and Lois Greiner

Published yearly on the farm at Wellman, Iowa

Subscription Rate---
One Christmas Note

Howard has been working with a group in Washington County trying to establish an activity center for the handicapped. Progress is slow but a good start has been made.

Dad Greiner is doing fine. He and Howard made a trip to Paris in March to the Exposition. It was dad's first trip abroad,and they saw cattle in France, Germany, Austria and England.

Clare and Linda are busy farming at the south farm, "Rawhide." This year Clare raised lots of milo and corn, as well as hogs and cattle. Besides cooking for all the visitors, Linda gardened and canned and froze so much, and has been helping outside, too. We sure enjoy having them so close.

Peter,our busy fourth-grader, likes school but loves the farm.He joined 4-H this fall and is busy planning a calf project. Pete started trapping for a hobby. His biggest catch to date is an opossum. He played ball with the pee-wees this summer, and had cousin Mark Sweeney here for a great visit.

Doug is a junior in Farm Operations at Iowa State in Ames. He has been home most weekends this fall, and all summer, helping Clare, as they plan to farm together. Everyone is looking forward to his graduation.

Cathy and John Conway plan to return to Iowa in March. John's hitch in the Marine Corps is to end then, and they plan to start farming. Cathy graduated from Iowa State last February in Home-Ec.-Education. John returned from Okinawa in March and they have enjoyed being stationed at Twenty-nine Palms, California ever since. We are very anxious to see them again.

Bev is also enjoying Iowa State, and is a sophomore this year. She works part time at Holiday Inn in Ames, a good new experience for her. Bev went to Europe with cousin Hila Blumenstein this summer, where they saw the country and visited friends in England, France and Germany.

Tommy will be thirteen this month and is in his fourth year at St. Coletta's. He was confirmed last May. We will drive to Jefferson, Wisconsin,for his annual Christmas program on December 19, and will bring him home for the holidays. He is doing well in school and growing up so fast now.

and Down On the Farm

We farmers in Eastern Iowa had a beautiful year, and raised the best corn crop in history. But our hog and corn prices are still very sick.

The cattle program is looking good. We imported four Charolais from England in July. Our German Fleckvieh will start to come in February. Ernie Dodd visited several times this year from England, and Ranald McDonald, Howard's partner in New Zealand, was here in December.

This fall Howard and Lois both took a course in Artificial Insemination and are using the new 'skill' trying to breed 200 Hereford heifers to Fleckvieh and Gelbvieh sires... time will tell what results we will have. Never did expect such an avocation---we have found it fascinating.

GOOD NEWS DEPARTMENT: Mother Clare will fly from Casper to spend the holidays with us. She has had a difficult year recovering from eye surgery. We are so very delighted she is over the worst and able to be here.

I COULD HAVE NEVER WRITTEN THIS BOOK HAD MY DEAR WIFE LOIS NOT STARTED PUBLISHING THE GREINER FARM NEWS IN 1949 AND FOR 35 YEARS SHE MADE THESE CHRISTMAS CARDS WHICH RECALLED ALLTHE THINGS WE DONE AS A FAMILY. BLESS HER

Part 3
Chapter 22 A
Russian Trip

Trip to Russia

Friday, July 22nd 1966

After early breakfast, a briefing in the hotel by an Attache to the American Embassy and to the airport at 10 a.m.. Then and every morning when we were departing we would put our baggage outside our hotel doors before breakfast and Fred took it from there. (Fred was our German guide who was with us the whole trip). Although we had an official limit of 44 pounds, we never had our bags weighed and could have carried and brought home much more if we had known. We took off had 12;20 p.m. Brussels time on Russia Aeroflot TU-104 (100 passenger), flying 800 KM\hr. it was very roomy and comparable, lots of leg room and five abreast. An excellent lunch: beef, new potatoes, beans, shrimp salad, caviar, hard rolls,a fresh orange,,crème puff and a ginger ale type bottled drink. We found we were served this drink at every meal in Russia. They called it fruit water and it has various flavors, Apple, pear, peach, etc. We never learned to like except that it was wet and we could only get water after a minor uproar. All so red wine, superb, and coffee. Hostess on Aeroflot were very sweet and wholesome (pleasantly plump). We were given the a brochure on the plane saying Soviet pilots and planes are so good that there is no need for life preservers, as are provided under the seats of all other overseas flights. They were equipped with emergency oxygen mask for all passengers. We landed at Moscow at 6: 25 p.m., Moscow time, losing two more hours. It was a beautiful flight over the North Sea.

Our first sight out of the plane window in Moscow: women shoveling dirt and a man standing with them smoking. In Moscow someone asked one of our Russian guides why the women did so much of the manual labor and their reply was, "In our country, you see, women have equal rights with man". This was to be one of our standard jokes, and we gals were all glad we had not achieved that at home.

While still on the plane we had to fill in this form:
First name
Last name
Year of birth
Nationality
Date of arrival
Purpose of trip
Date of departure
Number of bags

We had to fill out this form each time we changed hotels in Russia for Intourist agency. It was always printed in Russian and we were always confused.

And on through Moscow customs. Everyone had to fill out another form declaring how much money he carried, exactly, how many Jewels and uncut diamonds, etc.. This was a lengthy process as we all misunderstood and finally found even our wedding rings and watches had to be declared. We had to show our passports, visas and smallpox shot certificates. Howard and I used the ones we got last winter in Mexico. When we got back to New York that customs man showed us that it says right on them "Good only on the Mexican border", so it was a good thing that Russian could not read English too well. One lady in our party was held up for an hour because the date on her visa was July 21 instead of July 22. Finally they let her go on. Fred discovered every one of our visas was wrong and was afraid we would all be stopped.

We had an hour ride to Moscow over a very poor road and checked into the Ukrainian Hotel . Bob Hope once stayed here! A huge 1000 bed hotel, just for tourist, on the Moscow River this and all of our other accommodations in USSR, were run by the huge state run Intourist Agency. We had a late dinner at 9:30 p.m. of water, caviar, brown and white bread, small whole tomatoes, pear fruit, water, zucchini, new potatoes, beef, cabbage, pastries and good coffee. Onto our rooms by 11: 30 p.m..

We were met at the plane by Lelia and Marguerite, who are to be our guides in Russia. Both work for Intourist and were excellent linguists. They were attractive slender girls, both married, in their 20s, and each had a child who was in summer camp. All Russian children from 3 to17 must go to summer camp

303

all summer. It is obligatory, as Lelia said. Parents can visit one hour on Sunday. There were no children in Moscow, except for tourist.

We never had keys to our rooms in Russia. There was a lady on each floor who gave us the key as we entered our room and was ready to take it as we came out. We were all of the 24th floor

Saturday July 23rd 1966

We were brought out of our beds at 6;00 this morning by a horrible gonging noise. We could not for a while figure out what was happening, but it turned out that someone had left the room radio on full blast, and it was completely hidden by a drape. Each morning the one and only station starts by broadcasting the clock's chimes from the Kremlin tower. When our heads cleared we found we had an impressive view from our 24th floor window out over the river. Soon we could identify the buildings. We had a morning bus tour of this city of 7 million people, founded in 1147 by Ury Dolgaruki, meaning long armed. We drove a round the Kremlin, which means fortress, and was actually a fort built between two rivers. It is one hundred seventy-five acres and circled by the ancient wall with 16 towers--- what a place for all of us camera bugs. The Tower of Ivan the terrible was built in 1490 as was the Archangel Tower where the Czars are buried. St. Basil's Cathedral with its beautiful dome was erected in 1601. All these lovely old cathedrals are now Museums. Red Square dated from the 15th century and was the old marketplace. It has been used from the 18th-century for national celebrations. I am sure we will watch the TV pictures of their next May day parade with greater interest

Moscow, with its rivers and canals, can be reached by water from five seas. Moscow has one million tourists daily during the summer, and we believe this! We visited the Bolshoi Theater,Moli Theater, and Children's Theater. Tickets to the houses are just not available even as long as our trip had been planned.

Soviet means council. We keep learning. All over Russia we were taken to monuments, monuments and then more monuments, through the heroes of the glorious revolution, until one seemed just like the last. The people do have a lot of national

304

pride. Visited huge Pushkin (a poet) Square and of course his monument. We saw where Isvestia is published, where the international film festival is held. Also theTschaikowsky Music Hall, and the Puppet Show. By the American Embassy, only mildly impressive, with no flag out.

Moscow has 500,000 college students, and calls itself the city of students. We visited the big (40,000 students) University of Lomonov on Lenin Hills. The best looking buildings we saw in Russia, by far. All students from high school take exams and the top 10 percent are sent through college by the state. The others are out a luck and go on to trade schools and manual labor.

We visited the giant Exhibition of Economic Achievement, like a big continual fair. It was very colorful, but we were not permitted to see what we really wanted to, the agriculture and home exhibits. Those buildings looked empty. An exhibit of the Sputniks and a model of Lune 9 and the Cosmonauts was very interesting and the giant cinerama in a complete circle was fascinating. There were also continuous beautiful costume stage shows being put on by the people of the various 15th Soviet states.

Saturday night we went to a Russian Ice Circus. It was terribly crowded. The performers were excellent and put on a dandy show. Howard was standing in the back row as his legs were too long to wedge into the row of seats (the Russian people are short) , and a lady usher escorted him to a loge like seat in the front row. How is that for luck! He reported later that the aerialists were very lovely.

Sunday, July 241966

Most of our group did want to go to church to date and we found that there was one Catholic church and one Protestant church in Moscow. This one Protestant church is Baptist but takes care of something like 13 Protestant denominations, all that remain in Moscow. They both were to have services at 6: 30 p.m., and we planned to attend.

We toured the city more after breakfast—So many buildings going up but at no time saw anyone working on them. There seems to be a dreadful shortage of all materials, especially plumbing. Also, the pre-cast materials we saw were of poor or rough quality. We visited the G.U.M. Department Store, which is

305

famous as the largest of its kind in the world. What an experience! It is about three blocks wide and four blocks long and consists of many small shops arranged a round malls and balconies and walkways. It was dreadfully crowded and smelled of fish. People were trying to buy everything. Women's pushed to get into the dress shop. A few were let in at a time and a few shoved out. In each small shop the buying procedure was the same, as it is in each shop throughout Russia: you pick out what you want, and get inline and get a ticket on it from the clerk. Then go and stand in another line with the slip and pay the cashier, who marks the slip. And then go stand in a third line to get the item. This is true even in grocery stores. We bought a couple of abacuses and some small figurines. The girls in all the shops and offices we saw were really using abacuses as they figured.

We also visited a special tourist shop, run by Intourist for tourists. These shops accept only American or English money, and offer for sale merchandise which is the finest, and was not available in the regular stores. We were short on time, and the same shopping system was used. There were such long lines that it was hard to do much, but we did get some nice amber rings and bracelets for the girls.

And then we went on the Moscow Metro, or subway, and here is something terrific. They claimed it is the finest in the world and we are sure it is so. Each station was decorated in a different theme, some mosaic murals, some stainless-steel, others with sculpture, and all beautiful. It was fast, and very clean. You can ride anywhere in the city for one kopeck that is only 1.1 cent American. There are tremendous escalators to take you down to the two lower levels. We were sure that one went down 300 feet. We struck up a somewhat broken conversation with one pleasant Russian couple in one of the cars and gave them some give--a--ways, with which we had come well armed. Nearly everyone speaks some English they went out a head of us and when Howard reached the top of the first level they were there and showered him with five bouquets of fresh flowers. He was delighted and we nearly got lost from our group. He had enough posies for all the ladies.

Our visit to Lenin's Tomb was eerie. It's still seems incredible. On our bus rides we had seen the lines so often, always over a mile long, of people from all over the country, patiently waiting in the slow, slow line to see their hero. When Lelia and Marguerite told us that we would break into the lines so we would not have to wait, we all felt reluctant to do this. But the girls insisted, saying that the people knew we were tourists and had only a little time and wanted us to break in. We did, but felt from the steely looks on all the people's faces they might not be so delighted to have us. Even so, we did have about 45 minutes in line, then down some stairs and a round into the tomb, and there he lies, under glass, in flood lights. There were armed guards stationed all over, and one of them insisted that one of our men remove his hands from his pockets. It was there good revolutionary heroes, including Stalin, which is the only one in the long row without a head stone and marble bust. These are buried just behind the Kremlin wall. The guides refused to talk about Stalin. They proudly showed us the Kremlin wall where there are ashes of some American Communists. Tanja a special Kremlin guide, was horrified when none of us had ever heard of the American heroes.

Back at our hotel, which was always in turmoil with tours always arriving and leaving, we visited with many interesting folks. Tours are coming and going into every conceivable direction. Sometimes we wondered who was home minding the store. Howard mentioned to one New Yorker that we were going to the 6:30 Mass and he turned out to be a Priest from Fordham University who had been unable to contact the church in Moscow and his tour, an operatic one, was leaving at once. He gave us some prayer books and other items and money to give to the Russian Priest. It seemed simple enough. The bus loaded us up and delivered the one's going to the Protestant church first,then to the obscure address we had. It was a very old part of town and even the bus driver had trouble finding it. But we did and he let us out. We found the church was chained shut and there was no one about. There were some friendly folks in the backyard of a nearby house and we finally understood that the Priest had returned to Europe. Soon the kind bus driver became worried about us and drove back and took us to the hotel. So we missed Mass and did not deliver the goods. We finally sent the money to the Priest in the American Embassy to give to the Russian Priest and we carried the books home and sent them to the Priest in New York . Lelia and Marguerite had been shocked when so many of us wanted to go to church

Monday, July 25

We were called at 5:45, bags collected at 6:30, breakfast at 7:30, bus to terminal 9:00. We were to leave at 9:45 for Kharkov. We were taken to a tourist waiting room, where we were unbelievably held until 11:00 p.m., 14 hours. It was quite harrowing, the excuse given by our guides, who were helpless to, was bad weather. But people kept coming in saying the weather down south was great. We snacked, napped, bought gifts, (at Russian airports the tourist shops will only accept American or English money!) , played bridge and rummy and all grew annoyed in varying degrees. We had the impression they were trying to make us decide not to go to Kharkov. Some of the group did prefer not to go, and just stay in Moscow. We took a vote and the majority wanted to go on. Finally a plane was found and we boarded at 11 p.m., an Aeroflot Anioa, very huge, six abreast, full of Russians, and quite comfy. Landed at Kharkov at 12:40 p.m., at hotel Intourist at 1:45 a.m..

Tuesday July 26

Late breakfast , then bus tour of Kharkov, with two more Intourist guides, Nikoli and Sasha, very pleasant fellows about our age who we liked very much. Kharkov is a city of 2,500,000 people. It was occupied by the Germans for 22 months during World War II, and 250,000 people died here while it was occupied. Many buildings and monuments show battle scars. Both of these guides, and everyone else, we gathered still hate Germany. We saw some very old cathedrals. There are still 11 Orthodox cathedrals in Kharkov, fewer each year as the old people die. We saw Kharkov University and many monuments on Dzerginsky Square, the largest square in Russia, 22 acres.

That afternoon we saw the children's railroad in Gorky Park, five thousand acres, operated by 11 to 15 year old children as a reward to the smartest one's in their classes.

Wednesday July 27

We are in the bus by 9:30 and this is the big day we visit the collective farm. We had a nice hours drive through the countryside. This, the Ukraine Republic, has the richest soil in Russia and is called the 'Bread basket'. It is 602,000 square kilometers, 48 million people.

The farm we visited had its headquarters at a village called Sneshkovo. It consisted of 5000 Hectars grain, there were 2500 Horn cattle, 3750 acres cereal, 12000 acres total land, 2200 people of which 1097 were able-bodied workers,405 retired workers 700 milking Simmentahl cows, 3000 pigs, 1500 sheep, 2000 chickens, no bulls, 150 horses,1325 acres sugar beets,530 acres sunflowers, 450 acres barley, 2025 acres corn, and they have 16 inches annual rainfall. This is half the rain that we get in the state of Iowa. It is no wonder their crops do not yield like they do in this country.

The difference between a State Farm and a collective farm is that in the latter a quota is set by the state and a bonus is paid the manager and the workers if they exceed their quotas. Everything produced is delivered to the state. Every year they try to meet the quotas set by the state. This year they delivered136% of their wool quota, 85% of their milk, 127% of their wheat.

We had a reception in the farm office and met the farm manager, Popoff, the chief ageronomist , Anatu Theli, the keeper of the zoo (veternarian) and various other officials. They gave us a warm welcome and a lot of information about the management, operation, yields, etc.. The operators were young and aggressive and looked as if they could be farmers down the road from us.

They are very proud of their farm and the progress they have made since the war, when the village was completely leveled by fire by the Nazi's. Now all homes have thatched roofs, and water only in central open wells with windless. They said the whole village is scheduled to be rebuilt in 1967. We had the feeling they knew utterly nothing of the U.S. system of farming.

We kept an interesting tour of the farm--- first of the orchard where we all enjoyed apples and pears. These two fruits were the only ones we ever saw in Russia. The main crops are wheat, barley, and sugar beets. There are four hundred fifty milking cows, all Simmentahl, milked three times a day . They are milked and fed in open sheds in the summer and barns in the winter. We were not allowed to see the pigs.

309

The tractor pool was big and most of the machinery was obsolete by our standards. Tractors and combines, were old and looked unkept. Two men, on tractors were plowing about seven inches deep. One man drove the tractor while the other man changed the levers on the plow. One piece of machinery was pretty interesting in a gruesome way. Men brought manure to the fields on ox carts and put it in piles in a row. Then a machine driven by power take off with flails would sling the manure up into the air to scatter it. It was quite a sight.

Back at the headquarters, the ladies of the farm served us a dinner, and such fun!! All of the farm officials and our leader sat at the head table. Popoff began by proposing a toast to our good mutual relationship. We had been warned in advance that a toast means "bottom up" or it is an insult. We were served bottles of vodka, the official drink, dry wine (my choice and very nice), beer, and soda water, all in bottles on the table. The ladies watched closely and no bottle ever went dry before being replaced. With the first toasts we also enjoyed the salad course which consisted of small whole cucumbers and tomatoes served in compotes, a mild cheddar cheese, light and dark Russian breads and small slices of ham and sausage, all very good. Also little tubs of soft sweet butter, which served a real purpose we later learned. There were three or four more toasts during the salad, as each one obviously called for and answering toast by the other side. We toasted our heroic leaders on both sides, our fine interpreters, our beautiful guides Lelia and Marguerite, Nicoli, our sweet Kharkov guide was setting across from us doing a very good job of interpreting. Before each toast he ate a slice of black bread smeared very thickly with butter, and tried to convince Howard to do the same. But my stubborn Dutchman couldn't see wasting space eating bread when Vodka was so good and plentiful. Some time later we had big bowls of delicious borscht which the ladies kept refilling. Our group gave a glorious rendition of the Iowa corn song. We toasted the bumper wheat crop, the wonderful ladies who prepared the meal, People to People tours, then of the Cold War, and mutual understanding. Along here somewhere the leaders were discussing artificial insemination and some thought the Russians had it first and some felt we did. The keeper of the zoo (that is honestly what they called him) magnanimously announced he really felt the U.S. had it first. My hero's contribution here was to rise and declare it didn't really matter who had it first, Just so it helped us all and may we all continue to advance and prosper, etc.. It was shortly after that toast that Howard and a few others lost a little ground on our Ukrainian hosts. I am sure they didn't enjoy the excellent main course of roast beef, parslied new potatoes and beans, nor of the desert of more apples and pears heaped in bowls. The tables were still loaded with everything, but we finally thanked our hosts and made our way to the busses. We loaded them all with ballpoints, their favorite gift, and lots of other items we had brought, and they filled every bag and purse and pocket we had with apples and pears. We took loads of pictures. What a terrific day.

We were so glad we had lots of ballpoints--- a perfect tip for a waitress, in fact they begged for them. For their children in school, they said. We never saw any for sale there.

On on our way back to Kharkov, about an hour's ride, and of course there were no filling stations, we had to make a stop. The driver called out ladies to the bushes on the right, gentlemen on the left, and no one was too bashful to go. We did have considerable trouble here when Howard couldn't tell his left from his right. I was all for taking him back to the farm for good.

We had dinner in the hotel, but no one had any appetite, and on to the airport where we waited four hours and departed at 11:15 p.m. for Moscow. We were up only 10 minutes and turned around and landed again. There was a rain in Moscow and we had to wait it out. Their radar approach system is not so efficient as it is here. After an hour or so we all we reboarded and flew to Moscow. The terminals are very crowded with tourists, but had a lot of Russians, too, waiting for flights. We wondered how they could afford to fly and feel the state must furnish their tickets, as they did not look like prosperous travelers. We arrived in Moscow at 2:00 a.m. and back to check into the Ukrainian hotel again for a few hours sleep.

Somehow, we were all glad to be leaving the USSR. We were all more and more uncomfortable there for reasons we couldn't exactly explain. The drab, colorless streets, the grim, unsmiling faces, of the people. Their total resignation and helplessness frightening us more than anything.

Up and breakfast early and to International Jet Airport in Moscow and boarded Aeroflot Su 043y, landing at East Berlin's

Schonefeld Airport at 11: 30 a.m. gaining two hours. Arrived at the border via bus at 12: 30 where our passports are re-checked carefully. The East Berlin guards actually do check the motor, between each seat and run a little cart with a mirror on it under the bus to check for stowaways. No matter how many times we read it, it is still unbelievable. There it is a very elaborate labyrinth of thick concrete walls like interlocking fingers the buses have to maneuver so no one can just make a run for it. We passed without trouble through Checkpoint Charlie on into West Berlin where it seemed like we were entering a New World.

PostScript; I found this report in some old papers while researching for the writing of this book. My dear wife Lois had been making shorthand notes of the Russian trip and the rest of the countries we visited. I hope you have enjoyed what we saw in Russia during the Cold War. It was a terrible depressing place then and I'm sure it still is today. Thank God for America.

Dear Uncle Howdy & Aunt Lois,
    Happy Valentine's Day to the
two of you. You've always been
such a loving pair. I remember
when we were kids — we'd giggle
when we saw the two of you
necking ☺. It always appeared
to me that the two of you had
a really special relationship.

I LOVE IT!! I LOVE IT!!
313

YES!! WE DID HAVE A SPECIAL RELATIONSHIP, WE WERE ALWAYS TOGETHER

314

Part 3
Chapter 23
The Greiners in 1967

January of this year started out without having to worry about what I was going to do. I started doing remodeling work on our farrowing house so that everything could go to confinement. I was totally convinced that this was the coming way to raise hogs because there was less labor required, and the gain and the health of the hogs was much better. We know that the hog is the cleanest animal on the farm, if he is given an opportunity. It is the only animal that will go to a corner to do his bodily functions if given the opportunity. We were working to get the hog operation going full blast.

We had 300 sows to farrow in the spring, and between both farms, we have four hundred and fifty cows for spring calves. We would have our work cut out for us. At Rawhide we were trying to finish harvesting last year's corn crop, as it was so wet in the fall that we had trouble getting the crop out.

Green Valley chemical was in full production, and I was working on selling the extra anhydrous ammonia that I would not need for the farming operation. It looked as if it would not be a problem to dispose on my production. If the plant produced as we had expected, I would have 500 tons of anhydrous to use and dispose of. There was a board meeting every month at green Valley, and I always enjoyed these meetings. It was a good group of individuals from all over Iowa.

Lois and I decided that we would sell our airplane in March, and then we turned around and purchased a Dodge motor home that we could take our whole family on vacations. We had just plain outgrown the airplane. I hated to see it go, but there are some decisions that just have to be made.

We've got the crops in without any problems and the farming operation was moving along very well. When the first of July came, we decided to take a six week trip West and then south to Mexico.Seven of us went because Clare was old enough that he would rather be with his friends than with his family. This worked out well, as he could also take care of the farm. I think he many times regretted that he did not go with us because we had such a great time. We left in July, went out to Casper for a couple of days, and then headed south to all the great parks in Colorado and Arizona, then onto Mexico. We went down the West Coast of Mexico to Topolopampo, where I went sail fishing and caught a huge sail fish. It was a hell of a struggle, and had the boat not backed up and helped, I don't think this farmer would have ever landed that fish. Of course, they do this with every fish, so it really is not fair to the fish. They wanted to know if we wanted it and Lois said" No way do I want a mounted sail fish in my house". So we took pictures and gave the fish to the Mexicans. They were happy to have it. Unfortunately, the film later got wet in the mail, and we got no pictures of the sail fish. We then went on down to Mexico City where we all went to the bull fight. We boys enjoyed it, but not the women. Tom kept saying "He's bleeding! He's bleeding,! Don't bring out anymore bull's". He really did not enjoy it, and I have to admit the bull is not given a fair chance.

From there we went on down south through the mountains. There was just mountains after mountain until we've got to Guatemala. We toured Guatemala and had a couple of incidence's where someone tried to extort money from me on the highway. But I had been warned about it ahead of time, and refused to cooperate with the man, who was with their highway commission. He really was to control trucks, but he had a side racket of extorting money from Americans.

Lois wanted to go to a village where they did back strap weaving. We hired a guide and went to a village called San Antonio. It was established in the early 15th century and the Peace Corps had just build its first schoolhouse. As we approached that village we saw a home where a woman was weaving. We stopped the motor home, but just ahead of us was about fifty men with rifles shooting at man sized targets on the mountainside. I got out of the motor home and said to the guide laughing, " What do you have,a bunch of Communists here?" Jokingly I thought,. He said in a loud voice to me "Shut up!" Because that's exactly what they were. I did as he said. Meanwhile, we went down to the house or hut that was built out of corn stalks where this woman was weaving. The girls were very interested in this. Suddenly Peter said he had to go to the bathroom. So the guide took him back into the jungle, then this voice hollered, "Mother, come here. You won't believe this." It so happened these people did not have a bathroom of any kind and just went into the jungle for their personal hygiene. Believe me, mother did not go look. Just getting these people to use a toilet would have been a successful accomplishment.

We then went up the east coast of Mexico and stopped at Mission Texas to see Mary and Jack. Then it was on home to Iowa. It was a great trip that the kids will always remember.

Tom was in his second year at Prairie Flower school and had a different teacher who was not trained to work with brain damaged children. We could see he was not doing as well as he did the previous year we were very concerned about it. The rest of the children were growing up and in college and various schools. So ends 1967.

HOWARD WITH ONE OF THE BOYS BUT WITH OUT LOIS I CAN NOT TELL YOU WHICH ONE IT IS. BUT IT IS ONE OF THE FOUR..

Part 3
Chapter 24
The Greiners in1968

This was a year when we weren't overwhelmed by anything in the first part of the year of our farming operation, so it went a long well. I found out that the Canadian government was allowing the importation of Simmentahl cattle into Canada in a very limited way. A group of ranchers from Alberta, Providence had imported a bull named "Parisian." Carnation breeding service had made arrangements to import semen for breeding into the United States. I immediately ordered two hundred ampules of semen to breed cows with this year. That meant we would have half bred calves for next year. The United States would still not allow importation from Europe because of hoof and mouth disease. We would see what happens.

Our hog operation was functioning consistently. We had on hand about 3000 head of hogs all the time. I built another new confinement house on the Wilson farm. I bought an 80 acre farm north of the home farm. It is one where I used to go hunting all the time when I was a young boy. I also bought a hundred sixty acres of farm land two miles west of the home farm. So our farming operation was doing quite well for this year. We had added to the ranch so we had about 2000 acres down there.

I am still convinced that the Iowa farmer gives away half of his corn crop every year by not utilizing the corn stalks in some fashion. I had been experimenting with a machine that would make ensilage out of the corn stalks and save the ear which would have to be dried. This did not work for a big operation as it was far too slow. I then mounted a chopper on the back of a combine to chop the waste coming out of it and blowing it into a silage wagon. Then it was taken to a pit and water added to it to make silage. This also worked, but it was too slow of a process. A cow can live on corn stalks if fed a protein supplement. Some arguments are made that all of the corn stalks are needed to keep the organic matter high in the soil. The root system alone produces enough organic matter so the stalks are an item that can be used for other purposes. It takes so long for new ideas to develop, I'm sure in my lifetime I won't see it, but that day will come when we will be making paper, alcohol, or some other product. The farmer will be harvesting the corn stalks for sale just as he does the corn today. I put a lot of effort into trying to make this work, but like so many ideas of mine, I was about 10 years too soon.

In February, Lois and I received a letter, from the superintendent of the school where Tom was going, notifying us that they would not accept him for the next year. We were devastated and did not know what we would do. They did send us a catalog of schools and institutions that would take students like Tom. We found there were two possibilities for schools. One was a Catholic institution in St. Louis that required you bring the student Monday morning and pick him up Friday evening. Living 300 miles from St. Louis, we knew this would be impossible. The other institutions was also a Catholic institution, located at Jefferson, Wisconsin. Lois contacted the school in Wisconsin and made an appointment for us to take Tom for an interview. We went to Jefferson, saw this beautiful school, and wondered whether we could get Tom admitted. The interview was with the Sister who started the school in 1912. She asked us a few questions and all of the while she was watching Tom, who was always inquisitive. She sat there with her arms folded as Tom went over to her old antique desk and told her it needed fixing. He then examined and old antique clock sitting on the desk and asked her to wind it. She said "No, we have a man who does that every Friday when he cleans". Tom looked at it and said" Daddy, it's got two doors". She replied, "No, it has only one". I knew Tom well enough that I got up and went over and looked at the clock and said "Sister, I hate to tell you this, but it does have two doors". She laughed and said "That has been their 20 years and nobody knew it had two doors. "Tom then asked her to open her safe. She was quite elderly, but did hobble over and open the safe. She asked us a few more questions and informed us that they averaged 11 applications a day for entry into St. Coletta school. The interview was over.

We did find out that this is the school where Rosemary Kennedy, the sister of President Kennedy lived. The Kennedy family has been very generous to the school over the years.

We were just sick going home, because we felt there was

319

not a chance in the world of us getting Tom into this school with so many people applying. We did not know what we were going to do. We did not hear another word from the first week in March until June, when we had a packet from the school, with a lot of papers to be filled out, saying they would give Tom a chance to go to school at St. Coletta, if he could adjust to group living. We were convinced that it was Tom's interest in the interview that gave him the opportunity. Tom adjusted to the school and what a wonderful institution it was. It was the beginning of 12 years of Tom's life that prepared him for living. He could not have gotten this training anywhere else. At this time there was no government aid for handicapped children like Tom. Although we had to pay the full expense ourselves, we were so fortunate to find these people dedicated to special needs children.

Tom was growing up to be a handsome young boy and thanks to St. Coletta was able to read and absorbse and retain 90 percent of what he reads. He took the a great interest in the railroads, the Civil War, and the presidents of the United States. He can tell you anything you would want to know or need to know, about those three subjects. How lucky we were then, by the grace of God, to get him into that wonderful school.

My Mother and Father had a bad year. Mother was in the hospital six weeks with a bad infection but was able to conquer it. My Father had several bouts in the hospital with kidney infection. But they both were on the mend by the end of the year.

We had our usual number of visitors, which we were thankful for. We were also thankful for all of our local friends, as we were always going somewhere for dinner or just going to each other's house and having a great time. Mother Clare came for a month, as well as her brother, Jim and his wife Alice. We always enjoyed having them. Uncle Johnny Clare, and his wife came for a visit. (Johnny owns the cabin on Ten Sleep Creek in the Bighorn Mountains where I love to fish) it was another good year for Lois and I. What a wonderful life.

Tommy Greiner is a brain-damaged child. School officials told his parents, Mr. and Mrs. Howard Greiner of Wellman, that Prairie Flower school was not equipped to handle him. It would be up to the Greiners to find some place else to send him.

After a long and hard search, Tommy has been placed in a private school in Wisconsin where he is being trained to the full amount of his capabilities.

The search, though, brought realization to the Greiners that more facilities for the brain-damaged, mentally retarded and emotionally handicapped of the Washington area are needed.

Walt Farrell Sr. has a grandson who is a pupil at Prairie Flower. Young Wally is also a brain-damaged child, but exceptional in the eyes of his parents and grandparents. "He'll surprise you with what he knows," Walt stated.

The elder Farrell also sees the necessity for a rehabilitation center in the area, locally owned and situated. "These people like Wally are handicapped through no fault of their own and I feel it is up to those of us who are able to provide such facilities for them," he explained.

Leon Hilfman has never had the opportunity in the past to work in the field of the emotionally or physically handicapped. But the problem was presented to him by friends who are active in the Association for Retarded Children and realization dawned on him.

"Unless it touches you directly, you don't think about it," he explained. "But really, what do these people do after school is over? The way I see it, the funds are being expended anyway, through the state institutions, so why not bring them down to the local level?"

All three men are actively involved in the newly - formed Washington County Development Center, Inc., a local effort to provide training and activity facilities for the county's emotionally and physically handicapped.

Greiner and Farrell are president and vice - president while Hilfman is serving on the board of directors. Other officers are Lela Garton, secretary; and Cleo Orris, treasurer.

PUTTING TO GETHER THE WASHINGTON COUNTY
DEVELOPMENT CENTER FOR THE HANDICAPPED.

OUR CESSNA 185 ON THE FARM

NEED A WASH JOB

Part 3
Chapter 25
The Greiners in 1969

The big news in any family is when one of your children is married. Our daughter, Cathy married John Conway Jr., at the church we had built in Wellman. It was a beautiful ceremony and we had pitched a tent on the farm for their reception after the wedding. There were about 300 people in attendance and we had a great time. John was the son of John Conway, Sr., who worked for me in my plant at Melrose, Iowa. His brother Jim, was the plant manager. John was a lieutenant in the Marine Corps at the time of the wedding, he then came back and was with the farming operation until we quit farming. He now farms the home farm where I lived for 52 years. Both Cathy and John were graduates of Iowa State University.

The most important news we had for the year was that Tom was doing wonderfully at St. Coletta and had adapted to group living. Lois and I were so thankful and she worried so much about him. He was home for Cathy's wedding and was cross bearer. However, he was only able to be home a couple of weeks in the summer and a couple of weeks at each holiday. Since the older children were now gone or in college, it left Peter as the only child and allowed him to be spoiled rotten. He is always having a ball, and his teacher thought fun ranks too high in his interests.

Lois felt she had not caught up since the wedding. Her new project was trying to conquer a new knitting machine that we bought at the state fair. Lois loved to do that kind of work as well as needlepoint, sewing, and any kind of craft and artwork. She was always busy. During the summer, Lois flew back to Casper in August for Mother Clares 75th birthday and to spend a few days with her mother. The Clare family were altogether for the first time since Dad Clares funeral. They had a great time

The fall was busy for us as Lois was teaching high school religion. At the same time, she was having to cook for corn pickers, and all the extra help I had to get because Clare was called to the Army Reserves for six months of active duty and

Doug was in college. Lois and I went to Kansas City for the Royal Livestock Show. We wanted to see what reaction there was with Simmentahl. They sure looked good and we were enthusiastic about our crop of calves this year.

Dad Greiner helped a lot with the combine and he really enjoyed doing it since he could sit in an air-conditioned cab or use a heater if it got cold. He was a lot of help. We built a new modern corn drying set up at the Wilson farm, which was automated and made it very easy to handle all of these bushels of grain that we were harvesting. We built another 60 by100 foot storage building for corn as well as installed a 50,000 bushel grain bin. It seemed like all I got done was construct buildings and equipment, but I enjoyed it. The corn crop was quite good. We did have a late harvest, but when you're farming you always expect things like that to happen.

I flew to Calgary, Canada in August to a Simmentahl cattle meeting, where plans were made to form a new Simmentahl association for the United States. Interest was really starting to roll on this new breed of cattle. I was in the middle of it and was enjoying it very much. My enthusiasm had been aroused when I saw this breed in Russia and in Switzerland.

Lois, Beverly, and the little boys drove the motor home to Wyoming in August to visit Mother Clare. They had a great visit. We were enjoying the motor home. There were so many things going on around the farm that it was like a cyclone out of control.

I had been experimenting with no till farming and I found that it would work, but we just didn't have the proper equipment at that time. However, interest was starting to develop in the manufacture of equipment for that purpose. I could see no reason for plowing ground and had been playing with this for several years now already. I'm sure that a lot of local farmers thought I was nuts, but it was the type of challenge that I liked. My ideas weren't always successful, but it was my hobby. I played golf for several years after the course was built in Keota, but really never enjoyed it. I always enjoyed being home with Lois when I had free time, and of course, you find time to do what you'd like to do. So I gave up the game of golf. I never was one to hang out at taverns and Lois always appreciated this. She and I always had a great time just being together.

We never could figure out where the time went, as it

324

seemed the years were flying by. Life at that time was so challenging and so much fun. How could anybody not like it.

LOIS AND HOWARD READY TO LEAVE FOR CALIFORNIA ON A TEN DAY TRIP WITH INTERNATIONAL HARVESTOR. WHAT FUN

Part 3
Chapter 26
The Greiners in 1970

The year did not start very well because my mother, after battling arthritis for 40 years, passed away on January 23rd in Iowa City. We know the arthritis did not kill her, but she had a severe stroke which was too much. She fought a battle all those years without asking for sympathy. I always remember when the old doctor in Iowa City said "Francis, when you die, you should go straight to heaven as you had your hell on.earth. She had been a wonderful caring mother.

Our oldest son, Clare, finished the Army reserve training program. He and his girl friend, Linda Flynn, decided to get married on September 5th. They had a beautiful wedding in Keota and took a honeymoon into Canada. They moved to our Rawhide Ranch at Pulaski, Iowa to start their married life.

The farming operation was coming along great. But there was a severe outbreak of corn wilt disease which nearly devastated a lot of the corn crop. The hog operation was doing well, as far as numbers are concerned, but the price was 10 dollars per hundred weight lower than last year. This really hurt hog production and the profitability of that phase of operation.

I had made several trips to Denver for meetings of a proposed Simmentahl Registry for the United States, but it took a lot of meetings to get things hammered out for something like this. There would be calves of three quarter blood Simmentahl breeding the next year. Things were really starting to roll with the Simmentahl breed, and for the first time, there was a class at the state fair in Des Moines.

Because I had been attending meetings and was interested in the Simmentahl breed my name had been battered around. I received a letter from a man in England named Ernie Dodd. He had been granted importation rights for 12. Purebred German Fleckvieh heifers direct from Germany to England. These cattle had to be quarantined 60 days in Germany and 30 days in England before England would allow them into the country. He was interested in selling half interest in these 12 heifers to someone in the United States, because the United States would allow the progeny of these heifers to be imported by going through 30 days of quarantine in the United Kingdom and 30 days quarantine in the United States. He valued the heifers he had at 12 thousand dollars each. This was more money than I was interested in investing.

I was at the State Fair and showed the letter to some of my friends, Jack Shoup, Baxter Freese, Kay Statler, Keith and Bob Goode. They all decided that we should form a corporation and that I should fly over to England and look at the heifers. We raised between us the 72,000 dollars needed to buy a half interest in these animals. These would be some of the first purebred German cattle to get to the United States. I made arrangements to fly to England on September 6 to meet with Mr. Dodd on his farm to look at the cattle. They were an excellent set of heifers. Mr. Dodd was also a purebred breeder of Charolais cattle and he was interested in shipping those cattle to the United States.

The German DLG show was on at Frankfurt, which is the largest agriculture show in Germany. It is an absolute fantastic show of all aspects of German agriculture. Mr. Dodd and I flew to Germany for the show to see more of the German cattle and to tour the German bull studs in Germany. In Germany the Simmentahl breed is called Fleckvieh which in the German language Fleck means spotted, and vieh means cattle so Fleckvieh means spotted cattle. The Germans were 25 years ahead of us in animal genetics. We will never catch them. One of the reasons it is their agriculture is so controlled by the government where we have a free agriculture. The German farmer is not allowed to have a bull that does not have a license. A license has to be approved by the breed association, the government, and have a complete record of progeny on file. For this reason there are a few bull's on the farm in Germany, and almost all breeding of cattle is done by artificial insemination. This then allows some of the most fantastic breeding bull's I have ever seen. However, no seman from these bulls can be imported into the United States because they are all vaccinated for hoof and mouth disease. The German DLG show was fantastic. It was easy to see how much better the German cattle would fit into the American beef production than would the Swiss or French

Simmentahl. The Swiss and French Simmentahl were more like the American Holstein for milk where the Germans breed for meat and milk. I could see immediately the advantage of the German cattle over the Swiss and the French.

We went back to England and drew up an agreement between the new company, "German Fleckvieh of America" and Mr. Dodd. We now had cattle in England whose progeny we could import to America. We were all excited and had a lot of fun over it. We were also 72,000 dollars poorer.

This was the first of many trips I would make to Europe in the next few years. They were all learning experiences.

Tom had finished summer school at St. Coletta so Lois, Peter, and Beverly and I picked him up with the motor home and traveled north to Canada for a great trip across Canada. Beverly had spent some time in 1969 in Saskatchewan visiting a 4 H. exchange student that had stayed with us two years before. We went up to see her, also, in northern Saskatchewan. We then went on into Alberta, and looked at Simmentahl cattle. We just had a great time. We went on to lovely Lake Louise and then to Jasper, and then down into Wyoming for a visit with grandmother Clare. We just got home in time to get ready for the wedding of Clare and Linda.

Beverly was a freshman at Iowa State College and Doug was a sophomore. Peter was the only one left at home.

I was still involved in the fertilizer business with Green Valley Chemical, selling my anhydrous ammonia which was my share of production and going to the monthly board meetings. It was all very interesting and I loved every minute of it. Time has gone so fast that I couldn't believe it was already 1971.

A CHAMPION GELBVIEH COW IN GERMANY

"HAS" THE FAMOUS GELBVIEH BULL IN GERMANY

IN THE OFFICE AT THE FARM IN WELLMAN
330

Part 3
Chapter 27
The Greiners in 1971

It didn't seem possible but Lois and I celebrated our 25th wedding anniversary on Sept. 25th on the farm at Wellman. We barbecued a 200 lb. pig and had the whole Keota tribe there. We had a special ceremony at the church, a Mass, for the family and they were all there, except Cathy and Tom. Our blessings were great. We have been so fortunate in so many ways.

I had been working with some people in Washington, Iowa in trying to establish a program for the mentally handicapped. We made progress and called the program, Washington County Developmental Association. We had gotten it established and it has been very successful and has had a lot of good people involved in it since its conception. Of course, my interest was because of Tom. However, it turned out that Tom never made use of the facility. But it is fortunate that it is there, because it helps so many people. I am proud to have had a hand in developing this program and was President of it for a while. Again, my good friend and attorney, Bob Day, volunteered to help do the legal work to get this started. He and his wife Cornelius have been great supporters of projects like this for the community. When we started the program in Washington County, it was in the pioneer stage for this type of organization it was only because other dedicated groups of people assisting, that this project was successful. It took many meetings and trips to Washington to get this job done.

We had a beautiful year on the farm, and raised the best corn crop in history. However the hog prices were quite sick and we hoped for improvement. Our cattle program is looking good and we imported four purebred Charolais from England. Our German Fleckvieh were supposed to start coming the next February.

In March Dad Greiner and I flew to Paris for the Paris Agriculture Exhibition. The shows that these countries put on are so far superior to what we have over here that it is hard to believe

331

unless you go there. We all so went to England and stayed on the farm of Mr. Dodd for a couple of days before we went to Paris. My father really enjoyed meeting the German people, with the German Fleckvieh cattle, as he could talk German with them. One evening they took us to the Moulon Rouge nightclub. My father did not know shows like this existed. But he did enjoy the beautiful ladies. I became acquainted with Dr.Edwin Schwartz, who was with the German government and in charge of world exports of all German cattle. I really enjoyed these people. From the Paris show we went on to Germany into Bavaria where we toured various German farms. My Father really enjoyed this. Every farm we visited, we had to have a drink of schnapps. By the time night came we were feeling no pain. Our first crop of German cattle were in quarantine but we could not see them. We all so went to Austria and saw cattle there that are of the same German Fleckvieh breed. The Austrians use the same testing techniques as the German government. My Father really enjoyed this trip and it was the only time he ever went. I asked him several times to go later, but his answer was always the same, " I've been there and don't have any desire to go again".

Lois and I both took a course in artificial insemination. If anybody would have ever told me that Lois would do this, I would have laughed at the idea. But it turned out that she was better at it than I, because her hand was smaller and had better touch. What a girl!

We had been artificially inseminating and to aid in finding cows that were in the breeding cycle, we had what we called "Gommer" bulls. Now these were bulls that we operate on so their penis is redirected out their back. This is so they cannot breed a cow. We then put a marking halter with a chalk marker on the bull and we can tell which cows are ready for breeding. We had one gommer bull that was a Jersey that weighed about 900 pounds with horns sticking straight up. One day this bull had my father scared as he followed him alongside a fence for a quarter-mile all the time bellowing, and pawing the ground. Dad said to me "Get rid of that bull or he will kill someone." My reply was " He is the best gommer bull we have and he won't hurt you". A couple of days later I was up checking the cow herd and walked out into the lot when who came to greet me, but this bull. We had a face off in the middle of the field with the bull about five feet from me, pawing the ground, poking his horns in the dirt, and bellowing. I was scared to death because I knew if I'd turn to run he would have me in a minute. I could only stand my ground and shouted at him, but he continued. By the good luck of God, the herdsman also drove up to this farm to check on the cattle and scared him away with the truck. He would have killed me in an instant. He was not like the big bulls on the rodeo circuit that are fairly slow. But this bull would have been so quick and so furious, with his horns sticking straight up, he would have gored me to death in an instant. I took my father's advice and realized he was smarter than I. We loaded the bull up the next morning and he went to market. He would have killed someone as my father predicted. It was a close call and I said my prayers that night.

I purchased two more farms that fall west of Keota. They were good livestock farms adjoining each other. We were starting to get over 4000 acres of farmland, and of course, we were buying machinery to handle that type of acreage. Our local cattle operation was coming along well and we were anxious for the purebred cattle to arrive from Europe.

In January the group of guys with German Fleckvieh of America attended the National Western Livestock Show at Denver. I had been talking to a Mr. Jones who worked for that company about selling him a purebred bull from the German cattle that we were importing from England. He was very interested so we set up a meeting at a hotel in Denver for dinner. After dinner we started discussing with Mr. Jones having the first pick of any of the bulls from our 12 heifers in England. He asked me, since I always was the spokesman, what we wanted for that choice. I don't know why I said it, but my father always said start out high and you can come down. My reply was, 'Mr. Jones we want $125,000 dollars for that bull out of quarantine in New Jersey. There was no debate. He said," I will take it." We all about slid under the table, never dreaming that we would get this price. A contract was drawn up and was signed by both parties. He got the bull, and we got the money. I always marvel at that meeting!

Most of the cattlemen always stayed at the old Cosmopolitan Hotel in Denver. We had many good meetings there and a lot of good times. We had an unusual evening there once, but it is something I cannot describe in this book. It was unbelievable for a bunch of country boys from Iowa.

333

I had made acquaintances with some people from Ireland who also had German cattle that were eligible to come to the United States. I also had a couple heifers in the pipeline to come from Ireland. It takes a long time from the time you start the cattle to get them to the United States. It is a very expensive project as they must be flown across the ocean by airplane.

The children in school were doing fine. Beverly was a sophomore at Iowa State and Doug was a junior, taking farm operations. Our special son, Tom, was in his fourth year at St. Colletta and doing fine. Peter was in the fourth grade and planned to join 4-H as soon as he could, because he loves cattle.

It had been an exciting year and things were moving along, even though I met myself, coming and going. What a great life we were living.

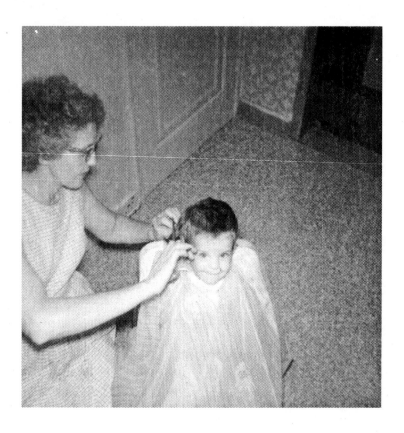

L TO R, CLARE, BEVERLEY, DOUGLAS, LOIS, TOMMY, PETER, HOWARD, CATHY.

Part 3
Chapter 28
The Greiners in 1972

The year started with the death of Mother Clare. She had survived Dad Clare by about 10 years, and could just never accept the fact that she was a widow. She was a wonderful Mother -in -law, and I could only have good things to say about her. We were always welcomed at their home. I always remember going out to a ranch west of Casper, and Dad Clare showed me where he was going to build their home. There was only one house on this ranch at that time, but Dad and Jim Clare developed the town of Paradise Valley on this ranch. Mother Clare's home was by the number one green on Paradise Valley golf course. We will miss going there.

With all the new products coming and new technology, we farmers are still at the mercy of the weatherman. We had a late planting season in 1972, because it was so cold and rainy. The crops look good, but in the fall, harvesting was a nightmare. Rains started in the forepart of October, and by the end of November winter was here in earnest. We always found it difficult when there was rainy weather on the ranch. The Des Moines River runs from Des Moines to the southeast corner of the state. When you buy land south of the river, you run into a type of soil that has a layer under it that is almost impervious to water. Tile do not work well here. If you get a lot of rain, and the soil slope does not allow,the water to run off, it remains very wet. It is so much different to farm than the soil north of the Des Moines river. I learned my lesson, as did a lot of other people, by buying land in that part of the state. The land was a lot cheaper and there was a reason for that. I always said at the ranch that we were two weeks away from a flood or a drought all the time. You could have a beautiful crop the first of August, but if it did not rain in a timely fashion, in two-weeks your crop could be reduced 50 percent. There was no sub soil holding capacity for water in this Seymour Idina soil.

I had been continuing to attend the National Simmentahl

Registry meetings and voice my opinion that a mistake was being made, in not keeping the German blood lines separate from the Swiss and French blood lines. I was ignored because at that time I was the only one bringing in German cattle. The Swiss and French Simmentahl have proven to be too big, give too much milk, are too hard to breed under range conditions. I finally had to accept defeat, that I would not get a separate Registry for the German breed of cattle. If you toured Germany, Switzerland, and France often enough, you would have to be blind to not see the difference. However, we had to blend our German cattle into the rest of the Simmentahl breed. Although it is 27 years later, a good cattleman will agree that I was right.

Our German cattle started coming in, and we delivered the the bull we sold to Curtis Breeding Company.

. I and our herdsman drove the semi out to Clifton, New Jersey to pick up about 20 head of German cattle that had cleared quarantine. In the meantime Mr. Dodd had received a permit to import 12 head of Gelbvieh cattle from Germany to England. These were the first cattle of this breed to be imported into England. I had been seeing these cattle in Germany and was very impressed with them. Although they did not have as much milk as the Simmentahl they were a smaller, superior beef animal that I thought would fit the American farmer better I later became involved, and eventually owned these heifers out right.

We took a pair of the purebred German Simmentahl to the Kansas City Royal show in October and they sold very well. The Simmentahl business in the United States and Canada was really starting to boom. This also aroused interest in other breeds that were being brought into Canada like the Chinina from Italy, Maine Anjou from France, The Saler and many other breeds. It was go-go-go time in the cattle business.

We were scheduling our own production sale for February the following year. We had a lot of half blood and three quarter blood heifers that were bred to sell in the spring, as well as other cows we had bred to various breeds. We had also bred cows to Chinina bulls, artificially, of course, for calves to have on the sale next February. Jack Shoup from Rhinebeck, was going to participate in the sale with us. It would be a new experience for me to have a production sale, as I have never done that before.

On the home farm, we had torn down some older buildings

and built a couple of new buildings, to better house the cattle we were importing. We were making plans to take cattle to the Las Vegas sale in a hotel there, and we needed a better place to individually house the cattle we were taking. We were also planning to take cattle to the Denver livestock show in January.

Things were so hectic this year that we did not find time to take a vacation. Dr. Schwartz had sent a boy over from Germany to get experience on the farm. His name was Tony Hoegele and he was an excellent worker and a good cow man. Tony was a delightful young fellow who fit into our family very well.

My father helped John and Clare with the corn harvesting in the fall and was kept busy running a thousand trips for parts and anything else that came up. He enjoyed it because he did not like being alone since mother has been gone. He loved to come to the farm.

John and Cathy Conway had their first baby,Sean Michael making Lois and me grandparents for the first time. They got home from the Marine Corps and were able to join us in the farming operation. John is an excellent worker and manager. Peter had his 4-H steers at the fair and won a couple of blues. Doug went to Europe with the college and enjoyed it. Beverly was a junior at Iowa State University and our beloved Tom was doing well at St. Colletta in Wisconsin. He came home on the 18th of December , his birthday. That was the first time in five years that we celebrated his birthday at home. They usually did not get out at St Colletta until the 20th of December.

Clare and Linda were working hard on the ranch. It has been a big job for them.

The meetings at Green Valley Chemical continued each month and the company was producing anhydrous ammonia at a good rate. We had been successful in selling our ammonia. I enjoyed these meetings because there was usually something exciting at each one. Green Valley had been become a successful company, and as I write this book in 1999, it is still running and I'm sure quite profitable. So the year of 1972 drew to a close and we all were healthy and enjoying a busy life.

338

Part 3
CHAPTER 29
The Greiners in 1973

     The year started off with our taking a load of cattle to a hotel in Las Vegas Nevada for the National Simmentahl Association sale. We were taking some of the purebred imported German Simmentahl, as well as three quarter bred cattle. It was a fancy sale held inside the hotel. Things were flying high in the purebred Simmentahl business. The sale was a success and some of the participants in our company, German Fleckvieh, had purchased some cattle at the Las Vegas show. However, we still had cattle that we had to take back to Denver to the Western Livestock Show. So it ended up that Lois, John Freese, and I drove the truck that was pulling a 24ft gooseneck trailer loaded with cattle back to Denver.

     Things went well until we got to Colorado, where we ran into a snowstorm. Now at this time Interstate 80 was not completed across Colorado, which meant we had to go over Loveland Pass with the load of cattle. We started up over the pass and although the snow plows were out, there was just a trail to follow. We were in low gear going about 15 mph. When young John Freese decided to get scared. This, of course, scared Lois. John was hollering," We will never get to the top! We will never get to the top!. We were about two miles from the top of the pass when a snowplow saw we were going slow. So he turned around, got behind us, and followed us to the top. He would have pushed us if we had stalled out. After we got to the top, John started saying," We will never get down! We will never get down!" This scared Lois some more. I had the urge to kill!! But needless to say, we did get down in fine shape and went along into Denver for the Western Livestock Show and sale.

     We had our first production sale in February at the Kalona, Iowa sale barn and the sale went very well. We sold a German Fleckvieh purebred, that had been imported from Ireland, for 20,000.00 dollars. We also sold a lot of other high priced three quarter blood Simmentahl, as well as other breeds.

We had bred some heifers to Chininia bulls and the calves were only about three weeks old. But people were buying them for $1000 each, putting them in trunks of cars, and leaving the cows. I can remember a lot of the old order Amish, who usually attended the sales at Kalona, just shaking their heads in disbelief.

It was a hectic spring because it was very wet during planting time and we got off to a late start. However the summer turned gorgeous and we had a near-perfect harvesting season. It was the kind of year that farmers dream of. The prices were good, hogs were doing well, and everything looked good. We were doing all minimum tillage farming, had been for several years, and now it became the big trend so most farmers begin doing it. I had been doing it for about 10 years already. It just made it a lot of sense.

We had another production sale in September and this also went very well. The exotic cattle business was really booming at this time. It was good and a lot of fun to be involved in it

We also took cattle to the Houston Fat Stock show and sale at Houston , Texas. It was a big job getting the cattle ready and running out to Clifton, New Jersey to pick up cattle that we imported from Europe.

Early in October Lois, and I flew to England to Mr. Dodds farm, where we purchased 12 head of purebred German Gelbvieh heifers that we could not import, although we did import their offspring. Gelbvieh in German means yellow cattle or gold cattle. The breed of cattle is a dark yellow color. I was convinced this would be a better breed for the American farmer than the Simmentahl. However, the Simmentahl had such a head start on this breed, it would be difficult for them to catch up.

Before Lois, Peter and I went to London I drove up to see my friend, Hugo Maguire, who lived just across the border from Northern Ireland. They had some German Fleckvieh cattle that I wanted to see. Hugo offered to take me up to County Donegal, which is on the north side of six counties that make up Northern Ireland. If we had driven up there and stayed in Ireland, the trip would have taken twice as long, because we would have had to go west quite a ways before going north.

We decided to leave early the next morning and driving across Northern Ireland to get to Donegal. It was apparent when we went across the border what an influence Great Britain had on it. In the South, the roads are narrow and crooked, but as soon as we crossed into Northern Ireland, there were four Lane highways. If the north were to join the South, obviously they would take a decrease in their standard of living. They are not anxious to do that. We drove across Northern Ireland into Donegal and spent all day looking at cattle. We were late starting back for Hugo's home and it was dark when we came through the last little town before getting to the border to cross into the South. As we came through this last village, we noticed all the British Tommies with their machine guns and rifles peeking around corners of the buildings.

Hugo's wife had planned a birthday party for his father that evening. He was driving quite rapidly when we popped up over a hill which was very close to the border, and there was a British tank in the middle-of-the-road with the British Tommies screaming to us for our own safety to turn out the lights. We were right in the middle of a shoot out. Hugo was scared to death and I guess I was too dumb to be scared. There was a lot of firing just before we got there, and then the IRA just disappeared into the hedge rows and were gone. It was exciting for a few minutes. Hugo and his father owned 80 acres of land right on the border, but they would never go back there at night. After dark the IRA used it as practice grounds and the Maguires would always find their empty shell casings. Why does a beautiful little country like this have to be torn apart?

Lois and I went on to Munich, Germany where we attended Octoberfest, which is a spectacle in itself. The Germans really get into it. Actually, Lois got a little bit scared, but I didn't think it was that bad. We loved Bavaria and toured cattle farms and the bull studs, where all the famous German sires are kept. The American farmer would not accept the restraints that are placed on the German farmer. Can't you imagine what an Iowa farmer would say if someone told him that he could not go out and buy and use a bull he liked. But this is the reason that Germans are so far ahead of us in animal genetics. This is true in cattle, swine, sheep and even dogs. After that we went back to Ireland, where we found fields as green as they are fabled to be. There we spent some time with friends and bought 22 Simmentahl to import to the United States for resale. We really enjoyed seeing these countries again and the new friends which we met.

In June Lois, Peter, and Tom drove out to Omaha to a Clare family reunion were they helped Aunt Nellie celebrate her birthday. They had a good time and met members of the family who they hadn't had an opportunity to meet before. We drove to St. Louis with the motor home and picked up Lois's sister's family. Then we headed for the Rio Grande Valley to visit Lois's other sister and her husband. All the children had a fun week together. On this trip when we were out on Padre Island, Tom told me the wheels were coming off, but I paid no attention to him. We were starting back to Mission, Texas from Brownsville, and sure enough, halfway, there the wheel did come off the motor home., Tom said "I told you Dad". He sure did, and from then on, I always paid attention to what Tom said.

The family was growing up. Doug graduated from farm operations and came home to join the farm. Beverly was a senior at Iowa State. Clare and Linda were on the south farm and John and Cathy moved to a farm we rent at the ranch. Tom was in his sixth year at St. Colletta and was 15 in December. Tom enjoyed attending this wonderful school to no end. Thank God for all those wonderful people who were willing to work with these children. Peter got a horse and did a lot of work on the farm. Although he was just 11 years old, he was doing a lot of tractor work which was a big help.

As we look back on 1973 it is hard to imagine that we did all the things that we did during the year. How could anybody had a more interesting and exciting life. I was blessed with good children and a wonderful wife, who was loved by all and everybody's friend. How lucky could a guy be.!!

342

VIEW OF OUR SIGOURNEY HOME FROM THE AIR

THE SWIMMING POOL, BATH HOUSE, AND SAUNA AT SIGOURNEY

Part 3
Chapter 30
On the farm 1974

This has been an exciting year for us and just as busy as always. We have been particularly fond of the way Tom has been doing at St. Coletta's. He is in his seventh year at St. Coletta's is five feet seven inches tall and a handsome young boy. He has made the swim team and won two gold medals at the Wisconsin state Special Olympics. He then went on to the regional Special Olympics in Minnesota in August and won a bronze medal. We are very happy with the way he is progressing. We are so thankful for this wonderful school. This overshadows for Lois and me anything else that could happen.

Things have gone well in the farming operation this year. The Simmentahl business has continued to grow in enthusiasm throughout the United States as well as other exotic breeds. Lois and I attended the Western Livestock Show at Denver as well as the Houston Fat Stock Show and the Kansas City Royal Livestock Show. We sold cattle at some of the sales. Peter especially likes fitting the cattle for the show's, even if it is a lot of work. I must admit this has never been one of my favorite jobs. There have been several sales held in the exhibition place in large hotels at various times. It really has been a fun time for Lois and me ,as we travel to these various shows. You get to meet a many wonderful people.

When John and Cathy came back to the farming operation we had rented a farm close to the ranch for them to live in. The people who owned this farm came back from a sabbatical quicker than they had planned originally. They were with a church group, which meant there was no place for the kids to live.

Lois and I purchased two farms over by Sigourney that totaled about 1000 acres of land. The two farms joined each other. One farm had a huge house that contained 6000 square feet of space. It had been built by a contractor who had decided to move to town. There also was a large outdoor swimming pool and bath house. Just below the house is a beautiful Lake that always seems to have some wildlife around. It is a beautiful home. We would not take possession until March 1st 1975. It is our plans next year to move into this house and then John and Cathy can move into the house on the home farm. Lois is thrilled with being able to plan how she will decorate the house when we move their next spring.

In the cattle business,the Gelbvieh are starting to attract breeders as they are being promoted by a Mr. Hall who is with the Carnation Breeding Service. He maintains that the Gelbveih Bulls in Germany are some of the best he has seen in his life. As he is so well respected a group of us decided that we should form the American Gelbvieh Association. The breed has caught on in Oklahoma. Therefore a group of us met there several times to form the American Gelbvieh association for the registration of the cattle for this breed. Jack Shoup from Rhinebeck Iowa and myself made several trips to Oklahoma and were on the original Board of Directors of this association. It takes a lot of work to get something like this started. The association now has its own headquarters north of Denver CO. As I no longer am involved, it is good to just know I had a part in forming this association and would use it till I left the cattle business.

We have 13 head of pure bred Gelbvieh that will be leaving England next January for their 30 day quarantine in the United States. We have a lot of half breed heifers that were from cows bred last year. Things look good for this breed of cattle however, they have not had the flashy money that the Simmentahl breed has had behind them because they came several years after the Simmentahl.

In June Lois, Beverly, Peter, and I flew to Ireland for a fantastic visit with the Culhane's who are good friends of ours in Ireland. Kevin was a young boy after the war and came to the United States to study the dairy industry by working on farms in our country. He saw how the American farmers worked and took care of their dairy cattle. He could see the way they were doing it in Ireland was very backward. After he went back to Ireland he would go around giving lectures about how the American farmers did their work. The Irish farmers laughed at him because they were used to milking their cows at 8 o'clock in the morning and then going to the creamery with their milk and spending the rest of the day in the pub. Kevin said okay you do it your way and I will do it the American way. As a result he became a very famous Irish farmer and dairyman. Kevin was one of the Irish farmers who was able to import German Fleckvieh and knew a lot of the Irish farmers who had done the same. And it was through him that I had bought other cattle in Ireland to import. They were wonderful hosts and gave us all a great tour of Ireland. Ireland is such a beautiful country but like every where it too is changing.

From Ireland we went on to England where I attended the British Royal livestock show. The Europeans do a tremendous job of putting on livestock shows. They really are superior to anything we do in this country as they add a lot of class to their shows. There is a lot of pomp and circumstances with their shows.

Beverly Peter and Lois toured London and Peter mastered the British subway system and they really enjoyed London which is not my favorite place. Beverly then flew on to Neustadt/Aisch in Bavaria where our good friends Dr. Schwartz lived with his family. Dr. Schwartz has been to our farm several times. Beverly stayed there until August 1 when she returned bringing with her Patrick Schwartz 11 and Oliver 8 for a visit to our farms. They were such wonderful well-trained young boys and we thoroughly enjoyed having them stay with us we took them to the state fair, the county fair, six flags in St. Louis and just had a good time with them. They loved sweet corn and root beer and took a case of root beer with them when they went home. Lois , Peter and I flew back home from London.

In August I flew back to Frankfurt Germany and took the two Schwartz boys with me and was met by Dr. Schwartz and his wife Barbara.. Dr. Schwartz and I then spent some time traveling Bavaria looking at Simmentahl and then up to the Wurtzburg area looking at Gelbvieh cattle. I am always amazed at how far breeding programs have progressed in Germany. Was totally amazed to find out that all male cattle are not castrated in Germany but grown and fed as Bulls. The rate of gain is higher than what we can obtain feeding steers. The meat is not as fat and the rate of gain is higher by doing it this way but in this country you will immediately take a penalty for feeding a young bull to maturity and trying to sell it. Just another tradition from the old days but someday it will change here also but not in my lifetime. We are so slow to change in so many ways in agriculture.

347

We had a good crop on the farm and the hog operation was doing well but since we were so involved with cattle we had cut down somewhat on hogs. So all in all agriculture was treating us well and our farming operation was approaching 5000 acres. It was a big job and Lois and I were glad the family was with us. We felt we primarily had an operation that the children could be involved in. And after all it is your children that give you an interest in life however it does not always work out that way.

Dad Greiner still lives in his house in Keota but is always available for running errands and enjoys going to some of the sales as he loves farm life and is the only thing he ever did. Until he and mother in later years started buying antiques he never had any kind of a hobby. He always thought people who chased little balls around had nothing better to do. He was always there when we needed him for anything.

Beverly started teaching which meant the four older children were through college and we could take a breather until Peter had to go. Tom was still doing very well at St. Coletta's and was home for the usual vacations. We got to know the road very well going back and forth to Jefferson Wisconsin. However, I flew him a lot by airplane back and forth.

We had our first granddaughter Brenna Conway born so we now had two grandchildren and Clare and Linda were trying to adopt a foster child they had. More on that later.

Peter and, Tom showed their calves at 4-H and had no big winners this year blue ribbons and red. Peter was very good about feeding the Calves for Tom while he was in school at St. Coletta's. Peter is in seventh grade and loves going out for football but is such a small child and is the runt of the family. He is good at getting up and taking care of his calves and doing a lot of farm work driving tractors and riding his horse. I had gotten the bug again for another airplane and in November I found an airplane that some young man in Chicago who was president of a steel Co. had bought. It was apparent his father was afraid he would kill himself and made him put the airplane up for sale. It was a beautiful Cessna 185 equipped with all the latest radio equipment and had a Robertson short take off and landing modification. This airplane was so much different and was so much safer to fly and land that you could not stall it. It's take off performance was unbelievable how I enjoyed flying this airplane

348

and the family enjoyed it also. What a machine it was. It only had twenty hours on it. I gave forty thousand dollars for it and to day it would cost a couple hundred thousand if it were still made but is no longer manufactured.

I had a very scary incident in the fall that could have ended up costing me my life. For some reason I seem to have to many of these kind of scares. In our first livestock sale at Kalona we sold an Irish purebred German Fleckvieh heifer that we imported. One of the guarantees in the cattle business on something like this is you guarantee the female to be a breeder. If she is not a breeder you replace her with an animal of equal quality. This is just part of the cattle business.

Clare and Linda were having a hearing at the court house in Bloomfield in front of a judge about adopting the little girl Aletha who we called Ali. I attended this hearing and while I was there and the hearing was going on the Balliff came and told me there was someone who wanted to see me in the hallway. I went out into the hall and there was a lady there with a cowboy hat and cowboy boots who said she and her husband were the people who had bought the Irish heifer that had turned out to be a non-breeder. I had absolutely no idea who this woman was as I had never seen her before in my life even at the sale where her husband had bought the animal. He had written to me and I contacted the people in Ireland and they had a replacement animal in Indiana and I had already flown out there to look at the animal which was to be a replacement. They had been notified of this.

She suggested that we go down and sit in her car and talk about it. I agreed seeing nothing wrong with that. When we got to her car she had me sit under the steering wheel and she said she would get in the back seat. She had the right front seat piled up with clothes or something. I agreed and got into the car and so did she.

Her next words were "How would you like to have this in the kidneys". I turned around to see that she had a revolver pointed in my back. She handed me the keys to her car and said "Back out I want you to go to your bank and return me the money we paid you for the heifer we bought." It was 3 p.m. then and the banks close at 3:00 and we were still 60 miles from the bank. I told her there was no way I could get the money. We went out

349

onto the highway and headed for Ottumwa. By this time I am beginning to see that this woman is crazy as a loon. I felt my only chance was to talk to her and just keep talking. After we got to Ottumwa she insisted I call the bank. We stopped on North Court Street by a phone booth and we both got out of the car where she held the gun under her coat or sweater. Of course by this time the bank was closed and nothing was accomplished. We got back into the car and I started driving all the time listening to her tell a bout her terrible childhood. Of various marriage problems, and of course, I was agreeing with her, knowing that my only chance was to keep talking to her. She had no idea where we were going, just to say take this road then that road to where we ended up in Des Moines, where we then went north out of Des Moines and later ended up at 10:00 p.m. NW of Webster City, Iowa. We had a full tank of gas when we left Bloomfield. It was easy to see she had this thought out quite well. It was about 10:30 pm when I said "Lady I don't care what you do but I have to pee" after setting that long I pulled onto a dirt road somewhere NW of Webster City and got out of the car. After I got back into the car she replied "Now you know my license number" my reply was " I really don't need it, why don't you put that gun away and we will go back to the Boondocks and go back home and talk about this tomorrow. After listening to her for eight hours I was feeling sorry for her also but I also knew she had something missing. She finally laid the gun on the floor and got out of the car and she took care of mother nature and got into the front seat.

We drove back to the Boondocks on Interstate 80 and I got on the phone to call Lois. By this time the family was frantic looking for me as the Mercedes was setting on the street in Bloomfield and I had completely disappeared. No one had any idea where I was. When Lois answered the phone she was frantic and I explained to her only that I had a lady with me and where I was and that I was all right and would be home in a couple of hours. By this time this woman was half starved to death so we ate a sandwich and headed back to the farm. When we arrived to the farm at Sigourney Lois could not believe what had happened. We put her in Beverly's bedroom and I will admit this is the first time we ever locked our bedroom door for the rest of the night.

The next morning I took her to Washington to where my attorney was. We then call her husband in Montana who had no idea where she was or what had happened. By this time she was begging me not tell her husband what had happened. I knew that they were under a lot of stress and that the bank was pressuring them for payment of the money they had used to buy the heifer and she admitted it was her idea to do it. We worked out an agreement and I then thought I wonder if there are any shells in that revolver. I went out to her car opened the trunk where I had put the revolver and sure enough, each chamber had a 22 long rifle shell in it. Had I tried to take this gun away this woman was in such a state of mind that she would have shot me.

After we left the attorney's office I made her return me to Bloomfield where I picked up the Mercedes and came on back home thanking my lucky stars that the family was not preparing for a funeral. Just another one of the times when it seems like the Lord has kept me here for some reason. This was another one of those experiences that I do not care to repeat. So ends the years history.

I could have charged her with kidnapping and attempted murder but what was to be gained by doing that. I was just happy to be alive and do more fun things in life. Thank you Lord for letting me live.

OUR IRISH FRIENDS IN IRELAND. KEVIN CULHANE ,PETER MARY CULHANE AND HOWARD ON TRIP TO IRELAND.

351

FRONT VIEW OF SIGOURNEY HOME

352

PETER AND HIS HORSE. HE WAS A GOOD RIDER.

PART 3
Chapter 31
The Greiners in 1975

      This is a big year for Lois and me as we are moving to the new farm we bought near Sigourney. I have lived on the farm at Wellman for 52 two years and I have always felt that when I moved from that farm the world would end. It has been my home for so many years and I had had so many wonderful times on that farm. But I never look back After we were moved into the new home it seemed like we had lived there all our married life. We would have many wonderful times in the next few years and also sometimes of stress.

      After we moved out of the home farm at Wellman our daughter Cathy and her husband John Conway moved into the home farm. They now had two children so they would enjoyed the home farm. Our son Doug then moved to a farm north of us at Sigourney where he was a confirmed bachelor at that time.

      Dad Greiner who is now 80 years old and has lived in his house in keota alone was a worry to us. We asked Dad if he would like to move in with us and he did not hesitate for a moment. His house was full of beautiful antique furniture and a lot of very high-quality cut glass and Bavarian China and cranberry glass. Before my mother passed away she decided which of us three children would get what piece or pieces of furniture. She had made a list so that settled a lot of problems that develop's in so many families . He then gave each of us three children and the grandchildren a credit of $3000.00 each and then he had an auction just among the family to dispose of the rest of his furniture and glassware. If you've spent over the amount he gave you credit for you had to come up with the cash. It worked beautifully and after Dad sold his house he moved in with us at Sigourney. He was quite healthy and still like to pick corn and cut weeds such as the thistle and burdock. He also continued to be the one called on when a trip was needed for parts or anything else. He enjoyed doing it and was always available and Lois and I felt very comfortable having him with us. My dear wife Lois was so good to my father and he also loved her although my old German father never could express himself the way younger people do. The word love was not in his vocabulary even though he expressed it physically. Lois was a wonderful cook and could make things that made your mouth water. Now my father loved to eat and one time Lois had made some custard where she always used Mexican vanilla to make it. It was wonderful and my father was eating some of this and he said to her " Lois keep plenty of this on hand". We always laughed because this was the closest thing to a complement I think I ever heard my father say. From his younger years he had mellowed as do we all.

The summer of 1975 was very hot and dry and it was not the greatest corn crop that we had ever raise and in the fall of the year we had a tremendous when storm that made it difficult to harvest a crop as so much of it had been blown down. But that is the one thing with farming you take what is handed to you can do the best with it that you can. I think that is one of the things that alloys frustrated me about farming. You had so little control over what you are doing and no control over the pricing of your product.

The cattle businesses continuing and we had a Gelbvieh sale in October which was quite successful but the prices of cattle had been slipping. Heifers we had hoped to bring 15 to 18 thousand dollars each averaged about $12,000 on the sale. Even though this sounds like a lot of money to import cattle paid to having flown across the ocean by airplane plus the quarantine expense is expensive. We had a large party at the house the night before the auction and of course we had it advertised quite well so a lot of local people attended the sale. They were quite flabbergasted when the first 10 animals averaged about 12,000 dollars each. This is just because they were not up on what was going on in the exotic cattle breeds. But it was fun but a lot of work.

We done our usual amount of traveling to various livestock shows throughout the country. Our good friends Mary and Kevin Culhane came over from Ireland. Along with Mary and Baxter Freese we took the motor home to the Houston Livestock show. After the show we headed west across Texas and then went down to Chihuahua Mexico and got on the train across the Sierra Madre Mountains to Copper Canyon. (This is larger than the Grand Canyon) and then onto Los Mochis on the West Coast where we stayed for four days and then returned on the same train. It was a fascinating trip and the engineering of that railroad across the Grand Canyon is really quite an accomplishment. It was a fascinating trip and we enjoyed it thoroughly. In this year 1999 it is advertised as a wonderful trip and I would agree. At each stop the little Mexican girls would get on the train and beg for lipstick and it would be so much fun to deal with the vendors. After returning to Chihuahua we picked up the motor home and came back to Iowa. It really was a fun trip.

Clare and Linda adopted a new son Brian . This was their second child and the number of our grandchildren is growing and Lois loves every minute of it. Our son, Tom is growing up and is still at St. Coletta's and was 17 and is in the senior program at that school. It has been such a wonderful experience for him and for us.

Peter and I went to Oklahoma City for a Gelbvieh cattle show and sale on December second. We also had some meetings with the organization of the national association and it was coming along quite good. Jack Shoup and I were both founding directors of the association.

We had our usual number of visitors and Lois was always cooking and planning for company. She was a wonderful hostess and everyone loved her. The swimming pool data a lot of use and the job of maintaining it pretty well fell to Peter and LOIS and if anyone thinks that a swimming pool outside does not take a lot of work had better not have a swimming pool. We certainly found that you become a slave to these things. Just below the swimming pool on the new farm was a beautiful pond. One morning LOIS looked out our bedroom window and said what is the matter with the swimming pool. Why does it looked like it is moving. I got up and went down to the pool and found it was alive with salamanders. We dipped out a five gallon bucket full of salamanders. Evidently they moved up from the pond to the swimming pool during the night. Always something new. We had a wonderful German shepherd named Rex who loved to take a daily dipp in the pool. He was huge and scared a lot of people but was really a big Bluff. In the wintertime the ground sloped down to the pool and when there was snow on the ground Rex would lay on his back and slide down the hill. We used to look out our kitchen window and laughed at his performance.

Before we moved from the farm at Wellman a couple of my good friends from Sigourney area David Noller and Wayne Morrison and there may have been a third person came over to our farm and presented a problem to me. In Keokuk County there was one fair grounds located at What Cheer Iowa which was in the North West corner of the county. This was privately owned and my friends did not think the 4-H children got a fair shake from them. They wanted to know if I would get involved with building a new 4-H fair grounds ,and help lead this project for the county's children. Since Peter was still in 4-H I thought I should and in the summer of 1975 we done all the necessary steps to get this accomplished. It took a lot of community effort and volunteers. I had a trench and a back hoe to lay all water lines and put in plumbing and so forth. Some of the group wanted to build small livestock barns and I was dead set against this and laid out a building that would hold all the livestock under one roof. Probably the only county fair in the state that has this potential. After the fair the building can be used for other things and rented for storage. We built a 78x380 ft.pole building that included in it a sales arena for judging and for livestock sales that will seat 500 people. We build an additional 50 by 140 ft. block building to house home economics and other uses.

At that time we instituted a carcass competition in an effort to broaden the 4-H and FFA members educational opportunities for livestock. It was a progressive step forward for a livestock buildings and a fair ground. I think until this day it is the only one in the state of Iowa that handles all the livestock under one roof. This did not happen without a lot of work from a lot of people none of home got paid. The fair has operated since 1976 the year it was built and it is my understanding that all the land has been paid for and it is doing well. I spent a lot of the summer working at the fair grounds.

TOM AND HIS TWO SPECIAL OLYMPIC MEDALS IN THE WISCONSIN STATE MEET HE WAS AN EXCELLENT SWIMMER WHILE AT SAINT COLLETA

Part 3
Chapter 32
The Greiners in1976

      On June 19th our second daughter, Beverly, was married at St. Mary's church in Sigourney to Russell Rutten. We held the reception out on the farm and it was a fun day. It is so good to see your children growing up and maturing. There were a couple hundred guests and the young kids had a great time swimming in the swimming pool, with plenty of room to run. We cleaned out the three-car garage and had a little dance band. The bar downstairs did a good amount of business. The only thing wrong was I should have been charging for the drinks. But we really had a great time and we welcomed Russell into the family. Lois was in the height of her glory, cooking and entertaining people. She was such a wonderful hostess.

      This seemed to be the year for our children to get married. Last year our son, Doug, and Marcia Vittetoe announced their plans to get married at the same time as Russell and Beverly. Doug and Marcia were married at St. James Church in Washington, Iowa on April 23rd. They had a lovely wedding and reception and moved into a house on the farm at Sigourney. We now had Tom and Peter left.

      Since I was mentioning Lois, this was the year that we went to Iowa City for a doctor's appointment on February 4th. I had taken a record player along for repair. We pulled into a parking space and got out of the car. There had been an ice storm previously, but all the ice was gone except for some on a curb that faced north. As Lois walked around the car to where I opened the trunk, she stepped on this ice and both feet went out from under her. I picked her up and she sat in the car a few minutes when she finally said, "I believe I hurt myself." She was to go to her gynecologist but instead we went to the Steinler orthopedic clinic. From the clinic we were sent to the hospital. She had badly broken her left shoulder. After we got home, I really found out how important she was to me. I can tell you that I became an expert on putting on pantyhose. It took a couple months for Lois to get back into the swing of things.

The following December third we had went to Washington to a party at our lawyers home. When we came home it was snowing quite badly and for some reason the automatic door opener on the garage would not work. Lois said "Honey I will open it for you". She then got out of the car opened the garage door and it was a heated garage. When she stepped on the warm floor with snow on her shoes both feet went out from under her again. I did not see it happen and I didn't know where she went as she was laying on the floor in front of the car. I got out of the car and picked her up and took her into the kitchen. She said "Honey I think I've done it again". It was now midnight and I called the doctor. We went into Sigourney to the hospital and they immediately sent us to Iowa City were x-ray showed she had broken her right shoulder. I was glad I had the experience of being trained in putting on pantyhose. Because we went through the same ritual again. From then on LOIS always said I don't do ceilings. As she could not raise her arms above her shoulders. Not one word of complaint had I ever heard from her lips or did she ever feel sorry for herself.

That summer Dr.Edwin Schwartz from Germany sent a young boy Karl Fraundorffer over to stay with us a month on the farm. He was to see how we done things in America. Then a young man from New Zealand by the name of Marcus Williams came and stayed with us a for a couple of months. Our house was always like a motel and it was a good thing the kitchen table would seat 12 people at a time. It usually was about full. For a lady who could not boil water when I married her her she had turned into a fantastic cook. She always said that our living with Mother and Dad Greiner for two years after we were married was a great education on cooking.

Tom was still at St. Coletta's and is on the swim team and is turning into quite a swimmer. He won two more gold medals in the special Olympics at Kenosha WI. How fortunate we have been for this wonderful school. He had a great time showing his calves at the fair along with Peter. Peter is now a freshman in high school. He had the grand champion heifer at the county fair in August and also showed in Des Moines, at the Iowa State Fair and the Kansas City royal livestock show. He really loves

360

showing cattle and has turned into quite a steer jockey.

We had a very dry fall but the corn crop was quite good. We had a Gelbvieh sale on Oct. 16 and a Simmentahl sale on December 18th. The cattle business has shown signs of slowing down.

My interest in green Valley chemical Co. was still there and I was wholesaling anhydrous ammonia and dry fertilizer. However I was finding it more difficult each year to sell my quota of anhydrous ammonia as I was getting too far removed from the fertilizer business. I was starting to entertain the possibility of selling my interest in green Valley chemical.

I had made a decision that turned out to be one of the worst decisions that I have made in whole life. But if you asked me today 23 years later why I done that I could not give you an intelligent answer. Only that I thought there was a need for this type of operation. This decision was to build a meat packing plant on the farm. I had spent considerable time in Germany and seeing how far ahead of the United States they were in processing meat by vacuum processing. We think nothing of it today to buy meat processed that way. But as time has showed me I again was 10 years at head of my time.

I flew to Germany to the DLG show where they displayed all of the latest meat packing equipment made in Germany. I had contracted with an architect from Omaha to design a packing plant for killing cows that would meet USDA rules and regulations for the processing of meat. I had a rough idea of the equipment I needed before going to Germany. It all was very expensive equipment the best that could be bought anywhere. I had started a new corporation called Rawhide Ranch Bavarian meats and made plans to bring to the United States a German sausage maker. Dr. Schwartz in Germany had lined up a young man who was interested in coming to the United States. I met with him in Germany and made plans to see if I could get a visa for him to come to the United States it took a longtime to get this visa approved.At that time Farmers Home Administration had a rural agriculture loan program that I applied for to build the meat plant. The loan was for just about one million dollars. However it was not approved in the year 1976 I had all these plans in the works as it takes a longtime and took several trips to Washington D.C. to the agriculture department to get these plans approved. I was going to be my own contractor and that part would work out okay. But plans had been made in 1976 to start construction of this project in 1977. You will see as we go long with the story of my life that this was a fateful decision. Everything we do in lifeis timing and luck. And I had had that for a number of years but my well was about to run dry because I could not foresee two things.One was the disastrous farm.period coming and the terrible high interest rates of the economy that developed during the Carter administration. The other disaster was my ideas on packaging and processing meat were 10 years too soon. This was the beginning of a very stressful time. However I did not see that in 1977 it was yet to come. But the groundwork was laid that year.

WOW! LOOK AT THAT HAIR AND THAT POLYESTER JACKET
TAKENAT THE WESTERN LIVESTOCK SHOW IN DENVER 1971

CONSTRUCTION OF THE MEAT PLANT AT SIGOURNEY

RETAIL SALES PORTION OF THE MEAT PLANT

SPEAKER AT THE NATIONAL GELBVIEH CONVENTION IN DENVER
IN 1976 AT WESTERN LIVESTOCK SHOW AND SALE

364

PART 3
CHAPTER 32
The Greiners In 1977

The good thing to say about 1977 was that good things came in pair is with the birth of two grandchildren. Suzanne Greiner and Kelly Conway entered into our families. The family keeps growing and we are getting older.

We got our corn crop and beans planted in good shape and are calf crop was good. The prices had slipped considerably but these kind of fluctuations go with the farm business. We always hope for better times.

I had received approval for the loan from the farmers home administration for the meat packing plant in early spring. As soon as the crops were planted I started the earth work for the two lagoons that were required to handle the wastewater. I had purchased a large scraper to pull behind one of the four-wheel-drive tractors and spends hours of hours moving dirt to build the lagoons. There were so many things to do to get started building. We had to meet all the environmental rules and regulations and were required to look for dead Indians and all the other nonsense required. There was no contracting done on building the plant except we did hire people who laid the concrete block, the refrigeration specialists, the roof work and the electrical work All of the rest of the work we did ourselves. That included installing all the insulation, glass board in all the coolers and freezers and in the kill floor. We also did all the labor and carpenter work in the offices and the retail office. Believe me all that involves many long hours and hard work. It was a big project and we would be until May of 1978 of getting the plant ready to start killing cows. To get all of this work completed, so that the USDA would approve, required many hours of working at night as well as working all-day. There was so much to do and so much to learn.

By October 1st we had the block work all done and brought in the big cranes to place that heady concrete beams and roof supports over the plant. After we got the plant enclosed it made it much easier to work as we were out of the weather. We had to send our semi to Casper, Wyoming five times to haul back bentonite to line the lagoons. I would have been ahead to have taken that money and throwing it into the wind but we had to show USDA the receipts for the material to satisfy them Much nonsense. It had become apparent to me that just satisfying the USDA meat inspectors would be a full-time job.

In June Lois and I had flown to Frankford Germany to the meat packers convention to order the equipment that I wanted for the plant. It was very expensive equipment however it was the best available. We also met again with the German sausage maker and his wife that we were trying to get to the United States. We still had not received approval for his visa but we were trying desperately to get it done so we could get him over here. There were long waiting periods to get equipment to the United States. As the I sit here thinking about all of the work and the frustration I went through it almost makes me sick to my stomach. But the worst was yet to come and unfortunately had I known then what I know now I would have stopped the project.

Several things happened this year some good some bad. Daughter Beverly and her husband Russ joined the farm operation and moved onto the one of our farms west of Keota. The bad thing was Lois was taking Dad Greiner to Iowa City on March 22 which was his birthday as he was feeling sick and needed to go to the hospital. It was a terrible day and it was raining and snowing and the roads became very slick. They were about five miles outside of Iowa City when a young man driving far too fast caught up with a string of cars and just as Lois came by lost control of his car and hit Lois and Dad head on. Totally demolishing both cars.

I was in Ottumwa at a meeting when I got the word. I left immediately for the Iowa City hospital. I found Lois in a wheelchair badly shaken but okay except for a broken clavicle. Fortunately the Mercedes had seat belts on it and Lois had hers hooked up. By this time already were the lap belt went across her legs she had hit the belts so hard that those places filled up with blood and water and they had to draw it off. The shoulder belt is what broke her clavicle. We had had the Mercedes about ten months and she felt so bad that she wrecked it and I could have cared less. The important thing was she was not hurt too bad.

It was a different story with my father as he was very badly hurt. He did not believe in seat belts and would never wear one.

He did wear them after that. At the time of the accident it threw him into the windshield in front of Lois and he was in intensive care at Mercy in Iowa City for four weeks. We did not know if he would live or not. He was delirious a lot of the time and was planning his funeral telling Lois and I that we were to be sure and feed the crowd real good. We often laughed at this because Dad did like to eat. However he did recover an and after he got back to the farm it took only about another four weeks and he was back to his old self. If he had not been a tough old bird he would not have made it. He was 81 years old the date of the accident

Between Lois and I, this was the third head on auto accident that we have had in our married life. Not a one of these were we at fault. We were just in the wrong place at the wrong time proving again that timing is everything. As I have always said timing and luck determines everything in business and in our life. There were six automobiles totaled out and yet we both were still alive even though we had suffered our share of injuries. Thank you Lord for letting us live.

The weather had been terrible this year we had a very dry summer for the corn crop , it did help me in doing the dirt work for the plant. Corn yields were cut considerably and then in the fall it turned terribly wet, and all but made corn harvesting impossible particularly on the ranch. That soil never dries out very fast. The farmers are all having protests about the low prices. It has been a tough year on the farm.

Tom will graduate from St. Coletta school in June. He will then enter their vocational training program. Tom is 19 years old and six-foot tall. We are proud of his progress and do not regret all the miles and time it has taken us over the years going back and forth to St. Coletta's. He was home during the 4-H fair and likes to show his calves, of course he has Peter looking over his shoulders, who by now has become what you could call a professional steer jockey.

Since my original investment in green Valley chemical I had doubled that investment. I had opportunity to sell my stock to a fellow stockholder for $600,000 to be paid in the next three years. It was an excellent time for me to sell my stock and I think it is the highest price per share of stock that was ever sold in Green Valley Chemical. I was relieved of not having to sell my quota of anhydrous ammonia. I had a full plate working with the meat plant and dealing with the terribly low values in farm products. I certainly had a great experience helping put this plant together and serving on the board those years. It was the most profitable business I have ever owned.

We had our usual number of visitors to the farm and Lois was always glad to have them. Everyone loved her because she made people feel so much at home. This was just the same way her parents treated me when I was in the service. Who says genetics aren't passed along.

We drove to Casper in February for the wedding of our niece Debby Clare. We had not been back to Casper for five years. Our traveling was somewhat reduced because I was so involved with the meat plant construction. So goes 1977

CONSTRUCTION IN PROGRESS

PART 3
CHAPTER 34
The Greiners in 1978

Things were so busy that I think I forgot to record that Collette Conway was born December 5th, 1977. She was be our seventh grandchild. Our oldest daughter Cathy and John Conway now had four children.

In February Joseph and Madelon Rohrmeier, our German sausage maker and his wife, showed up at the Cedar Rapids airport unannounced, because we had sent the visas that we received in January to them. The people at the airport finally figured out where these people were trying to get to and called us, so we drove to Cedar Rapids to welcome them into our home. We had to find a place for them to live and get settled in Sigourney. They had two young children so our motel (our house) was full again. But Lois enjoyed having them.

We were still working frantically on the plant and Joseph pitched into help with the construction. We finished with the construction about May 8th and had our first run at killing cows that day. It went rather slow as the help was all inexperienced, and of course, we had three USDA inspectors looking down our necks. We had a beautiful retail section and Joseph was ready to start filling the cases with his specialty sausages.

The conditions in agriculture were starting to get quite severe. The same year that I opened our plant two identical cow kill plants closed in Iowa. It had turned into an unprofitable business and they could not survive. After killing cows for about six months and losing from one hundred fifty to two hundred dollars per head, I could see it was a losing battle and we closed the kill floor. It was apparent that this could not be turned into a profitable operation quick enough to continue.

As we did not have problems enough, the meat packers union decided to organize the union at our plant. This was just what I needed! We protested, but I did not want to spend the money fighting it, so a vote was held and they won. However, it did them

369

little good in the end because we never were profitable and we did not have to deal with their nonsense.

I had brought vacuum packaging equipment from Germany to package meat in individual packages. We sent our salesmen out with these products to call on the supermarkets and we met one hundred percent resistance to this packaging. The comment we heard at that time was "Who will buy meat looking like that?" As we all know today, we buy vacuum packaged meat everywhere. However, we were 10 to 15 years too soon. The story of my life.

We started manufacturing meat snacks, which were comparable to the "Slim Jim" product that is sold today in every convenience store. That product was made from beef, and we also developed a product that we called "Porkey Stick" that was made from all pork. The convenience store market was just beginning to develop and we made some progress into that market.

We had a terrible scare in the summer. When Peter's cousin, Mark Sweeney, was up visiting, he was showing off the kill chute and tripped it. Peter made the mistake of having his fingers under the heavy iron chute which nearly severed three of his fingers. I raced him to the hospital and our Thai Doctor scrubbed and cleaned, and scrubbed and cleaned, before sewing Peter's fingers back. For three or four days, it looked like his fingers would be all right when he suddenly started getting red streaks up his hand into his arm. We took him back to the doctor and he took one look and ordered us to go immediately to Iowa City. We took Peter to Iowa City and they soon discovered that he had gaseous gangrene. He was one sick boy and the doctors really went to work on him to try and get ahead of the infection. They told Lois and I that it was a very serious situation. When I told our doctor who was from Thailand that he had gaseous gangrene, he later told me that he thought Peter would die. So many people died from that in Thailand. However, it worked out that Peter did recover and has some fingers that are scarred. But he was one mighty lucky boy!

Tom was still at Saint Colletta's at Jefferson, Wisconsin and was attending their vocational training program. They were training him for apartment living and basically how to take care of himself. He had become an expert on the presidents of the United

States and anything you want to know about the Civil War or the railroads in America he could tell you.

Peter was still having a ball working with livestock shows and cattle. This year he showed calves at our local fair and also the Kansas City Royal livestock show. However, my father always said, "Did you ever see a rich steer jockey?"

Our oldest son, Clare, and his wife decided to leave the ranch. If there was anything I needed at this time it was to have him leave when I was so involved with the meat packing plant. I had made up my mind to list the ranch for sale and rid ourselves of that responsibility so far away. Farm prices were still up good, even though the livestock business was slipping. I had put the ranch together at about an average cost of 700 dollars per acre and had a chance to sell it for 1400 dollars per acre and I took it. That relieved me of some responsibility.

Our cattle business was just holding its own and our oldest son, Doug, and sons-in-law, John Conway and Ross Rutten, were doing a good job handling that phase of the business, as well as the farming. I was one hundred percent tied up with the packing plant at that time.

Dad Greiner turned 82 this year, and was doing very well. He still loved to be involved with the boys in the farming operation. However, he was convinced that Peter was spoiled rotten and would never amount to anything. I will agree he was his mother's favorite.

In January, six of us farm couples flew to Cancun, Mexico. Cancun was just getting started and we rented a wonderful Villa and just had a perfect holiday exploring the Mayan ruins. We planned to do it again the next year. There was no trip to Europe this year as I was too involved in trying to get the packing plant into the black. Lois planned for all the family to be at our house for Christmas. She really enjoyed doing this. What would I do without her!

I spent some time in traction in November with a bad back and was beginning to think there had to be an easier way. By this time I was thoroughly enjoying my acquaintances with the Indian Hills Community College at Ottumwa. I enjoyed this very much as all the board members were terrific people, as well as the staff. It was an unusual institution and still is today.

LOIS AND HOWARD LEAVING FOR TEN DAYS IN NEW YORK
AND PHILADELPHIA IN1962

Part 3
Chapter 35
The Greiners in 1979

       The fateful decision I had made to build the meat plant was starting to tear at the farm operation as I tried to keep both going. However I found it necessary to start selling off some of the other farmland. At this time I was still convinced I could get this plant into the black. At least my old stubborn German heritage was telling me that. We were losing 25 to 30,000 dollars per month in the meat plant. I was desperate to come up with something to make it profitable.

       We were manufacturing a lot of meat snacks but we could not get enough volume to carry the overhead of this large of a plant. About the middle of the year I developed a pork snack that we called" Porkey Stick". This was a product that was made of one hundred percent pork and was a very good item. We packaged them just as a slim Jim product is packed today. I took this product to North Carolina to Goodmark a company that makes slim Jim and has a national market. They contracted with us to manufacture this product for them. We geared up to do this but as business conditions deteriorated under the Carter administration at the close of this year they notified us they would no longer honor their contract. Just what I needed. There were times when my spirits weren't too high but fortunately my dear wife was there for me to lean on and to give me encouragement. All through these stressful times my father never once criticized me for making the decision of building the plant. He realized how hard I was working at trying to make this operation succeed.

       My son-in-law Russell and daughter Beverly informed Lois and I that they were going to be leaving the farm and moving to Waterloo. I therefore decided to sell the farms they were living on and cut down some more the farming operation. This was starting to leave us shorthanded for the cattle operation.In the middle of the summer I decided to completely liquidate our cattle operation and we scheduled a dispersal sale to be held at Platte City MO on October 22nd and 23rd. This would remove from my back the cattle operation. John Conway and Doug done a great job in preparing the cattle for the dispersal sale and it when quite well.

Our crops in 1979 were wonderful and set new records due to favorable weather conditions all year so we could not complain on that phase of our operation. In the fall Doug joined me in trying to get the meat plant into production. There were so many things that I wanted to try such as feeding cattle with no hormones or growth stimulants but I could never get any of these programs approved by the USDA. They now allow this but again I was too soon showing again timing is everything.

Lois and I vacationed in Cancun Mexico with the same friends that were with us last year. We stayed at the same Villa and I became a little restless so Lois and I took one of the vans and headed south towards Belize. We saw a crude little sign that said Resorta with a trail leading through the jungle toward the coast. We thought what the heck we will follow that trail and see where it goes. It led us to a Mexican resort on the most beautiful Beach you can imagine. It was not fancy at all but just fascinating. It was owned by a Mexican and had small concrete block cabins and a restaurant. We stayed two days and spent our time walking up-and-down this beautiful Beach that saw very few people. The restaurant faced the jungle and was wide open for cooling as there was no air conditioning. While we were eating breakfast we saw a rat come out of the jungle and run into the restaurant. I motioned to the waiter and told him what he had behind his refrigerator. His reply was"OH we used to have cats to keep the rats away but they would set on the tables and we would rather have the rats". LOIS and I enjoyed this place so much and its beautiful beaches that we thought what the heck if it don't bother them it won't bother us. My attitude has always been if you cannot accept what the people in another country does then stay home.

Tom has completed all his courses at St Colletta and we have enrolled him in the Strauss Kephart program at Indian Hills community college for two years. We are so thankful that this has turned out the way it has for Tom. Lois has always been so concerned about this son.

Lois and I went to New Orleans to a convention where we were displaying our line of meat snacks and we had been making numerous shows in Chicago at McCormick Place and other places promoting our products. You never know whether these shows will do you good or not. But it did give me a break away from the meat plant. As we went through Jackson MS the Mercedes had some kind of a problem that I cannot now recall but it was not very serious. We stopped at a Mercedes and Audi dealer and there was this beautiful red Audi that LOIS just loved. We were in need of a second car and it ended up that I bought it and she and I drove both cars back to Sigourney. It was the first new car Lois ever had to drive in our married life that she could call her own. She really enjoyed this automobile and it served as well. I had the Mercedes for many years and when I get rid of it in had over 300,000 miles on it. It to serve me well.

That summer Lois's family had a reunion in Casper at her brother Jim's home and all her brothers and sisters were there. Lois enjoyed her family very much.

In October of that year Pope John Paul II came to Des Moines. Lois's cousin Sister Timothia was administrator of Mercy hospital in Des Moines and along with other relatives asked us to join them. Now if anybody would have ever told me that I would spend five hours standing in a field waiting for someone to come I would have told them they were crazy. But we done just that and I will have to admit that it was very stimulating experience to see so many people in such a happy mood. It just so happens that 20 years later in fact today he he is arriving in St. Louis MO and I would enjoy seeing him again. So the year 1979 comes to a close with all of the family being with us for Christmas and this is the most important thing of all.

PART 3
Chapter 36
The Greiners in 1980

We always have to start with one of the things that is important to most people and that is your children and your grandchildren. Doug and Marcia had a new baby boy in January who they named Ross Albert after Grandpa Albert. Russ and Beverly showed up at a family party in May with a beautiful adopted girl born May 11th named Marisa Anne. Needless to say this makes LOIS very happy as she is a wonderful grandmother. I must admit that I am not the greatest grandfather in the world and rarely found time to spend with my grandchildren. We are now manufacturing little Smokey's for Dubuque, 'Morrell, and Rath packing Co. It has been quite a battle and maybe we are gaining on it. I'm still trying to find a volume product that would utilize the whole plant. With the 20 plus percent interest rates and poor farm economy nothing is easy.This year Doug and Marcia made a difficult decision and Doug decided to leave the farm and the meat plant and go back to Iowa State University to enter computer engineering. Doug found it very difficult to come and tell Lois and I however we had to agree with him that this was a smart decision. It has turned out to be so and we both encouraged him to do it. So they moved to Ames and started school again. Marcia who was a court reporter started doing that again to help pay for school.

Peter was state district vice president of FFA and this has been a wonderful experience for him. He has been doing a lot of traveling and speaking at various meetings and has enrolled at Iowa State University as a freshman this year. He showed the grand champion heifer at the fair last summer and was thrilled to know end.

Dad greiner is 84 this year and his health is quite good. Clare and Linda bought a farm south of Chariton Iowa and he dearly loves to go over and stay with them. Linda is so good to him and such a good cook that I think he thoroughly enjoys being withthem. Farm life will never be taken out of my father. That is all he has ever known and all he will ever open up his mind for.

Tom is in his second year at the Strauss Kephart program in Indian Hills Community College. And is doing quite well and talks everybody to death about the railroads. His mind is like a computer but it is closed to things like mathematics as this just does not interest him.John is doing the farming and thoroughly enjoys it. He is the only one of the family who is still involved in the farming operation. I guess I have to thank the Lord for a great son-in-law. Lois had her 40th class reunion in Casper and we drove out for it. She graduated from Casper high school and a quite large reunion. She thoroughly enjoyed it and I enjoyed it also. We stayed with her brother Jim and Alice for a great time. Her sister Mary and Jack also came from Texas and we had a terrific visit.1980 was a good year on the farm as we had perfect summer weather and a beautiful fall harvest. We still have a lot to be thankful for.

I'm still very much enjoying serving on Indian Hills Board of Directors. It is a great institution and there are always new ideas coming up so the board meetings always have something to look forward to.

TOM GRADUATING FROM INDIAN HILLS COLLEGE IN THE STRAUSS KEPHART PROGRAM

SISTER PATRICIA CLARE SULLIVAN PRESIDENT
OF MERCY HOSPITAL MEDICAL CENTER DSM.

PART 3
Chapter 37
The Greiners In 1981

In May we had to take Peter to Sioux City Iowa to participate in an FFA convention of which he was a state vice president. Our son Tom asked if he could go along and go to South Dakota and visit Renee who lived at Parkston. Renee and Tom went to school together all the years they were both at St. Colletta's. They had started school at the same time and many times when we were at the school we would be with her folks and go out for dinner together. Lois said it would be fine so we took Tom to South Dakota after leaving Peter off at Sioux City for his convention.

Tom and Renee were glad to see each other and while the two children were together they decided they would like to get married. This came as a shock to us as well as her folks. Neither of us parents had ever thought that our children would get married. After discussing it between both sets of parents we decided why not. Neither of the children had any close friends because they were in school away from home all those years.

So on Sept. 26, Tom and Renee were married in Parkston South Dakota in a big wedding. All of our family was there as were all of friends of the Borman's. Tom and Renee moved into the little house where John and Cathy live and they will look after their needs and Tom will help John on the farm.

The meat plant continues to go through some pretty rough times. We had an agreement with a packing company. to package and process bacon for them. We just started doing this in October and we really are just starting to get our feet on the ground with that project. Frustrations, frustrations

Dad Greiner was hospitalized in Iowa City and had prostate surgery and seem to recover from it in very good shape. He was 86 years old and doing quite well and looks at about 75. Something that affected my life developed with my dear Lois in November Lois had always gone to a gynecologist religiously every six months in Iowa City. She had an appointment June 29th with her regular doctor and at that time told him she'd had a tender spot on her breast and thought she was getting an inverted nipple. This quack just felt of her breast and said you are all right come back in six months. November 22nd she found a lump in her breast while taking a shower. She did not want to worry me with all the problems I had so she made an appointment with the doctor in Sigourney. She did not tell me until she came home that evening that the doctor at Sigourney wanted to perform a biopsy immediately. It about rolled me over however I did not show that to Lois but said we would conquer it. The biopsy proved to be positive and we immediately made appointments to go to Iowa City with doctors at Mercy hospital.

They informed us that Lois needed a modified radical mastectomy and the sooner the better. So on December 3rd Lois was operated on for the removal of her right breast and lymph nodes. The lymph nodes proved to be positive and it was recommended that chemotherapy be started soon as possible. Mercy hospital did not do chemotherapy at that time and we would have had to go to University Hospitals. Sister Pat who was the administrator of Mercy hospital of Des Moines said that we should come up there and we were as close to Des Moines now as we were to Iowa City. How thankful we were to have someone we know help us. At Iowa City they made such a big fuss to me about my wife losing a breast and how I should accept it. Evidently a lot of men can't accept that. I can't imagine what kind of a man you would have to be to let this be a problem. It was no problem to me and only drew Lois and I closer together.

When sister Pat had the medical records from Iowa City she informed me that it was not good. She told me that if I got two years with Lois I would be lucky. We started chemotherapy and I took her to Des Moines regularly for treatment. They would make her quite sick and she would always hang her head and sleep most of the way home from Des Moines. But after a day she would be the same wonderful person as always. She was such a wonderful person about never complaining.

John had done a good job with the crops and the weather cooperated for the harvest. We had been doing minimum tillage farming now for quite some time and it was working for us quite well. However the farm prices and farm agriculture was in a terrible recession due to the high interest rates that the Carter

380

administration was causing. Many farmers were going through terrible times and we were no different.

I was enjoying my time on the Indian Hills college board and it was a diversion for me at this time in my life and I was thankful that I had it. They were such a great group of people to work with. Things were getting to the point where great things would be happening for the community college program in Iowa. we had merged with Ottumwa Heights College for two years and as far as we knew were the only public tax supported college to do that. Since this was the mother house of the Sisters of Humility of Mary and they could no longer afford the large campus. Dr Lyle Hellyer , Al Effner and I met with them several times and in the end bought the campus and 120 acres of land. This included all of the equipment relating to education. It was hard for the Nuns to sell this as there whole life was there but with the changing times they knew it was the only thing to do. We bought the campus for$2,800,000 dollars. It was a real bargain for us as there were dormitory's, class rooms for a total of 185,000sguare feet of buildings. We announced this on May 4 th and made plans to add class rooms as soon as possible. I have been on most college campuses in Iowa and am proud to say none are as nice a setting or as beautiful. Believe me the Nuns were good negotiators. If we had stayed at the old navy base we would have had nothing today. It was great to be apart of this growing college.

Just to have something different I decided to try and raise some geese for the pond in the spring. I have to agree I was not very successful because between the coons and Rex our dog the score was 28 to the coons and 12 to Rex. I found Rex had been killing them and burying them in the garden. I walked into the garden one-day and saw two feet sticking up and I knew were my geese were going. I survived with three geese.

381

Part 3
Chapter 38
The Greiners in1982

This is a year that all of us will remember as it constituted a large change in our family. I guess you could call at the year of the calamity I don't know what else.

On March 1st I received a registered letter from the company we were processing bacon for telling us they were canceling their contract. I had to realize and accept the fact that I had reached the end of the road both financially and physically. Rawhide Ranch Meats was a separate corporation and I had to declare Chapter 11 bankruptcy for that corporation. The problem was although it was a separate corporation I had personally endorsed the notes and of course expanded a tremendous amount of capital from the farming operations to keep the plant running these four years. Had I turned the key after the first year I could have survived but determination to make it work cost LOIS and me our entire life's work. But I am a person who never looks back because we know you can not undo what was done yesterday, you can only do something about tomorrow.

It is easy for me to see how some people when faced with a disaster like this let it get the better of you and do something foolish like taking your own life. I had the support of LOIS and all she ever said was" All that matters is that you love us, we will get by". My father never once criticized me, nor did any of the children, but it is easy for me to see that if they did constantly remind you of your mistake that you would do something foolish.

After I closed the plant, my friend John Hatfield from Green Valley Chemical was trying to put the old group back together to buy a fertilizer plant at Kellogg Idaho. This was part of the old Bunker Hill Mining Corp. that had closed down and had all of the equipment of a fertilizer manufacturing plant setting their. I spent a lot of time that summer in Idaho working on trying to put this program together and stayed in a small hotel in Kellogg. We held several meetings in Idaho with the people from Green Valley Chemical and it was becoming apparent that nobody was really interested seriously in putting this program together. Looking back now it is easy to see that this program would have had troubles also as this site turned into a super contaminated area and came under the control of the Environmental Protection Agency due to the high contamination of lead everywhere. This was an old silver mine and the area around Kellogg looked like an atomic bomb had went off. In September I washed my hands of this project and came back to Iowa.

Lois had came out to Kellogg and was not too crazy about the area as she did not like the idea of leaving the children and all of our friends so far away.

After Lois and I came back to Iowa we discussed what we would need to do toward making a living as it was apparent that we were going to lose everything. After staying in the motel in Idaho the thought occurred to me that if I could find a motel in Iowa and scare up the money to buy it that we could make a living. I looked at several motels a round the state and did not find what I wanted. I was watching the ads in our state paper and I saw a motel advertised at Albia Iowa. I remember this motel because I drove buy it going to green Valley chemical meetings and going to my fertilizer operation at Melrose when I had it. The motel was a very nice brick building and had 20 rooms in it. I made an appointment with the owner and while visiting with him he also said the motel across the street which was also a 20 rooms motel was for sale also. I began to think maybe I could buy both motels making a total of 40 rooms which would be a more profitable operation and eliminate the competition. These two buildings were the only motels in Monroe County. They still are today.

I worked out an agreement with the two ladies across the street and found I could buy both motels on contract if I could come up with enough money. I must give thanks to my father who helped me come up with the necessary funds to buy these two motels on contract. I had taken Lois down to look at the apartment that was in the motel on the south side. We saw where we could remodel the apartment to where it would make us nice living quarters and still have room for my father and Peter who was still at home.

We had the privilege for 10 years of living in a 6000 square foot house with a three-car garage a family room and a separate bar a separate swimming pool and bath house and a large yard to mow. After looking at the apartment LOIS remarked to me"Honey from here on in my life all I want is a bedroom, a bathroom, and a kitchen" we did not realize it at the time but when you have these huge large homes that you become a slave to them and they own you ,you do not own them.

Although I was able to get the money to buy the two motels I was faced with a problem of trying to get the two motels hooked together with a phone system that they could operate in a businesslike manner. That would allow us to have the office and living quarters on the south side of the road and the motel on the north side of the road would be an annex. I found that to do this would require a phone system that at that time would cause thirty thousand dollars. I did not have that and of course you could buy the same system today for probably five thousand dollars or less. Lois had talked to her sister Mary and Jack in Texas and was just telling them what we were doing as we were so close to all of her brothers and sisters. She had happened to mention the telephone problem in the conversation and that was all that was said about it. Two days later we got a call from Mary and Jack telling us they would loan us the money for the telephone exchange. We did not ask them for it. There are few family members who would do this for someone. Do you know any? That is how wonderful this family has been to us.

I came down and took possession of the two motels on December 1st and immediately started remodeling the office in the Annex into a lounge as we did not need two lobbies. The Annex also had a small restaurant that was leased out to an individual. I spent the whole month of December running the motel alone however I did have some guidance from local people who had worked at the motel over the years. We did not hire a full-time desk clerk to start out. LOIS would come down and spend some weekends with me and the rest of the time took care of what needed to be done at the farms. It was a changing time for us.

I had already sold my beloved airplane early that year. It was a sad day when I stood there at the airport and watched it fly away because it was such a beautiful and high performing machine. At the time I had bought the airplane I had paid forty thousand dollars for it and that is what I got for it the day I sold it. So I had the use of it for about 10 years but you cannot look back.

My son-in-law had made arrangements to farm my father's land and he'd also done all the work in preparing for our liquidation sale of all of our machinery and equipment. I just could not bring myself to doing that. It was a large sale with 4 four wheel drive tractors two combines with eight row corn heads and all the trucks and equipment. The sale went very well and of course the proceeds went to someone other than me. I did not attend the sale as it was not in my heart to do so.

Through all of this I was taking LOIS to Des Moines for her chemotherapy treatments and never for getting what sister Pat had told me about LOIS and the two years that I would get if we were lucky. I never ever told LOIS or indicated to her what I knew. She has completed her treatments and we were so thankful that we had sister Pat in Des Moines who was so kind to us. It made it much easier to go to Des Moines on those trips.

My father was doing quite well and LOIS was taking care of him at the farm while I was in Idaho during the summer and in Albia after we bought the motels. He did come down and stay with me several times on his way to our sons farm but he just did not feel comfortable. He wanted to look out the window and see cows as this was his kind of life. We were hoping he would be satisfied when LOIS moved down because he did love being with her more than with me. I was too busy running the motel and doing fix up work and did not have the time to spend with him.

Peter is now a junior at Iowa State University and spent the summer working as a counselor at a boy's camp in Maine. It is apparent that he has been spoiled rotten as he was the only child who was allowed to do things like this. There is no question but what he was his mothers favorite. I'm sure it was because he was so far behind the older children that he was raised as an only child. TOM is on the farm helping John and being provided for by them.

People reading this will wonder why I failed at this packing plant. The meat business is a tough business. When I worked out an agreement with the company who I had the contract with to do bacon for that I thought would help save the plant turned out to be anything but honest. I am enclosing a letter here for you to read that I wrote to that company and you will see what I mean. The letter is as follows

385

Dear------------

This is a very difficult letter for me to write. We have had trouble with settlement problems since we started. You are also aware we made several trips to Dubuque to get that straightened out and get to our original agreement, which again was not written to the agreement but to circumspect the union.

Let me refresh your memory. You made an approach to us for processing bacon. The agreement was very simple. You furnish and install all equipment and start-up costs needed for processing bacon at our plant. We agreed on 18 cents per pound for No. 1 and No. 2 and 14 cents per pound for Carnation. We were to do 125, 000 to 150, 000 pounds per week. We were to furnish all labor sanitation and repairs on equipment under 250 dollars and you were to stand repairs that were over $250. Labor to be deducted from the payment per pound.

A very simple arrangement, but it did not worked out that way. It now is very apparent that we were to never do that much bacon as the equipment sent to us was incapable of doing that. It is now apparent why you would never furnish the second slicer to get those pounds sliced. It is very evident that we were used as a means for Dubuque to wring concessions from the union in the Dubuque plant.

You also are aware and so am I, that the agreement was written so that the union could not make any issue of it. These are all facts and you know it.

Had you not gotten your concessions from the union, we would have been your hero. Since you did, we were used as a tool, in your game. After you purchased the Rochelle plant and transferred equipment to that plant and got the wage reduction at the Dubuque plant, we then became surplus to you.

We do not expect to be used as your tool to gain what you want. We have spent over $40, 771.39 at your request from the beginning to do the things you requested for us to do to process bacon. We are presenting those bills to you now and expects settlement on them.

I do not like these kind of games, but I am forced into then by your actions. The records show the start-up and equipment costs are yours and these bills are start-up costs we incurred at your request to do 125, 000 pounds of bacon per week or more.

You sent your engineer down to size the refrigeration equipment to do 30, 000 pounds a day. We done that and spent the money at your request. After the Rochelle plant came on you found this production not needed. We never were allowed to run that many pounds.

We hope this does not have to become a battle of the lawyers as I'm sure it could get rather sticky for both sides. I do not want to get involved in that unless I am forced to. We spent this money for you to gain what you needed. You got your concessions by using us as the means.

It would be well if you came down and we made a settlement on this so it can be dropped by both sides.

This is to let you know we will release no equipment until this issue is settled. Since we spent the money for you at your request, we expect this to be settled. We have spent this money and if we cannot slice bacon, you have, by your actions and promises, put us out of business.

Under the circumstances, we expect settlement on our bacon processing as per the original agreement, not aa you had your accountants do so you could get what you wanted your statement to show and for these bills enclosed. We will then release the equipment.

All supplies and meat may be picked up as soon as possible.

Sincerely

Howard W. greiner

This just gives you a little idea of the many problems that were involved with trying to make this meat plant work. I put my heart and soul into it but again my timing was wrong and the disastrous farm economy that we moved into was just too much. Everything I had done in my life up until that time worked for me I just could not get on top of this. However I was not worried about this it was that lady named LOIS who was my big concern. I have shed a bucket of tears writing this even though it is about 18 years ago.

In the November/December 1996 issue of beef to day is an

article about a wonderful farm family by the name of Jorgensen from South Dakota who were 10 years behind me but ran into the same kind of problems with USDA that I had put up with 10 years sooner. What happened to them should happen to no one in this country. We both had new ideas to help our communities and make jobs for people in our areas but it would turn out that we would end up being the losers. When I read this article about the family in South Dakota my heart goes out to them as I had been through just about the same thing. Our government is becoming a bureaucracy that runs wild with a president who can lie under oath and obstruct justice and get a way with it. Here was a simple farm family who built a packing plant on there farm like I did and some how mislabeled some meat that is so easy to do. They were invaded by federal agents and in the end Mr Jorgensen Was sent to prison and the family ruined. It was almost a repeat of what happened to my family. Any one who has an idea of ever getting into the meat processing business with USDA approval should look up and read this article. It is sickening but is almost a duplication of the ideas that I had only I was several years sooner.

THE CLARE GIRLS,L TO R MARJORIE, LOIS, MARY
SISTER-IN –LAW ALICE CLARE

388

Part 3
Chapter 39
The Greiners in 1983

Our life was changing and since I was in Albia at the motels and Lois was on the farm at Sigourney we had our Christmas with the family on December 17th. It would be the last Christmas we would have in the big house at Sigourney. The children were growing up and by this time we had nine grandchildren. They all have their different things that they wish to do. It was a joyous Christmas and yet although no one said it we all new that our life would never be the same. John and Cathy were the only ones left in our farm family and even the captain had to abandon ship. Lois and I were hoping for many years together and we faced that with a positive attitude.

In March my father had driven down to Clare and Linda's farm as he always like to go there. He started not feeling well there and Linda drove him over to Albia and I had him at the motel. I could see he was not feeling well at all and I arranged for him to go to the hospital for a few days for checkups. He started rapidly going downhill. A week after we had put him in the hospital my father passed away. It was at this time I did something on the spur of the moment that I have hated myself for ever since. While Dad was in the hospital he became very hard to handle. One of the nurse's called me in a state of panic that dad had taken after them with his cane. I went out to the hospital and of course I was mad. I went in, took his cane and broke it over my knee. What a terrible thing to do. I know he was not in a mental state to realize it but I have regretted that ever since. Dad had a a habit of using his cane to poke Peter when he was small. This was the only thing that ever made Lois made at Dad. This was on my mind but it was a terrible thing to do. What a wonderful way for him to go. With his strong German will we were all concerned about how we would handle it if he ever had to go into a rest home. Although we hated to see him leave us, we were relieved for his sake that a rest home was not in his future. In spite of his temper in his younger days, he mellowed in his older years, as I have done. We

389

all missed him. He would have been 88 years old on the 22nd, of March. He was always good to Lois and would do any thing for her. She always said "Dad has been good to us".

Lois had her checkup at the oncology clinic at Mercy hospital and we had a good report which we were delighted with. However we never mentioned it to each other but we knew that the threat of her cancer returning was there with us. She was feeling very good as she was always the healthy one in the family and if anybody got sick it usually was me. Other than an occasional cold and problems caused by outside forces she was a very healthy woman.

I worked long hours in building the lounge in the Annex and hired a lady who operated it for me by the name of Sue Archer who dID a very good job and had good public relations with the CUSTOMERS. It was very nice when it was completed and although we have made some minor changes it is still the same as one I built in 1983. The lounge has never been a real large money maker but it has just been consistent over the years.

I finally got permission from the state highway commission to go ahead with the installation of the new phone system as we had to bring the telephone cable across the road to the Annex. I found a local man who had the equipment to help me do that. During the summer after the lounge with completed I started a project to double the size of the restaurant which was quite small. Their was no place to hold meetings and this would work for that. I thought by having more meeting space we would draw more people into the motel.

Tom and Renee had a serious auto accident near Sigourney. Renee had ruptured her spleen and had to be taken by helicopter to Iowa City for immediate surgery. Tom had a concussion, but they both were lucky kids.

I had been having some chest sensations and would wake up at night short of breath with my heart not beating. I would take a deep breath and then everything would be all right. I thought I had better go to Mercy in Des Monies for a checkup. They gave me an AKG and would not let me come home as they informed that I was a prime candidate for a stroke or a heart attack. They scheduled the the next morning for an angiogram. The doctor came in the night before and told me that one out of 10,000 die when they do this operation. I thought that was very good odds.

The next morning while doing the angiogram they run the probe into my heart and injected the die. I was allergic to the die and immediately went into the state of shock. The doctor was hollering inject , inject, as they were all very excited and I'm thinking "My God I'm the number 10,000 ." it all turned out great as I had no blockages at all in my heart so the next day they allowed me to go home and put me on some medication. However I continued waking up at night being out of breath AND thought nothing of it.

After Dad Greiner passed away I immediately had Lois, with the help of John move all of our furniture to Albia, so Lois and I could start leading a normal life. We did not like being separated whatsoever. However Dad just was not happy at the motel which is why she was still at Sigourney. The farm was still in his blood.

That fall Indian Hills College had an Amtrak trip to Chicago to see the Vatican art collection and we both went. It was a nice little side trip which we enjoyed. How ever Lois fell on the train leaving Ottumwa and hurt herself very bad . As look back I am sure it was connected to her cancer. After arriving in Chicago she was better and enjoyed the trip. The Clare family had a reunion at the YMCA camp in Estes Park Colorado. We were there along with 27 other family members and had a great reunion. My sister Cordell and her husband came and stayed a few days in the summer we enjoyed having them.

John is still farming, Doug graduated from computer engineering and took a job in Boulder Colorado. Peter again spent the summer as a counselor in a camp in New England.

I had to resign my position from the Indian Hills Community College board since I moved to Albia as I would be in a different district. However in September there was another school board election and I signed nomination papers for this district. I was opposed by a local businessman here in Albia and I thought I had no chance of getting re-elected to the board. I was starting to modernize the kitchen in the restaurant and there was a sale at Webster City, Iowa that I went to the day before the election.. I had Elroy Fry and his son go with me the next day to dismantle and get the equipment I had bought. We left before the polls opened and I never even voted as I thought my chance was about zero of being elected. When we came home the next day Lois had a smile on her face and said I have something to show you.

The headlines in the local paper showed that I won the seat back on the board of Indian Hills Community College. The only person to ever be elected to the board from two different districts.

This is always been one of my proud achievements as I served on this board for 19 years and was chairman of the board for eight years. Again I am probably the only man in the United States who has been chairman of a college board without a year of high school let alone college.

We soon found out that the motel business is like farming in many ways. It is a 24-hour a day business. If you wanted to shut down at 10 p.m. and disconnect the phone you could do so. We had to many customers who would stop by after that an I did not like to turn away business. But you do adjust to that. However you have to like people and if you don't stay out of the motel business.

PART 3
Chapter 40
The Greiners in 1984

We had completed the lounge and made an addition to the restaurant. My usual need to build something took a hold again and I drew up plans to build a 60 by 140 ft. two-story addition to the Annex. I felt we needed to have more than just a motel with 40 rooms but an operation that could be more modern.. The plans included 16 more rooms banquet facilities that would seat 200 people a swimming pool, sauna, and a hot tub with dressing rooms for the swimming pool and a large exercise room upstairs. Because we were the only motel in town I felt this would also make some one think twice before building another motel in a town of 3800 people. So far it has worked but people do get crazy ideas and if there were another motel in this town neither of us would make any money.

One of my cousins, Paddy and Elroy Fry, live close to Albia. He is a very good carpenter, electrician and all-around good worker. He and his two sons helped me and we started construction in June I had the dozer work done and the site prepared. I drew the plans up and basically started building this project from cash flow. Lois managed the desk for the hotel operation while my time was spent working on the new addition. It was a large challenge but for some reason I liked to build things.

Our business was good and we had some very good employees and people who helped us when we needed them who had more motel experience then did I.

Peter graduated from Iowa state University in May and was gone for the summer again as a counselor in New Hampshire. That fall he left to go work in a ski resort in Tahoe, Nevada. I certainly could have used him here but his mother felt he should be able to do what he wanted to do. Each year Indian Hills college takes some of the board members to the national convention which is held in different cities throughout the United States and Canada. This year the convention was to be held in San Antonio Texas . Lois and I thought it would be good to go as we would call Mary and Jack who lives in the Rio Grande Valley to come to San Antonio and we would spend some time together. We were feeling so great as Lois had a checkup at the oncology department at Mercy and the doctors told her she was doing great and to come back once more and if everything was fine she would not have to come back for a year. We really were celebrating this good news.

Along towards the last of September Lois started complaining that she had what she thought was a cold and started complaining that she ached all over. We went on to San Antonio for the convention with the Indian Hills group who always had a great time at these meetings. The president of the college Lyle Hellyer always went along and was a great host for the board. We always managed to mix business and pleasure. Mary and Jack were at San Antonio and we just had a great time.

After we got home Lois started complaining more. This was something that she was not one to do. The convention was in the last of October and by the end of November I could start to see that something was going wrong. She never once asked about going to the doctor and I wish she had of. The first week in December I called Sister Pat at Mercy and she said for me to bring her up immediately.

When we got to Mercy we got the bad news that the cancer had spread to Lois 's bones and that she immediately had to start chemotherapy and radiation treatments as it had all so moved to her brain after getting a brain scan. The news was devastating to both of us even though we both put up a big front. I knew it was just a matter of time because that at the time Lois had her mastectomy Sister Pat had told me that if we had two years we would be lucky. Maybe we were lucky because we got three years. After the chemotherapy and radiation in December we had our family Christmas on about the 20th of December. Gene and Marjorie Sweeney came up from St. Louis and if my memory serves me correct the whole family except Peter were there. He was at Tahoe. Nevada

I made plans for a Clare family reunion in January and we were looking forward for that and it is with this unpleasant news and developments that Lois and I closed out 1984..Although we never mentioned it to each other, I am sure we knew we were on borrowed time. A terrible time for any one who love each other.

LOIS ON DECEMBER 17,1984 JUST AS SHE WAS STARTING THE HEAVY DOSES OF RADIATION THAT WE KNOW DID NO GOOD

Part 3
Chapter 41
The Dreaded Year 1985

January came and we had our Clare reunion. Lois was feeling fairly good and of course had lost all of her hair , which she did not do the first time she had all of her chemotherapy. But this really never bothered her and I always made light of it like I did with her mastectomy. I would kid her and tell her that I always wanted a woman with one boob and no hair. While her brother Jim and wife Alice came from Casper, Mary and Jack from the Rio Grande Valley of Texas, Gene and Marjorie came from St. Louis for a week for a grand and glorious reunion. All of the children except Peter would be there and Lois was in the height of her glory. Sister Pat came down from Mercy in Des Monies and Lois was always glad to see her. It was a very good family reunion.

In between times I was working on the new addition as much as possible but Elroy and his two sons were doing a great job of continuing what had to be done. The building enclosed last fall so the work was all inside work. We had hired Arlene Bernard who lived behind the motel to manage the desk and take care of that part of it. Elberta Friday helped me very much during this time of stress and for that I am very thankful to them.

After the reunion was over there seemed to be a letdown for Lois. The first week in February it was apparent that I would have to take her back to Mercy again. I remember very plainly while working in the swimming pool we had dug I looked up to a walkway that would be in front of the rooms facing the pool. I drove Lois to the front of the building and on the walkway where we had planned to put a steel railing I made the comment that when I was in the pool and you looked up as some lady was walking from room to room you could see under her skirt. Lois made me promise that I would put a different railing along the walkway and of course we done that. We then left for Mercy and she hung her head and never said another word all the way to Des Moines. She felt so bad and I think she knew she would never be back.

After she was in the hospital a couple weeks she felt a little better and then her sister Mary and Marjorie came to Des Moines and stayed at the hospital and spent a week with Lois. She dearly loved this and had such a wonderful time visiting with her sisters. Sister Pat had all so accommodated them with a room at the hospital. It was wonderful of them to come as it was such a spiritual lift for Lois. Although Sister Pat was the administrator of that large institution she always found time every day to see Lois and visit with her. She was a wonderful help through that stressful time.

After Lois was admitted and they started treating her for pain we started a two-month stay at Mercy. Sister Patricia was so kind to us. Lois of course was her first cousin. Sister made the statement to me that she had spent her whole life taking care of people who were ill and this was the first time she could do something for her own family. She carried that out to the very end.

I rarely left the hospital and Sister Pat gave me a room at the hospital and spent most of my nights however I would leave occasionally to come to Albia and maybe work during the day. Lois wanted me there all the time and I complied as much as was possible. She continued to go downhill and at the end of the first month in the hospital the doctors would go in and tell her how well she was doing. Then come out of her room and say to me "Pray that she can go to sleep'.

Sister Pat in her wisdom could see the end coming. Peter was still in Tahoe Nevada working as a groomer on the ski slopes and like all young people was having a good time. Sister Pat called Peter and I'm sure in no certain words told him to come home that his mother was dying. He quit his job and came home immediately and was able to be with his mother for a couple of weeks. The cancer had moved into Lois's lungs and sister told me I had better call the family in. The all came except Doug and Marcia who were on there way from Colorado. We all were all in the room including Sister Pat about nine pm and had finished saying the Rosary when Sister said "Listen. "My best friend had stopped breathing and was with the Lord. Doug and Marcia arrived a couple of hours later and we all said our good byes as this was the last time we would ever see her.

On our various trips to Des Moines Lois and I discussed

how we wanted to handle our funerals when the time came for us to leave this earth. When I was younger if anyone would have ever told me that cremation was the way to go I would have put up a vigorous defense. In this changing world ,and due to the fact that neither Lois or I were cemetery people, and by that I mean going to the cemetery to look at a tombstone we both decided we preferred to be cremated. Over the years Lois had always said when I die I don't care what you do with my bones you can throw them over the fence if you want I'm going to be with the Lord.

Sister Pat had suggested to me that we do an autopsy. I questioned why an her reply was that may it someday could help our daughters and other people. Since she was going to be cremated I agreed. After the autopsy I met with the doctor at Mercy who does all the autopsies and he told me what I already knew. That once the cancer is in the lymph nodes it is final and that Lois had cancer throughout her entire body. She was 62 years old and had had to aunts previous to her who had died with breast cancer who were also that same age. There has been a long history of cancer in the Clare family.

All of Lois's family had to come from some distance and since there was no body we delayed the funeral mass for a week so that everyone could make arrangements to be here. We had an 11:00 mass at St. Mary's church in Albia and since we did not have to make that. awful trip to the cemetery to bury the body we were able to go directly into the hall and have dinner. The ladies at the church had a terrific meal and Lois wanted all of her friends to come out to the motel and just have a good time celebrating her being with the Lord. We done just what she wanted.

Father Martin Manning who had been our priest at Wellman for 10 years gave the eulogy address. He started out by saying

"A Princess, a Saint, a Royal lady, is what you
will think when you think of Lois". She was
a unique person and I knew that a new phase of my
life would start. I was lucky to have her for 38
years but I knew that was over. I was not about to let
my burdens become the burdens of others. I would   I
live my life and the rest of my years thanking
the Lord for letting me have her as long as I did.

It was my privilege.

At the funeral there was a sizable Memorial left for Lois. That Memorial was given to Mercy hospital. Sister Pat had an idea of remodeling a couple of rooms that would make into a large room where the family could be in one end of the room and the patient would be there all so. Making it so much nicer for a family who had someone in the hospital. This was on the eighth floor if I remember correctly of Mercy and as far as I know it is still there today in her memory.

When Lois lived in Wyoming she worked in Jenny Lake Lodge at Jackson Hole Wyoming which is in Grand Teton national Park. It is very close to Jenny Lake and you had the most beautiful view of the Grand Tetons. She loved this place very much. I had spent time up in the high country hunting and I thought it was the most beautiful place I have seen. I certainly have been over a lot of the world and this is the most beautiful place I know. We made a pact that we would spread our ashes at hidden falls which is up Cascade Canyon at the base of grand Teton Mountain. The following August all of our family including all of the grandchildren made a trip to Jackson hole Wyoming. All of the grandchildren, young and old, made the hike of over five miles to hidden falls to spread Lois's ashes. It really turned out to be a fun trip for the family and the grandchildren all called it Grandma's trip. Our oldest son Clare and Linda had never been able to have children and had adopted Ali and Brian. However Linda on this trip got pregnant and she said she knew Lois said "Lord give these kids a baby'. This is when Valerie came into our family nine months later. Instead of a terrible trip to the cemetery we made a wonderful trip to Wyoming and one the grandchildren won't forget. All of Lois's children and grandchildren large and small walk the five and a half miles to hidden falls and I spread her ashes on the beautiful clear water coming down Cascade Canyon.

After the funeral both Peter and I threw our hearts into finishing the addition on the motel annex. We had all of the rooms booked for Memorial Day and we needed to get it finished. We did get it done and we had a lovely new addition that has been a great asset to our motel. The swimming pool is beautiful and although we have had some problems with humidity and it is a real pain in the you know what to keep it up it is a great asset for us. I did make the terrible mistake of putting a couple exhaust

399

fans above the pool venting them into the attic. I did not think what the end results would be. One cold day I went up into the attic and found huge icicle's hanging from the roof. This was a disaster when they melted. After a period of trial and errors this problem was eventually conquered. But we felt the consequences of it for a long time as we had used chipboard for sheeting and when it got wet it went to pieces. We are this year having to replace the roof because of that. What the heck just a 15,000 dollar mistake.

Peter decided he wanted to travel again and left after the trip to Wyoming to go to Australia for a year. Around the first of September he had left and would be gone for a year. He left around the first of September. I was fortunate in the motel that I always had people around me and when I got lonesome I could always walk into the office and be with someone. Later in the year I met a lady in Des Moines and she was a little like the one who kidnapped me. She had such a terrible life that I felt sorry for her and in my desire of not being alone made a stupid decision. But what the heck I don't like to look back and it was not one of the better years in my life so we will move on to another year.

400

ON THE TRAIL TO HIDDEN FALLS TO SPREAD LOIS'S ASHES AT JENNY LAKE WITH THE ALL OF THE FAMILY.

BEVERLEY AND HUSBAND RUSS AND MARISA AT HIDDEN FALLS

THE GRAND CHILDREN AND MY CHILDREN ON OUR WAY TO HIDDEN FALLS

BEAUTIFUL HIDDEN FALLS AT CASCADE CANYON JUST BELOW
THE GRAND TETON. HOW COULD YOU ASK FOR A MORE
BEAUTIFUL MONUMENT. THE RUSHING WATER AND ANIMALS.
I WILL JOIN MY BELOVED HERE WHEN MY TIME COMES.

LOIS PASSED AWAY APRIL 2 ,1985.THE FAMILY MADE THIS TRIP
IN AUGUST WHICH GAVE US TIME TO ADJUST. WE DID NOT
HAVE TO MAKE THAT AWFUL TRIP TO A HOLE IN THE GROUND
WE HAD A MASS AND THE DINNER AND LOIS WANTED HER
FRIENDS TO COME TO THE MOTEL AND TOAST HER BEING
WITH THE LORD. IT WAS DONE AS SHE LIVED WITH CLASS.

HOWARD AT JENNY LAKE IN AUGUST 1985. THE WHOLE FAMILY
WAS THERE TEN DAYS ON GRANDMA'S TRIP
406

Part 4
Chapter 1
The Motel in 1986

The year 1986 was another year for a new grand daughter. Beverley and Russ adopted a new girl born April 17, 1986 in Des Monies. Her name is Lauren Clare Rutten. Seems my grandchildren just keep growing.

Running a motel is a day-to-day business that more falls into the category of routine. It is so much different from the farming operations where every day you have a new project or some crisis to face. People come and register into your motel and may stay one day or one-week. Some you get very well acquainted with and although you like them very much you never become friends in the sense that we had in our old areas. To operate a small motel in a town of 3800 people you have to be as efficiently as possible to make it profitable. It is a 24-hour a day business and because you cannot afford a 24-hour a day staff you find yourself as manager handling all the night telephone calls and the night check-ins. But after you do it a while you become accustomed to this type of operation. We were going through a very severe economic depression in the town of Albia. We lost a company employing a large number of people as well as several other plants. The farm economy is in shambles at this time but being in the eternal optimist you always think that it will be much better in the future.

Since we bought the hotel the restaurant had always been leased out to another individual. I really did not want to get into the restaurant business but the lease was coming up for renewal and I could not stand some of the things that were going on in the restaurant. The annex had a very small inefficient kitchen and the leasee had a couple of freezers in the basement that I had turned into a shop and repair place. He would thaw frozen meat out on the floor in the basement and the place begin to smell like a rendering plant instead of a shop. The only rest rooms for the restaurant were down in the basement which required people to go down a very steep stairway and I knew it would be a matter of time until some senior citizen fell and we would have a lawsuit on our hands. So I made the decision to cancel the lease and remodel the restaurant.

I called on my good friend Elroy Friday again to help me remodel the restaurant. We had no walk in freezers or coolers which were needed if you ran a good restaurant. I drew out a new floor plan that would put the two restrooms in the restaurant upstairs. I more than doubled the size of the kitchen previously so it was of an adiquit a size. All of the equipment in the restaurant was to be removed as none of it belonged to the motel and most of it was old and not adequate for what I wanted.

I also designed a very large walk-in freezer in cooler on the north side of the annex. I had had so much experience building walk-in coolers and freezers when I had the meat plant and this was no different only on a very small scale. We certainly are glad that we have those large freezers in coolers now as they are usually always full of items that are needed in the operation of the restaurant. The I contacted my friend Don White who had decorated our home at the farm near Sigourney and was a very good interior decorator. He had done work for the Armstrong department-store in Cedar Rapids for years and was a very good friend. I had decided the equipment that we needed as I had went to the national restaurant convention in Chicago at the McCormick Place. Needless to say I picked out some very good equipment. Don certainly knew more about the restaurant business than I did and designed a very efficient kitchen. Over the past years it has worked out very well.

Don designed the interior of the restaurant and it has turned turned out to be very durable and still is the same today. I had a couple of very large tables that we had in our home at Sigourney and are of the finest quality. Since I no longer needed them in our apartment I placed them in the restaurant. One is a 60 in. round captains table with very sturdy captains chairs and a lot of people use that as their favorite table today. The other was our kitchen table on the farm which seats 12 people and that all so has a lot of family use. To this day that always pleases me to see a family setting around this table as it reminds me of all the good times that LOIS than I had raising our family around this table.

We planned as opening for the middle of October and it went quite well. We had a lot of complements on the the quality of

408

the furniture and the large oak chairs that I had gotten because I wanted a comfortable chair for people to set on. I hate to eat in a restaurant in uncomfortable chairs and did spend a lot of money for them. I also had installed a large refrigerated salad bar that had a total openings for 40 different items. Sometimes this is good and sometimes not as it is always a problem to have enough salad and items for the salad bar. But people do love it. It too was a very expensive item at the time but I could not see dragging ice every day for a big salad bar. This way we can flip the switch on the compressor and we are in business.

Help was not to big of a problem to get help then but like all new restaurants you have to have a shakedown. And believe me we went through that. Also this was a good thing for me as it kept in my mind off of all my other troubles. There was still a lot of things left in over from closing out the meat plant and the farming operation.

Things had turned so sour in my new relationship and being stupid enough to think that you could change someone who has lived their whole life being unhappy to a state of happiness was crashing around my shoulders. I had quickly made up my mind after having 38 wonderful years with Lois I was not about to live that way. So ended and emotional time in my life that had became very depressing for me.

Peter was in Australia having a good time showing cattle and working on various farms throughout Australia. It was a great experience for him and he was a very lucky young man as none of the older children would have ever gotten to do all of the things that he has done. It was an education for him and he is more like his father than any of the other boys. What do we call that? Inherited genetics. So went the year and it really was a busy year.

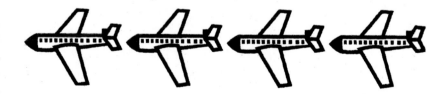

SWIMMING POOL AT INDIAN HILLS INN , ALBIA, IOWA BUILT 1985.
410

CHAIRMAN OF THE BOARD AT TEACHERS CONFERENCE

BREAKING GROUND FOR HELLYER CENTER , INDIAN HILLS COLLEGE

411

Part 4
Chapter 2
The Greiners in 1987

We had a fair winter as far as business was concerned in the motel and the restaurant dID quite well. There were the usual problems with help as far as the restaurant was concerned. We never seem to have a problem with help in the motel but they're always was a coming and going of the waitresses and most of the cooks. However we did hire one lady Fran Knowels at the time we started the restaurant and she has been with us ever since. She is a jewel.

I was wanting to get out and do some different things and for some reason I wanted to river raft down the Grand Canyon on the Colorado River. We had done some of that when we had taken Lois's ashes out to Jackson WY. The whole family went and we had a great time. I contacted a river runner at Flagstaff, AZ and made reservations for the twelve day trip to float the entire length of the Colorado River through the Grand Canyon for 240 miles. In April of that spring, I had met a lady in Des Moines and we had gone out to dinner several times and I asked her to go along on the trip to float the Grand Canyon. She thought about it for 10 minutes and decided it would be a fun thing to do. So I made then confirmed the reservations for the both of us to float the River in August. I had help to run the motel and decided to make a little longer trip of it. Sylvia had never been to the Southwest so we made plans to go to Mesa Verde Co to the National Park . We then continued to Zion National Park and Bryce Canyon Park and then up through Utah to Dinosaur National Park ,then back to Iowa.

When the time came, Sylvia and I drove down to Flagstaff AZ and checked into the rafting company that we were to go with. Now there are two ways you can go the length of the Canyon and one is by motorized raft which to me would be no fun at all or you could go in the six person rubber rafts and row. This is what we did and it took us twelve days to make the journey and we had a great time and it is an unbelievable experience if you have never done it. I would recommended it to anyone. We left from just below the Glenn Canyon Dam where the water is very,very cold about 46 six degrees Fahrenheit. There were various sand bars that we would camp on and stop and have our meals. We ate like Kings and Queens and the food was absolutely wonderful. We had a great bunch of people and everyone did their share in cleaning up the campsite as we could leave nothing. Our personal waste also had to be brought out of the canyon. It is understandable that the park service requires this as there is such a small place that if it were not done it would soon turn into a mess. The rough water was wonderful and a lot of fun however we did have two of our boats over turn. One was at Lava Falls which is the worst rapid on the Colorado River. We were the first boat to go through the rapids and we completely submerged but managed to get on through. It was then our job to pick up anybody who was thrown out of their boat. The next boat went airborne and turned upside down and came down on top of one lady who could have been severely injured. We managed to fish out all of the people but it was very hard work. Did you ever try pulling somebody who weighs a couple hundred pounds into a boat?It's a struggle.

Sylvia and I got back to Iowa both agreeing that it was a wonderful trip. She had never been to the West and really enjoyed the trip and said she learned so much. This was just a trip that two friends took and enjoyed. I would see her occasionally in Des Moines and she would come to the motel occasionally for a visit there was nothing more serious.

That summer Peter called from Australia and said he was going to South Africa to visit his friend Brian Owens. I did not really want him to go as there was turmoil in South Africa at that time. But of course he didn't listen to me and went on to South Africa. He was there for about six months with his friend Brian who he had met as a counselor when he worked in Vermont and New Hampshire.

When Christmas came I was ready for him to come home. He called about 10 days before Christmas and I told him I needed him at home very bad. He did not argue and said he would be right home. As I recall he got home Christmas day and I was pleased to have somebody who was ready to help run the motel

413

and restaurant. When I bought the hotels I had put them in the name of Peter and Beverly. I thought the least he could do was come home and help run the place.

At our annual board meeting at Indian Hills College I was elected to be chairman of the board.What an honor that was for this country kid. My years on this board were always so exciting as we were always building some thing or Dr Hellyer would have another great idea for us.That is what has turned it into the wonderful college that it is.

PETER LOVES TO SKI AND SO DO I HOWEVER AN ARTIFICAL KNEE HAS GROUNDED ME

LAVA FALLS,THE BIG ONE ON THE COLORADO

THE BIG CAVE ON THE COLORADO

THE POWER BOAT THAT RESCUED THE YOUNG LADY AT GRANITE RAPIDS IN GRAND CANYON

I'M ALL RIGHT MOM I JUST HAD THE HELL SCARED OUT OF ME

417

SILVIA MY TRAVELING COMPANION IN THE CANYON

VASEY'S PARADISE,32 MILES DOWN THE CANYON FROM
LEE'S FERRY.THE START OF THE RAFTING TRIP

ON THE WATER IN THE GRAND CANYON

ON THE RIVER WITH THE UPSIDE DOWN RAFT. "SCARY FOR SOME".

PART 4
Chapter 3
The Greiners in 1988

Peter had come home and it was a very big help and a relief to me as he could do so much of the maintenance that needs to be done in a motel all the time. The business had been very good because Cargill Inc. had started building their huge complex at Eddeville Iowa and there was a large number of workers and the motel had been running full for some time. It really is the way you like to have business as a full house is always better as any poker player knows.

The restaurant had been doing quite well and of course there were the usual problems of trying to get everything paid for because when you do things with out cash in the bank it always makes it more difficult to accomplish your motives. I had learned a very good lesson when I had to close out the meat plant. I had learned in life what it is like to have a little money when you needed it and what it is like to not have any and it is a hell of a lot more fun to have a little money. But we take what life gives us and go on.

Our weekends in the motel business are always great in the summertime. This is caused by having weddings and reunions and various functions in the area. Weddings are always one of our biggest problems in the motel on the weekends. Mostly because there will always be a bunch of young people who will have a can of beer in each hand and think they are Gods gift to mankind. Before we had the pool completely closed off we had a wedding party one night were some of the guests were jumping into the pool from the second floor balcony and since the pool is only five feet deep there was great danger in someone getting seriously hurt. Of course this would mean a lawsuit to us even if they had to much to drink. This was taking place at about 1:00 in the morning and the rest of the guests of course were complaining they could not sleep because of the noise. I must qualify that by saying it is rare when we have problems like this as most are very thoughtful of the other guests.

420

I came over to the motel and of course chased them out of a pool, I was walking down the hallway when a young woman stuck her head out of the door and said" Grandpa you gray haired old son of a bitch what are you doing over here? I went directly to the telephone and called the police, who were Johnny on the spot. They ordered them to their room. One little guy who had a red handkerchief tied around his neck started to give one of the policemen a bad time. His reply to him was" We have a nice warm room for you uptown and if you don't get in that room and shut up you are going". After the police finally left I sat in a chair at the far end of the pool where I could look down the long hallway. They would peek out of their rooms and see me sitting their and it reminded me of mice hiding in Swiss cheese. But after an hour they settled down and I went back to bed. It is just one of the many things that happen in the motel business.

I will say the young lady who addressed me so eloquently apologized to me the next morning. I just laughed cause I know that goes with the motel business.

All of my life I have been using the national parks and I felt that it was my turn to do something for the environment so early in the summer I signed up with the Sierra Club to spend 11 days up on the Grand Teton Mountain working on mountain trails by repairing them and building new ones for hikers. This was at an average altitude of 11,000 to 11,500 feet.

I left in August and drove out to Briggs Idaho where I met with the group to hike the 11 miles up the backside of the Teton range. Most of us see the Teton mountain's from the Jackson Hole side and Grand Teton Park. We see the beautiful tall peaks however on the backside there is a gradual up slope with smaller hills and valleys that gets you to the very top of the Teton mountain's. I had no problems hiking up and we spent 11 days with a a pulaski in our hands , sleeping in tents, and taking turns cooking for the group. It was just on the other side of the mountain where we had spread Lois's ashes and if we were to walk across the top and down the east side we would have came out at Cascade Canyon and Hidden Falls. It was kind of a strange experience as I did feel very close to Lois while I was doing this. Incidentally a pulaski is a form of a hoe and an axe that is used by the forest service to fight fires and do just this kind of work. The tools had all been packed up by horseback for us to use and we did not have to carry them up but only our packs.

This was the summer that Yellowstone National Park had all the big fires. From where we were we could see that huge fires burning in Yellowstone 50 miles away. It was unbelievable the amount of smoke and flames that we could see. We knew it had to be a devastating fire. However it was one of the best things that ever happened to Yellowstone Park. I remember when we were hunting up on the headwaters of the Yellowstone the dead timber and underbrush was so thick in places that you could not ride a horse through it. When this did catch on fire because they had not let it burn for so many years, it burned so hot that it done a lot more damage than had they let nature do over the years what it has done for centuries. There would have been much less damage to the environment. I was back in Yellowstone Park in the fall of 1998 and mother nature is recovering nicely. There will be more food for the wildlife then there ever has been in recent years.

When it came time for us to come down off of the mountain I was lucky enough to have one of the Rangers bring my pack down on a pack horse. I started the walk down and although I did not realize that at the time I'm sure it was the beginning of my heart troubles. I became so light headed and felt so funny that I was not sure that I would make it to the Mercedes that was parked where I met the group. By the time I got to the car I could hardly track my feet one a head of the other. I was so light headed that I was not sure I could drive the car safely into Briggs. Upon arriving in Briggs I got a motel room and slept for 24 hours and when I awoke I felt just fine. My heart problem is that I do have a good heart which I do not have a good electrical system. The top part of my heart would beat faster than the bottom part and evidently that is what happened to me on my way down off of the mountain. I was one lucky person to not have something more serious develop.

Indian Hills was doing fine. That fall in October we made a trip to San Francisco for the yearly convention and had a great time. I met a lady from Omaha and had dated her several times and she went along on the trip. We always had a great time on these trips as our Board of Directors were such a great group of people. I enjoyed being chairman of the board and felt very honored to have that position. I enjoyed Marie in Omaha very much as she was a lovely lady and had a lovely home. I knew that there was no way for us to continue a close friendship when she was 200 miles away so that relationship came to an end even though we both enjoyed each other. It was another little experience on life's way. So ends the year.

LOIS ALWAYS TEASED ME BY CALLING ME BIRD LEGS
IN LOOKING AT THIS BIG REDWOOD AND ME I AGREE

423

Part 4
Chapter 4
The Motel in 1989

Things were moving along in great shape at the motel and the restaurant. We were still very busy with construction workers from the building that Cargill Corporation. was doing at Eddyville, and we were very appreciative of that business. The restaurant and lounge settled down to a daily business of so much income that there is not a lot you can do to increase the amount of business when you are limited to the number of people in your area. We always have a special Sunday buffet and had for years that is a very steady business.

Because I have always loved to do white water rafting I had signed up to float the River of No Return across the state of Idaho. I had made plans to do this in July.

Earlier that spring I had met a lady in Marshalltown who lived at Alden, Iowa. Her name was Maxine Madsen and as I had lost Lois in 1985 she had lost her husband from lung cancer from smoking in 1986. We seemed to have a lot in common as Maxine was a farm girl raised in that area of the state. She grew up with strong German parents the same as I and her husband had been a submarine sailor who came back to Alden after the war and started an electrical business. And of course we both agree that after losing our mates life goes on
and you have to make your own way because nobody else wants to hear about your troubles. After losing her husband Maxine and her good friend Helen had been doing a lot of traveling. Her friend Helen, had a good friend in Henry, Idaho and was staying with them for a short time.

I had asked Max if she wanted to ride along out to Idaho with me. She could visit Helen and then take me up to Salmon, Idaho where we would start our float trip across Idaho on the Salmon River which was called the River of No Return. We drove out through Yellowstone Park and spent some time in Jackson Hole and went on down to Henry, Idaho. Now Henry, Idaho is not very

424

much in that it amounts to a country store, over 100 years old, by a large lake on the Black Foot Indian Reservation. Helen's friend and her husband had a mobile home there and just spend three months during the summer at this location because of the fishing.

When the day came for me to be at Salmon, Max and her friends drove me to Salmon, Idaho which was a very nice drive so that Max would know how to come back to Salmon to pick me up. We really enjoyed the trip up there as the area has so much history about the mountain men who used to travel that country and I always love that kind of history.

The trip down the River of No Return was to take six days and there was about 15 of us in the four rubber rafts. The trip through the Frank Church River of No Return Wilderness Area was really a beautiful trip. For six days we floated down this river never seeing another human being camping on beautiful sand bars along the shore and getting a glimpse of bighorn sheep and other wildlife. It truly is a great relaxing experience and I would recommended it to anyone. The river is not anyway near as rough as the Colorado through the Grand Canyon but is more of a peaceful and relaxing trip. There are always great people on these trips who seem to be easy to get along with and a kind of people you enjoy being with.

After we got to McCall, Idaho which is where our trip ended ,I had made arrangements to fly back to Salmon, Idaho by plane. We flew back in a Cessna 206 and it was a beautiful trip back to Salmon where Maxine was waiting with the Mercedes. It always is a beautiful trip flying across the mountains at a low altitude in a private plane. However in 1990 the same airplane flying some men back from McCall crashed killing the pilot and all aboard. I was lucky again.

After leaving Salmon we drove north to Coeur 'd'Alene, Idaho and then on up to Sandpoint and on into Canada. We then drove up through the beautiful mountains to Banff and Lake Louise. From there up to Jasper for a couple days and then on to Edmonton where we attended a good stage play at the Edmonton College. We went to Fiddler on the Roof. It was a very good production. We went down to Calgary where we attended the Calgary Stampede which was a tremendous show and where I hopE to go again this summer. The chuck wagon races are terrific. We came on home and just had a delightful time.

425

During the winter, Max and I went out to Colorado to the town of Leadville which has the highest altitude of any town in the United States. It is above 11,000 feet. I decided to take up skiing so Max thought she would try it also. After a great try and being down more then up, Max thought she had best abandon the project before she broke some bones. After about an hour the instructor turned me loose and said go for it. I really found it quite easy but because I knew how to water ski. I continued skiing until I got an artificial knee and then I also decided I had best give it up. We have been back to Leadville many times since and like to stay at the Old Delaware Hotel. It is a neat old place. Cooper Mountain is a great place for a family to go skiing and it is inexpensive. This is where the ski troops trained during World War II.

Things were going great at the college and I was elected again at the annual meeting to be chairman of the board. I guess I am doing things right or I would not have that honor. The rest of the year was a pretty average year. I have been so thankful that my health has been good and I can continue to do these things. Life is wonderful.

ON A TRIP WITH INDIAN HILLS BOARD OF DIRECTORS

426

RAFTING THE RIVER OF NO RETURN ACROSS IDAHO

427

NEAR MY GOD TO THEE

In June Max and I went to Yellowstone for a quick trip. I really enjoyed water rafting and after floating the Colorado River through the Grand Canyon, the Arkansas River, and the Lower Snake River. I decided that I would buy a raft of my own, that I could carry with me in the pickup camper, as Max and I were traveling around the country.

We had planned a trip in the pickup camper to go Yellowstone and spend a couple of days there. I wanted to pay a visit to Hidden Falls, where we had spread Lois' ashes, in the Grand Teton Mountains. Helen, who is Maxine's good friend from Alden, wanted to go along so that she could visit her friends in Henry, Idaho.

We got to Yellowstone Park, drove down to the Grand Teton Mountains, and Max and I made the hike of five plus miles back to Hidden Falls. We had made plans that morning to go to Moose, Wyoming, where the Park Service Headquarters for the Grand Teton Park are. We got our permit to float the Snake River. Since it was just the first week of June, they were breaking in new college students to issue the permits for the summer and they were not very familiar with what they were doing.

We drove up the Snake River where we were about halfway to Jackson Dam, which creates Jackson Lake. We had planned to send Helen down to Jackson Hole and we were going to float to where she would be waiting for us along the Snake River at Jackson. At this point we would take out the boat and go on to Henry, Idaho.

We unloaded the raft, pumped it up, loaded our cameras, and since we were going to float all the way to Jackson, we attached our six horsepower outboard motor, knowing we could not use it in Grand Teton Park. We shoved off, bid goodbye to Helen, and started floating down the Snake. It was a very beautiful as the Grand Tetons were off to our right and it was a bright sunny day.

We probably floated about three miles when we suddenly came to a place in the River where it split into about five fingers. Max said, "Which way are we going?" I took a quick look and thought it made sense to take the finger with the most water, so

428

that is what we did. The water was very swift. Then we swept around a curve and there was a huge logjam completely across the River.

There was nothing I could do because the current was too swift and it took us down to the logjam. With a big wuff!!, it set the whole raft, including Max and me up on the log jam! My concern was to get Max to shore, which we did with no trouble. We then found that we were on an island and there was no way off. What I was thinking, I don't know, but I thought I could walk out on the jam and push our raft into the water. Then I could walk around the jam, load up, and go on our merry way. I crawled out on the logjam and pushed the boat off into the water. I had no more than gotten it into the water when the water grabbed it so fast that I could not let loose. It sucked the boat and me under the jam. However, what I had a hold of I held onto desperately because I knew if I let loose, I would be in the bottom of the jam. There was only about three feet of boat sticking out of the water. The rest, including me, was under the logs. The water was very cold because it was freshly melted snow coming off the mountain. However, at the time I didn't feel it. My legs were thrashing around and I had this terrible roar in my ears from the water. My life vest was pushing me up against the logs and I was having a struggle to get my head up for air. Max, who was watching from shore, said to herself, "Howard's gone", when suddenly my head popped up, looking like a drowned muskrat.

It took me a good 15 minutes to struggle and pull myself up onto the log jam. By this time I was weak and so cold that I was near exhaustion. My body was as red as a tomato from the cold. We knew we had to get off of this island, so Max and I picked up some stakes to use as probes and walked across the next stream. We walked around and spotted a car on the other side of the next stream.

Max started screaming, "Help! Help!" A lady who had driven there was sitting in a chair, enjoying the nice day. She happened to be a flight nurse and wanted to know how many of us there were. When we told her two, she said that she would go get the Rangers, and left at once, telling us to get out of the sun. This was the last thing I wanted to do as I was nearly frozen.

In a short time, the Rangers came and put a raft in up river, floated down, and picked us up, taking us to the other side where the flight nurse was. By this time the sun had warmed me up a little bit. We then filled out the accident report for the Rangers. I was so shaky I could not write so the Rangers had to fill it out. We told them what our plans had been and they replied that we should have been told not to float below where we put in. But due to the new inexperienced help that morning, we did not get that information.

The Rangers volunteered to take us to Jackson where Helen was waiting with the camper. Then they told us that they needed to practice a recovery, and for us to come back at 3:00 p.m. and they would get the boat out for us. I gradually was warming up, and when we got to the camper, I put some medications on my legs which were scratched up from swirling around under the logjam.

The Rangers took a power winch with a long cable and pulled the boat out from under the logjam and brought it back to Rangers Headquarters, where we picked it up about 4 p.m. A couple of them were very frank in saying, "We don't know how you got out from under there because usually we would be looking for a body." That made me realize how lucky I was that I was strong enough to pull myself out from under that log jam!

Other than taking a trip on a jet boat down Hell's Canyon on the Snake River, I have not done any more white water rafting since then, but I am ready to go again. I was a mighty lucky individual and I do know how easy it would be to drown under these circumstances. The water never stops.

Although it has been ten years since this happened I can still hear the roar of the water in my ears and the thrashing my body was taking. Yes it did scare the living devil out of me but not enough to prevent me from water rafting.

Part 4
Chapter 5
The Motel in 1990

There are not a lot of things that change in the motel business from year to year. There is a constant need to keep upgrading rooms and to keep fixing the small items that are constantly breaking down. Business has been average for the winter months meaning January and February are usually very slow months as there are few construction projects that require people to stay at your property. Restaurant business goes on from day to day and becomes a routine. I do not know why but routine has a tendency to drive me crazy. Maybe that is one of the reasons I am looking for something new.

My friend Maxine and I decided to buy a camper that we would put on the new pickup that we bought at the motel. After having motor homes for 20 years I knew I did not want another big motor home. When you have one of these monsters you are always looking for a place to park or waiting to get out of someone's way. I mounted a 6000 watt generator on the front of the pickup so now we had electricity and not only that we could park anywhere.

We had made our plans to go to Alaska and left about the middle of June going to great Falls Montana were we spent a delightful day at the Charles Russell Museum. We have a lot of Western art in the motel and Charlie Russell of course was one of the real Western artists who actually lived the life. We then drove up into Canada to Kamloops and worked our way up to Prince George then over to Prince Rupert. Here we decided to take that inland ferry up to Haines, Alaska. We did not have reservations on the ferry and had to take our chance of getting on. We were successful and of course every port we came to we had to unload and take our chance of getting back on.   We unloaded at Ketchikan and were the last vehicle to get back on when we left. When we got to Sitka we stayed three days and just had a delightful time taking in several shows and just plain enjoying it. We then went for Juneau and of course the ferry stopped at various locations along the way where we would have to unload. However we were always successful in getting back on the ferry We had a great time in Juneau the capitol of Alaska..

We spent about three days in Juneau before boarding the ferry to go up to Haines where we unloaded and started our motor tour of Alaska. We had a delightful tour of Alaska going to Anchorage, Homer, Seward ,Valdez and every other city we could find. We took the delightful train trip from Anchorage to Seward and spend time there. After we finished the territory in the Anchorage area we headed north to Denali National Park where we were fortunate in being able to see the top of Mount McKinley which is the highest peak in North America. It really is a beautiful mountain when you can see it on a clear day. And of course we saw numerous grizzly bears and caribou plus a couple of wolves. It is great that these areas are being held for posterity

From the park we went to Fairbanks and spend three or four days going to every Museum we could find and also to ride on the riverboat that is a must for every tourist who comes to Fairbanks. I wanted to see the pipeline so we headed north on the Dalton highway. We followed the pipeline for a couple hundred miles north, which is all gravel road, to the little village of Coldfoot. Coldfoot got its name because the gold miners got that far north and got cold feet and turned around and went back to Fairbanks..

They would not let us go any further north toward Prudhoe Bay. So we stayed overnight in Coldfoot there will always remember that I ordered blueberry pancakes for breakfast where I had more blueberries that I did pancake. They were wonderful.

We started back towards Fairbanks when I blew out a tire on the right front of the pickup. I know more than had gotten out of the pickup when one of the men who patrols the pipeline stopped and helped me change the tire. It was most appreciated. We came on back to Fairbanks and started our journey toward home. We decided to go through Dawson,Yukon Territory and got as far as Chicken, Alaska where we stayed overnight. Chicken got its name because the miners wanted to name it after a local bird the Ptarmigan and since they could not spell it they just used the name of chicken. From chicken on the road was not too good and people told us not to go to Eagle which I wanted to do. Maxine was scared so I did not go but took the top of the world highway

432

on over to Dawson in the Yukon. However, the road was muddy enough that we did have to use the four-wheel-drive in various places.

When we got to Dawson we thoroughly enjoyed that city and the history of it. As a kid I always read all the Jack London stories and wanted to take a trip down the Yukon river. We got on a jet boat at Dawson and went a hundred miles down stream to Eagle where I wanted to go in the first-place. It was a delightful trip and we thoroughly enjoyed the trip being able to see the fish traps that the Indians used to get salmon for themselves and for their dogs in the winter. The captain of our boat took us out to his home and showed us his dogs that he used in the winter time for running his trap lines. He lived at Eagle. We got back to Dawson that evening for a stage show where I was up on the stage doing the can-can and just having a great time.

We left Dawson and went to Whitehorse where we stayed a couple days. We attended one of the great shows there about the cremation of Sam McGee. That was a reading that Robert Service ,who was so famous as an author, in the gold rush days at Dawson City had written It really was a great show.

After leaving Fairbanks we worked our way back to the United States down the Yukon highway. We were gone about a total of six weeks and drove over 11,000 miles. It was a delightful journey as I had to get back for a meeting at the college the end of August.

Every fall at Indian Hills we have indoctrination and a meeting for all of our staff. We introduced the new staff members and just give a rundown of what we will be doing the coming year. One of the things we do each fall is honor three people for outstanding leadership in the community and for Indian Hills college. I did not know that I was to be so honored at this meeting. However, when I received the reward and was giving my thanks for it I suddenly noticed that I was feeling short of breath and felt like I had a 10 ton block of cement setting on my shoulders. Some of my family was there as well as Maxine. We went to the cafeteria and everyone knows how well I like to eat but I just could not see anything I wanted. Maxine knew something was wrong.

I went to the table with the family and decided I had better go to Dr. Hellyers office and lay down. Our instructor for the nursing

433

program came in and took my blood pressure and suggested they call the ambulance and take me to the hospital. I really was getting ready to drive home. When they got me to the hospital they found the top part of my heart was beating about 240 beats per minute so they had to put me to sleep and stop my heart and re-start it again. They kept me at the hospital for a day, which I don't remember, and the Dr. then informed me that I had to have a pacemaker as my electrical system for my heart was shot. They took me to Des Moines to Mercy hospital where they installed the pacemaker and everything has been fine since. Thank God for technology or I would be pushing up daisies somewhere.

It really has been a wonderful year in spite of the little heart problem so how could you be complaining about anything. I have a good family, good friends, a good place to live, and plenty to eat so what more could you ask for to close out the year.

WE FOLLOWED THE PIPE LINE THREE HUNDRED MILES NORTH OF FAIRBANKS TO COLDFOOT.PICKED BLUE BERRIES ON ARTIC . CIRCLE. ALL GRAVEL ROAD

Part 4

Chapter 6
The Motel in 1991

Our hometown Albia, is 10 miles from Rathbun Lake which is about 11,000 acres in size. Peter had been doing a lot of work helping to promote fishing tournaments on the Lake. These usually meant more motel rooms and were quite successful for several years. A lot of people who use the Lake were wishing for some kind of a dinner boat on the Lake. In October of last year we received a flyer of a Mississippi River boat that was being auctioned off in Quincy IL. It was a very nice looking boat that was licensed for 150 passengers and was a true side Wheeler as the old riverboats used to be. We drove down to Quincy the night before the auction and looked over the boat and thought it would be very nice if it were on the Lake here. However the day of the auction the boat did not sell and we came home and forgot about it. A month or so later the owner called Peter and I and asked if we were still interested in buying the boat. We ended up and bought the boat the last days of December of 1990.

This meant the boat had to be moved from the Mississippi River to Lake Rathbun. Before we bought the boat we checked with the Iowa highway commission to see if we could move a boat that was 26 feet wide and 62 feet long over the highway. They assured as they would allow this under special permit. This boat was a double deck boat that meant we had to cut the top deck completely off to get it under 16 feet in height. So in February we started cutting off the top deck and the pilot house to get it ready to truck home. We then figured that we would have to find a trucking company that could haul something this large which we were able to do. We could not load the boat at Quincy but had to have it towed to Keokuk where we could load it on the truck as the state of Missouri would not allow any width over 16 feet.

We had made the arrangements to dock the boat at the Rathbun Marina however we had to build walkways and a barge that we could anchor the boat to and a office reception room for people waiting to ride the boat. This all sounds very simple but to

435

meet all the requirements of the U.S. Army Corps of engineers is one hell of a job. Engineering plans had to be submitted and it all run into much more money than we ever expected. However, it was a class job once we got the boat to Rathbun.

We succeeded in loading the boat at Keokuk with the aide of several large cranes and had it all tied down ready to start the trip to Lake Rathbun. The Iowa state highway commission showed up and weighed the truck and found out we were a few thousand pounds too heavy on an axle and refused to let it move. After a few frantic calls to the governor's office and every office we could think of they finally granted permission for us to leave the next day. The trucking company was charging us $1000,00 a day demurrage if we could not move it. We left Keokuk with it the next morning and about six hours later we arrived at the Lake with the boat. It created quite a stir going down the highway and we were escorted by six Iowa state highway commission patrol cars.

After arriving at the Lake and getting it unloaded we started the work immediately of putting it all back together. It was like a jigsaw puzzle but we knew exactly how to do it. We did not drive the boat at Quincy and as soon as we got it into the Lake we discovered part of the hydraulic systems needed some very expensive repairs. This was just the begining as we would soon find out. We had figured we could cater the meals on the boat from the restaurant in Albia which we did the first year and had fairly successful year. Peter and I drove the boat most of the time at Lake Rathbun as this was not controlled by the Coast Guard. We only had to deal with the state of Iowa which was not too difficult however all the rules of the Corps of Engineers had to be constantly adhered to.

We were beginning to find out many problems on the boat. The air conditioners were unsatisfactory and would shut off when the temperature got hot in the boat and you needed them the worst. Peter was excellent at solving a lot of these problems and we were constantly making improvements to the boat. However all of the improvements were costing a lot of money that we were not planning on spending. By the end of the first year we had learned a lot about the boat business that we did not know that the start of the year.

The motel did fairly well this year but we found we were expanding most of our time working with the boat. There was no

436

time for any side trips this year as we were spending full-time on the boat and at the Lake. People who would take a dinner cruise on the Princess were now enjoying it very much and we had high hopes for the next year and continued during the winter to improve the boat. We found it was quite a drag to haul the food from the restaurant so built a kitchen on our dock where we tied the Princess for the winter. We had a real education in the boat business the first year we were hoping for better things for the year 1992.

"PRINCESS" WITH THE TOP DECK CUT OFF.WHAT A LOAD

THE "PRINCESS" ON LAKE RATHBUN WITH CAPTAIN HOWARD AT THE WHEEL

I NEED HELP!!! CAN'T YOU SEE THIS SHOVEL IS TO HEAVY

BREAKING GROUND FOR DAY CARE CENTER AT INDIAN HILLS

439

TIME FOR A GLASS OF MILLER LIGHT FOLKS

440

MY FAMILY AT OUR WHITE BUFFALO REST.ON MY 70TH BIRTHDAY L TO R BACK
ROW TOM.CLARE DOUGLAS. CATHY ,BEVERLEY , HOWARD AND PETER 1993

DEDICATION AT TRUSTEE HALL WITH PRESIDENT HELLYER AND THE BOARD CHAIRMAN

JUDGEING ART WORK AT CENTERVILLE CAMPUS
443

Part 4
Chapter 7
The Motel in 1992

The motel had a decent winter and we had continued doing a lot of improvements on the boat hoping for a real good summer. Peter had hired a new cook for the summer and we had a very good amount of booking for the summer months.

One of the things we underestimated and did not consider when we bought the boat to Lake Rathbun was that the population density of this area is very light. After people ride something like a dinner cruise boat or something similar to that a couple of times they will say" Been there, done that" and suddenly you run out of people which happened to us later in the summer. We could see that we had a problem on our hands.

Max and I went to Branson, Missouri and after seeing the number of people coming there I thought there might be some way we could move the boat to Branson where we had a large population of tourists. I looked the place over and could not see a place where we could dock the boat either on table rock Lake or on Lake Tanneycomo. I came home and told Peter what I saw and that I felt he should go down and look. He did and found a place at an old hotel where a young couple had just bought it. Peter discussed the business arrangement with them and they came up to Lake Rathbun to look at the boat and thought it would be a good thing for both of us. We could see we were having a problem and started figuring out how we could move the boat to Branson Missouri.

I suggested that we cut the boat in half since the state of Missouri would not allow us to ship anything that wide over the Missouri highways. We tried every angle possible and run into a roadblock at every turn. Since the Lake Tannycomo came under U.S. Coast Guard rules and regulations we had to get their permission to move the boat to Branson. We drew up plans and submitted them to the Coast Guard as to how we would cut the boat into and how we would put it back together. It took a little time to get all of this approved and by then we were into the winter months. We finally got all of the approvals and we started stripping the top deck off of the boat. I purchased a laser cutter to cut the boat into two pieces.

We loaded the boat on one truck and then pulled another truck alongside and finished cutting it into. And after a lot of work and frustration we were off to Branson Missouri. We had found a place just below Rockaway Beach to put it back together. A gentleman had given us permission to unload the boat there and that evening just before we were going to unload the boat we got a call from the electric Co. telling us that man did not own the land and that we could not unload the boat there. More trouble but finely at 10 p.m. we got a promise from the electric Co. to give us two months to get the boat back together and vacate their land.

I spent the winter in Branson , having rented an apartment, working to put the boat back together. Peter would come down as much as he possibly could and help. Since we were going to be operating on a Lake under the control of the Coast Guard I had to get a captain's license to operate the boat. I did a lot of studying and went to St. Louis for the Coast Guard exam. I passed that and then had to take a physical. Since I have a pacemaker the Coast Guard in Washington D.C. turned down my application. However if I would go take a stress test and a full physical they might pass my physical which is what I did and was able to get my license. A pacemaker also has taken away my pilots license to fly an airplane which is really silly because since I have my pacemaker my health has been better than before. We had to do a lot of remodeling at the old hotel and spent considerable money and labor getting it all done and getting a new dock to meet the Corps of Engineers specifications for anchoring the boat.

I had to make numerous trips to Little Rock AR where the headquarters of the Army Corps of Engineers is located to get plans approved and to argue with them about various things. What a bureaucracy everything is cut in stone and there is no give anywhere. To this bureaucracy the word commonsense does not exist in their vocabulary.

Max would come down and stay a few days at which time she would cook a meal for us in the apartment which always tasted very good. We were working on the banks of the Lake and it was quite chilly so a warm meal at noon always tasted good to Jim and I and whoever else was helping on the boat getting it put

445

back together.

I made arrangements to get back to Indian Hills college for each board meeting. Although I was spending most of my time in Branson I did not consider it home. It was just a place where I had to be at this time in my life.

I had decided to make a run for the state senate in our district I would run on the republican ticket and had a good candidate to run against in the primary. Since he had paid his dues to the party and in all honesty I had not done so. I was lucky enough not to get the nomination I would make a poor politician as I like to get things done and the way politics work it would drive me crazy.

Part 4
Chapter 8
The Motel in 1993

We worked on putting the Princess back together at Branson for the months of January February March and had the boat ready to launch a bout the 15th of April. I had hired a couple of good welders and of course they both had to be certified welders to satisfy the Coast Guard. I have been around a lot of welders in my life but the one gentleman I hired who had spent 20 years as a welder in the California oil fields was the best I ever saw. The Coast Guard was going to make us x-ray the welds in the hull and it was going to cost us around $5000 dollars. When Scott finished welding the hull the lieutenant from the Coast Guard made the comment that he had never seen a job of welding that good. He then suggested that we run a die test on the entire welds and checked for pin holes. We did that and found no pin holes in the Welds. He made the statement he was going to bat for us in headquarters at St. Louis and see if we could eliminate the x-raying of the hull. Lucky for us they left us off the hook.

About the 15th of April we again launched the Princess by getting a bulldozer and greasing a bunch of railroad ties and slid it into the lake and we headed for Branson and our new dock.

About the first of May the buses started arriving and we had a lot of bookings for this summer and fall. Our location was not good as some of the buses had trouble getting into the parking lot and this was always a bone of contention for the drivers.

The summer when quite well for us and I did most of the driving however we did have captain who used to live in Albia and then moved to Springfield that would spell me off when I had to come to Iowa for anything. Allen Young was a very able captain and did a good job handling the Princess and entertaining the passengers.

I was looking for places and talking to people about finding a different place to dock the boat. This was right in the middle of Branson's big boom and of course every businessman thought it would last forever. I had approached the city of Branson several times about different locations and always got a cold shoulder. The main reason being there was another boat on the Lake and the owner of that boat had some buddies on the city council and believe you me the good old boy southern network is at play in Branson.

We made our last run for the year on New Year's Day and closed the boat down for the year. Max had been down several times as well as other friends of mine and of course after we closed the boat down I would come to Albia and spent most of my time up here. Peter was busy running the motel and was also deeply involved in keeping the boat running. It seemed there was always something that needed to be changed or fixed.

I had been re-elected as chairman of the board again at Indian Hills college and in February of each year we would go to Washington D.C. for the annual community college convention. It was always interesting going to Washington as we would meet with our representatives and senators. There are always many things to do there and I loved to go to the Smithsonian Institute. The president of our college was a very unusual man in that we can go anywhere in the United States and he would find somebody or see somebody that he would know. He has been a great leader in all the years that I have been on the board.

The years have been hard since we've owned the boat. It has cut down on Max and my traveling time. However being in Branson and in business entitled us to go to the shows free and we done a lot of that when it worked into our schedule. So ends the year.

448

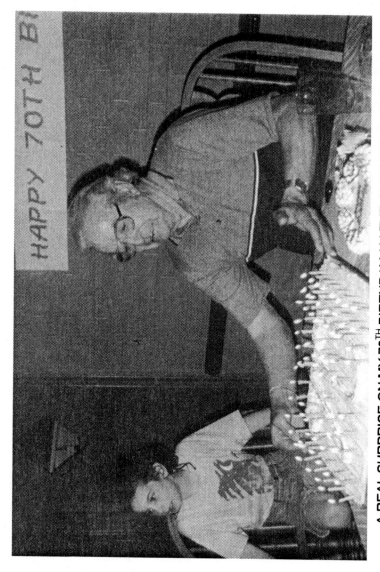

HAPPY 70TH B[...]

A REAL SURPRISE ON MY 70TH BIRTHDAY ALLTHE CHILDREN WERE THERE

449

SON TOM AND WIFE RENEE ON TRIP TO HIDDEN FALLS 1985

MY 70TH BIRTHDAY ,GRANDSON BRIAN ,SON DOUG AND WIFE MARSHA

Part 4
Chapter 9
The Motel in 1994

The months of January, February, and March were very slow, for the people who had bought the motel, where we had the boat docked in Branson. It was apparent they had paid too much for this old motel. There monthly payments were impossible to meet and it appeared as though the man who sold it to them was going to take it back. This man was not the kind you want to do business with and his reputation in Branson and Hollister with the police was not the greatest as this motel was always being checked for drugs and other things.

When we moved the boat to Hollister which is just across the river from Branson, we leased the whole downstairs for our waiting room and kitchen to do our cooking for the meals on the boat. After he repossessed the motel we came to the boat and found he had taken over our waiting room and turned it into a bar. This motel did not have people of good reputation staying in it. So you can imagine what the clientele was like. When we started running the boat in the spring of 1994 we would have to walk our customers through the bar and it was just a terrible situation. However we had no choice but to put up with it for the summer It was one hell of a mess. After he had taken over the waiting room he decided he wanted to sell food also and took over the restaurant and our cooking equipment. In the morning when we would come down to start breakfast for our early cruise the kitchen would usually be dirty and in a heck of a mess. But we put up with it for the year, as we had no other choice.

I doubled my efforts trying to find a location on the Branson side at one of the fishing docks. I succeeded in working out an agreement with one of the docks by the City Park. I had to hire an engineer to redesign and anchoring system for the Princess at that dock before I could approach the city council for permission to move the boat to the Branson side. I made two or three trips to Little Rock AR to the corps of army engineers headquarters getting these plans approved and spending a couple thousand dollars for engineering fees. The core had a new policy of making all anchors now meet the hundred year flood meaning the anchor would be strong enough to hold the boat and dock for the flood that might come once in a hundred years. We hired an attorney and appeared before the city council three different times and each time the man who owned the other boat on the Lake succeeded in getting his friends on the council to reject our request each time. One of their excuses used was that the River was too narrow and congested. We had the Coast Guard come down from St. Louis and testified in our behalf that this was not so but we could not convince the city council who were friends of the other owner.

And We went on through the year in this terrible situation and although the people riding the Princess enjoyed it thoroughly it was depressing for them to have to load and unload through this type of operation.

In starting to tell on both Peter and I. The stress we were under trying to make this thing work. Nevertheless, hope springs eternal and we were looking for better days ahead.

Fortunately for me, Max would come down and spend a few days, and this would help shorten the time. Allen would take over running the boat when I had to leave. Once the people were loaded on the Princess it was always a beautiful trip going up and down the river.

Most of the traveling Max and I would do would be back and forth to Albia so that I could attend board meetings at Indian Hills College. It was always a pleasure for me to attend the board meetings because this was such a good group of people and the college was growing and we were building new buildings so something was always going on. I really like that. So that's the way the year went and we were hoping for something better next year.

CAPTAIN HOWARD AT BRANSON MISSOURI WITH THE PRINCESS

Part 4
Chapter 10
The Motel in 1995

It looked like the year was not going to be a fun one in Branson, as the people we had the original contract with were no longer there and we were dealing with the man who owned the motel. At the end of the last year, where we were cooking our food turned into an impossible situation. Peter and I discussed the possibility of putting a kitchen on the upper deck of the boat so we could do all the cooking aboard the Princess. So about mid-January, I went back to Branson and started construction on this. Peter would come down and help me as much as possible. It ended up that we were able to do this and still serve our good prime rib dinners and breakfasts and lunches, as we had been doing before. I wonder now why we didn't think of this before we bought the boat. It ended up for the year of 1995 that I would do most of the cooking, and we had several really good employees who worked as waitresses.

Our night cruises always took a little longer, as I would have to wait until the boat was cleaned because the waitresses were afraid of the clientele in the motel where we.. I cannot blame them.

I continued trying to get approval from the council and at that time they elected a new mayor. I really felt I had the mayor's ear as he could see where this type of entertainment was needed. Unfortunately he did not vote on the council, so my efforts were all in vain. Terribly frustrating! However, no one said it would be easy.

The motel at Albia was doing all right, and the restaurant continued making people happy with its Sunday buffets. Peter was busy doing work on the swimming pool, and trying to keep up with all the new regulations that the state was now putting on swimming pools and hot tubs. It seemed like everyday there was some new inspector coming into the motel for something. However, I am sure this will continue to get worse, before it gets any better.

456

I told Lyle Hellyer at the college that I did not feel like running for election that fall. He encouraged me, but my heart was not in it and there was another candidate campaigning for the office. I have always felt that maybe people were thinking that because I was spending so much time in Branson, I wasn't representing the school. However, I seldom missed the board meetings. In the end, I did put my name on the ballot and lost the election, after 19 years. At the time I did not feel sorry about it. However, I must confess that I do miss these people yet today.

I spent the summer running the Princess in Branson under almost impossible conditions. I was to make a last cruise for a bus load of people at 9:00 a.m. on January 1, which would have been the last cruise for the winter. I went down to the boat at 7 a.m. to start cooking for the cruise. It was then that I discovered a dead man floating in the water by the boat. His body had been caught on one of our anchor cables. I went in immediately and called the Hollister police. In about 30 minutes, we had 10 police cars there and the whole area was closed off.

It turned out the man, who was about 50 years old, had been beaten to a pulp in a fight. His face was beaten and swollen up, and his shoes were laying outside the door where we would have to bring our customers in. You could see on the gravel where there had been a terrible fight.

I continued cooking breakfast for our cruise and was not sure how I would handle the bus when it came. At about 8:45 a.m. it pulled in. I went out and got on the bus and told the people that we had a little problem with a dead man floating in the water next to our dock. Since our waiting room was fenced off, I could not take them that way, but we could get on the boat another way. All 40 people said, "Yea, we want to go". So I led them over another route and we got on the Princess and had a delightful cruise. By the time we came back, they had pulled the man out and covered him with an old rug. The cruise was one of the best the most fun we had all year. In fact the tour group leader said, "When we come back next year, have somebody else floating in the water."

So I closed out the year at Branson and was ready to go home. I had a nice apartment in Branson, and fortunately Max would come down occasionally, which certainly helped. But I missed being around the motel and the people I knew because I found it difficult to make friends in Branson. Due to all the uncertainties, this was not one of my better years.

Postscript: here it is February 10, 1999. As I write this, it is strange how things happen in your life. I was having breakfast in the motel last week and a man came in. I thought he looked familiar to me. He was a Deputy Sheriff from Branson, Missouri in Albia looking for someone. This deputy was one of the deputies on duty the morning I found the body in the water near the motel in Branson. I asked the deputy if they had ever solved the murder. It turned out the bartender at the motel bar had beaten the victim because the victim was gay and had made a pass at the wrong person. Evidently no one had enough evidence to prosecute the case and it was tucked away in the archives. Small world.

PRINCESS AT DOCK IN BRANSON MISSOURI ON LAKE TANNYCOMO.

Part 4
Chapter 11
The Motel in 1996

After I made the last cruise on January 1 came back to Albia as I knew we would have no cruises in the coming year if we could not get a better docking location. I had been talking to a marina at Rockaway Beach and there was a possibility that we could dock there however we felt it was too far away from Branson. To get buses to go down there was a 10 mile trip from Branson to Rockaway Beach and there was a lot of road construction under way that made it more difficult.

I had been having some difficulty with my knee that I injured in the first auto accident that Lois and I had in 1962. I had been up to Iowa City to the Steinler orthopedic clinic for x-rays and was told that I needed a new knee. After the x-rays the doctor told me that he had a new one in the box whenever I was ready for it. I declined his offer and maintained as long as I could use the old one I was going to do so.

We had made an arrangement later in the month to move the Princess to Rockaway Beach. We had worked out and agreement with a dock in Rockaway Beach to tie the Princess up at that location. They had a marina which was two stories and wanted to build a restaurant on the top floor of the marina. In the last part of January Peter and I had gone to Branson and the next morning we started the Princess and headed for Rockaway Beach. We got about halfway to Rockaway Beach where we were overtaken by the water patrol wanting to know where we were going with the Princess and whether we owned it. The owner of the hotel was trying to claim ownership of the Princess. We were dealing with a real winner. We proceeded onto Rockaway Beach and tied the Princess up to the marina.

We still had our dock and all the walkways we had built plus all of the rest of our restaurant equipment in the old hotel which we had let them use after we put the kitchen on the Princess. We figured we would have trouble getting this equipment and we were proved right. Peter got a court order and we spent several days dismantling the walkways and removing our kitchen equipment and all the time there was a deputy sheriff their packing his pistol and telling the owner of the motel to stay in Springfield as he would put up with no-nonsense from him. After we got the walkways loaded on the dock and all the restaurant equipment removed from the motel I brought the Princess backup and tied on to the barge and took it to Rockaway Beach. We tied the barge along the Lake where we had put the Princess together and then brought the equipment back to Albia as well as the lumber from the dock.

By this time it was getting into April and Beverly was getting her master's degree from a college at Fort Collins Colorado and wanted me to come out for the graduation. I really was having a lot of knee problems but I decided to go even though I could hardly walk. I went to her graduation which was very nice, and would have liked to have handed her diploma to her as I had done so often at Indian Hills College and was very pleased for her. She now had her master's in special education. By this time I could hardly walk and spent all my time sitting in a chair at their house. I got on the phone and called the Steinler orthopedic clinic at Iowa City and told the doctor to get that thing out of a box that he said he had. I made an appointment for the next day after I got home from Denver and although it usually took six weeks to get into the schedule for knee replacement he got me in the next week.

Now the knee operation was not bad at all but I had so messed up my back that after the surgery I was not able to take the proper exercises at all which created a problem for me. They had given me a blood thinner so therefore could not give me the necessary treatment for my back so after a week in the hospital sent me home. My back was so bad I could not lay in a bed and slept in a chair for three weeks waiting to go back to try and get my back fixed. When the day came I went to Iowa City to get the shot in my back and since I am allergic to angiogram dye the doctor was not too confident but fortunately he gave me the shot at about 6 p.m.. Peter waited with me till about 7 p.m. to make sure there was no allergic reaction and we then came back to Albia. At about 10 o'clock that night I was feeling so good that I was able to lay in the bed with no pain whatsoever in my back. My God isn't modern medicine wonderful. I had dugout those same crutches that I had used in the prison camp in Germany 52 years before and was up and around the next day. My only advice out of this is if they ever tell you that you need a new knee don't be stubborn like I was, but go get it done.

I see people coming into our restaurant day after day who need a new knee but just will not go get it done because of the fear of it. It wasn't the knee that caused all my pain but my back that I wrecked favoring the knee.

By the middle of the summer I had went back to Branson and was starting to work helping the marina build a restaurant. We decided that we would not even try to do any cruises the summer and fall but would start preparing for the next season. Peter and I both felt that it was going to be a tough struggle to get the Branson market to come to Rockaway Beach but we continued working our tails off through the rest of the summer.

Fortunately the motels were doing fine and we had some good help that would handle things here in Albia when we were both gone. A labor shortage was developing but we have some very good loyal employees here at the motel. The restaurant was continuing with our Sunday buffets

That fall the owner of the marina at Rockaway Beach looked out on the Lake and saw our barge being pulled back towards Branson with a motor boat. He knew this wasn't right so he called the water patrol who then intercepted the barge and the boat pulling it. One of the men was wanted by the police and was handcuffed and taken to jail. They were all taken into custody and the barge was then taken back to the marina. The owner of the old motel was a person who just never gave up. He knew the law and knew that he could get away with anything and he just kept trying.

All the time I was at Branson and working at Rockaway Max would occasionally come down and we would go to a few shows and she loves to go to the factory outlet malls and all the shops. We enjoy each other when we are together. In spite of all the troubles life is good and you always have to think that tomorrow will be better. You can't do anything about yesterday but you sure can about tomorrow. I always look forward to tomorrow.

461

Part 4
Chapter 12
The Motel in 1997

I was home awhile in January and then went back down to Branson to help the people who owned the Marina work on the restaurant in the Marina. The manager of the Marina thought the cooking should be done for the Princess in the restaurant rather than on the boat as we had been doing. The little galley that we had on the boat really worked great and I knew that this idea was not a good one as I had been doing all the cooking on the boat and knew how easy it was with a galley right there. Cooking off the boat meant you had to drag all of the food down a flight of stairs to where the Princess was docked. But because he insisted I went ahead and tore out the galley. It was a mistake.

The Princess needed to be painted again and we undertook to do that job and lay down new carpet on the upper deck to where we had it looking very good again. We were working on sales but it was a slow project to get buses to come to Rockaway Beach. We could see that this was going to be a bad year, so Peter elected to get rid of the boat which we did in June and I was able to pack my baggage what little there was and come back to Albia. We had put tons of work in moving the boat to Branson and putting it back together but our efforts were not rewarded. I will say that we had a ton of learning experience.

It was good to just be able to get back into the old routine at the motel. Over the past few years while working with the Princess we had gotten off of our usual routine of painting and constantly improving the motel. This year after coming back from Branson we painted and improved all the rooms on the south side of the road and Peter laid new carpet in all of those rooms over their. We have constantly kept after that program throughout the whole year.

It was a great relief for Peter and I to just get back to the business of the motel and restaurant.

462

TOP-MAX AT QUEBEC CANADA ON 8100 MILE RR TRIP
BOTTOM-MAXINE MADSEN AND I AT BRECKENRIDGE CO

Part 4
Chapter 13
The Motel in 1998

The year started out with Max and I going to Orlando Florida to visit my sister, who has been quite ill with three surgeries in a month. It was in January and we came home through Pensacola Florida and stopped and visited the naval air Museum which is a terrific Museum and anyone who is interested in aviation should stop and see. We then went on to mobile Alabama and toured the battleship Alabama, which was fascinating to me. To be able to go into those huge gun turrets and see the size of the shells and how they were made was very interesting. We then came on to Biloxi, MS and on up to Tunica, MS were all the gambling casinos are built out in the country about 30 miles south of Memphis. It really is amazing to see how the gambling industry has grown.

We arrived home in February and Peter and his friend Lisa had decided to go to Australia and get married. Peter of course had spent a year in Australia and had some friends over their so that is where they decided to get married. So guess who was taking care of the motel and painting rooms during that time. They returned after having a great time in Australia. That is the end of the marriages for all six children.

Max and I like to ride trains, so I put a trip together leaving in May to go to Chicago then to New Orleans for four days. On to San Antonio for four days, and from there to Los Angeles for a couple days. We then took the train on up to San Francisco and after spending a couple days in San Francisco, rented a car and went up into Napa Valley. Then we caught the train back to Denver, CO where Beverly and Doug both live. We had a delightful time visiting them before we left to get on back home.

After putting the trip together a couple of friends who used to live in Albia, but now reside in Fort Smith, Arkansas decided to go with us. Kenny and Mary Brewer were great traveling friends and we had a good time on the trip. They had never been to California so they thoroughly enjoyed the trip and having a tour guide. Max and I enjoyed them very much.

I had no sooner gotten home when I saw in the paper that Amtrak and Via rail in Canada had just made an agreement similar to the rail passes in Europe. I called Max and asked her if she wanted to go on another long railroad trip. She replied in the positive so I contacted the travel agent in Des Moines who had never done this before and after a couple months had put together another railroad trip on Amtrak and Via in Canada.

We left Ottumwa on Amtrack Aug. 16th and went to Chicago and then the next day caught the train to Glacier National park. We stayed there two days and then onto Seattle where we caught the high-speed ferry to Victoria BC. What a lovely city and what a great time we had at Victoria. After three days there we went to Vancouver and caught the Via to Jasper national Park and spent two wonderful days there. After leaving we went on to Edmonton and stayed there a couple days before going on to Toronto. An overnight in Toronto and the next morning left for Montreal which was supposed to be a four-hour trip.

About half way to Montreal the train came to a sudden stop and started backing up. We were riding in the last car when one of the train men came running down the aisle and we backed up a couple miles to the town of Brockline. We set there a short time and the train started up again and then suddenly backed up again to the town. About that time a passenger train came from the opposite direction going to Toronto. They came on their speaker system and said they had mechanical problems and that we would have to unload from the train by the little depot and wait for buses to come pick us up to take us on to Montreal. So about 300 people sat at this little depot for four and half hours waiting for buses that never came. Then about 1130 p.m. another train came from Toronto and hooked on to our train and we all loaded up on the same train again. As this was going on and people were loading on the train I was talking to one of the train crewmen about what was going on. I asked him whether the engineer had run a red light and he replied in a very quiet voice" It was worse than that because the engineer had picked up the wrong train orders when we left Toronto" needless to say when the railroad finally figured out what happened they grounded the engineer and the train right there. So mistakes do happened on the railroad and we were lucky we did not have a serious head on accident. After

465

all passengers were loaded we went on to Montreal and got their about 130 a.m. in the morning.

Funny things happen on a trip like this. Our hotel reservations according to the travel agent was a quarter of a mile from the railroad station. We got into a taxi and I told the driver the name of the hotel. He started driving and after about three miles I told the driver something was wrong because we were to be close to the railroad station. He replied he would take us to the hotel and if he were wrong I would not need to pay him. After about 20 mile and a 25 dollar taxi ride we arrived at our hotel close to a railroad station but in a different town. However it all worked out as we took the gray line tour the next morning and got to see Montreal. On the way back with the gray line tour we told the driver what happened and he said he would pick us up the next morning for free and take us back downtown to where we could catch our train that evening. We had the whole day to spend in Montreal. That evening we left for Quebec.

We love the old city of Quebec and had a delightful time there. It is a very fun place when you are in the old section and we had one of the best lunches on our trip at the old hotel Lechateau Frontenac. From Quebec our reservations said catch the train to Halifax NS. So we took our bags to the train station and checked them and spent the most of the day in the old city. We stopped for our usual ice cream cone about 4 p.m. and was visiting with the owner who we told that we were catching the train at the depot for Halifax. He gave us a strange look and said could I see your ticket please? I gave him a ticket and he looked at it and called the depot and told us there was no train leaving from the depot but we would have to catch the ferry and cross the St. Lawrence River and catch the train at Levis. We hurried back and got our bags and headed for the ferry. After arriving at Levis we found several other couples who had the same experience, we laughed about it but they were quite irate.

We went on up to Halifax and this time our hotel was attached to the railroad station. This was the night the TWA plane went down with all 200 plus people aboard in Peggys Cove. We had planned to go there the next day but that ended that trip. We enjoyed Halifax NS and while there took a gray line tour. On the tour someone asked where I was from and I said Iowa. After we unloaded this gentlemen come up to me and told me he was from

Iowa also. He introduced himself and I told him my name was Greiner to which he replied" I knew a Greiner down by Sigourney that built a meat packing plant. To which I replied I was the one. He then replied" You are the one who had that beautiful copper kitchen that looked out over the lake". What a small world that he remembered something like that. It turned out he had worked for Iowa electric and had a meeting with me about getting three phase electricity for the plant. I had forgotten completely about it. We thoroughly enjoyed Halifax and plan to go back again. While at Halifax I got to see one of the little Corvettes that was a ship a couple hundred feet long that escorted our convoy across the Atlantic Ocean for 17 days in January of 1945. We had hit such a terrible storm that these little boats were underwater as much as they were above water. Out of 120 built this boat was the only surviving Corvette from the war. The sailors who spent their time on these do not deserve a metal but a whole pocket full of metals.

We then left Halifax for Chicago where we had to stay overnight to return back to Albia. We had kept our baggage with us as we had bought new luggage with the big six inch wheels that were wonderful as we knew we would be doing a lot of walking. I then suggested to Max the next morning that we could check our luggage and then walk on to downtown Chicago to have lunch and then catch the train at 3:00 which we did. Guess what, when we arrived at Ottumwa there was no luggage. It went on to Omaha and came back the next day. Never check your luggage on the train.

We arrived home about the middle of September and I started putting the camper back on the pickup as we had not had it on since we had the Princess. Max and I then left on a trip to the Black Hills and on up to devil's tower and on to Cody Wyoming. In Cody we spent the whole day at the Buffalo Bill Museum which is wonderful if you like Western art. We then went northwest out of Cody to the Northeast entrance of the park which was a beautiful drive and one I had never ever taken before. It was the Chief Joseph highway. We went on to old faithful and stayed a couple days and then on down to Jenny lake. I had not been back to Jenny lake and hidden falls where the family had spread Lois's ashes since we had bought the Princess. I wanted to walk back to the falls which is a five and a half mile hike. Max and I went back to the falls and it is not and easy walk. Max did

467

it in great shape. After returning to our car a couple we had become acquainted with at Yellowstone were at Jenny Lake and we agreed to meet them for dinner that evening. He was an old B-24 pilot and he and I had a lot in common and we just had a great time talking airplanes. They were from Delaware and he was retired from Du Pont and had been involved over the years in developing weeds sprays so we had a lot in common there also. It was a fun evening.

Max and I went on down South to flaming gorge dam and then on to Vernal Utah and then on out to dinosaur national Park before heading back to Denver and spending some time with the children. It was a great trip and Max and I had spent most of the year traveling and enjoying life.

It was about the middle of October when I mentioned something to Cathy about someday writing a book whenever they would get a computer that I could talk to. She replied" Daddy they have them now' '. So the last day of October I bought a computer with a software package that I can talk to the computer with and I have been having a ball writing this book digging up a lot of my past. Most of it was good memories however there were a few bumps on the way.

This will end the adventures that I have had and I hope you will agree that I have had an interesting life.

Memories

It has been a wonderful experience writing these memories and recalling many of the things in my life, that I had either forgotten about, or just put into that part of the mind where it cannot be recalled unless there is a prior incident to bring it back.

As I write this I think of the wonderful life that I had as a child growing up and although we were poor we were still very rich because we had love, a home where there was always plenty to eat, and things to do. I would not change my childhood for what the children of today have. Although my teen years would have been better had I been able to go to high school. I do not feel as if it has handicapped me in any way or any form.

I have many wonderful memories of my mother and I think the reason I was so close to her was because of her illness. And although it was hard for her to write hardly a day went by, when I spent three years in the service, that I did not get a letter from her everyday. I also tried to write to her at least three or four times a week because I knew how she wanted to hear from me.

My years in the military were a great experience and it was my high school and college combined. Without it I would have never met the wonderful lady who was to be my partner. And that is exactly what she was, a partner.

The most wonderful years of my life were the 38 years that Lois and I had together. She was such a good mother and so loving to everyone. It was devastating to all us when we found out that she had cancer. I remember my father crying like a baby when we found out the bad news. This was very unusual for this strong old German. It truly was a wonderful life I'm so glad that we were able to do all the traveling that we did. Any woman who has four children before the oldest one is five and never complained has to be close to a Saint. We enjoyed being together so much.

We had so many wonderful memories together raising our six children and the children too have many fond memories of their mother.

I knew Lois would be leaving and being one to never look

back I had made up my mind to live my life and not look back. I knew nobody cared about my troubles and I was not going to burden anyone with them. I needed to be with people or someone as I cannot stand being alone.

In 1989 I met Maxine Madsen who had lost her husband to lung cancer in 1986. Maxine was raised on an Iowa farm and we both like to do the same things as we try to never pass up a Museum or any points of interest when we travel. Although we live 120 miles apart we usually get together every couple of weeks for a couple days. She's a great traveling companion and never complains. She has two daughters and I enjoy them and she enjoys my family also.

Although I have a few spare parts my health is very good and so is Maxine's. So the remaining years of our life, God willing, we will be seeing more of this wonderful country of ours.

I thank God for allowing me to survive the many things that have happened to me and wonder why he took the lives of so many of my close friends so young. I guess we are not meant to understand it.

Over the years I have had so many wonderful people working for me because I could not have done many of the things I have done without there knowledge and assistance. To all of the wonderful friends in the areas where I have lived I can only say thank you for making my life so fulfilling. I tell my children when my time comes do not mourn me, because I had a wonderful life.

Quick Order Form

Fax orders: (515)932-7181

Telephone orders: Call 1-800=728-4286 toll free
Have your credit card ready.

E-mail orders:GREINER@CKNET.NET

Postal orders: Indian Hills Publishing
100 Highway 34 East
Albia, Iowa 52531 USA   Telephone (515) 932-7181

Please send _____ books to the following address

_____

_____

_____

_____

Price per book is $24.95. shipping is $2.50 per book Iowa
residents must add 5% sales tax per book.

Payment; _____Check_____ Credit card _____Visa

_____Master Card _____AMEX _____Discover

Card
number_____

Name on
card_____ Exp.Date. ____/____

If more than one book is ordered we will send them to any address
that you wish. We will be happy to have the books autographed as you
desire. That may delay shipping the book a few days .